The Migration of L... .

# The Migration of Labor

## *Oded Stark*

Basil Blackwell

First published 1991

Basil Blackwell, Inc.
3 Cambridge Center
Cambridge, Massachusetts 02142, USA

Basil Blackwell Ltd
108 Cowley Road, Oxford, OX4 1JF, UK

*Library of Congress Cataloging in Publication Data*

Stark, Oded.
    The migration of labor/Oded Stark.
        p.   cm.
    Includes bibliographical references.
    ISBN 1–55786–030–0
    1. Migrant labor—Developing countries.   2. Economics of migration
I. Title.
HD5856.D44S73   1991
331.12'791—dc20                                           91–30980
                                                               CIP

*British Library Cataloguing in Publication Data*

A CIP catalogue record for this book is available from the British Library.

Typeset in 10 on 12pt Times
by TecSet Ltd, Wallington, Surrey
Printed in Great Britain by T J Press Ltd, Padstow, Cornwall

# Contents

# Preface

The work reported in this book was carried out over nearly a decade with most of the research undertaken during my tenure as the Director of the Migration and Development Program at Harvard University. The long time span involved in carrying out the work and the intense engagement in research and teaching have produced ample opportunities for interactions with colleagues, students, and collaborators. Many served beyond the call of duty to provide inspiration and support that led me to explore yet another dimension of labor migration. I am particularly indebted to B. Douglas Bernheim, David E. Bloom, Oded Galor, Eliakim Katz, Jennifer Lauby, David Levhari, Robert E. B. Lucas, Mark R. Rosenzweig, Vibhooti Shukla, J. Edward Taylor, and Shlomo Yitzhaki. The support and guidance of the Faculty Advisory Committee of the Migration and Development Program must also be gratefully acknowledged. In particular, C. Peter Timmer and Zvi Griliches, chairman and committee member respectively, provided inexhaustible encouragement and invaluable help. The Andrew W. Mellon Foundation, the Alfred P. Sloan Foundation, and the Ford Foundation have supported most of my work. I was also supported by the World Bank and the David Horowitz Institute for the Research of Developing Countries at Tel-Aviv University. It is my hope that these foundations and institutions will accept this book as a modest return for the confidence they have placed in my research. Having accounted for my academic and financial indebtedness, I would like to acknowledge the spiritual and emotional support of my wife, Shua Amorai Stark. While my passion for migration research resulted in numerous migrations from home, her love, trust, and sound judgment, together with the understanding, kindness, and patience of our children, Eran and Alit, repeatedly replenished my dwindling stock of perseverance, insight, and optimism.

This collection includes my more interesting papers on labor migration. Many were first disseminated in the Migration and Development Program

Discussion Paper Series and subsequently appeared as journal articles in the *American Economic Review*, *Demography*, *Economic Development and Cultural Change*, the *Economic Journal*, *Economics Letters*, *European Economic Review*, *International Economic Review*, *Journal of Development Economics*, *Journal of Development Studies*, *Journal of Labor Economics*, *Journal of Political Economy*, *Journal of Population Economics*, *Journal of Urban Economics*, *Population and Development Review*, and *World Development*. I thank all the publishers for graciously granting me permission to include the articles in this book. One advantage of incorporating journal articles as chapters is that to a considerable extent they are self-contained, and the reader need not go beyond chapters that are of immediate interest. The obvious disadvantage is that there may be some overlapping and repetition. A preference for accessibility and ease of use rather than chapter-by-chapter innovation resulted in a decision to leave most of the chapters that had earlier appeared in print more or less in their original form.

*Introduction*

# Introduction

This book models afresh labor migration and various phenomena and processes associated with it. It builds on three premises.

First, even though the entities that engage in migration are often individual agents, there is more to labor migration than an individualistic optimizing behavior. Migration by one person can be due to, fully consistent with, or undertaken in pursuit of rational optimizing behavior by another person or by a group of persons, such as the family. As the book amply demonstrates, this premise shifts the focus of migration research from individual independence to mutual interdependence. Various implicit and explicit intra-family exchanges, such as remittances, are thus integral to migration, not unintended by-products of it. And given the overall pattern of the demand for labor, the performance of individual migrants in the absorbing labor market can largely be accounted for not just (as in standard human capital theory) by the migrants' skill levels and endowments but also by the preferences and constraints of their families who stay behind.

Second, there is more to labor migration than a response to wage differentials. Thus migration in the absence of (meaningful) wage differentials, or the absence of migration in the presence of significant wage differentials, does not imply irrationality. Migration is fundamentally dissimilar to the flow of water, which will always be observed in the presence of height differentials. This premise compels consideration of new variables, such as income uncertainty and relative deprivation, and invites the study of associated phenomena, which include migrant – family pooling of risks, the returns from migrant children and hence the demand for them, and the size and composition of human capital investments in children.

Third, a great many migratory phenomena would not have occurred if the set of markets and financial institutions were perfect and complete. Furthermore, markets are usually far from free of asymmetries, externalities, cross-over effects, and technological lumpiness. A family in rural Maine can capitalize on the industrial development of California's Silicon Valley by buying shares on the New York Stock Exchange. Migration out of Maine is not necessary. But, especially in less developed economies, entry to a specific labor market is often barred by constraints in capital, commodity, or financial markets. These characteristics tend to encourage migratory phenomena that would not have arisen if, for example, information were completely symmetric, if financial (insurance, credit) institutions functioned smoothly, or if returns to exchange among agents exhibited linear regularities. And the often quoted "golden rules" of migration, such as the inverse relationship with distance, become subject to an unconventional twist: when informational asymmetries and lower income covariance are conducive to migration gains, distance as an explanatory variable enters positively.

This book attempts to explain labor migration in light of these three premises and, as hard as the task may be, in light of their interactions. It offers new insights on why and when entities such as families may find it optimal to behave strategically, to act simultaneously in, and to distribute their human capital across, several markets, and to sequence their actions in a particular fashion. This book demonstrates how in the larger scheme of things migration is ingeniously and efficiently harnessed to assume a variety of tasks. It also takes a novel look at how migratory outcomes are fed back into and modify the very market environments that stimulated migration.

A prolonged study of a topic is bound to be associated with a progression of thinking. This entails a change in focus and a shift of interest that should not be confused with a change in belief. Early on I spent considerable energy in an effort to cool down the profession's over-fascination with the expected income approach to the study of migration. I suspected the behavioral foundation of the approach to be rather slim, and doubted that the inducement to migrate would be eliminated when the differential between the expected urban wage and the certain rural wage was zero. For example, since risk-averse individuals, by definition, would prefer a given certain wage to a probability mixture of wages the expected value of which is equal to that certain wage, a zero intersectoral wage differential would imply urban-to-rural migration, and a zero (net) rural-to-urban migration would entail a positive equilibrium differential; in other words, the no inducement and no differential conditions are mutually exclusive. As yet another example, I also argued that, if risk-neutral individuals attach any value to leisure, they cannot possibly be indifferent between a given rural sector wage $W_R$ and a higher urban sector wage $W_U$ conditional on a probability $p > 0$ of attaining it (and a $1 - p$ probability of not working and thus having an urban wage of zero). To simplify matters, assume that a standard unit of work time $S$ exists in both sectors implying, for example, that $S$ days of work fetch $W_R$ in the rural sector or $W_U$ in the urban sector. With a zero intersectoral wage differential $pW_U - W_R = 0$, the rural sector pair of leisure and wage $(0, W_R)$ is dominated by the urban sector pair $[(1 - p)S, pW_U]$, and thus rural-to-urban migration *will* take place (see Stark, 1982). It was thus a matter of natural evolution to place considerable and increasing emphasis on the families' decision-making process leading to migration. I believed then, as now, that in social science research in general and in migration research in particular we need not necessarily search for the explanation where we observe the phenomenon. (As an old Russian proverb has it, it is not the horse that draws the cart, but the oats.) Placing the family, rather than the individual, at the center of the migration decision (this need not imply/result in migration *by* the family) was a relatively new direction. This must not be interpreted to suggest that the behavior of individuals should be ignored, but rather that it should be analyzed in the context of a decision-making unit operating as a group. And the group, to wit, the family, should not be treated as if it were an individual. I even postulated that migration research could turn out to be a highly profitable means of studying the family. I thus suggested that real advances will be made in migration research upon substitution of a principal agent study for a lone agent study. The family can be conceived as a "coalition," a group of players committed by choice to act as one unit *vis-à-vis* the rest of the world. This not only facilitates protection from attempts to exploit individual weaknesses but also renders it possible to obtain more together than separately. Migration by family members can be interpreted as a manifestation of the viability of the family: substituting space (scope) economies for scale diseconomies that limit the capacity for coinsurance; simultaneously sampling from a number of separate markets (that is, investing in one without completely liquidating and shifting holdings from another); sharing both costs (for example, financing the move) and rewards (for example, through remittances); and so forth (see chapters 4, 6, 15, and 16). There are, of course, interesting interactions within the family coalition concerning how to share what has been obtained together through specialization (migration by some, nonmigration by others) and cooperation (for example, exchange of risks). Here the notions of relative powers, bargaining, altruism, and so forth count (Stark, 1983, 1984).

The idea that the family involved in migration is an alliance of agents that engage in a game with each other as well as against a "common enemy" directly or indirectly inspired several of the chapters in the book.

A particularly interesting line of inquiry is that where the "common enemy" – against whom the game is played – constitutes an entire distribution of a set of families. The consideration that the well-defined outcome of a particular inter-familial comparison at origin results in differential inducements to have family members sent out as migrants is taken up in several chapters (notably 6, 8, and 9). The dual game approach also established the framework for a more recent interest in the particular forces that govern the results of the last of the games described above. Here I felt that to obtain a significant improvement in our understanding of the economic performance of migrants it would be productive to study the structure of incentives that migrants face, rather than their vector of characteristics (see chapters 27 and 28, and Lauby and Stark, 1988). In addition, I felt that the unexplored issue of what rules govern the interactions between migrants in the receiving economy on the one hand, and between migrants and nonmigrants on the other hand, could tell us a great deal about several aspects of migration, such as the distribution and clustering of migrants in the receiving economy, the optimal size of the concentrations of migrants, and the rationales for the creation and disposition of "network and kinship capital" (chapter 3). The payoff to future research in this direction could be quite high.

## References

Lauby, Jennifer and Stark, Oded (1988) "Individual Migration as a Family Strategy: Young Women in the Philippines." *Population Studies* 42: 473–86.

Stark, Oded (1982) "Rural–Urban Migration and Surplus Labour: Reservations on Bhatia." *Oxford Economic Papers* 34: 569–73.

Stark, Oded (1983) "Towards a Theory of Remittances in LDCs." Discussion Paper 971, Harvard Institute of Economic Research.

Stark, Oded (1984) "Bargaining, Altruism and Demographic Phenomena." *Population and Development Review* 10: 679–92.

# Part I

## Overviews

# 1

# Research on Rural-to-Urban Migration in Less Developed Countries: The Confusion Frontier and Why We Should Pause to Rethink Afresh

## 1 Introduction

Researchers in the field of social sciences are often placed on the defensive when challenged by planners and practitioners: "This or that idea of yours may be good publication material, but what can *I* learn from it?" Planners and practitioners often have cause to be in an aggressive mood: pressing issues must be attended to, while researchers busy themselves in the pursuit of other avenues, perfecting and expanding works that they initiated long before specific topical concerns have arisen. This conflict stems partly from practitioners and researchers having different time preferences and discount rates, no doubt reflecting different things being maximized (for example, being reappointed versus producing a definitive, scholarly, or scientific work). But it often mars the field as well as the life of conscientious researchers.

To the casual observer or the scholar seeking to make a contribution only to find the arena overcrowded, the study of rural-to-urban migration, especially of labor, in less developed countries (LDCs) appears to be an unusual and enviable exception – a rare convergence of real-world concerns, professional interest, and productive research activity.

However, recent intensive research in the field of rural-to-urban migration – the high surge in research activity appears to have started off with Todaro's pioneering article (Todaro, 1969) – has left the field beset with loss of direction, considerable confusion, and serious doubts as to (a) whether research has really provided practitioners with finer, more *specific* means of intervention, if it should be deemed desirable, (b) a proper understanding of such intervention, its justification, and results, (c) the areas in which the marginal benefit of extra research amounts to zero, (d) those areas in which some solid consensus has emerged, and a clear formulation of this consensus, (e) which problem areas and specific issues in them merit additional intensive migration research in the coming years, and (f) whether or not the academic profession has based its migration research effort in the recent past largely on an inappropriate set of presuppositions or, even worse, on invalid postulates.

To render this list and the accusations leveled in it more concrete, we shall present and document a few examples of confusion and/or fallacies that come readily to mind. Rather than suggesting the simultaneous existence of competing schools of thought – often a healthy sign of a dynamic and competitively developing field of research – these examples illustrate what appear to be conflicting axiomatic stands leading to the deliberate bending (or neglect) of evidence rather than to its accumulation and unbiased interpretation. No less serious, such stands are often sublimely transformed into doctrines which (naturally) give rise to conflicting policy prescriptions.

## 2  Migration and Fertility

The macro long-term statistical association between rural-to-urban migration and fertility is unequivocal: when the former increases the latter declines (possibly with some lags and variations, for example, with destination – city size). The underlying reason is that the urban environment and labor market, with their different relative prices and income constraints, are less conducive to large families than are rural areas. It is also possible that a self-selection process operates here whereby locational preferences – migration – reflect and serve pre-migration-formed fertility preferences (Ribe and Schultz, 1980; Lee et al., 1981).

However, there is no very sound migration, fertility, or economic theory here. If bearing and raising children is more costly in an urban environment then, although exposure to that environment could produce the postulated effect, it is not clear from this argument why families should subject themselves to that environment in the first place. Obviously, it makes good economic sense for them to raise children in rural areas – where it costs less – and then have them (or their families, with them included) migrate to the urban sector.

The preoccupation with the fertility behavior of rural-to-urban *migrants* has led to a complete disregard of another variable in the migration–fertility linkage. This variable has to do with the micro decision-making association. Consider a modal agricultural family, assumed to be the decision-making entity,[1] which attempts to transform "familial" into "capitalist" production. It usually faces two major constraints. First, there is the "investment capital" constraint: the transformation (for example, to high-yielding varieties) requires some investment funds which a small farmer family with its existing resource endowment and a "pre-capitalist" mode of production is unlikely to possess or generate. It is both relevant and interesting to note that most of the recent "relevant technological transformations" depend crucially on new factors and inputs – elements in which the very transformation, the new technology, is embodied. This in itself (apart from the component complementarity that characterizes these technologies) creates strong discrete needs for investment capital and produces a new pattern of technological change which differs from traditional technological progress – a continuous change involving gradual increments to the quantities of *existing* factors facilitated, in turn, by a continuous accumulation of savings.

The second constraint is that of risk. The transformation to a new technology magnifies the subjective risks involved in agricultural production, whereas the family unit is assumed to be risk averse. Thus the major obstacles encountered are bridging the gap between the family's desired investment capital and its necessary cash outlays (including existing savings) and, once this is accomplished, resolving the conflict between the family's aversion to risk and the increased risk element in its portfolio.

In the absence of smoothly functioning credit markets or appropriate institutional facilities, and when insurance markets either do not exist or charge prohibitive premiums, the family must reorganize the utilization of its *own* resources. It is here that rural-to-urban migration by the most suitable family member – a mature son or daughter (especially if educated) – comes into the picture. In bypassing the credit and insurance markets (with their bias against small farmers) migration facilitates the transformation; it succeeds in doing this via its dual role in the accumulation of investment capital (acting as an intermediate investment between technological investments, which have a certain lumpiness, and investment in financial assets, which, if feasible, has a low (or even negative) return), usually generating significant urban-to-rural flows of remittances,[2] and, through diversification of income sources, controlling the level of risk. This "portfolio investment" in urban earning activity (migration by a maturing family member) as a risk-alleviating device assumes, in particular, that the urban sector is statistically independent of agricultural production.[3]

In an economy where transformation of production modes cannot be performed directly, grown children *as migrants* thus assume the unique role of financial intermediaries. From a private parental point of view, and considering lifetime utility, children are generally seen to yield various direct and indirect utilities which may be conveniently designated "consumption utility" (children are a source of personal pleasure and satisfaction), "income utility" (children directly contribute to the family's income by working), and "status, security, and insurance utility" (status, for example, when position and power are established through child-generated familial ties, security, especially old-age security, and insurance as an extra child can generate various utilities if other children fail to do so, mainly because of early mortality). The alleged role of children as migrants implies that a new element is added to the utilities-from-children vector, namely facilitating production transformation. This element is distinct from the others, especially from the income utility element, in that children's primary role as migrants is not to generate an income stream *per se*, but to act as catalysts for the generation of such a stream by precipitating an income-increasing technological change on the family farm.[4]

This is an intriguing assertion because, if thoroughly tested and verified,[5] it will imply that, whereas with an adaptation lag that could last as long as a whole generation, rural-to-urban migration may lower the fertility of the migrants or of their urban-born offspring, the specific valuable task that children *as migrants* fulfill may induce higher demand for children and *higher fertility* – the very birth of the migrants themselves.

## 3 Migration and Education

Conflicting views also abound on migration and education. On the one hand it is argued that the better educated rural youngsters who acquire nonrural specific human capital and possess more human capital – and hence are also less risk averse – are induced to migrate townwards (Barnum and Sabot, 1976). On the other hand, poor educational opportunities in rural areas induce rural families, especially the wealthier ones, to send their children to school-rich urban areas. So, should the absence of education or its availability be held responsible for generating rural-to-urban migration?[6] Or, perhaps, will nonhomogeneous education (in quality or orientation) differentially affect migration propensity, with education of the "right kind" discouraging it and other types of education enhancing it?

Note that in both cases, if educational expansion is universal, externalities can no longer be ignored; the end result could be very near homogeneity of degree zero throughout. Higher returns to more education (and to more human capital in general) inversely relate to its scarcity. Rural educated youth may find that acquisition of more urban-specific education fails to enhance their employment prospects in the urban sector and is of no (or limited) use in making them more proficient in rural occupations. And if what migrants really care about is their relative position (rank) (Stark, 1984), the end result could be exactly homogeneity of degree zero.

It is probable that there are richer layers of explanation on both sides. We shall proceed with just two illustrations linking the argument to the issue of fertility dealt with in the preceding section. First, in a time series context, education may very well correlate negatively with migration. An educated rural girl is likely to desire and achieve lower fertility which, in the long run, will reduce rural-to-urban migration.

Second, take for example the case of the small farmer and the credit crunch raised in the preceding section. Whereas the small farmer has no effective (or sufficient) access to institutional or other credit, nor can he expect this situation to change,[7] his children usually have access to some sort of state education which is often a pure public good, largely financed by government subsidies and not (directly) by the pupils' parents. Thus a small farmer's vicarious entrance into a less discriminating market can be viewed as a surrogate for participation in one into which his entrance is effectively barred. Banking on the expectation of a high cross-return to the joint decision of educating a child and then "expelling" him or her to the urban sector, migration (and the education preceding it) thus substitute for the credit deficiency, the alleviation of which is mandatory in facilitating technological change on the family farm. Farmers therefore deliberately use the educational system to prepare for their children's migration.

## 4 Migration and the Distribution of Income by Size

Another popular view held by some of the better writers in the field is that migrants are twice to blame for increasing inequality. Because of the selective nature of migration, rural areas are depleted of scarce human capital, entrepreneurial skills, and leadership for agricultural development. At the urban end, migrants, even if employed, join the less productive earners at the lower end of the income distribution (Lipton, 1977, 1980). However, if we view the income-receiving unit as the family as a whole, *including* its young migrant member, the argument is reversed.

The family, excluding the migrant, and the migrant himself are "bound together" for a considerable period of time in a cooperative game. By taking a *joint* decision as to what course of action each party (player) will adopt, they secure a mutually advantageous coordination. This produces a result (total income or utility) which, from the point of view of any one of the players, cannot be bettered by "going his own way," that is, compared with his noncooperative prospects. The cooperation, evidenced in the maintenance of close economic ties for a considerable period of time (for example, urban-to-rural migrant-to-family remittances, or provision of rural-based insurance against upheavals in turbulent urban labor markets), the implied pooling of resources, and the joint decision-making with respect to income plans, both earnings and disposition, can then easily be shown to reduce inequality in the distribution of income by size, as measured by the Gini coefficient, or to increase welfare directly as discerned by application of stochastic dominance and Pareto criteria (Stark and Yitzhaki, 1980; Stark, 1984).

In addition, some macro simulation exercises have unmasked the real equilibrating beauty of rural-to-urban migration, especially in a non-short-run perspective (Ahluwalia, 1976; Adelman and Robinson, 1977; Knowles and Anker, 1977).

## 5 Migration and Urban Employment

Many rural-to-urban migrants rationally, although involuntarily, join the ranks of the urban unemployed since there are fewer high-paying formal sector jobs than rural laborers who migrate in response to their creation (Todaro, 1979, 1980a). Yet, drawing on their own savings or on familial or similar support, migrants may willingly go through a prolonged period of urban unemployment as an optimal strategy of investment in search of high-paying jobs, particularly when free-entry informal sector employment is available at a competitively determined market-clearing wage. There are thus two labor market equilibrium conditions. The first is the usual intersectoral one. To specify the second, assume for simplicity that migration decisions are based on a two-period planning horizon, that is, all future periods collapse into the second planning period. When formal sector employment cannot be secured in the first period, two competing strategies are feasible: (a) accept informal sector employment in the first period, and in the second period move with probability $p$ into a higher-paying urban job or pursue (with the complementary probability) informal sector employment; (b) reject informal sector employment and remain unemployed, but invest in information and engage in intensive formal sector job searching to enhance the probability of being employed in that sector in the second planning period from $p$ to $q > p$. Alternatively, take up, with the complementary probability, an informal sector job. At equilibrium, the expected return discounted to the present of adopting each of these two strategies is the same. As long as $q$ is larger than $p$, urban unemployment could well make sense as a deliberate *post*-migration choice.

Whereas standard economic theory maintains that downward supply pressures will prevail when the price of a commodity is set artificially (institutionally) high, it fails to provide any insight into the operation of the "inverse black-market mechanism" through which the limited slots are allocated among the many participants (because of the homogeneity assumption). Rather than passively awaiting their turn to be randomly selected, rural-to-urban migrants may choose unemployment so as to engage in the resource- and *time*-consuming operation of acquiring preferential treatment, say, by cultivating oligopolistic shop stewards. This process may convey a positive externality onto a specific community – the migrant's extended family or his fellow villagers – and could therefore be sustained by that community.

Note that rural-to-urban migrants may choose to remain unemployed for yet another reason. Their acceptance of a low-paying low-skill informal sector job could be construed as a signal, albeit an imperfect one, by the *formal* sector, reflecting their (apparently) inferior labor force qualifications and personal traits. Thus a revealed low supply price, suggestive of a low level of human capital and general skills, could consequently reduce the expected urban income stream by more than immediate acceptance of informal sector employment would increase it.

## 6 Migration and the Politics of Economics

A widely held view is that rural-to-urban migration raises food prices and increases urban revolutionary potential; underemployed, unemployed, and low-income urban laborers whose absolute or relative deprivation and frustration might be converted into political action threaten the stable political order that is so crucial for smooth production and continued profit-taking. Governments are impatient, and researchers are often called upon to produce virtually unanimous prescriptions designed to contain the "drift of rural migrants into the large urban centers," for action-prone governments to act upon (United Nations, 1979).

However, an equally powerful argument can be advanced to show why governments do not really want to stem the "tide of migrants to the cities" (Stark, 1980a). It will draw upon the profit-maximization motive of profit-seekers who participate in government, influence its decision-making, or provide it with crucial, tacit, or explicit support. By dampening urban wages, or mitigating their rise, migration increases profits and thus, statically and dynamically, serves the fundamental interests of these profit-earners. In a similar vein, migration serves the interests of urban landlords in raising or putting an upward pressure on urban rents.

In recent years increasing emphasis has been placed on the argument that a great deal of rural-to-urban migration is due to urban bias in the allocation of national resources, especially public investment and public expenditure. Political priorities manifested through economic strategies are the root cause; rural-to-urban migration is the observed malady (Lipton, 1977; Newland, 1980). But rural-to-urban migration may also be the healing agent. The political economic biases are more likely to be toppled by relatively new urbanites who gradually acquire access to the decision-making apparatus without abandoning their familial ties and property rights in the rural sector. The equilibrating beauty of rural-to-urban migration may be manifested once again.

## 7 Migration and Policy Measures

Another widely held view is that, since expected utility maximization under substantial intersectoral income differentials induces rural-to-urban migration, policy measures designed to dampen urban incomes (a freeze on urban real wages) or to increase rural incomes (farm price supports) are essential (Todaro, 1980b). Development strategies must be restructured to redress past unbalanced growth and urban biases, and to take proper account of agricultural and rural development (Lipton, 1977). At the same time, leading international development agencies frequently and increasingly adopt accommodationist policies that "aspire to improve the lot of migrants" (Laquian, 1979). Such policies (for example, sites and services projects, reception centers for new migrants) run counter to the perceptions mentioned earlier, since, virtually by definition, they increase the attractiveness of the urban destination, often not so much by increasing expected income as by decreasing uncertainty (income variance). But this does not really matter, since in a utility-maximizing exercise both expectations and variance count. Accommodationist policies are thus conducive to rural-to-urban migration rather than being an added constraint on it. It is worth expanding this point a little.

It can be shown (Stark and Levhari, 1982) that risk avoidance, *not risk seeking*, is a major explanatory variable in rural-to-urban migration decisions. This is so not only when the migration decision-making entity is the family (as already mentioned, migration implies a risk-reducing portfolio diversification of income sources) but also when it is the individual. If he were to pursue agricultural production he would have to endure some level of risk per period emanating from the low immunity, especially of traditional agriculture, to stochastic variability in rainfall and weather conditions, plant disease, attacks by pests, etc., all of which affect both grown and stored crops. This low immunity is especially hazardous as it is usually coupled with an absence of institutional insurance arrangements. If an individual migrates from the rural to the urban sector, he is not subjected to similar periodic risks. At first, risks are very high. Entry attempts into high-paying sectors may fail. Entry into low-paying sectors, which may be relatively easy, entails a high probability of discontinuity of employment because of high sensitivity and hence vulnerability of these sectors to market fluctuations. But risks associated with urban employment diminish with time and may be relatively low – that is, lower than the typical risk associated with agricultural production – after some initial high-risk period. An individual who engages in rural-to-urban migration under such circumstances is obviously one who attaches a premium to an early resolution of (much of) his lifelong income-associated risks. He trades in "medium-level" risks for immediate higher, but thereafter lower, risks.

This hypothesis, if substantiated, opens up a new range of policy measures. If institutional intervention aimed at reducing migration is deemed desirable, it will be efficient to shift away from exclusive (so far largely futile) attempts to narrow the intersectoral wage differential toward transformation of rural income-earning activity into a less risky proposition, for example through the creation and/or perfection of rural insurance markets, direct provision of technological insurance to small farmers, etc.

Similarly, optimal techniques in urban industry must be relatively capital intensive (rather than labor intensive) so as to avoid inducing extra migration through "excessive" job creation (Todaro, 1980b). However, migrants' saving behavior may enhance, not impede, investment and growth, and thus the optimal choice could favor labor intensity after all, compatible with national resource endowments and scarcities (Stark, 1981b). A new urban job may attract so many productive rural laborers that the shadow wage pertaining to an urban marginal new project could be pushed high above the market ruling wage (Todaro, 1980b). Yet, again, migrants' saving behavior could be shown to generate a shadow wage *lower* than the market wage relationship as the negative net contribution of changed consumption to the shadow wage outpaces the positive production opportunity cost (Stark, 1980c, 1981a).

It is also not quite clear why "disequilibrium" in the labor market – manifested by a continuous rural-to-urban migration – should be addressed by intervention in *that* market. In a general equilibrium context, disequilibrium in one market must coincide with disequilibrium in another and the two are causally related. As made clear in section 2, the roots of rural-to-urban migration can be found outside the labor market, that is, in the ill-functioning capital market. Improving the operational efficiency of *financial* markets (where major imperfections are asymmetry in information and transaction costs which create barriers to trade) could bring about the desired impact in the *labor* market. (A good example is India's Farmers' Protection Deposit Scheme, whereby depositors who are paid only a low interest rate are granted the right to borrow up to twice the outstanding deposit at a modest rate of interest in the event of crop failure (Bhatt, 1978). Thus a reason for migration – aversion to increased production risks which cannot be effectively hedged against given the existing structure of the insurance market – is, at least partially, removed.)

## 8 Conclusions

This list could be extended further, but it suffices to illustrate the conflicting views, biases, confusion, and fallacies, and hence the disappointing dissipation of enormous cumulative research effort.

Responsibility for the present dire state of the art probably rests on the overcrowding of researchers in a narrow zone (undercrowding in the "real" field), which is rapidly decreasing the usefulness of their work. Furthermore, more often than not it has implied repeated reference to an unwarranted expansion of conventional notions emanating from a theoretically weak (yet often staunchly defended) center. A great deal of work has been produced through sheer inertia, and very little from fresh departures. Presuppositions necessary to facilitate analysis and improve the understanding of migration have stiffened into doctrines rather than being revised, let alone superseded, in light of the advances that have been made. It is time to pause for a major re-evaluation which could and should prove a turning point in academic work and institutional thought.

Perhaps the most crucial element in opening up the field should be the reformulation of the policy-related presumptions on which recent research has been based. Rather than trying to reach a better understanding of the decision-making process generating rural-to-urban migration and its sectoral and overall social implications so as to devise more effective measures to contain/reverse it, the starting point should be an effort to manipulate the phenomenon effectively so as to turn it into a vehicle of national development and personal betterment. The formidable, but amply rewarding, challenge is to exploit skillfully, not to tame coercively. Rural-to-urban migration carries with it a large array of potentially desirable repercussions, often realized and manifested. Good policies should employ effective means to minimize or eliminate the few (if any) undesirable consequences of migration, but not eliminate migration itself.

A general argument often gains force by an excellent example. Such is provided by the issue of urban-to-rural transfer of remittances. By now there is sufficient reason to believe, and evidence to suggest, that rural-to-urban migration and urban-to-rural remittances have actually been used to transform agricultural modes of production (Stark, 1978, 1980b). What a new constructive approach should focus on is the analysis of why, in some cases but not in others, urban-to-rural remittances have had very little impact on agricultural development. Remittances can be turned into a vehicle of rural prosperity even if in the past they were not always conducive to agricultural development. This *may* require some – minimal – institutional intervention to induce migrants to remit more and their rural families to utilize what they receive more productively. (Special remittance bank accounts and matching grants or loans to be extended on the disbursement of receipts of remittances toward the introduction of new technologies may serve such a system.)

Consider, as yet another example, one of the most often repeated statements in the field, that by historical yardsticks the urbanization process in present-day LDCs is second to none (which may not be true at all) and that the phenomenon far exceeds "the absorptive capacity" of cities in present LDCs (Todaro, 1979). A fresh approach may very well demolish even this "conventional wisdom." By now, the advance of social science and technological knowhow has outpaced that of urbanization rates. There is no *a priori* reason why modern knowledge and tools should be unable to provide excellent means to handle the "excessive" growth; migrants' skills and time can be combined to expand this so-called "constrained absorptive capacity" and if we do not yet know exactly how to manipulate them, assuming that such manipulation is warranted, that is exactly what new research efforts should be about.[8]

In the evolution of science and technology, breakthroughs were often autonomous and incidental – an apple happened to fall when Newton was in a contemplative mood. In recent times, however, trail-blazing advances have become increasingly induced. It is time to initiate a coordinated endeavor of the best minds in a concerted effort to redefine the research agenda, to inject a new sense of direction, and to infuse a new vitality and sense of purpose into rural-to-urban migration research.

**Notes**

Reprinted from *World Development* 10, 1982. Published by Pergamon Journals Ltd, Oxford, United Kingdom. An earlier version of this paper was circulated as Center for Policy Studies, Population Council, CPS Notes No. 31, November 1980. Another version was presented at the Population Association of America Annual Meeting, Washington, DC, March 26–28, 1981. A large number of people read the earlier versions and furnished me with enlightening comments and constructive critique. I am indebted to all of them and, in particular, to Ansley Coale, Arthur Lewis, Geoffrey McNicoll, Simon Kuznets, Mark Perlman, Theodore Schultz, Amartya Sen, Paul Streeten, and an anonymous reader. The financial support of the Center for Policy Studies, Population Council, is gratefully acknowledged.

1   There are some strong empirical and theoretical reasons for this assumption. See, *inter alia*, Stark (1978, 1982a, b).
2   Significant urban-to-rural transfer of remittances is one of the most important observed regularities of rural-to-urban migration in LDCs (Stark, 1978, ch. III, 1980b).
3   For formal and fuller treatments see, respectively, Stark (1978, appendix II) and Stark and Levhari (1982).
4   In a lifetime utility-maximization exercise, where discounted streams of benefits and costs associated with bearing and rearing children are considered, a lower net price (cost *minus* benefit) of children implies that more of them will be desired (through the positive impacts of both the substitution and the income effects, assuming that children are a normal good).
5   For some empirical evidence see Stark (1978, ch. III).
6   For given studies containing conflicting views see Lipton (1976) and Findley (1977).
7   Credit markets are imperfect, not fully formed, and highly fragmented, the quantity of marketable assets possessed by the small farmer as collateral for credit is very limited, and so forth.
8   In comparing the urbanization rate in present-day LDCs with that experienced in the past by present developed countries (DCs), proper account should be given to "the impression that in current LDCs, urban mortality is not signifi-

cantly greater than rural, and perhaps may be lower – whereas the excess of mortality in the cities in the earlier decades in the now DCs was substantial until the beginning of the twentieth century" (Simon Kuznets, personal communication).

## References

Adelman, Irma and Robinson, Sherman (1977) "Migration, Demographic Change and Income Distribution in a Model of a Developing Country." Research Program in Development Studies, Discussion Paper 71, Woodrow Wilson School of Public and International Affairs, Princeton University.

Ahluwalia, Montek S. (1976) "Inequality, Poverty and Development." *Journal of Development Economics* 3 (4): 307–42.

Barnum, H. N. and Sabot, R. H. (1976) "Migration, Education and Urban Surplus Labour: The Case of Tanzania." Development Centre Studies, Employment Series 13, Development Centre of the Organization for Economic Co-operation and Development.

Bhatt, V. V. (1978) "Interest Rates, Transaction Costs and Financial Innovations." Domestic Finance Studies 47, World Bank.

Findley, Sally (1977) *Planning for Internal Migration: A Review of Issues and Policies in Developing Countries.* US Department of Commerce, Bureau of the Census.

Knowles, James C. and Anker, Richard (1977) "An Analysis of Income Transfers in a Developing Country: The Case of Kenya." Population and Employment Working Paper 59, World Employment Programme Research, International Labour Office.

Laquian, Aprodicio A. (1979) "Review and Evaluation of Accommodationist Policies in Population Redistribution." Presented at a United Nations/UNFPA Workshop on Population Distribution Policies in Development Planning, Bangkok, September 1979.

Lee, Bun Song, Farber, Stephen C., Jamal, A. M. M. and Rulison, Michael V. E. (1981) "The Influence of Rural–Urban Migration on the Fertility of Migrants in Developing Countries: Analysis of Korean Data." Mimeo, Louisiana State University.

Lipton, Michael (1977) *Why Poor People Stay Poor: A Study of Urban Bias in World Development.* London: Temple Smith.

—— (1980) "Migration from Rural Areas of Poor Countries: The Impact on Rural Productivity and Income Distribution." *World Development* 8 (1): 1–24.

Newland, Kathleen (1980) "City Limits: Emerging Constraints on Urban Growth." Paper 38, Worldwatch Institute.

Ribe, Helena and Schultz, T. Paul (1980) "Migrant and Native Fertility in Colombia in 1973: Are Migrants Selected According to Their Reproductive Preferences?" Discussion Paper 355, Economic Growth Center, Yale University.

Stark, Oded (1978) *Economic–Demographic Interactions in Agricultural Develop-ment: The Case of Rural-to-Urban Migration.* Rome: UN Food and Agriculture Organization.

—— (1980a) "On Slowing Metropolitan City Growth." *Population and Develop-ment Review* 6 (1): 95–102 (reprinted as ch. 20 in this volume).

—— (1980b) "On the Role of Urban-to-Rural Remittances in Rural Develop-ment." *Journal of Development Studies* 16 (3): 369–74 (reprinted as ch. 14 in this volume).

—— (1980c) "A Note on the Shadow Wage in LDCs with Migration and Formal and Informal Sectors." *Economics Letters* 5 (3).

—— (1981a) "Urban Project Appraisal with Migration: The Issue of the Shadow Wage." Presented at the European Meeting of the Econometric Society, Amsterdam, August 31 – September 4, 1981.

—— (1981b) "On the Optimal Choice of Capital Intensity in LDCs with Migra-tion." *Journal of Development Economics* 9 (1): 31–41 (reprinted as ch. 19 in this volume).

—— (1982a) "Rural–Urban Migration and Surplus Labour: Reservations on Bhatia." *Oxford Economic Papers* 34 (3): 569–73.

—— (1982b) "Game Theory, Migration Theory and the Family." Mimeo, Harvard University.

—— (1984) "Rural-to-Urban Migration in LDCs: A Relative Deprivation Approach." *Economic Development and Cultural Change* 32 (3): 475–86 (re-printed as ch. 7 in this volume).

—— and Levhari, David (1982) "On Migration and Risk in LDCs." *Economic Development and Cultural Change* 31 (1): 191–6 (reprinted as ch. 4 in this volume).

—— and Yitzhaki, Shlomo (1980) "A Welfare Economic Approach to Growth and Distribution in the Dual Economy: Comment." Discussion Paper 8006, Econo-mics Research Institute, Bar-Ilan University.

Todaro, Michael P. (1969) "A Model of Labor Migration and Urban Unemploy-ment in Less Developed Countries." *American Economic Review* 59 (1): 138–48.

—— (1979) "Urbanization in Developing Nations: Trends, Prospects, and Poli-cies." Working Paper 50, Population Council, Center for Policy Studies.

—— (1980a) "Internal Migration in Developing Countries: A Survey." In Richard A. Easterlin (ed.), *Population and Economic Change in Developing Countries.* Chicago, IL: University of Chicago Press for National Bureau of Economic Research.

—— (1980b) "Internal Migration, Urban Population Growth and Unemployment in Developing Nations: Issues and Controversies." Mimeo.

United Nations (1979) *World Population Trends and Policies: 1977 Monitoring Report,* vol.2. New York: United Nations.

# 2

# The New Economics of Labor Migration

Research on the economics of labor migration has undergone an exciting and significant transformation during the past few years. At a theoretical level, migration research has expanded the domain of variables that seem to impinge upon and are affected by spatial labor supply decisions, it has highlighted the role of wider social entities and interactions within them in conditioning migration behavior, it has identified new linkages between migration as a distinct labor market phenomenon and other labor market and nonlabor market phenomena, and it has contributed to our understanding of the processes of economic betterment and development. At an empirical level, recent work on the economics of labor migration has confirmed the usefulness of old and well-established models of labor migration. It has also provided better estimates of key behavioral parameters, many of which are important ingredients in ongoing debates over public policies relating to migration. With such an impressive score, it is a wonder that more of the profession has not shifted into migration research. Perhaps this has to do with lack of information.

Our goal here is to summarize the actively evolving ideas, findings, and difficulties in the economics of labor migration. We do this mainly by illustrating selected theoretical and empirical developments which we believe to be on the frontier of research in this area. We also identify several new research topics that comprise part of the next research frontier. Prior to proceeding with these tasks, we wish to point out that much of the more interesting recent research is associated with migration within and from developing economies. This situation might be partly explained by the fact that the impact of wage differentials on migration tends to be offset by unemployment compensation programs and other fiscal policies in the developed economies. The scene in the less developed countries (LDCs) thus constitutes a good migration research laboratory for studying migration in general.

## 1 Theoretical Issues

Whereas owners of production inputs or commodities, such as bricks or bottles of wine, can ordinarily ship them away (so as to maximize profits or utility) while themselves staying put, owners of labor must usually move along with their labor. Furthermore, owners of labor have both feelings and independent will. Indeed, most aspects of human behavior, including migratory behavior, are both a response to feelings and an exercise of independent will. These simple observations divorce migration research from traditional trade theory as the former cannot be construed from the latter merely by effecting a change of labels.

People engage quite regularly in interpersonal income comparisons within their reference group. These comparisons generate psychological costs or benefits, feelings of relative deprivation or relative satisfaction. A person may migrate from one location to another to change his relative position in the same reference group, or to change his reference group. Membership in a reference group with low relative deprivation may well be preferred to membership in a reference group with high relative deprivation even if in the former a person's absolute income is lower. In general, a person who is more relatively deprived can be expected to have a stronger incentive to migrate than a person who is less relatively deprived. Moreover, a reference group characterized by more income inequality is likely to generate more relative deprivation and higher propensities to migrate. Note also that, as particular individuals migrate, the relative deprivation perceived by nonmigrants may change, thereby creating second-round inducements to migrate. For example, if relative deprivation is gauged through a comparison with a reference group statistic such as average income, migration by low-income (that is, relatively deprived) individuals will cause this statistic to increase and thereby induce migration by other individuals who become increasingly relatively deprived.

Not only can the migration behavior of individuals be expected to differ in accordance with their perceived relative deprivation, it can also be expected to differ according to their skill levels. This outcome results when the assumption of heterogeneous workers is paired with the assumption of imperfect skill information on the part of employers. To obtain some strong illustrative results, consider the following polar case. In a given profession, workers with skill $S$ receive wages $W_P(S)$ and $W_R(S)$ from employers at P and R. Assume that skill follows a uniform distribution along a unit interval, that the functions $W_P(S)$ and $W_R(S)$ are nondecreasing and linear, and that $S$ is known by P and R employers. Assume further that for low levels of $S$, say $S < S^*$, $W_P(S) > W_R(S)$, whereas for $S \geqslant S^*$ the reverse inequality holds. Clearly, the lowest-skilled workers will not wish to migrate from P to R. Assume now that R employers cannot observe the true skill level of individual P workers (that is, that skill information is asymmetric), but that they know the distribution of $S$ and will pay migrants from P a wage that is equal to the average productivity of the migrant group. The interior solution $S^*$ now vanishes and is replaced by one of two corner solutions: either there is no migration at all, or there is migration by all. This result follows essentially because the highly skilled workers who migrate under perfect information may not do so if the pooled wage is too low. But if they do not, the pooled wage is lowered so that the next highly skilled group also does not find it advantageous to migrate and so on.

Just as it is clear that neither a brick nor a bottle of wine can *decide* to move between markets, so should it be equally clear that a migrant is not necessarily the decision-making entity accountable for his or her migration. Migration decisions are often made jointly by the migrant and by some group of nonmigrants. Costs and returns are shared, with the rule governing the distribution of both spelled out in an implicit contractual arrangement between the two parties. For example, one important component of the direct returns to the nonmigrating family from the migration of a family member are his or her remittances. Theory suggests the view, that empirical evidence seems to support, that patterns of remittances are better explained as an intertemporal contractual arrangement between the migrant and the family than as the result of purely altruistic considerations.

Theory also offers reasons for the migrant and the family to enter voluntarily into a mutually beneficial contractual arrangement with each other – rather than with a third party – and identifies conditions under which the contract is self-enforcing. Since the chosen contractual arrangement reflects the relative bargaining powers of the parties, this approach can also be used to generate empirically falsifiable predictions about remittance patterns, that is, that variables that enhance the bargaining power of the family and the importance of its support (such as a high-unemployment urban labor market) will *positively* influence the magnitude of migrant-to-family remittances. Note that this approach demonstrates the efficiency, flexibility, and what we might call the dynamic comparative advantage of the family. In other words, it does not view the family as an entity that is split apart as its independence-seeking younger members move away in an attempt to dissociate themselves from familial and traditional bondage, regardless of the negative externalities thereby imposed upon their families. Moreover, this approach shifts the focus of migration theory from individual independence (optimization against nature) to mutual interdependence (optimization against one another), that is, it views migration as a "calculated strategy" and not as an act of desperation or boundless optimism.

Risk handling provides another illuminating example in which a wider social entity is collectively responsible for individual migration. Clearly, the family is a very small group within which to pool risks. But the disadvantages of small scale may be made up by an ability to realize scale economies and yet remain a cohesive group. Such scale economies are achieved by the migration of one or more family members into a sector where earnings are negatively correlated, statistically independent, or not highly positively correlated with earnings in the origin sector. Again, as in the remittances example, the important point to note is that *both* parties are better off as a result of migration since, in this case, an exchange of commitments to share income provides coinsurance. Note, in addition, that just as it explains migration by part of the family, this example also accounts for nonmigration by the remainder.[1]

The nature of intra-group interaction could also help to explain features of the economic performance of migrants. To begin with, migrants often outperform the native born in the receiving economy. (We say more on this in section 2.) In addition, heavy reliance upon "network and kinship capital" is another prominent characteristic of migrant behavior patterns. The latter may explain the former quite readily in the context of an economy with a large number of agents whose transactions are governed by a prisoner's dilemma super-game. Briefly, a migrant who offers to cooperate in his trade with *anyone* in the first game, whereas thereafter the choice in each game is that of the other agent in the previous game, will tend to be better off than a native who never behaves cooperatively, provided that a sufficiently high proportion of trades by migrants are conducted among migrants. This result provides an interesting explanation for the observation that new migrants are assisted by those who have migrated earlier; one good way of having a higher proportion of all trades conducted among migrants when there are few of them is to have additional migrants. The arrival of new migrants confers benefits upon the earlier migrants. It also suggests a resolution of the apparent inconsistency of altruistic behavior within a small group (say, a family) and selfish behavior within larger groups (say, a marketplace); the same strategy, that is, cooperate in the first game and thereafter reciprocate, is systematically applied throughout.

This appeal to strategic behavior may also be used to derive further migration-related insights. Consider first a typical village economy in an LDC where farming landlords are in an oligopsonistic position with respect to the determination of wages and employment. Through collusion, the farmers can increase their profits. However, labor migration can constitute a credible counter-strategy to this possibility, provided that, from time to time, some undertake it. Note that, once again, migration confers benefits upon those who stay behind, in addition to those associated with a leftward shift in the supply curve of labor. Second, consider the case of employers who, in static and dynamic contexts alike, are better off with a larger labor pool than with a smaller labor pool. Since a large labor pool can be developed by cultivating an image of worker success, it might be worth-while for employers to create high-paying jobs in order to attract more migrants. As long as a large number of workers believe that high-paying employment can be obtained, or that it is worth waiting for, a migratory response will be produced. High "institutionally determined" wages in urban labor markets in LDCs are thus not necessarily externally imposed upon reluctant employers by government legislation and trade unions. Instead, they may result from endogenously determined strategies de-signed to maximize profits in dynamic settings. Also, generating a few very high-paying jobs and heavily advertising, so to speak, the rewards asso-ciated with them may help to maintain a large labor pool in the presence of high levels of unemployment. This strategy will tend to confuse migrant calculations, which may suggest that expected urban income is less than rural income. Thus high-paying jobs might also be created *in response* to high levels of unemployment rather than preceding them and bringing them about.

Since the endowments and preferences of economic agents are always heterogeneous in practice, selectivity, as such, in response to a given set of prices and opportunities and changes in it, by way of migration or otherwise, is quite obvious. In many cases, whether migration selectivity prevails is not as interesting as the extent to which the migration response diffuses. Indeed, migration can be looked upon as a process of innovation, adoption, and diffusion. As time goes by, what proportion of a given group of *potential* migrants have migrated? To illustrate, assume that there are a number of migration destinations and that there is some prior belief that one particular destination is better than the others. In this setting, the experience of actual migrants provides valuable information that presu-mably reduces future uncertainty of the remaining pool of potential migrants. Under these circumstances, the most interesting research issues relate to the determination of the speed of adoption of migration as an innovation and the characteristics associated with the delay in the adoption of the innovation (rather than whether it takes place). That is, why are some individuals quicker to migrate than others? For the case of rural-to-urban migration in LDCs where, if history were to repeat itself, most rural people will end up as migrants, such an approach seems particularly appropriate. Note that, as with a demonstration effect in the case of innovation adoption, a stock of past migrants at a given destination (particularly a large stock) represents evidence that might lead to an upward revision of beliefs that migration is a worthy investment. Moreover, the impact of migration upon the society from which it takes place is now stage specific. Thus the divergence of views concerning the consequences of migration (for example, its impact upon the distribution of income by size) can partly be attributed to the simple fact that the underlying observations are made at distinct stages of the diffusion process.

## 2 Empirical Considerations

Recent empirical research on the economics of labor migration has benefited a great deal more from the development of new econometric techniques than from new theoretical ideas. The techniques that have substantially improved our ability to use micro data sets in the estimation of relatively standard models of labor migration include techniques for the analysis of qualitative dependent variables, techniques that correct for sample selection bias, and techniques for the analysis of longitudinal and pseudolongitudinal data. At the micro level, most empirical studies have attempted to test simple microeconomic models of migration according to which individuals (or families) make locational decisions primarily by comparing their income opportunities at alternative locations. The key feature of recent studies of this type is their focus on the estimation of structural, as opposed to reduced-form, models of the migration decision. In the past, a major problem that made the estimation of such models difficult was the absence of data on the wages that particular individuals would receive at two or more locations at the same point(s) in time. In other words, survey data sets typically provide researchers with information on the wages received by individuals at their residential location at the time of the survey, their migrant or nonmigrant status at that location, and selected individual characteristics (for example, age, education, and marital status). To the extent that particular *unobserved* characteristics of individuals are rewarded differently at different locations, the average wage of individuals (conditional on their observed characteristics) at location A, who migrated there from location B, will provide a biased estimate of the wage that individuals who remained at location B would receive if they moved to location A.

Largely as a result of advances in the statistical analysis of selected samples, however, we now have fairly simple methods that we can use to test and correct for the bias associated with this unobserved wage problem. To date, estimates of these structural models of labor migration uniformly support the hypothesis that individuals respond to income incentives in making decisions to migrate. However, further application of these models is desirable, using different data sets and more carefully formulated and tested empirical specifications. It would be interesting to examine whether the strength of the migration response to wage differentials decreases over time, while the response to variables such as relative deprivation increases. We should also like to point out that longitudinal data may prove particularly useful in analyzing the determinants of migration, insofar as they permit a distinctly different approach to the problem of sample selection (that is, longitudinal data permit researchers to control more directly for unobserved variables that affect wages and that are correlated with the migration decision).

Furthermore, much empirical research has been conducted on the labor market progress of migrants, with special attention paid to the behavior of international migrants. To date, most studies of this topic have involved the estimation of cross-sectional wage equations in which "years since migration" is entered as an independent variable and its coefficient is interpreted as a measure of migrant progress. Typically, these studies find that migrant workers earn less than native-born workers with similar characteristics during the first few years after migration but more there-after. It has been suggested, however, that this longitudinal conclusion, based on analyses of cross-sectional data, may be an artifact of either the declining quality of migrant labor over time (that is, a vintage effect) or the outmigration of the least successful migrants. In view of the contradictory nature of extant empirical conclusions, and given the academic and policy importance of this issue, additional research on the pace of migrants' labor market progress is clearly needed. Further analysis of longitudinal data on migrant earnings would also be helpful.

In addition to the two focal points for empirical work discussed above, there are four other areas that empirical economists have touched upon and which we think should receive further attention. The first of these areas involves estimation of the macroeconomic effects of migration. There is a surprising lack of empirical work on the effects of labor migration on wages and employment in net sending and net receiving locations, especially for different types of labor (for example, skilled and unskilled labor). Further work on this topic would be of interest, perhaps involving estimation of the wage and employment effects of migration in the context of well-defined structural models of equilibrium and disequilibrium labor markets. Analysis of the distributional impacts of migration and the degree of substitutability between international and internal migration in the process of labor market adjustment would also be helpful.

Second, the microeconomic and macroeconomic relationships between aging and labor migration are topics which have received only scant and indirect empirical attention (for example, age is usually a right-hand side variable in microeconomic studies of migration decision-making). Indeed, empirical evidence strongly suggests that older workers are less mobile than younger workers. This finding is quite plausible for a variety of reasons relating to the differential preferences and opportunities of older and younger workers. It therefore seems likely that workforces in many low-fertility countries will show a declining propensity to respond to exogenous economic change by migration as they age over the next two decades. Thus, to the extent that mobility is one of the key requirements for economic efficiency, it would be useful to know more about the extent to which the aggregate migration behavior of a population is influenced by its age distribution and the underlying bases for this relationship. Such information could be very helpful in debates over public policies that provide incentives to migrate.

The third topic that deserves further empirical attention is the migration behavior of dual-earner families. In its most general form, this issue relates to the broader one of the appropriate unit of analysis for studying migration behavior to which we alluded in section 1, that is, the individual or the family. In this connection we can consider the extent to which the labor market activities of one family member are conducive to the migration of another family member, especially in the context of LDCs, or, alternatively, the extent to which the labor market activities of one family member impose a constraint on the migration behavior of another family member, especially in the context of developed countries (DCs). In view of the dramatic rise in the labor force participation rates of females in many DCs, such constraints may have noticeable effects on aggregate migration rates. It would be fruitful to conduct further empirical work on this problem, developed in the context of a structural model of constrained consumer choice and focusing on occupational characteristics as well as earnings.

Finally, at this point in time, we still await the empirical implementation of many of the new theoretical ideas relating to labor migration. Part of the lag stems from the fact that much of the inspiration for recent theoretical work on labor migration is provided by the experience of developing economies in which data on migration are either nonexistent or of poor quality. Nevertheless, given the contribution that careful econometric analysis of the new ideas can make to the fullness of our understanding of migration, it seems clear that such efforts cannot be very far off.

**Notes**

Co-authored with David E. Bloom. Reprinted from *The American Economic Review* 75, 1985. Comments by participants in the Harvard-MIT Research Seminar on Migration and Development are gratefully acknowledged. Bloom's research was supported by NIH Grant HD18844-02.
1  The insurance attribute of migration also applies to the individualistic case. For example, just as general human capital provides self-insurance, so does migration in conjunction with specific human capital. Thus, in easing risk bearing associated with investment in specific human capital, migration facilitates such investment, thereby conferring efficiency gains.

# 3

# Migrants and Markets

In recent research considerable effort has been devoted to studying the determinants of migration. In our own work we have examined various factors such as informational asymmetries, attitudes toward risk, relative deprivation and intra-household interactions *as causes*. The subject of the returns to migration or the performance of migrants in the receiving economy has received less attention. To a large extent the question "Why do migrants fare as they do?" has been answered through an inspection of the vector of migrants' characteristics. Possession or lack of human capital assets such as skills has been taken to account for migrants' earnings – an approach which is in consonance with that accorded to nonmigrants. The idea that special features characterize the interaction between migrants and the markets they join and that *market* characteristics largely account for the labor market performance of *individual* migrants has not been pursued. It is this idea which constitutes the main theme of this chapter.

Our motivating example is recent migration to the United States. Several stylized facts stand out. First, migrants from a given origin, for example, source country, are not randomly dispersed across the absorbing economy nor are they all concentrated in one single labor market. Migrants tend to form clusters. For example, returns from the 1980 US census indicate that Asian male migrants who arrived during the five year period preceding the census concentrate in four main Standard Metropolitan Statistical Areas (SMSAs): Los Angeles, New York, San Francisco, and Chicago. Second, the intertemporal distribution of the clusters of migrants is not stationary. The distribution across labor markets of migrants of high-order waves does not replicate the existing distribution. For example, a comparison of the distribution of Mexican male migrants who arrived in the United States during the five year period preceding the 1980 census with Mexican male migrants who arrived in the United States during the five year period preceding the 1970 census reveals less clustering; only 60 percent of the recent arrivals chose Chicago and Los Angeles, whereas a full 76 percent of the earlier arrivals chose these cities.

Third, even though the absolute size of a migrant group within a given labor market is often large, in comparison with the absorbing population (for example, the native born) migrants do not constitute large groups. Fourth, recent migrants are assisted by established migrants; there is heavy reliance upon and usage by the new migrants of "network and kinship capital." Fifth, virtually by definition, migrants have several traits distinguishing them from the population they join. Some characteristics are (costlessly) observable. The differentiation by traits often results in a *statistical* discrimination, that is, migrants *as a group* are treated differentially by the nonmigrants compared with the way that nonmigrants are treated by the nonmigrants. For example, migrants are paid less, on average, than equally skilled nonmigrants. Sixth, in many circumstances, migrants outperform the native born. Usually this result is obtained after a time lag from the migrants' arrival. It tends to hold even after allowance is made for the standard controls.

Although each of these stylized facts can be explained separately with greater or lesser ease, no explanation which causally links all of them appears to exist. It might be useful to attempt to sketch the outline of a possible explanation. We begin by explaining the clustering of migrants through an application of a random walk rule in conjunction with scale economies to trade. Suppose that, at the start, migrants choose the labor markets that they join randomly. Successive migrants arrive and each chooses a labor market, taking into consideration several factors one of which may be the presence of migrants who have arrived in the preceding period(s). Even if each new migrant were to choose randomly among the labor markets, after several waves of migration, say at time *t*, a specific market will probably have more migrants than others. When each of several players repeatedly tosses a die, at some point one player will have scored more odd numbers than the other players even though after many rounds all would score odd numbers exactly the same number of times.

Suppose that the concentration of migrants is subject to scale economies which are quite sensitive to changes in the number of migrants when this number is small. The scale economies (and diseconomies) arise from trade considerations, as explained below. Consequently, from some point in time *t*, a particular market will become more attractive to all subsequent migrants and clustering will occur. Now suppose that, in contrast, the native population, which is much larger, is subject to decreasing returns to scale. Then, from some point in time, the migrants may obtain an edge and outperform the natives. To the extent that migrants of an early vintage are aware of the sensitivity of the onslaught of scale economies to the overall number of migrants in their particular location they may well undertake steps to support and induce new migrants to join them. Consequently, the choice of destination by the new migrants is less likely to be random. This process will not continue if increasing returns at a specific location no longer prevail while they do in another location. The intensity of the pull exerted by that other location will then transform it into the more attractive destination and hence the pattern of several clusters will develop. As long as migrants constitute a distinct group from the natives in the sense that there is no cross-over between "their" increasing returns and "the natives' " decreasing returns, the explanation as outlined above can account for all six stylized facts.

Scale economies leading to differences in the returns to trade (exchange activities) may arise from differences in the structure of interactions, that is, in the manner in which trades are being conducted. This manner, in turn, is largely determined by the likelihood of trades being repeated. This likelihood affects the incentive to invest in reputation and the choice whether to execute trade cooperatively or not. When the number of migrants is very small the likelihood of repeated trades with fellow migrants is low since, by necessity, many trades will be conducted with members of the host community. When the number of migrants becomes very large, the need for a repeated trade with any given agent or subset of agents dwindles, and even among migrants trades are conducted in an environment of anonymity. With a negligible likelihood of trades being repeated, tomorrow's reaction by a partner to today's trade will not matter and hence there will be no inducement to undertake steps either to build and sustain reputation or to protect against retaliation. If, however, the number of migrants is neither too small nor too large and the likelihood of repeated trades amongst them is reasonably high, short-term gains from noncooperation will be more than offset by losses from adverse reputational effects and a pattern of cooperative trades could ensue. Somewhat paradoxically, variables tending to raise the likelihood of a repeat meeting among migrants, for example, barriers of various types to trades with outsiders, may be to the migrants' advantage in inducing a pattern of cooperative trade amongst them which accounts for, or contributes to, their superior performance. Whereas for a relatively small migrant population being distinct from the absorbing population is cost free (recall the migrants' possession of visible distinguishing traits such as color, language, accent, pattern of behavior, etc.), forming a distinct group might be quite costly for a subgroup of agents of the absorbing population who recognize the advantages associated with cooperative trades. This is so especially because there is an incentive for members of the complementary portion of the absorbing population to "raid" the subgroup with noncooperative trades, hoping not to be recognized for what they are.

This line of reasoning, rudimentary as it is, leads to several interesting predictions and policies. These differ from predictions offered and policies mandated by existing models or theories. New migrants may not necessarily receive the greatest degree of help from an established community of migrants when such a community is large since the advantage accruing to the latter from a marginal increase in its size might be much smaller than the advantage accruing to a smaller community from a similar increase. Efforts to disperse migrants across a large number of receiving markets or communities may fail inasmuch as migrants recognize the advantage associated with regrouping and the formation of optimal size clusters. Likewise, efforts to direct new migrants to existing concentrations of migrants guided, for example, by a reasoning that the established migrants could provide social (welfare) services, thereby substituting for public outlays, will fail if clusters are already at their optimal size; large concentrations will tend to disgorge rather than absorb the new arrivals. Since clustering rewards "distinguishable migrants" but not others, it would be reasonable to expect the former to be much more concentrated than the latter. If, for example, the US distribution of migrants were to be compared with that of native-born persons of the same ethnic origin, the native ethnic groups should be expected to be more dispersed throughout the United States than the migrants. In addition, given the pace and the extent of the assimilation of migrants into a host population, markets characterized by quicker and fuller absorption will be more "able" to accommodate additional migrants than will markets characterized by slower and partial assimilation. Markets of the former type will find it possible to absorb migrants continuously without reaching the optimal capacity constraint. Finally, by undermining the returns from, and thereby the incentive for, cooperative trades, efforts to hasten the integration of migrants into the host economy and render the integration more complete (a process assisted by acculturation and socialization efforts) may not be in the migrants' best interest.

# Part II

## Migration and Risk

# 4

## On Migration and Risk in Less Developed Countries

### 1

From the 1970s to the early 1980s, the ruling economic explanation for rural-to-urban migration taking place in less developed countries (LDCs) has been the response to the intersectoral expected incomes differential. Originating largely in Todaro's pioneering article (Todaro, 1969), the dominance of the expected-income motive soon became virtually exclusive. This is somewhat surprising, especially since during the very same period both risk and (especially) risk avoidance have assumed major significance in mainstream economics. Yet the expected-income hypothesis, even in its revised formulations, is void of any explicit decisional risk content (Todaro, 1976, 1980); the hypothesis does not incorporate a random variable (multiplicative or other), and the implied utility function is linear.

Confronted with the evidence that rural-to-urban migration often results not in high-paying formal sector jobs but in urban unemployment or employment remunerated by income that is meager even by rural standards, the hypothesis offers the long-planning-horizon explanation: future urban expected earnings are sufficiently high (discounting notwithstanding) to compensate for a temporary reduction in earnings. However, the higher short-run *variability* in earnings as a source of direct disutility and the way variability in alternative rural earnings and in future urban earnings must figure in migrants' calculations is beyond the grasp of the expected-income hypothesis.

This chapter is devoted entirely to risk as an explanatory variable of rural-to-urban migration in LDCs. In making the argument, it may seem that we are overplaying our hand. Clearly, both risk and return count with entities that are making a decision concerning migration, and the focus here on risk is a heuristic device: we wish to draw attention to an overneglected dimension.

To the best of our knowledge, the argument that aversion to risk is a major cause of rural-to-urban migration has appeared only in Stark (1978, 1981). In section 2 of this chapter, that argument is distilled. In a nutshell, it is suggested that an optimizing risk-averse small-farmer family confronted with a subjectively risk-increasing situation manages to control the risk through diversification of its incomes portfolio via the placing of its best-suited member in the urban sector, which is independent of agricultural production. The severely limited possibilities for diversification that generally characterize human capital thus cause no special problem in this case (Levhari and Weiss, 1974). Section 3 takes up the possibility that the decision-making unit is the individual and suggests an argument why in such a context, too, rural-to-urban migration may be adopted as a means of resolving aversion to risk. The suggested policy content of the arguments is brought up at the end of each section.

**2**

Consider a small-farmer family with a strong desire to innovate but deterred from adopting a new technology because of its subjective high-risk content.[1] A necessary condition for technological transformation is thus the resolution of familial aversion to risk intersected with a risk-increasing component in the family's incomes portfolio. If insurance markets either do not prevail or do not form, or they exist but require prohibitive premiums, the conflict between increased risk and risk avoidance must be resolved internally – that is, through reorganized utilization of the family's own resources.

That *objectively* the higher risk entailed in pursuing the new technology is rewarded by higher expected output is of no avail to the small farmer. It is his *subjective* risk that counts. If the small farmer were to be portrayed on a risk–expected-return plane, a necessary condition for his moving upward from his present equilibrium position on a given efficiency frontier is that the risk involved in obtaining the higher expected return should exactly match his subjective preferences, represented by the frontier. (This, of course, assumes that none of the variables determining the location of the frontier change.) Although, as figure 4.1 shows, the new technology involves an initial objective move from A to D,[2] the small farmer considers his new (subjective) position to be represented by B, whereas, given $e_2$, what he is willing to bear is a move to C. To avoid B and

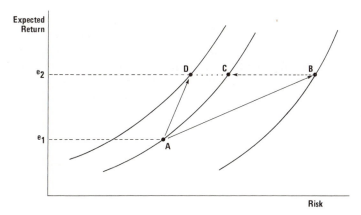

**Figure 4.1**

to locate on C, a simultaneous adoption of a risk-depressing strategy must accompany the introduction of the new technology.

"Spreading of risks being the great way of diminishing risk" (Hicks, 1967), the small-farmer family will attempt to diversify its incomes portfolio. When diversification cum technological transformation on the farm is insufficient or impractical,[3] and when ex-farm agricultural or rural diversification options either do not exist or are too closely positively correlated with stochastic farm production, a portfolio "investment" in urban earning activity – namely, migration of a family member – is the clear strategy to follow. If it is assumed that the urban "investment" is distributed independently of all other "investments" and has a mean that is at least as large as that of any other "investment," it is mandatory to enter the urban "investment" in the optimal "investments" portfolio regardless of the variance of each investment, provided only that it is finite (and nonzero).[4]

This is an interesting result: rural-to-urban migration is taking place in the presence of a positive urban–rural expected-income differential, yet the motive may not be expected-income maximization *per se*. A strong force – aversion to risk – which prevailing explanations do not capture, may be churning below the surface. That this deeper relation is not easily made explicit using present data should provide an incentive to generate the appropriate data set; it should not discourage an attempt to uncover a deeper reality than that accessible to the naked eye.

The relation between risk aversion, expected-income differential, and migration has a distinct policy implication. Assume that risk avoidance is an underlying cause of rural-to-urban migration. Assume further that an institutional interference aimed at reducing migration is deemed desirable. Under these circumstances, it would be efficient to shift away from exclusive (so far largely futile) attempts to narrow down the intersectoral wage differential toward the creation and/or perfection of rural insurance markets, even toward a direct provision of technological insurance to small farmers.

3

Assume, alternatively, that the entity that engages in choice-making – to migrate townward or to pursue agricultural production – is the individual. The individual derives pleasure from income, but the accompanying risk (variability) is a source of dissatisfaction. In every period throughout his planning horizon, the individual receives a bundle – expected income and risk – but risk levels (and return) are sectorally dependent. To focus on risk, however, it is convenient for a moment to assume intersectoral equality of expected returns. If the individual were to pursue agricultural production, he would have to endure some level of risk per period emanating from the low immunity, especially of traditional agriculture, to stochastic variability in rainfall and weather conditions, plant disease, attacks by pests, and so forth, all affecting both grown and stored crops. This low immunity is especially hazardous as it is usually coupled with absence of institutional insurance arrangements. If the individual migrates from the rural to the urban sector, he is not subjected to similar period risks.

Initial risks on migrating are very high; attempts to enter high-paying sectors may fail. Entry into low-paying sectors, which may be relatively easy, entails a high probability of discontinuity of employment because of the high sensitivity (and hence vulnerability) of these sectors to market fluctuations. There is, of course, also the distinct possibility of involuntary unemployment. But risks (variability) associated with urban employment diminish with time and may be relatively low – that is, lower than the typical risk (variability) associated with agricultural production – after some initial high-risk period.[5]

An individual who under such circumstances engages in rural-to-urban migration obviously attaches a premium to the early resolution of (much of) his lifelong income-associated risks. He trades in "medium-level" risks for immediate higher, but thereafter lower, risks. Obviously, his time rate of discount cannot be high and his planning horizon cannot be short. These

are thus especially likely to apply if he is young. He is also one whose
degree of risk aversion cannot be small.

The underlying reason why an individual who is risk averse – and whose
time rate of discount is not very high – engages in the said trade of risks is
that the disutility from periodic future risks – hence the intensity of the
incentive to resolve them – is an increasing function of the length of the
future envisaged. In considering migration, the individual compares two
levels of expected utility-of-lifetime earnings: (a) that associated with the
rural income stream and (b) that associated with the urban income stream.
We assume that "income" in every period is a bundle of expected income
(a source of utility) and variability (a source of disutility). Through the
expected utility operator, the two-variable characterization of each bundle
is reduced to a single-variable characterization.[6] This, in turn, is discounted and added to present values of other bundles transformed and
then discounted in a similar way. The individual thus faces the easy task of
comparing two unidimensional numbers – "urban utility" and "rural utility." It is clear from the procedure described here that, for an individual
who is more risk averse, the net utility associated with a given expected
income–variability bundle is lower. Other things being equal, the sectoral
expected level of utility-of-lifetime earnings will consequently be lower. If,
through the "purchase" of some relatively high-risk bundles in the near
future, all remaining more distant bundles turn out to be relatively low
risk, the game may be worth the candle.

One interesting implication of this argument is that rural-to-urban
migration decisions by individuals can now be seen not as a response to
their risk-taking or risk-loving properties – the argument so far, and for
long dominating the literature[7] – but as a manifestation of their risk
avoidance.

A second interesting implication is the policy-related one already
mentioned in the preceding section: if stemming the migration flow were
the order of the day, transformation of rural income earning activity into a
less risky proposition might be highly effective.

**Notes**

Co-authored with David Levhari. Reprinted from *Economic Development and
Cultural Change* 31, 1982. Comments from participants in a seminar held at the
World Bank, Washington, DC, are gratefully acknowledged.
1   For some early, excellent, and succinct expositions of the deterrent impact of
    risk aversion on technological change in agricultural production at the microlevel,
    see Holmes (1959, p. 191), Sen (1966), and Brewster (1967).

2 Once the new technology is utilized, familiarity with it and experience in its application, apart from reducing the subjective risk, also ensure a greater expected return.

3 An illustration of this impracticability is provided by the shift from traditional to high-yielding varieties. Widespread *traditional* risk-reducing practices are staggered planting, whereby deviations from optimal planting time (reduction in expected yields) are traded in particular for minimization of the effects of randomly incurred periods of water stress, and the interplanting of one crop with another (intercropping), where the various crops differ substantially in their "environmental resistance" to stochastic environmental variability (for example, to drought, local pest damage, and bird damage). However, under the new technology – where a new variety is involved – similar intercropping may be useless, even harmful (for example, when the mixed crops, directly or indirectly, interact negatively) or may simply be out of the question (for example, when considerations of future use demand the preservation of the purity of the seed). Likewise, extreme sensitivity to deviations from optimal planting time effectively eliminates staggered planting. In addition, it is of interest to note that in an agrarian sector of a less developed economy, where economic and social variables interact strongly, adoption of the new technology of high-yielding varieties may impede traditional risk-sharing, and hence risk-reducing, arrangements.

4 A formal proof is provided by Stark (1978, appendix 2).

5 For evidence on the employment experience of rural-to-urban migrants, see Stark (1978, ch.3).

6 In the case of the $\mu$–$\sigma$ approach, this "reduced form" is obtained through a slide southwestward along the indifference curve drawn in the expected income–income standard deviation plane to the intersection point of the curve with the expected-income axis.

7 Those who have the highest propensity to migrate are "the dynamic *risk-taking* beings who have a high capacity to detach themselves from the traditional surroundings and adapt themselves to the unfamiliar environment" (Sahota, 1968; emphasis added). See also Kuznets (1964, p. xxxii) and Myrdal (1968, pp. 2140, 2148).

### References

Brewster, John M. (1967) "Traditional Social Structures as Barriers to Change." In Herman M. Southworth and Bruce F. Johnston (eds), *Agricultural Development and Economic Growth*. Ithaca, NY: Cornell University Press, pp. 67–8.

Hicks, John (1967) *Critical Essays in Monetary Theory*. Oxford: Clarendon Press.

Holmes, Horace (1959) "Helping the Asian Villager Help Himself." In *Community Education: Principles and Practices from World-Wide Experience*, Fifty-eight Yearbook, Part 1. Chicago, IL: National Society for the Study of Education, pp. 191–207.

Kuznets, Simon (1964) "Introduction: Population Redistribution, Migration and Economic Growth." In Hope T. Eldridge and Dorothy S. Thomas (eds), *Population Redistribution and Economic Growth in the United States, 1870–1950: Demographic Analysis and Interrelations*. Philadelphia, PA: American Philosophical Society.

Levhari, David and Weiss, Yoram (1974) "The Effect of Risk on the Investment in Human Capital." *American Economic Review* 64 (6): 950–63.

Myrdal, Gunnar (1968) *Asian Drama: An Inquiry into the Poverty of Nations*. New York: Twentieth Century Fund.

Sahota, Gian S. (1968) "An Econometric Analysis of Internal Migration in Brazil." *Journal of Political Economy* 76 (2): 218–45.

Sen, Amartya K. (1966) "Peasants and Dualism With or Without Surplus Labor." *Journal of Political Economy* 74 (5): 425–50.

Stark, Oded (1978) *Economic–Demographic Interactions in Agricultural Development: The Case of Rural-to-Urban Migration*. Rome: UN Food and Agriculture Organization.

—— (1981) "On the Optimal Choice of Capital Intensity in LDCs with Migration." *Journal of Development Economics* 9 (1): 31–41 (reprinted as ch. 19 in this volume).

Todaro, Michael P. (1969) "A Model of Labor Migration and Urban Unemployment in Less Developed Countries." *American Economic Review* 59 (1): 138–48.

—— (1976) "Urban Job Expansion, Induced Migration and Rising Unemployment." *Journal of Development Economics* 3 (3): 211–25.

—— (1980) "Internal Migration in Developing Countries: A Survey." In Richard A. Easterlin (ed.), *Population and Economic Change in Developing Countries*. Chicago, IL: University of Chicago Press for National Bureau of Economic Research.

# 5

## Labor Migration and Risk Aversion in Less Developed Countries

### 1

That poor people in less developed countries (LDCs) undertake migration and, in particular, rural-to-urban migration as an act of rational choice has long been a major theme in development economics research. There is also wide recognition that, at least in some cases, migration constitutes an actuarially unfair risk with income earning in the urban sector often not being guaranteed prior to the migrants' arrival there. When subjected to empirical testing, the popular expected-income hypothesis of rural-to-urban migration (associated most closely with Todaro (1969)) does not fare well in terms of either the sign of the coefficients or their statistical significance.[1] In addition, in many cases the expected income in the urban area is not larger than the expected income in the rural area. Combined, these observations point to an empirical paradox: how is it that calculative behavior by rational people results in the choice of an actuarially unfair risky prospect? In this chapter we offer two explanations, but first list and briefly discuss four additional responses to this question. We reject the first two; the third and fourth have been proposed elsewhere (see Stark and Levhari, 1982) and require the acceptance of special assumptions.

One possible response to the problem posed above is that rural-to-urban migrants are risk loving. Such a characterization draws particularly on the evidence that migrants are usually selectively drawn from the rural areas with respect to characteristics that are closely correlated with love of risks: youth, low ratio of location-specific to location-transferable human capital, and so forth (Kuznets, 1964; Myrdal, 1968; Sahota, 1968). Thus an argument can be made that a sample selection problem might creep in: only the risk-preferring leave, and so the remaining people are risk averse. What induces us to reject this explanation is the evidence that in other domains of economic life farm people in LDCs (including those who subsequently turn out to be migrants) ordinarily shirk risks (Schultz, 1964; Roumasset, 1976).

A second explanation is bounded rationality: human rationality is limited and bounded by the situation and by human computational powers (Simon, 1983). People can deal with only one major problem at a time; therefore they may not be able to deal with all the possible implications of their migration decision. What makes us uncomfortable about this explanation is that bounded rationality seems to be a useful explanation in situations in which the world is mostly intersectionally "empty" in the sense that most variables are only weakly related to other variables. Then the world may be factorable into separate problems. But such factorability does not seem to apply when a different risk is inherent in every alternative of income earning.

A third response is that rural-to-urban migration is perfectly consistent with a person's aversion toward risk even if the risks associated with urban income earnings are initially high. Clearly, this line of reasoning introduces an intertemporal utility function. It seems that risks (variability) associated with urban employment diminish with time and, after some initial high-risk period, may be relatively low, that is, lower than the typical risk associated with agricultural production. A person will therefore engage in rural-to-urban migration if he attaches a premium to the early resolution of (much of) his lifelong risks. He trades in "medium-level risks" for immediate higher, but subsequent lower, risks. This is, of course, likely to be particularly relevant if the individual is young, so that the low-risk period he faces after migrating is particularly long. However, accepting this explanation imposes narrow bounds on the time discount factor.

A fourth response rests on broadening the decision-making entity perspective rather than deepening the time perspective. Although the modal rural-to-urban migrating unit in LDCs is an individual, there are strong theoretical and empirical reasons to suggest that the decision-making entity is often the family, of which the individual is a member. Migration by a family member is then warranted when it facilitates reduction in total familial risk via diversification of earning sources. For the migration strategy to make sense in this context, one of the following two conditions is required: the head of the family, for example, keeps perfect control over the migrant, or a cooperative arrangement is struck between the two decision-makers – the family and the migrant – involving intra-familial trade in risks, coinsurance arrangements, devices to handle principal agent problems, moral hazard problems (the migrant understates his success in the urban area or the migrant increases his standard of living appreciably, thus producing a smaller surplus), and contract enforcement problems (the migrant admits his success but refuses to share it with his family) such that, overall, a mutually beneficial intertemporal self-enforcing contractual arrangement is struck. If migration by two or more family members is allowed, these problems are compounded as issues of coalition formation and prisoner's dilemma creep in. (The latter situation might arise when every migrant member wishes the family to enjoy remittances yet prefers that another migrant member remits more and himself less.) This promising approach is presented in related papers (Stark, 1983; Lucas and Stark, 1985).

However, we depart from this direction here for three specific reasons. First, in many situations rural-to-urban migration in LDCs is an act of individual choice. Second, we wish to relate our analysis to the pioneering work of Todaro (1969), which is cast in an individualistic context. This enables us to criticize the work constructively and fairly and to offer an alternative theory drawing on the characteristic features of LDCs' capital markets. Furthermore, it also enables us to explain temporary migration, which Todaro's theory certainly does not. Third, while it is interesting and relevant in some important contexts, the portfolio diversification approach must be pursued with care; the delineation of an efficient portfolio is highly complex and very sensitive to small changes in the parameters of the distributions involved, namely, their means, their spreads, and their correlations. Consequently, the conclusion about whether all, some, or no family members will migrate is not that clear cut. But the very question we are addressing requires an all-or-nothing approach. Might a risk-averse person migrate or not? Is migration consistent with global risk aversion? In this chapter we attempt to provide a positive answer to both these questions.

Before turning to our analysis, we wish to address briefly one final point. The explanation of the rural-to-urban migration phenomenon has many policy implications. Suppose that in an LDC an institutional action aimed at reducing rural-to-urban migration is deemed desirable. Clearly, different sets of policies would be relevant, depending on what it is that fuels migration. For example, if migration is fueled by risk diversification resulting from the incompleteness of insurance markets, then it would be efficient to shift from exclusive attempts to reduce urban-to-rural wage differentials (which have not been very successful) toward the creation and/or perfection of insurance markets. If, as we shall suggest here, a main cause of rural-to-urban migration – a labor market phenomenon – is capital market imperfections, then policy to constrain migration should aim at enhancing access to, and improving the competitiveness of, capital markets.

**2**

As is well known, an individual who is not everywhere risk averse may rationally engage in both insurance and actuarially unfair gambling. Thus, following the classic work of Friedman and Savage (1948), if the individual's utility function is in turn concave, convex, and concave, this might explain why under certain circumstances he may expose himself to some risks at the very same time that he pays to shield himself against others. The migration decision might then be explained by the existence of a Friedman–Savage utility function, where the migrant is on the convex part.

Yet Friedman and Savage's explanation has been recognized as an essentially *ad hoc* formulation of the utility function created specifically to accommodate a bothersome economic phenomenon, namely simultaneous gambling and insurance. In contrast, it has been suggested (see Appelbaum and Katz, 1981) that, even if individuals are everywhere risk averse, they may still undertake actuarially unfair risks. A circumstance under which this is likely to occur is a situation in which the yield to investment is an increasing function of the amount of money invested, that is, in the presence of imperfect capital markets which are a critical feature of LDCs.

Let us demonstrate how this approach applies in the context of the migration decision. An individual with an initial wealth of $A$ rupees is faced with the decision to migrate when the parameters facing him are as follows: if he migrates, there is a probability $q$ that he will obtain a job in the city. In the event that he does obtain a job, the net reward will be $W$ rupees. Alternatively, he may find himself jobless with a probability $1 - q$, in which case his net reward will be $-C$ rupees (as he will be eating into his own wealth).[2]

If, on the other hand, the individual stays at home, then, because of the institutions of perfect intra-familial sharing and some inter-familial sharing, his net reward will be $X$ rupees with certainty. To make the analysis simple without losing generality, let $X = 0$.

Clearly, if the individual is everywhere risk averse and the story ends here, then a sufficient condition for him to choose not to migrate is that

$$(1 - q)C \geqslant qW \qquad (5.1)$$

that is, that migration yields no more (and possibly less) than an actuarially fair return.

However, if migration is viewed in a broader context, the story does not end here. Specifically, a number of recent studies discuss the effects of uncertainty, imperfect information, and various transaction costs on capital markets and show that the result may be that capital markets are characterized by certain imperfections. These studies establish both strong theoretical reasons (Barro, 1976; Jaffee and Modigliani, 1976; Benjamin, 1978; Braverman and Stiglitz, 1982) and empirical evidence (Eckstein, 1961; Nerlove, 1968) for believing that capital market imperfections of one kind or another are very likely to emerge when informational imperfections, high transaction costs, and so forth are present.

Clearly, within the context of the rural areas of LDCs, the imperfections described above are likely to be of even greater importance than within a developed economy; information in LDCs is, of course, very sparse and costly, given the lack of a modern communication infrastructure. Further, and perhaps for the same reason, several asset markets that exist in modern economies are completely absent in LDCs. This particularly applies to futures markets. The implication of the incompleteness of these markets is that a person will typically be unable to realize, on the current set of markets, the full potential value of his future wealth.

For example, a potential migrant might be able to obtain a loan locally, but this could require him to provide unpaid labor services to the money lender (cum landlord) at peak periods (thereby lowering his social status) and to accept a collateral valuation (for example, for land or draft animals) below that given by the relevant local asset market (thereby devaluing his initial wealth). In such a case, migration may serve to evade the institutional complexities and asymmetric bargaining power that characterize the incipient fragmented capital markets in villages in LDCs. These considerations, and the fact that at an early stage of the development process the return to physical investments may be extremely high, suggest that, at least for a certain range of wealth (that which, for example, enables a farmer to adopt modern techniques), the rate of return $R$ on assets is an increasing function of the level of investment $Y$. Hence we can write

$$R = R(Y) \tag{5.2}$$

where $R'(Y) > 0$ for at least some range of $Y$.[3]

If these considerations are included in the individual's migration decision, an individual whose initial level of wealth is $A$ will be indifferent between migrating and not migrating if

$$U\{A[1 + R(A)]\} = qU\{(A + W)[1 + R(A + W)]\}$$
$$+ (1 - q)U\{(A - C)[1 + R(A - C)]\} \tag{5.3}$$

where $U$ is the von Neumann–Morgenstern utility function defined on final wealth.

This indifference (iso-utility) curve can be written as

$$C = G(W, A) \tag{5.4}$$

As is well known, a necessary and sufficient condition for an individual with initial wealth $A$ not to engage in a fair bet is that the set of acceptable gambles is convex, implying that the boundary set as defined by $G(W, A)$ is concave.

Consider, therefore, the shape of the function $G$. As is proved in the appendix, locally, at $W = C = 0$,

$$\frac{dC}{dW} = \frac{q}{1 - q} > 0 \tag{5.5}$$

and

$$\frac{d^2C}{dW^2} = \frac{q}{(1 - q)^2} \left[ \frac{U''(\cdot)}{U'(\cdot)} + \frac{2R' + AR''}{(1 + R + AR')^2} \right] (1 + R + AR') \tag{5.6}$$

where $U''(\cdot)$ and $U'(\cdot)$ are evaluated at $A[1 + R(A)]$. Thus locally, at $W = C = 0$, the iso-utility curve is increasing, but its curvature is unknown. The expression in square brackets in (5.6) may be positive or negative, depending on $A$ and the exact characteristics of the rate of return function $R(A)$. Therefore the set of acceptable gambles may or may not be convex. Thus the concavity of the utility function is neither necessary nor sufficient for the convexity of the acceptable gambles set. The conclusion, then, is that the individual may migrate and thus accept an unfair gamble even if his utility function is a concave function of wealth.

An examination of (5.6) shows that there are two effects to consider: (a) the effect of an increase in wealth on marginal utility, that is, the curvature of the utility function, and (b) the effect of an increase in wealth on the return to wealth, that is, the curvature of the wealth return function. The first effect, $U''(\cdot)/U'(\cdot)$, is (minus) the Arrow–Pratt measure of (local) absolute risk aversion. In this case, however, we cannot look at this risk-aversion measure only; both effects determine whether an individual with initial wealth $A$ undertakes an actuarially unfair migration gamble.

Hence, given a sufficiently large $R'$, it is clear that the potential migrant may overcome his risk aversion and migrate to the urban area even if this involves an unfair gamble. This is because migration gives a person a chance of being able to reap for himself the high rewards associated with, for example, drastic modernization of farm production techniques.[4]

Finally, it is important to note that most of the results are local in the sense that they correspond to a given level of initial wealth. As the level of wealth changes, the individual may modify his behavior even if his preferences remain the same. Hence, as the level of wealth increases, the likely decline in the effect of capital market constraints may reduce his apparent risk-loving behavior. This suggests that the rural rich will not migrate even if their preference function is no different from that of the rural poor.

Note that we have identified a new mechanism that accounts for rural-to-urban migration in LDCs: migration takes place because it enables a person to overcome a constraint imposed by the rural capital markets. Furnishing a person with even a small chance of reaping a large reward may make migration a game well worth the candle.

## 3

In this section we provide an alternative interpretation of the acceptance by migrants of an actuarially unfair gamble by migrating from rural to urban areas. Once again this is done without the need to relax the universal assumption of risk aversion. The explanation provided here is essentially an adaptation of that offered by Katz (1983) and Stark (1984a, b).

It has recently become accepted that individuals derive utility from their wealth in two distinct ways. First, wealth yields benefits in terms of consumption. Second, wealth may provide a social status such that, the greater the wealth of an individual in comparison with others, the greater his utility. To enable us to capture these two effects, let an individual's utility $U$ be defined on his wealth $W$ and his social rank $S$, such that $S$ depends on $W$; that is, let

$$U = U(W, S) \qquad (5.7)$$

be the individual's utility function and, to ensure risk aversion, assume that $U$ is strictly concave in $W$ and $S$. This implies that

$$U_1 > 0, U_2 > 0, U_{11} < 0, U_{22} < 0$$

and

$$U_{11}U_{22} - U_{12}^2 > 0$$

The social rank $S$ can be measured as that proportion of the population (with which the migrant compares himself) that has an amount of wealth smaller than that of the individual.[5] Thus the lowest ranking is 0 and the top ranking is 1.

If $g(W)$ is the wealth density function for the relevant population, the social status of an individual with wealth $W$ is given by

$$S = \int_0^W g(W)dW = R(W) \tag{5.8}$$

If we now use our earlier assumptions about the parameters of the migration decision and ignore the complications generated by possible investment, we can show that the boundary of the set of acceptable gambles is defined by

$$U[A, S(A)] = qU[A + W, S(A + W)] + (1 - q)U[(A - C), S(A - C)] \tag{5.9}$$

Now, as mentioned earlier, the individual will not accept a fair gamble if and only if the boundary set is convex, that is, if the iso-utility curve defined by (5.9) is concave. Defining the iso-utility curve as

$$C = G(W, A) \tag{5.10}$$

we prove in the appendix to this chapter that, locally, at $W = C = 0$,

$$\frac{dC}{dW} = \frac{q}{1 - q} \tag{5.11}$$

and

$$\frac{d^2C}{dW^2} = \frac{q(U_1 + U_2S')^{-1}}{(1 - q)^2} [(U_{11} + 2U_{12}S' + U_{22}S'^2) + U_2S''] \tag{5.12}$$

Clearly, by concavity, the first term inside the square brackets, that is, $U_{11} + 2U_{12}S' + U_{22}S'^2$, is negative. However, for the concavity of $G$, the concavity of $U$ is neither necessary nor sufficient since it also depends on $U_2S''$.

It transpires that $S''$ may well be positive within low wealth ranges, given commonly accepted shapes of wealth distribution. For example, if the wealth distribution is normal, then the relation between $S$ and $W$ is as plotted in figure 5.1. Clearly, $S''$ is positive between $W_1$ and $W_2$, and if this

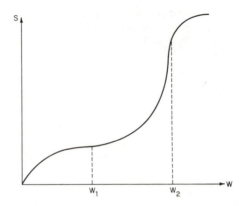

**Figure 5.1**

effect is sufficiently strong and the marginal utility of status is sufficiently high, it may cause risk-averse individuals to engage in an actuarially unfair gamble through migration.

Holding the identity of the population with which the migrant compares himself as given, we obtain the same result as before but through an alternative route: a small prospect for a greatly enhanced status fueled by increased wealth – along with the increase in wealth itself – is sufficient to make migration preferable to nonmigration, even though the migrant is universally risk averse in both rank and wealth.

### 4

We now offer some concluding comments. The assertion of the pioneering work of Todaro (1969) and Harris and Todaro (1970) that rural-to-urban migration in LDCs is an individual response to a higher urban expected income has been transformed by hundreds of articles and dozens of textbooks on development economics to an axiomatic postulate. In this chapter we have questioned this status, demonstrating that rural-to-urban migration is rational even if urban expected income is lower than the rural income. We achieve this under a set of fairly stringent conditions – an individual decision-making entity, a one-period planning horizon, and global risk aversion – and we obtain a quite powerful result: a small chance of reaping a high reward is sufficient to trigger rural-to-urban migration. Our result hinges on one of two explanations. The first is an explicit and, in our view, realistic assumption concerning the incompleteness of capital markets. Hence there is a cross-market spillover from cause to conduct.

(Of course, in a general equilibrium context, disequilibrium in one market coincides with, and is causally related to, disequilibrium in another.) The policy implication suggested by this analysis is that manipulation of rural-to-urban migration of labor may require interference in capital markets. Improving the operational efficiency of financial markets, especially in rural areas, is very distinct from narrowing an intersectoral (expected) wage differential. At least in part, migration may be the intermediary between capital markets and labor markets where deficiency in the former is partially corrected. When we relate our analysis to the recent work on migration and relative deprivation, we present the second explanation, which demonstrates that migration may occur even if it constitutes an actuarially unfair risk. Individuals who care about both wealth (or income) and rank (relative deprivation or satisfaction) and who are globally risk averse in wealth and rank might still be better off taking actuarially unfair risks with respect to wealth in migrating to the urban area if by so doing they face even a small prospect of greatly enhancing their rank. The likelihood that migration will pay off depends crucially on the shape of the population wealth (or income) density function. Indeed, the strength of our results lies in the fact that, in general, wealth density functions are of the requisite shapes.

Our analysis leads us to identify a new research direction. We believe that in real life people not only derive utility from rank and from absolute income but also use one to obtain more of the other. The underlying "production functions" may be such that rural-to-urban migration could render the transformation process of one into the other more productive. Thus, for example, migration may be used to improve rank in the rural-origin reference group by more than would have been possible by staying behind. If absolute income positively depends on relative position, migration advantageous with respect to the latter may subsequently facilitate improvement in the former. Given the interaction between rank and absolute income, the interesting effect of migration on the conversion of one into the other has been little explored. Perhaps particularly in LDCs, where, because of capital market imperfections, extension of credit by local moneylenders may critically depend on rank (social status) as collateral, enhanced rank (status) captured through migration may translate quite powerfully into pecuniary gains.

Finally, it may be worthwhile to consider the difference between the testable implications of our explanations and the implications of Todaro's approach. Let us begin with our imperfect capital markets explanation. There are two major differences between our predictions and those of Todaro. First, our model would predict that rural-to-urban migration will be mainly from rural areas characterized by a high marginal product of capital, coupled with a significant absence of capital markets. Todaro's approach does not require such a bias. Put somewhat more bluntly, given the expected urban wage, Todaro's hypothesis would predict least migration from rural areas of high production potential, while ours would seem to predict most migration from precisely such areas if and only if significant capital market imperfections existed there. Second, our model requires that the earnings of urban migrants are mainly channeled into investment activity. Todaro's approach would predict a similar consumption-to-investment ratio in both the rural and the urban areas.

As for our rank explanation, our model would predict migration by individuals whose rank is very sensitive to changes in income. Thus we would predict that rural-to-urban migrants are concentrated among rural individuals whose income position is in an upward-sloping portion of the income density function. Such a prediction would not be made by Todaro.

## Appendix

### A1

Deriving the curvature of $C = G(W, A)$ as in (5.3), let

$$J = U\{(A + W)[1 + R(A + W)]\} \qquad (5.A1)$$

and

$$K = U\{(A - C)[1 + R(A - C)]\} \qquad (5.A2)$$

Then, totally differentiating (5.3), we have

$$qJ_W dW + (1 - q)K_C dC = 0 \qquad (5.A3)$$

so that

$$\frac{dC}{dW} = -\frac{qJ_W}{(1 - q)K_C} \qquad (5.A4)$$

Now

$$J_W = [(A + W)R'(A + W) + R(A + W) + 1]U'\{(A + W)[1 + R(A + W)]\} \qquad (5.A5)$$

and

$$K_C = -[(A - C)R'(A - C) + R(A - C) + 1]U'\{(A - C)[1 + R(A - C)]\} \qquad (5.A6)$$

Therefore, at $W = C = 0$,

$$J_W = -K_C = (AR' + R + 1)U'\{A[1 + R(A)]\} \tag{5.A7}$$

and hence

$$\left.\frac{dC}{dW}\right|_{W=C=0} = \frac{q}{1-q} \tag{5.A8}$$

From (5.A4),

$$\frac{d^2C}{dW^2} = -\frac{q}{1-q}\left(\frac{K_C J_{WW} - K_{CC} J_W \, dC/dW}{K_C^2}\right) \tag{5.A9}$$

since $K_{CW} = J_{WC} = 0$.
  Now from (5.A5)

$$\begin{aligned}
J_{WW} &= [(A + W)R'(A + W) + R(A + W) + 1]^2 \\
&\quad \times U''\{(A + W)[1 + R(A + W)]\} + U'\{(A + W)[1 + R(A + W)]\} \\
&\quad \times [(A + W)R''(A + W) + 2R'(A + W)]
\end{aligned} \tag{5.A10}$$

and from (5.A6)

$$\begin{aligned}
K_{CC} &= [(A - C)R'(A - C) + R(A - C) + 1]^2 \\
&\quad \times U''\{(A - C)[1 + R(A - C)]\} + U'\{(A - C)[1 + R(A - C)]\} \\
&\quad \times [(A - C)R''(A - C) + 2R'(A - C)]
\end{aligned} \tag{5.A11}$$

so that at $W = C = 0$

$$J_{WW} = K_{CC} = (AR' + R + 1)^2 U'' + (AR'' + 2R')U' \tag{5.A12}$$

Hence, noting that

$$1 + \frac{dC}{dW} = \frac{1}{1-q} \tag{5.A13}$$

we know that

$$\frac{d^2C}{dW^2} = \frac{q}{(1-q)^2}\left[\frac{U''}{U'} + \frac{2R' + AR''}{(1 + R + AR')^2}\right](1 + R + AR') \tag{5.A14}$$

which is equation (5.6).

*A2*

Deriving the curvature of $C = G(W, A)$, as in (5.A9), let

$$L = U[A + W, S(A + W)] \tag{5.A15}$$

and

$$M = U[A - C, S(A - C)] \tag{5.A16}$$

Then, totally differentiating (5.9), we have

$$qL_W dW + (1 - q)M_C dC = 0 \tag{5.A17}$$

so that

$$\frac{dC}{dW} = -\frac{qL_W}{(1 - q)M_C} \tag{5.A18}$$

But

$$L_W = U_1[A + W, S(A + W)] + U_2[A + W, S(A + W)]S'(A + W) \tag{5.A19}$$

and

$$M_C = -U_1[A - C, S(A - C)] - U_2[A - C, S(A - C)]S'(A - C) \tag{5.A20}$$

so that at $W = C = 0$

$$L_W = -M_C = U_1 + U_2 S' \tag{5.A21}$$

and hence

$$\left.\frac{dC}{dW}\right|_{W=C=0} = \frac{q}{1 - q} \tag{5.A22}$$

Hence, from (5.A18), we have

$$\frac{d^2C}{dW^2} = -\frac{q}{1 - q}\left(\frac{M_C L_{WW} - M_{CC} L_W \, dC/dW}{M_C^2}\right) \tag{5.A23}$$

since $M_{CW} = L_{WC} = 0$.

Hence, from (5.A19),

$$L_{WW} = U_{11}[A + W, S(A + W)] + U_{22}[A + W, S(A + W)]S'^2(A + W)$$
$$+ 2U_{12}[(A + W), S(A + W)]S'$$
$$+ U_2[A + W, S(A + W)]S''(A + W) \tag{5.A24}$$

and from (5.A20),

$$M_{CC} = U_{11}[A - C, S(A - C)] + U_{22}[A - C, S(A - C)] S'^2(A - C)$$
$$+ 2U_{12}[A - C, S(A - C)]S'$$
$$+ U_2[A - C, S(A - C)]S''(A - C) \tag{5.A25}$$

so that at $W = C = 0$

$$L_{WW} = M_{CC} = U_{11} + U_{22}S'^2 + 2U_{12}S' + U_2S'' \tag{5.A26}$$

Hence, using (5.A13), we know that

$$\frac{d^2C}{dW^2} = \frac{q}{(1 - q)^2}(U_1 + U_2S')^{-1}(U_{11} + U_{22}S'^2 + 2U_{12}S' + U_2S'') \tag{5.A27}$$

which is equation (5.12).

## Notes

Co-authored with Eliakim Katz. Reprinted from *Journal of Labor Economics* 4, 1986. This is a revised version of Discussion Paper 9, Harvard University Migration and Development Program.

1   Good examples of recent studies that reach this conclusion are Banerjee and Kanbur's (1981) study of India, Salvatore's (1981) study of migration from the rural south to the urban north in Italy, and Garrison's (1982) study of Mexico.
2   We rule out unemployment insurance payments from public agencies.
3   The dramatic increase in the rate of return associated with a shift from traditional to high-yielding varieties (HYVs) – a shift that is contingent on investment in a bundled package of modern inputs – provides an excellent illustration. See Stark (1978); this study also provides evidence that the proceeds of migrants who do earn high wages are used to undertake investment in projects with increasing returns.
4   There is extensive evidence that migration income facilitates technological change in agricultural production (Stark, 1978) and is utilized to accumulate

productive capital assets in the rural areas. For example, in Botswana migrants remit heavily and rely on their families back in the rural areas to act as trustworthy intermediaries in accumulating and maintaining capital – including human capital in the form of the education and upbringing of their own children left behind in the rural areas (Lucas and Stark, 1985).

5  Such a comparison generates levels of relative satisfaction – or depriva-tion – that, in turn, can be modeled to impinge on migratory decisions. This direction is pursued by Stark (1984a) for the case of rural-to-urban migration and by Stark (1984b) in the context of international migration.

## References

Appelbaum, Elie and Katz, Eliakim (1981) "Market Constraints as a Rationale for the Friedman-Savage Utility Function." *Journal of Political Economy* 89 (4): 819–25.

Banerjee, Biswajit and Kanbur, S. M. (1981) "On the Specification and Estimation of Macro Rural-Urban Migration Functions: With an Application to Indian Data." *Oxford Bulletin of Economics and Statistics* 43 (1): 7–29.

Barro, R. J. (1976) "The Loan Market, Collateral, and Rates of Interest." *Journal of Money, Credit and Banking* 8 (4): 439–56.

Benjamin, D. K. (1978) "The Use of Collateral to Enforce Debt Contracts." *Economic Inquiry* 16: 333–59.

Braverman, Avishay and Stiglitz, Joseph E. (1982) "Sharecropping and the Interlinking of Agrarian Markets." *American Economic Review* 72: 695–715.

Eckstein, O. (1961) "A Survey of the Theory of Public Expenditure Criteria: Reply." In Conference of the Universities, National Bureau Committee for Economic Research, *Public Finances: Needs, Sources and Utilization*. Princeton, NJ: Princeton University Press.

Friedman, M. and Savage, L. J. (1948) "The Utility Analysis of Choices Involving Risk." *Journal of Political Economy* 56 (4): 279–304.

Garrison, Helen (1982) "Internal Migration in Mexico: A Test of the Todaro Model." *Food Research Institute Studies* 18: 197–214.

Harris, John R. and Todaro, Michael P. (1970) "Migration, Unemployment and Development: A Two-Sector Analysis." *American Economic Review* 60: 126–42.

Jaffee, D. M. and Modigliani, F. (1976) "A Theory and Test of Credit Rationing: Reply." *American Economic Review* 66: 918–20.

Katz, Eliakim (1983) "Wealth, Rank, Risk Aversion and the Friedman–Savage Utility Function." *Australian Economic Papers* 22: 187–90.

Kuznets, Simon (1964) "Introduction: Population Redistribution, Migration and Economic Growth." In Hope T. Eldridge and Dorothy S. Thomas (eds), *Population Redistribution and Economic Growth in the United States, 1870–1950: Demographic Analysis and Interrelations*. Philadelphia, PA: American Philoso-phical Society.

Lucas, Robert E. B. and Stark, Oded (1985) "Motivations to Remit: Evidence from Botswana." *Journal of Political Economy* 93 (5): 901–18 (reprinted as ch. 16 in this volume).

Myrdal, Gunnar (1968) *Asian Drama: An Inquiry into the Poverty of Nations.* New York: Twentieth Century Fund.

Nerlove, Marc (1968) "Factors Affecting Differences among Rates of Return on Investments in Individual Common Stocks." *Review of Economics and Statistics* 50 (3): 312–31.

Roumasset, J. A. (1976) *Rice and Risk: Decision-Making among Low-Income Farmers.* Amsterdam: North-Holland.

Sahota, Gian S. (1968) "An Econometric Analysis of Internal Migration in Brazil." *Journal of Political Economy* 76 (2): 218–45.

Salvatore, Dominick (1981) "A Theoretical and Empirical Evaluation and Extension of the Todaro Migration Model." *Regional Science and Urban Economics* 11: 499–508.

Schultz, Theodore W. (1964) *Transforming Traditional Agriculture.* New Haven, CT: Yale University Press.

Simon, Herbert A. (1983) *Reason in Human Affairs.* Stanford, CA.: Stanford University Press.

Stark, Oded (1978) *Economic–Demographic Interactions in the Course of Agricultural Development: The Case of Rural-to-Urban Migration.* Rome: UN Food and Agriculture Organization.

—— (1983) "Towards a Theory of Remittances in LDCs." Discussion paper 971, Harvard Institute of Economic Research.

—— (1984a) "Rural-to-Urban Migration in LDCs: A Relative Deprivation Approach." *Economic Development and Cultural Change* 32 (3): 475–86 (reprinted as ch. 7 in this volume).

—— (1984b) "Discontinuity and the Theory of International Migration." *Kyklos* 37: 206–22.

Stark, Oded and Levhari, David (1982) "On Migration and Risk in LDCs." *Economic Development and Cultural Change* 31 (1): 191–6 (reprinted as ch. 4 in this volume).

Todaro, Michael P. (1969) "A Model of Labor Migration and Urban Unemployment in Less Developed Countries." *American Economic Review* 59: 138–48.

# 6

# Consumption Smoothing, Migration, and Marriage: Evidence from Rural India

Studies of migration in low-income countries have been principally concerned with the flows of individuals and families from rural to urban areas. For the most part such studies have been based on theories of migration in which agents seek income gains (or expected income gains), and migration is viewed as a wage (or expected wage) equilibrating mechanism. However, rural-to-urban migration propelled by earnings incentives is only one component of spatial mobility. Indeed, in one major low-income country, India, rural-to-urban migration plays a relatively small role in total migration. Analyses of the 1981 Population Census of India (Skeldon, 1986; Sundaram, 1989), which for the first time provides reasons for migration on the basis of a 5 percent sample, indicate that the net outflow from rural to urban areas between 1971 and 1982 represented only 2.2 percent of the 1971 rural population, with the net outflow of migrants for reasons of employment representing only 1.6 percent of the rural population in 1971 and only a little more than 8 percent of the 1971 urban workforce. Net rural-to-urban migration contributed less than 19 percent to the total growth in the Indian urban population between 1971 and 1981.[1]

However, overall geographical mobility and hence rural-to-rural migration in India are not low. The 5 percent sample from the 1981 Population Census also reveals that almost 30 percent of the Indian population in 1981 (196.3 million people) was composed of individuals who resided in a place other than their place of birth. Most important, approximately 80 percent of these "lifetime migrants" were women who gave marriage as the principal reason for their move. Migration in India is thus predominantly a marital phenomenon, for which conventional employment-based explanations of migration, motivated by the incentives of spatial income differentials, would appear ill suited.

The importance of marital migration, particularly for women, is not confined to India, although it is more prevalent in that context. Our analysis of the Malaysian Family Life Survey (MFLS) data, a probability sample of 1262 households in Malaysia containing at least one ever-married woman less than 50 years of age (Butz and DaVanzo, 1978), indicates, on the basis of the matching of retrospective migration and marriage dates, that 69 percent of all women who had ever moved from one town to another did so at the time of their marriage, with 32 percent of all moves (town to town) by women accounted for by marriage. As in India, marriage migration is significantly less important for Malaysian men: only 13 percent of men changed their town of residence at the time of their marriage.[2]

On the basis of unique longitudinal data from India, in this chapter we develop and test a framework capable of explaining marriage cum migration patterns. Our central hypothesis is that marital arrangements among households, in particular, the "exchange" of individuals among households, characterized by the distance between households and assortative mating patterns, are manifestations of implicit contractual arrangements serving to mitigate income risk and facilitate consumption smoothing under conditions in which there are informational costs and spatially covariant risks.[3] Problems of information asymmetries and returns to risk diversification have previously been fruitfully incorporated in models of such formal rural institutions as banks and sharecropping contracts and of the landholding arrangements of cultivating households (McCloskey, 1976). While insurance considerations have only recently been brought to bear on the study of actual migration phenomena (Lucas and Stark, 1985), the pervasiveness of risk and its important spatial character in rural agricultural societies suggest that attention to consumption smoothing arrangements and insurance mechanisms may be useful in understanding marriage migration processes.

Anthropological and econometric studies indicate that inter-household family transfers are an important source of income insurance in low-income countries. Indeed, there is evidence (Caldwell et al., 1986; Rosenzweig, 1988a) that nonresident in-laws in India are the principal source of income transfers for households experiencing income shortfalls associated with the exigencies of weather.[4] The MFLS data suggest similar patterns in Malaysia: 39 percent of the value of all goods and cash transfers for purposes of "emergency" help and for "maintaining expenditures" and sent at least 20 miles from the sample Malaysian households went to the

in-laws of the male head of the household (22 percent to his parents).[5]
Eighty-four percent of the value of the longer-distance transfers received
by the sample households was sent by the children of the head, but the
MFLS does not identify the sex of these donors.

In section 1 we briefly describe our framework for examining the
locational and sorting patterns of marriages under a regime of spatially
covariant risks, and we compare the implications of the framework with
those derived from models of marriage and migration that ignore payoffs
to risk diversification. Section 2 provides a description of the sample used
and its statistics on spatial correlations in rainfall and incomes, mobility,
marital arrangements, and the extent of occupational, locational, and
marital diversification characterizing Indian farm households. In section 3
an econometric analysis is performed to test directly the proposition that
marital arrangements contribute to mitigating the influence of farm income
variability on household consumption. Section 4 tests the implications for
how household wealth holdings and the degree of risk characterizing crop
production jointly influence the average quality of marital matches and
the mobility – via marriage and migration – and occupational choices of
household members. The results support the hypothesized consumption
smoothing role of marital arrangements and indicate, consistent with the
insurance-theoretic framework, that the exogenous income riskiness faced
by a household and its ability to self-insure via its own wealth holdings
jointly and in a similar way influence (a) the distance between it and the
households with which it is engaged in marital cum insurance contracts and
(b) the probability that the household has among its members temporary
migrants or resident persons with nonvolatile incomes. However, the
wealth–contract–distance relationships estimated appear to be inconsistent
with models of marriage (or migration) concerned only with costs of search
and static income gains.

## 1  Spatial Risk Patterns and the Gains from Marriage Migration

A distinguishing feature of the agricultural sector is that income risk has a
strong spatial dimension. As a consequence, the pooling of risks entails the
transfer of funds or resources across space. The spatial separation (distance) of agents who might benefit from a risk-pooling arrangement,
however, makes such arrangements difficult, given the need to monitor
performance as a consequence of moral hazard. Thus, while the distance
between contracting agents provides a risk-pooling benefit, it also
increases costs of enforcement. The nonexistence of competitively pro-

vided crop insurance and the difficulties of credit provision in most low-income rural areas are in part consequences of the spatial character of agricultural risks. Protection against risks, however, is an important need of households engaged in agricultural production.

One means by which a household may spatially diversify its sources of income, using the bonds of kinship to mitigate the consequences of enforcement costs, is to locate its members in areas characterized by low covariances in income. The transfer of a family member to another established household confers diversification benefits to both households with minimal setup costs, which may be high in settings in which there are important area-specific experiential returns.[6] The presence in household $i$ of a member of household $j$ not only supplies household $j$ with an incentive to contribute to consumption smoothing in $i$ (altruism) but also introduces a verification and monitoring capacity.

Thus marriage across villages, whereby one of the marital partners "migrates" to the household of the other partner, in part fulfills the role of an institution providing income insurance benefits for households in the presence of spatially covariant risks. Note that this form of migration is welfare improving even in the absence of any (expected) inter-village wage differentials and even if village-specific risk distributions are identical, as long as the timing of states of nature is not perfectly synchronized. Indeed, in that case migration by entire households would never occur.

If households connected by marriage are also related because of some past marriages, an additional layer of enforcement is enjoyed. Moreover, if kinship facilitates information flows, marital matches among partners already related by kinship will be desirable. Thus risk considerations suggest that marriages will take place between partners in different rather than the same villages, but not in order to avoid marriages between close kin. Rather, marriages are likely to be among kin groups because they take place across spatially separated locations.

Considerations of the returns to risk via cross-household sharing arrangements and problems of incentives imply a particular assortative mating pattern: the "permanent" characteristics or endowments of origin and destination households that influence the level and variability in incomes will be similar (positive assortative mating with respect to the persistent attributes of agricultural incomes), but the correlation between income outcomes will be as low as possible. Close matching by endowments is desirable because a difference in endowments that determines susceptibility to risk (such as the size of irrigated landholdings) leaves the better-endowed household poorly insured.

Information considerations appear to suggest that marriages arranged by a household with many daughters, for example, would often take place

with multiple sons from another household, particularly given the desirability of matching households. While multiple transactions with the same
household do minimize transaction costs, gains from diversification are not
fully exploited. The insurance-conscientious village household will best
subdivide its risk by sharing it among different villages.

The risk-theoretic approach to marriage migration thus implies the
following: (a) households engaged in a marriage exchange will be closely
matched by the permanent traits of the members; (b) gains in income levels
associated with marriage migration moves will be small or nonexistent;
(c) individuals from the same origin household will tend not to have the
same destinations; (d) households with more wealth, and thus better able
to self-insure, will invest less in marriage migration, and the distance
between households linked by marriage will be less for the wealthier, to the
extent that distance confers a diversification benefit; (e) households facing
greater income risk, for given wealth levels, will be more willing to finance
moves of longer distance.[7]

Risk-theoretic considerations provide predictions about marital arrangements and migration that diverge in some important respects from those of
standard migration and marriage models. Economic models of marriage
(Becker, 1973, 1974; Keeley, 1977) and migration incorporate income gain
and search cost considerations with marriage models, unlike those of
migration, also concerned with the matching of individuals' traits, although
this is implicit in migration models in which individuals seek locations most
complementary to their skills.

Positive assortative mating is predicted by income gain marriage models
on the basis of the notion that individuals' traits are for the most part
complementary. While this implication is the same for the risk diversification framework, the existence of income gains from closely matching traits
implies that those individuals with relatively rare traits will invest more in
search. In a spatial context, therefore, using the income gain framework,
we would expect that the wealthier would tend to search over a greater
area for a marital match and to be engaged, on average, in longer-distance
marital arrangements. In contrast, the risk model implies that the primary
payoff to distance is the reduction in risk covariances, which is less valued
by the wealthy who are better able to self-insure. The wealth–distance
relationship provides a strong test of the two approaches to marriage in the
Indian setting.

A well-known finding of migration studies is the high serial correlation in
migration flows between specific origins and destinations. In the migration
literature this finding is often attributed to the role of information
(Greenwood, 1971). As noted, such search-theoretic considerations thus
suggest that the correlation between the destinations of individuals from

the same origin (household) will be positive, while risk diversification suggests the desirability of diversity among destinations. The sign of the correlation between the destinations of marital migrants thus discriminates between the risk and income gain approaches to migration. Risk-diversifying behavior is indicated if households distribute their migrant members across destinations with differing mean incomes rather than concentrating them at the higher mean income destination. Finally, in contrast with the income gain models applied to marriage migration, the risk framework suggests that (origin) income riskiness will increase the distances of marriage–migration linkages.

## 2 Mobility, Marital Arrangements, and Spatial Risk Diversification among Indian Farm Households

*The Sample and Spatial Covariances in Rainfall, Income, and Wages*

Examination of marriage and migration patterns in the context of household arrangements facilitating the minimization of consumption risk requires information not only on the characteristics of household members and household asset portfolios, but also on income flows, their spatial correlations, and consumption behavior over time. We use a unique longitudinal data set from southern India that provides most of the necessary information. In 1975–6 the International Crops Research Institute for the Semi-arid Tropics (ICRISAT) initiated a survey in six villages in three agroclimatic regions of the Indian semi-arid tropics. In three villages, information on family membership, incomes, expenditures, and production resources was collected continuously over a ten year period for 40 (30 cultivating) households in each village. A supplementary retrospective questionnaire was employed in 1984 to elicit additional information on family background, marriages, and inheritances for 400 households, including the households in the original six villages and households in four additional villages that ICRISAT had begun to survey in 1979–80. In addition, in 1985 more details were obtained from households in the three "continuous" villages on the kinship relationships between marital partners and on the distances associated with marital migration.

The availability of a ten year time series on daily rainfall, agricultural profits, and wages for six villages affords an opportunity to test directly whether increasing the distance between households can potentially reduce their intertemporal covariances in weather conditions and in incomes. As the number of locations provides $N = \Sigma_{i=1}^{n} (n - i)$ bivariate correlations for each variable, we can construct a cross-sectional sample of 15 correla-

*Migration and Risk*

tion–distance pairings from the six ICRISAT villages. The direct regression of the $N$ estimated pairwise correlations on inter-village distances would yield biased coefficient standard errors because the variance of the distribution of each estimated correlation $r$ depends on both the number of time series observations, which in this case is the same for each village (ten years), and the magnitudes of the true bivariate correlation, which clearly varies across the $N$ village pairs. However, the variance of the monotonic transform $z$ of $r$, where

$$z = 0.5 \ln\left(\frac{1 + r}{1 - r}\right) \tag{6.1}$$

depends solely on the size of the sample from which the correlation is computed.[8] Regressions of the transform $z$ on distance yield homoskedastic errors, so that valid hypothesis tests are possible, and, from (6.1), enable computations of the effects of distance on the actual correlations.

Table 6.1 provides the regression estimates of the effects of distance on the $z$ values of the ten year correlations for daily rainfall (in the critical agricultural months of July–October), real mean profits net of the value of family labor, and real agricultural (male) wage rates based on the six

**Table 6.1** Regressions of transformed pairwise intervillage correlations for rainfall. Real agricultural profits, and wages on distance for six ICRISAT villages. 1975–1984

| Variable | Village correlations between | | |
| | Daily rainfall[a] | Mean profits[b] | Wages[c] |
| --- | --- | --- | --- |
| Distances between villages | −0.122 | −0.0912 | −0.0998 |
| (km × $10^{-3}$) | (5.44) | (2.48) | (1.96) |
| Constant | 1.05 | 0.665 | 1.17 |
| | (8.84) | (3.42) | (4.33) |
| $R^2$ | 0.694 | 0.322 | 0.227 |
| $F$ | 29.5 | 6.27 | 3.82 |
| No. of observations | 15 | 15 | 15 |

Dependent variables = $0.5 \ln[(1 + r)/(1 - r)]$, where $r$ is the correlation coefficient; $t$-ratios are in parentheses beneath the coefficients.
[a] Averages for the months of July–October.
[b] For all sample farm households, in 1975 rupees.
[c] Daily wages for male agricultural workers, in 1975 rupees.

village ICRISAT sample. The results indicate that distance decreases the correlations significantly in all three variables: the point estimates suggest that for each 100 km increase in the distance between locations, the correlations in rainfall, profits, and wages decline by 0.073 (18 percent), 0.083 (49 percent), and 0.038 (7 percent) respectively.[9]

## Mobility and Marriage

In the analysis of marriage and migration, we shall use data principally on farm households in the three villages (Aurepalle, Shirapur, and Kanzara) for which there is both continuous information over the ten years on farm profits and food expenditures and the supplemental marital information. Each village represents a distinct agroclimatic area. Aurepalle is located in a region marked by low levels of erratically distributed rainfall and by soils with limited water storage capacity. Shirapur is characterized by soils with somewhat better storage capacities but is in an area with equally irregular and low levels of rainfall and little irrigation. Kanzara is also characterized by low levels of rainfall, but rainfall is somewhat more reliable and the soils have storage capacities equal to those of Shirapur. The principal crops grown in the villages are sorghum, pigeon peas, pearl millet, chick-peas, and groundnuts – crops unaffected by the Indian "Green Revolution." Table 6.2 provides descriptive statistics on the farm (cultivating) households in the sample.[10] Agricultural incomes are quite variable: the ten year standard deviation in farm profits net of the value of family labor is 25 percent greater than mean profits for the average farm household.

The three villages appear to conform to the general Indian mobility pattern. Only eight of 108 (male) heads of households inclusive of nonfarm households (less than 7 percent) were born outside the village, while almost 94 percent of married women were not residents of the village prior to marriage.[11] "Temporary" migration is more prevalent than male "permanent" migration but less pervasive than marital migration in the sample. Only 28 percent of the sample farm households reported having at least one migrant member, a person 18 years of age or over not resident in the village household nor residing in an independent household. While all these household members were located outside the sample villages and only two of the 57 migrants worked in agriculture, less than half the migrants represented a potential steady source of income since 40 percent were attending school. Migrants with regular salaries or with incomes not highly covariant with those of the sample households are still more prevalent than *resident* household members holding salaried jobs, who are found in only 10 percent of the farm households.

**Table 6.2** Descriptive Statistics: farm households, 1975–1984

|  | Mean | Standard deviation |
|---|---|---|
| Mean food expenditure | 3,101 | 10.98 |
| Intertemporal food expenditure variance ($\times 10^{-5}$) | 15.1 | 20.5 |
| Mean profits | 3,243 | 4,137 |
| Intertemporal profit variance ($\times 10^{-5}$) | 86.6 | 162 |
| Value of head's inheritance | 78,869 | 135,905 |
| Distance of marital partner households (km)[a] | 30.0 | 60.5 |
| No. of married women | 1.70 | 0.838 |
| No. of male household migrants | 0.25 | 1.27 |
| No. of female household migrants | 0.14 | 1.38 |
| No. of permanent servants (attached laborers) | 0.10 | 0.284 |
| No. of male market workers | 1.08 | 1.20 |
| No. of female market workers | 0.65 | 0.80 |
| Inherited dry land (acres) | 12.7 | 19.1 |
| Inherited wet land (acres) | 1.82 | 3.47 |

All values are in 1983 rupees.
[a]Includes marriages between households within the village (7.8 percent); distance is assigned the value of zero for within-village matches.

With respect to spatial diversification via marriage, the mean distance from a sample household to the origin villages of the daughters-in-law is 30 km. Most important, *within* all but two of the 49 percent of households with two or more married women, each married woman came from a different village. The mean of the maximum distances between the origin villages of the married women within these households, inclusive of any women born in the same village, is 47.7 km. The observed within-household diversification of marriage partners by origin location appears to be inconsistent with pure search-theoretic income gain theories of migration or marriage.[12]

To assess the degree to which there is positive assortative mating with respect to the mean income-generating characteristics of the parents of the marital partners, we performed a confirmatory factor analysis (Jöreskog, 1969) based on the survey information describing the family backgrounds of the heads and their wives in the ten ICRISAT villages. We assumed that the permanent income potential or "quality" of each partner's origin household, a latent variable, is measured by the dry and irrigated landholdings (in tenths of acres) in each partner's household when each was 15 years of age and the educational level (in five categories) of their fathers. Table 6.3 presents the correlations between the three individual background variables of the marital partners, the correlation between the latent indices estimated from the two-factor latent variable model, and the associated $t$ statistics. The coefficient estimates and test statistics of the full factor analysis are presented in table 6.A1 in the appendix to the chapter. The results in table 6.3 indicate a significant degree of positive association between the origin households of the heads and those of their wives, which is underestimated, however, by the individual correlations between any one of their background characteristics.

**Table 6.3** Correlations between individual measures and latent index of marital partners' origin families in ten ICRISAT villages

|                          | Correlation | t-statistic |
|--------------------------|-------------|-------------|
| Father's schooling       | 0.461       | 10.11       |
| Owned dry acreage        | 0.319       | 6.55        |
| Owned irrigated acreage  | 0.267       | 5.40        |
| Latent family quality    | 0.964[a]    | 7.03[a]     |
| No. of pairs             | 382         |             |

[a] From maximum likelihood estimates of latent variable model; see text and table 6.A1.

### 3 Household Characteristics and Consumption Smoothing

The close matching of marital partners with respect to origin household variables and the diversity and distance characterizing the marriage portfolios of the ICRISAT households are consistent with the hypothesis that marital arrangements influence a household's ability to smooth its consumption when confronted with highly variable income streams. In this section we exploit the longitudinal feature of the ICRISAT data to estimate directly the contribution of marriage migration, as well as of endowed wealth, to consumption smoothing.

Consider a household that in each year $t$ produces a stochastically determined amount of income from own-crop production $\pi_t$. Consumption $c_{ti}$ for household $i$ in year $t$ is then

$$c_{ti} = \pi_{ti} + \tau_{ti} \tag{6.2}$$

where $\tau_{ti}$ (other income) represents other sources of the household's net income, from the sale or purchase of assets, from increasing or decreasing debt, and from inter-household and possibly intra-family net transfers. The amount of other income $\tau_t$ in period $t$ used for consumption depends on the household's own-crop income $\pi_t$ at $t$, since how much the household would like to borrow (or repay) or how much transfer income is received (or sent out) will depend on $\pi_t$ and on the household's expectations of future own-crop incomes. Moreover, if capital markets are imperfect, the *sensitivity* of other income to the household's current realization of $\pi_t$ will depend on its owned stock of assets. Consider, for example, two households, one with assets and one without, facing a transitory decrease in own-crop income. In the absence of a credit market the second household cannot smooth its income; the first household, however, can sell off its assets and compensate for the loss in own-crop income. More generally, since $\tau$ in any period cannot exceed the total value of owned assets, given credit constraints, the capacity to respond to a transitory decline in own-crop income depends on the value of assets held. Our hypothesis suggests that a household's other income also depends on the crop incomes of household partners connected via marriage. In particular, we assume that

$$\tau_{ti} = \alpha(w_{ti})(\pi_{ti} - \mu_{it}) + \Sigma\gamma_k(\pi_{ti} - \pi_{tk}) \tag{6.3}$$

where $w_{ti}$ is household wealth at time $t$, $\mu_{it}$ is household expected future crop income at time $t$, $\pi_{tk}$ is the crop income at time $t$ of the $k$th potential transfer partner, and $\alpha$ and the $\gamma_k$ measure the extent to which own-wealth and transfer households respectively contribute to smoothing income, where $\alpha < 0$, $\alpha' \leq 0$, and $\gamma_k \leq 0$. Note that because $\tau$ captures what is conventionally defined as "savings," that is, the change in net wealth, as well as net transfer income, both of which contribute to smoothing income, expression (6.3) is not the standard income–consumption–saving relationship in a regime of imperfect capital markets.

If households have an infinite horizon and the stochastic income process is characterized by stationarity, assumptions which are not unreasonable for the environment we are studying, we can treat $\mu_{it}$ as a constant for a given household $i$; that is, any current realization of crop income will not affect income expectations. Changes in consumption for a household $i$, given (6.2) and (6.3), are thus related to changes $d\pi_i$ in its crop income by

$$dc_i = [1 + \alpha(w)]d\pi_i + \Sigma\gamma_k\left(1 - \frac{d\pi_k}{d\pi_i}\right)d\pi_i \qquad (6.4)$$

where $d\pi_k/d\pi_i$ expresses the intertemporal relationship between the crop income of household $i$ and the incomes of its transfer partners.

Two extreme views of low-income country environments are nested in (6.4). If there are perfect credit markets or all households are able to self-insure perfectly, then $\alpha = -1$ and $\gamma_k = 0$; for each household, consumption will be constant (given stationarity and an infinite horizon), independent of stochastic realizations of income. If, however, no household can "store" income and there are no risk-pooling arrangements via credit markets or via implicit familial contracts, then $\alpha = 0$ and $\gamma_k = 0$; current consumption is then dependent solely on current crop income. We believe that neither of these extreme cases characterizes the Indian setting well; instead, we expect that $-1 < \alpha < 0$ and $\gamma_k < 0$, that a household's ability to smooth consumption depends on its owned asset stock, $\alpha' < 0$, and on its ability to engage in risk pooling with partners with low covariant incomes.

We can use the ICRISAT data to estimate a variant of (6.4). On the basis of the ten year time series, we computed intertemporal variances for both farm profits (net of the value of family labor) and food expenditures (85 percent of all expenditures) for each farm household in 1983 rupees.[13] For the household's wealth stock, we used the value of the household head's inheritance, again in 1983 rupees, which we assume to be exogenous to the household's consumption-smoothing preferences. The most difficult component to measure in equation (6.4) is the covariation in incomes between the (potential) transfer partners and the farm household. To obtain such information would require a survey that followed over time all households or individuals *potentially* engaged in risk pooling/income sharing, not just the sampled (representative) households. We know of no such survey. However, the incomes of household migrants, almost none of whom are engaged in agricultural production, are unlikely to be correlated with the sample household's farm profits. With respect to the origin households of the resident married women, we can use the information collected on the distance to these households, based on the findings in table 6.1 that distance is negatively related to the covariation in agricultural incomes. Thus we can test whether there is a payoff to increasing the distance between the households of marital partners in terms of the enhanced ability of the household to smooth consumption via income sharing.

Let $d\pi_i/d\pi_k = \delta d_{ik}$, where $d_{ik}$ is the distance between household $i$ and "partner" household $k$ and $\delta < 0$ (from table 6.1). Then the basic equation we estimate is

$$\sigma_i^2(c) = \beta_0 + \beta_1\sigma_i^2(\pi) + \beta_2 I_i\sigma_i^2(\pi) + \beta_3 W_i\sigma_i^2(\pi)$$
$$+ \beta_4 M\sigma_i^2(\pi) + \beta_5 D\sigma_i^2(\pi) + \epsilon_i \qquad (6.5)$$

where $\sigma_i^2(c)$ and $\sigma_i^2(\pi)$ are the ten year food expenditure and profit variances respectively, $I$ is inherited wealth, $W$ is the number of resident married women, $M$ is the number of household migrants, $D$ is the mean distance between the sample household $i$ and the origin households of the resident married women, $\epsilon_i$ is the household-specific error term, and $\beta_5 = -\gamma_k\delta$. Perfect intertemporal markets would imply all $\beta_k = 0$; alternatively, the absence of any mechanisms to transfer income either over time or contemporaneously across households implies that $\beta_1$ is close to 0.8, the proportion of food in total expenditures, and $\beta_l = 0, l = 2, \ldots, 5$. With self-insurance and with spatial risk pooling associated with migrants and marriages, $\beta_l < 0, l = 3, \ldots, 5$.

Table 6.4 reports estimates obtained from three specifications of equation (6.5), all of which additionally include village dummy variables.[14] In the first column, we exclude the possibility of spatial income pooling. The results reject the hypotheses that households, independent of their endowed wealth, can perfectly smooth consumption or that households cannot smooth consumption at all via asset transactions. The joint hypotheses that (a) both the profit variance and inherited wealth profit variance interaction coefficients are zero ($F(2, 57) = 4.7$) and (b) the profit variance coefficient equals 0.85 while the wealth interaction coefficient is zero ($F(2, 47) = 5.3$) are rejected at the 0.0001 level of significance. Indeed, inherited wealth significantly contributes to consumption smoothing. An increase in wealth of one standard deviation, at the sample means, reduces the impact of profit variance in food consumption by 12 percent.[15]

In the second column of table 6.4 we add the migration and marriage profit variance interaction variables. These results indicate that both the number of married women and the distance between the origin households of the marital partners contribute significantly (statistically) to reducing the variability in household food consumption, for a given variability in farm profits. The presence of household "temporary" migrants also reduces the impact of profit variability, but only marginally. The point estimates

**Table 6.4**   Determinants of variability in real food expenditures in farm households, 1975–1984

| Variable | (1) | (2) | (3) |
|---|---|---|---|
| Profit variance | 0.114 | 0.229 | 0.227 |
|  | (14.9) | (7.91) | (7.18) |
| Inherited wealth × profit variance | −0.147 | −0.107 | −0.197 |
| (× $10^{-6}$) | (4.08) | (4.97) | (4.53) |
| Number of married women × | — | −0.0346 | −0.0340 |
| profit variance |  | (2.82) | (1.97) |
| Marriage distance × profit | — | −0.000228 | −0.000231 |
| variance |  | (4.31) | (4.33) |
| Number of migrants × profit | — | −0.00719 | −0.00695 |
| variance |  | (1.32) | (1.03) |
| Number of adult male market | — | — | −0.0003 |
| workers × profit variance |  |  | (1.24) |
| Number of adult female market | — | — | −0.0708 |
| workers × profit variance |  |  | (1.34) |
| Shirapur village (× $10^5$) | 11.0 | 11.1 | 11.4 |
|  | (4.29) | (3.75) | (3.50) |
| Kanzara village (× $10^5$) | 3.37 | 6.18 | 6.89 |
|  | (1.39) | (2.10) | (2.14) |
| Constant (× $10^5$) | 1.10 | −1.64 | −1.20 |
|  | (0.59) | (0.64) | (0.44) |
| $R^2$ | 0.764 | 0.846 | 0.852 |
| $F$ | 63.3 | 43.4 | 33.9 |

*t*-ratios are in parentheses beneath the coefficients.

indicate that at the sample means the (positive) effect of profit variability on the variability in food expenditures is reduced by 15 percent when the number of resident married women increases by one, and by 6 percent for each increase of one standard deviation (60 km) in the mean distance between the farm household and the origin households of the resident married women. The addition of a household migrant has a weaker effect, reducing the effect of profit variance by 3 percent. In the last column of table 6.4, we assess the robustness of our results to the addition of variables representing the number of resident adult male and female market (off-farm) workers. The presence of such workers may reduce the effects of profit variability on the variability in household consumption to the extent that off-farm labor supply responds flexibly to own-farm profits, and off-farm earnings opportunities in the village are not perfectly correlated with own-farm profits. The estimates indicate that the null hypothesis that the number of off-farm workers does not reduce consumption variability among farm households cannot be rejected ($F(2, 53) = 0.91$). Moreover, the influence of marriage migration in reducing the impact of profit variability on consumption variability is essentially unchanged when the family worker variables are included. It is not the presence of adult women (or men) in the household willing or able to work but their marital status, with its associated inter-household bonds, that contributes to income risk mitigation.

## 4 The Determinants of Spatial Income Diversification

The preceding results suggest that the distance between the origin locations of marital partners contributes to the mitigation of consumption variability, as do the household's asset holdings and, marginally, household migrants. In this section we test the hypothesis that farm households facing *exogenously* riskier incomes associated with spatially covariant risks will be more likely to invest in spatial risk diversification. We also examine the influence of endowed wealth on such arrangements.

A difficulty in relating variability in incomes to household arrangements is that income volatility can in part be influenced by household resource allocations. Even fluctuations in farm profits, net of family labor costs and thus net of family labor supply decisions, can be modified by households, for example, via crop or plot diversification strategies or investments in water control mechanisms. Both farm profit variability and arrangements facilitating *ex post* income transfers may thus reflect a household's attitudes toward risk. Therefore the covariation between profit variance and *ex post* insurance arrangements does not necessarily provide evidence on the appropriate experiment, which would alter exogenously the riskiness of incomes for a given household, when households are heterogeneous in risk preferences.

As noted, the ICRISAT data provide information on daily rainfall for the ten year period. We constructed monthly rainfall variances for each of the critical agricultural months (July–October) for each of the villages. We used as instruments these weather variables interacted with each household's *inherited* dry and wet landholdings to predict each household's mean and variance in profits for the ten years. Under the assumption that village rainfall and inheritances do not reflect household risk preferences, these predicted measures of household income risk should be orthogonal to preferences.[16]

To test the influence of wealth on marriage migration, we used the value of the head's inheritance, again because a household's post-inheritance wealth state will reflect in part its desire for self-insurance and thus its attitudes toward risk, while the head's inheritance is less likely to be correlated with preferences. We expect, as noted, that households with more variable profits, for given mean profits, and households with less endowed wealth, *ceteris paribus*, will be more likely to invest in temporary migration, to have some of their members participate as regular salaried workers, and to invest in marriages with partners whose origin households are separated by greater distances. Riskiness in incomes raises the return to such investments, while wealth is a substitute for such income insurance mechanisms, as is evident in table 6.4. Moreover, while higher wealth and profits in the head's (parents') household should attract a spouse from a higher-wealth household, greater variability in incomes is a liability and should lower the mean value of the match, *ceteris paribus*.

Table 6.5 reports estimates of the effects of profit variability and endowed wealth on the number of migrants, on the presence or absence in the household of a worker with a regular salaried job (assured yearly income), and on the mean distance between the origin village of the resident daughters-in-law and the sample household, on the basis of two-stage tobit, two-stage probit, and two-stage least-squares procedures respectively.[17] We also assess whether the inheritance of the head's father and profit variability influence the value of the landholdings of the father-in-law of the head. The estimating procedures take into account both the possible endogeneity of the profit variables and the specific properties of the dependent variable; that is, no households had more than one salaried worker or a member who was a farm servant, and 76 percent of the households had no temporary migrant. In all cases, we could reject the hypothesis that the variance in profits is orthogonal to the error terms. Heterogeneity in risk preferences does appear to influence jointly both realized profit variability and *ex post* income insurance arrangements.

Two specifications are reported for each dependent variable, one with and one without (predicted) mean profits for the household. The results appear to support the view that exogenously imposed income variability induces households to alter the sources of their incomes. In particular, among farm households with equal endowments of wealth, those afflicted with more variable profits from cultivation are more likely to initiate arrangements conducive to income risk-pooling that encompass greater

**Table 6.5** Effects of agricultural profit levels and profit variability on household labor force and marital arrangements

| | Dependent variable (estimation procedure) | | | |
|---|---|---|---|---|
| | Number of migrants (two-stage maximum likelihood tobit) | Attached laborer/salaried worker (two-stage maximum likelihood probit) | Mean marriage distance (two-stage least squares) | Value of landholdings of head's father-in-law[a] (two-stage maximum likelihood tobit) |
| Profit variance[b] | 1.32 (5.26) | -0.0381 (1.85) | 0.707 (2.98) | 0.00490 (0.51) |
| | — | 0.137 (2.05) | 54.8 (0.52)[c] | -0.0580 (1.37) |
| Profit mean[b] ($\times 10^{-5}$) | -0.152 (0.33) | -7.40 (2.66) | 2.98 (0.15)[c] | 0.00126 (1.58) |
| Value of inheritance ($\times 10^{-4}$) | -2.57 (2.20) | 0.0286 (0.59) | -2.21 (1.85) | 7,26[d] (1.16) |
| | -0.0356 (0.21) | -0.134 (1.41) | -2.03 (1.32) | 8,618 (1.72) |
| | -0.280 (1.51) | 0.287 (0.37) | -10.31 (0.47) | 88,964 (0.95) |
| Constant | -6.42 (3.23) | 5.94 (2.41) | -7.71 (0.30) | 129,574 (1.25) |
| $\chi^2$, F | 37.8   32.9 | 21.0   10.2 | 4.45   3.87 | 8.75   11.2 |
| Hausman–Wu | 9.93   7.08 | 13.1   2.46 | 19.4   10.6 | 2.12   2.48 |

Asymptotic t-ratios are in parentheses beneath the coefficients.

[a] In 1983 rupees.

[b] Endogenous variable; instruments include village-level means and variances of rainfall in July–October 1975–84, and interactions between the rainfall statistics and head's dry and irrigated landholdings at inheritance.

[c] Jointly significant: $F(2,59) = 5.78$.

[d] Inheritance of head's father (in 1983 rupees).

distances via both "temporary" migrants and longer-distance migration associated with marriage. Moreover, greater (predicted) variability in incomes reduces the mean value of the marital match that the household was able to obtain, consistent with risk-avoidance behavior in the marriage market.

The negative wealth coefficients in the distance regression also conform to the risk insurance model of marriage cum migration but are inconsistent with the conventional theory of marriage, in which families with greater wealth are predicted to search for marital partners over a larger area. Although high-wealth households are evidently more likely to contract marriages with other high-wealth households, in conformity with the assortative mating prediction, farm families with greater wealth, among those households facing the same income risk, are less likely to be characterized by marriages extending over long distances, despite their enhanced ability to finance a search over a wider area and their greater difficulty in finding a desirable marital match.[18] As is consistent with the results in table 6.4, the usefulness of asset holdings for reducing consumption volatility, for given income variability, appears to be reflected in households' decisions about migration and marriage cum migration arrangements. Wealth is thus not merely a matching trait or a source of investment funds, and marriage and migration are not merely mechanisms for increasing income levels.

## 5 Conclusion

In this chapter we have examined from a risk-theoretic perspective a major component of migration in low-income rural areas, that associated with the movement of women for the purpose of marriage. In particular, we have hypothesized that the spatial distribution and characteristics of matches associated with the marriage of daughters are in part manifestations of implicit inter-household contractual arrangements facilitating consumption smoothing in an environment characterized by information costs and spatially covariant risks. Analysis of longitudinal data from villages in South India provided support for the hypothesis, indicating that marriage cum migration contributes to a reduction in the variability in consumption, for given variability in income from crop production, and that households exposed to higher income risk are more likely to invest in longer-distance migration–marriage arrangements.

The hypothesized and observed patterns of migration and marriage do not appear consistent with standard models of marriage or migration that

*Migration and Risk*

are concerned solely with search costs and differentials in expected income levels. Thus these patterns suggest that spatial differences in the average returns to skills (or wage levels) may not importantly account for population movements within rural India. However, our framework also implies that agricultural technical change may significantly alter spatial marriage patterns, if not the stability of the marriage institution, since such change not only alters the spatial covariances and levels of risk but renders more difficult the assessment of risk and thus the establishment of implicit risk arrangements. Conversely, improvements in formal institutional arrangements (for example, credit markets) that facilitate consumption smoothing may reduce the role played by risk considerations in marital arrangements and rural migration, perhaps resulting in diminished rural mobility. Finally, our results suggest that the value to parents of having a girl relative to having a boy in environments characterized by underdeveloped insurance markets and spatially covariant risks may be substantially understated by sex differentials in expected labor market returns. Moreover, attention to the returns arising from the specialized role of daughters accruing from their dispersion suggests that policies lowering *ex ante* income risks in such settings may result in diminished resources allocated to young girls if intra-household resource allocations are influenced by economic incentives.

**Appendix**

**Table 6.A1**  Maximum likelihood estimates: latent variable analysis of marital partner quality

| Indicator | Head | Wife |
|---|---|---|
| Father's schooling | 1.00[a] | 1.00[a] |
| Owned irrigated acreage | 22.65 | 1.07 |
|  | (6.73) | (4.75) |
| Owned dry acreage | 3.28 | 5.75 |
|  | (7.26) | (7.27) |
| $\chi^2(8)$ | 75.89 | |
| No. of observations | 382 | |

Asymptotic *t*-values are in parentheses beneath the coefficients.
[a] Reference (scaling) variable.

**Notes**

Co-authored with Mark R. Rosenzweig. Reprinted from *Journal of Political Economy* 97, 1989. This is a revised version of Discussion Paper 32, Harvard University Migration and Development Program. We are grateful to Sam Peltzman, Zvi Griliches, and a referee for helpful comments, and to R. P. Singh for valuable assistance in obtaining and interpreting the data.

1 Urbanization in India appears particularly slow in the context of the productivity gains in the urban sector (Mills and Becker, 1986).

2 Twelve percent of the women in the Malaysian sample were of South Asian Indian ethnic origin. These women exhibited behavior more akin to Malaysians than to Indians residing in India. Although 42.3 percent of this group moved at the time of marriage, only 27.5 percent of all their moves were for marriage. Among males of Indian ethnic origin, 13.7 percent migrated when married and 5.6 percent of all their moves were for marriage. The "Indian" pattern of marriage migration appears to depend more on the environment than on ethnicity *per se*.

3 We do not investigate the role of dowry payments in marital arrangements. Such payments are part of the set of intergenerational relationships, along with inheritances, whose study we are pursuing in other work.

4 Caldwell et al. (1986) found in their study of nine villages in Karnataka in South India that 56 percent of the relatives providing aid during droughts were either relatives of the head's wife or those of the husbands of the head's daughters. None of these relatives was located within the study villages. Using a subset of the data described below, Rosenzweig (1988a) found that almost 60 percent of income transfers (in value terms), representing 10 percent of agricultural profits on average, originated outside the village, that such transfers moved inversely with agricultural profits, and that the inverse association between net transfers (exclusive of marriage-related gifts and dowries) and profits was stronger among households with greater numbers of resident daughters-in-law.

5 Seventy-nine (36) percent of the value of household transfer inflows (outflows) of cash and goods for emergency support and consumption maintenance traversed distances of 20 or more miles. Because of small cell sizes, it is not possible to distinguish precisely differences in the patterns of these transfers among Malaysian ethnic groups.

6 Rosenzweig and Wolpin (1985) formulate and test a model that explains the immobility of farm household males as a consequence of land-specific returns to experience associated with weather variability. For additional evidence on the returns to experience, see Rosenzweig (1988b).

7 Cooper (1987) demonstrates that in a model in which agricultural income is uncertain, nondecreasing relative risk aversion with a value less than or equal to unity or nonincreasing absolute risk aversion is a sufficient condition for a

mean-preserving increase in risk to increase a household's demand for insurance via the allocation of additional household time (migration) to riskless activities. Quizon et al. (1984) show that the experimental evidence on risk aversion (Binswanger, 1981) based on lottery games played with residents of the Indian villages from which our survey data were obtained (see below) is consistent with increasing relative risk aversion. The experimental evidence suggests a high degree of risk aversion for games involving large payoffs (500 rupees) and is also consistent with prospect theory risk models. However, the evidence appears to reject standard economic models of risk behavior incorporating linear probability weights on von Neumann–Morgenstern utilities of final wealth levels.

8  The standard error of $z$ is $(t - 3)^{-1/2}$, where $t$ is the number of time series observations. The attainment of homoskedastic errors by the transformation of the correlations according to (6.1) also requires that each of the correlated variables is normally distributed (Hoel, 1971).

9  The sample of six ICRISAT villages provides estimates that may overstate the extent to which distance generally reduces the covariation in agricultural incomes since sample site selection was based in part on the criterion of minimizing the similarity in agroclimatic conditions across regions. Thus the pairs of villages within each of three regions are likely to experience similar conditions and are proximate (the intra-region mean distance is 22 km), while the mean cross-region distance between villages, for which conditions are dissimilar, is 583 km.

10  Included in the sample are all cultivating households in the three villages that remained in the survey over the ten year period from 1975–6 to 1984–5, when the retrospective questionnaires were applied. Of the 90 original farm households in 1975–6, 70 were present in 1984–5, but seven of these were not able to be interviewed for purposes of obtaining information on the distances of marriages. Unfortunately, households were dropped from the sample when there was a change in the head of the household. In almost all cases this was due to the death of the head.

11  A supplementary retrospective survey on the kinship relations associated with all marriages in the sample households in one of the villages, Shirapur, indicates that despite geographical exogamy, or more precisely because of it, almost all marital partners were also related by kinship. Of the 115 marriages, only 14 (12.2 percent) involved partners who were not also relatives. Daughters-in-law of the head, for example, were most typically daughters of a sibling of either the head's father or the father of the head's wife. Thus the ties between spatially separated households are typically reinforced by marriages, not just initiated by them.

12  A farm household may diversify its income sources and thus reduce the intertemporal variability in its income by cultivating plots of land differentiated by their sensitivities to given states of nature in addition to diversifying the geographical location of potential income sources in the face of spatially covariant income risks. However, while almost three-fourths of farm house-

holds in the three villages own two or more plots of land, less than half own plots that are distinct from each other in terms of soil quality (among seven types), irrigation, or location. Moreover, the households do not appear to view plot fragmentation as advantageous: of the plots purchased by the households in the three villages since inheritance, 42 percent were acquired in order to consolidate landholdings or because the plot was close to the household's residence. Diversification was never mentioned as a reason for either buying or selling plots.

13  We use food expenditures rather than total expenditures because of the well-known difficulties of correcting for the lumpiness of consumer durable expenditures. Food expenditures include the value of consumption from own production and from own foodstocks.

14  The village dummy variables pick up all permanent characteristics of villages inclusive of the means and variances of village-level 25 aggregate incomes.

15  In equation (6.5) we also included inherited wealth not interacted with the profit variance to assess whether the variances in consumption are greater among the wealthier for given variability in incomes. The coefficient on this variable was not statistically significant in any specification ($t$-ratios were 0.14, 0.13, and 0.06 in the three variants of (6.5)), and its inclusion only trivially altered the coefficients and $t$-ratios reported in table 6.4.

16  The estimates from the first-stage regressions are available on request.

17  The two-stage maximum likelihood tobit and probit procedures are described by Smith and Blundell (1986).

18  The location of the wealthy households is not the reason for this result. While there is a tendency for wealthier households to cluster among themselves *within* villages, the sample villages are not situated in "wealthy" areas, that is, in closer proximity to villages with higher proportions of wealthy households.

## References

Becker, Gary S. (1973) "A Theory of Marriage: Part I." *Journal of Political Economy* 81 (4): 813–46.

—— (1974) "A Theory of Marriage: Part II." *Journal of Political Economy* 82(2), part 2: S11–26.

Binswanger, Hans P. (1981) "Attitudes Toward Risk: Theoretical Implications of an Experiment in Rural India." *Economic Journal* 91: 867–90.

Butz, William P. and DaVanzo, Julie (1978) "The Malaysian Family Life Survey: Summary Report." Rand Report R-2351-AID, Rand Corporation, Santa Monica, CA.

Caldwell, John C., Reddy, P. H. and Caldwell, Pat (1986) "Periodic High Risk as a Cause of Fertility Decline in a Changing Rural Environment: Survival Strategies in the 1980–1983 South Indian Drought." *Economic Development and Cultural Change* 34: 677–701.

Cooper, Joyce M. R. (1987) "A Note on the Intersectoral Allocation of Agricultural Household Labor under Uncertainty." Mimeo, University of Iowa, Iowa City.

Greenwood, Michael J. (1971) "A Regression Analysis of Migration to Urban Areas of Less-Developed Countries: The Case of India." *Journal of Regional Science* 11: 253–62.

Hoel, Paul G. (1971) *Introduction to Mathematical Statistics*, 4th edn. New York: Wiley.

Jöreskog, Karl G. (1969) "A General Approach to Confirmatory Maximum Likelihood Factor Analysis." *Psychometrika* 34(2), part 1: 183–202.

Keeley, Michael C. (1977) "The Economics of Family Formation." *Economic Inquiry* 15: 238–50.

Lucas, Robert E. B. and Stark, Oded (1985) "Motivations to Remit: Evidence from Botswana." *Journal of Political Economy* 93 (5): 901–18 (reprinted as ch. 16 in this volume).

McCloskey, Donald N. (1976) "English Open Fields as Behavior towards Risk." In Paul Uselding (ed.), *Research in Economic History*, vol. 1. Greenwich, CT: JAI Press.

Mills, Edwin S. and Becker, Charles M. (1986) *Studies in Indian Urban Development*. New York: Oxford University Press for World Bank.

Quizon, Jaime B., Binswanger, Hans P. and Machina, Mark J. (1984) "Attitudes toward Risk: Further Remarks." *Economic Journal* 94: 144–8.

Rosenzweig, Mark R. (1988a) "Risk, Implicit Contracts and the Family in Rural Areas of Low-Income Countries." *Economic Journal* 98: 1148–70.

—— (1988b) "Risk, Private Information, and the Family." *American Economic Review, Papers and Proceedings* 78: 245–50.

—— and Wolpin, Kenneth I. (1985) "Specific Experience, Household Structure, and Intergenerational Transfers: Farm Family Land and Labor Arrangements in Developing Countries." *Quarterly Journal of Economics* 100 (suppl.): 961–87.

Skeldon, Ronald (1986) "On Migration Patterns in India during the 1970s." *Population and Development Review* 12 (4): 759–79.

Smith, Richard J. and Blundell, Richard W. (1986) "An Exogeneity Test for a Simultaneous Equation Tobit Model with an Application to Labor Supply." *Econometrica* 54 (3): 679–85.

Sundaram, K. (1989) "Agriculture–Industry Interactions in India: Issues of Migration." In Sukhamoy Chakravarty (ed.), *The Balance Between Industry and Agriculture in Economic Development, Proceedings of the 8th World Congress of the International Economic Association, New Delhi*, vol. 3, *Manpower and Transfers*. New York: St Martin's Press, pp. 177–206.

# Part III

## A Relative Deprivation Approach to Migration

7

# Rural-to-Urban Migration in Less Developed Countries: A Relative Deprivation Approach

1

The basic premises of this chapter are (a) that, given a person's own (current) income, his satisfaction or deprivation is some function of income statistics other than this income (for example, a statistic based on the incomes of some (not necessarily all) other persons) and (b) that rural-to-urban migration is undertaken in order to improve a person's position in terms of the *latter statistic*. As is often the case when an old approach (relative deprivation) is applied to a new area (migration),[1] the ideas presented here are exploratory and illustrative and have not yet been subjected to complete and formal empirical verification. Nonetheless, the usefulness of this approach in offering novel explanations to migration-related phenomena opens a promising avenue of research in a field where empirical work abounds but theory is still fairly weak (and all too often somewhat *ad hoc*).

Premise (a) builds on the notion that people are engaged in interpersonal income comparisons which are internalized, thus generating psychological costs or benefits, frustrations or elations, relative deprivation or satisfaction. Viewing migration as an act of choice, premise (b) builds on the notion that these factors motivate locational decisions. Relative deprivation is an important factor affecting people's choices which has been overlooked by the received migration theory.

Working through a large number of village studies,[2] we have observed several interesting and largely unexplained regularities: (a) rural-to-urban migration rates are not highest from the poorest villages; (b) migration rates are higher from villages where the distribution of income by size is more unequal; (c) it is the very poor whose propensity to migrate from these villages is highest. Conventional migration theory, linking migration propensities causally and positively to intersectoral income differentials, fails to predict (a), nor does it offer sound clues that carry (b) and (c).[3] Moreover, the Pareto welfare implications of observations (b) and (c) have not yet been examined systematically. A prime purpose of this chapter is to model these relationships and to pursue such an examination.

Although the issue addressed in this chapter is that of rural-to-urban migration, the analysis has a bearing on a wider area of social study: do individuals, motivated by self-betterment, undertake actions that improve their own welfare as well as that of the community (society) at large? The ensuing analysis can be construed as a special yet important case, where such a favorable result holds.

Section 2 defines a simple deprivation concept and causally relates it to rural-to-urban migration. The Pareto welfare implications as well as some migration theory implications are examined. Section 3 adopts an alternative relative deprivation concept and again examines the Pareto welfare implications of the induced migration. Although the concepts utilized in these sections are fairly stringent, they seem to share many of the important features of broader more realistic concepts and serve to elucidate the possibilities inherent in them. Section 4 addresses the intriguing question of whether the distributional consequences of migration motivated by absolute income maximization, rather than by relative deprivation minimization, nevertheless imply a diminution of societal relative deprivation. Conclusions and some complementary remarks are offered in the concluding section.

**2**

Consider a small rural community – a village – in which everyone compares his income $y$ with the community's average income $\bar{y}$. For simplicity, assume that the income distribution in this village is uniform, or very close to uniform, over the range $y^l$, $y^h$ – the lowest and highest incomes in the village. We thus have a discrete distribution approximated by the uniform distribution. Affiliation is so strong that the village average income continues to be a reference statistic irrespective of the villagers' location (that is, the village is a stable and consistent reference group).[4] Those whose income $y$ is less than $\bar{y}$ may constitute the relatively deprived,[5] but we shall adopt a more specific concept:

$$RD(y) = \begin{cases} 1 & y < \bar{y} - d \\ 0 & y \geq \bar{y} - d \end{cases}$$

Clearly, the case in which the reference statistic generating relative deprivation is exactly $\bar{y}$ is a special one in which $d = 0$. The relatively deprived (those whose income falls short of $\bar{y}$ by more than $d$ and who assume that by migrating to the urban sector they will secure an income closer to $\bar{y}$) migrate, taking, so to speak, their income with them. The average income in the village is now higher than $\bar{y}$. Therefore a villager whose income prior to the migration was closer than $d$ to the village average is now relatively deprived, and he also decides to migrate. Again, the average village income rises, and someone else feels deprived and dissatisfied, resents being so, and decides to migrate. Eventually, only those whose income is higher than $y^h - 2d$ are left; when $y^l = y^h - 2d$ no villager has an income less than $\bar{y} - d$, that is, the necessary condition for rural-to-urban migration. Substituting $y^l = y^h - 2d$ into $\bar{y} = \frac{1}{2}(y^l + y^h)$ yields $\bar{y} = y^h - d$. Obviously, we assume that the urban income is sufficiently high (no lower than $y^h - 2d$). Note that in the specific case $d = 0$ those left in the village are the ones whose income is highest.

    This highly abstract stationary process raises a number of interesting issues. First, is the outcome Pareto optimal? Clearly, the standard operative form of the Pareto criterion – a community is better off when the income of some individuals increases whereas the income of all the others remains intact – collapses, since people in this model consider their position *relatively*. Yet it is possible to overcome this difficulty by observing each of three distinct groups: (a) Pavement dwellers in Bombay are definitely worse off relative to the average Bombay resident than they were relative to the average in their own village prior to migrating to Bombay. With the assumption that incomes are evaluated relatively, a possible explanation for these migrants' location and behavior is that in assessing their own welfare they indeed continue to relate to the village community as their reference group, and hence register an improvement. (b) Those who stay behind are the ones who were not relatively deprived before migration and will not become deprived after it. (c) We are left with those who constitute the host community. If, numerically, this community is substantially larger than the number of migrants, which is very often the case, the urban average income will hardly be affected at all and hence nothing, in terms of relative deprivation (or satisfaction), will change. Note the asymmetry: whereas migrants alter the position of members of the community that they leave, they have no effect on the position of members in the community that they join. Suppose now that migrants do constitute a significant proportion of the receiving urban community. As they are likely to secure a lower income than the urban average,[6] all the urban dwellers will decrease their deprivation or increase their satisfaction in comparing their income with the new *lower* urban average income.

Thus, without a straight application of the standard operative form of the Pareto criterion, rural-to-urban migration with relative deprivation as the motivating force is seen to constitute a collectively preferred state.

A second interesting implication of the postulated process is that it offers a new explanation for one of the most widely observed migration pheno-mena – its apparent self-perpetuating tendency. The received theory is that once migration from a *given* sending community begins, there are good reasons for it to continue. Migration usually occurs amid imperfect and scarce information on the characteristics of the destination and uncertainty with respect to future receiving-end employment prospects. Acquisition of information (search) and insurance are costly (often prohi-bitively so), yet some level of each may be a necessary condition for migration. This is why migration should be expected to be, and often actually is, closely associated with the creation and utilization of social networks, with the presence at the receiving end of friends and relat-ives – fellow villagers constituting an earlier vintage of migrants – who can provide destination-specific information, hedge against the initial high risks associated with attempts to enter a new labor market and/or secure continuous employment in it, and so forth. The perpetuation phenomenon is thus explained by a receiving-end factor – paucity or possession of crucial destination-specific capital (DaVanzo and Morrison, 1981). The alternative suggested here is that such perpetuity stems from a sending-end factor – relative deprivation which brings about migration that leads, in turn, to further relative deprivation and discontent (by others), resulting in additional migration, and so on.[7]

Another interesting implication of the present model concerns the interaction between rural-to-urban migration and the persistence of inter-sectoral inequality in labor incomes (wage rates). The received theory postulates that while "excessive" rural-to-urban migration (in terms of urban job slots) does not bring about equalization of actual labor incomes, it does equalize *expected* incomes, and rural-to-urban migration ceases precisely when equilibrium in these terms obtains (Todaro, 1969, 1980). Put differently, the only explanation offered by existing migration theory for the *simultaneous* cessation of rural-to-urban migration and prevalence of urban-to-rural positive wage differentials (which often fails when subjected to empirical verification) is that (risk-neutral) migrants respond to expected differentials (wagees multiplied by probabilities of securing them) and not to actual differentials. The process described here provides both a new stopping rule for rural-to-urban migration and a new explanation for the persistence of the intersectoral wage gap. Since migration halts at $y^l = y^h - 2d$, actual (average labor) urban income can be, and remains, higher than (average labor) rural income at this point. In a (pure) relative deprivation model, and as seen from the perspective of the "potential migrant," a higher urban than rural wage rate is a necessary condition for rural-to-urban migration, but elimination of the intersectoral differential, although sufficient, is not a necessary condition for migration to cease. (A possible marriage between a relative deprivation model and an expected income model of rural-to-urban migration is demonstrated in section 5.)

## 3

Now consider a village in which everyone compares his income $y$ not with the village average but with all other villagers' incomes. Retain the assumption that villagers regard the village as their reference group irrespective of their location. Relative deprivation is a function of the village incomes of which a person is deprived and of their relative frequency. Formally,

$$\text{RD}(y) = \int_y^{y^h} [1 - F(x)]dx$$

That is, the relative deprivation of a person whose income is $y$ is a summation over the range $y$ to $y^h$ (the highest income obtained in the village) of one minus the cumulative income distribution (the proportion of the villagers in the total village population whose income exceeds $y$) (Atkinson, 1970; Yitzhaki, 1979; Hey and Lambert, 1980). Some villagers feel so relatively deprived that they decide to migrate to the urban sector, assuming that they will thereby succeed in securing an income higher than their initial income $y$. Consequently, all the remaining villagers become more relatively deprived, since as $1 - F(x)$ increases $F(x)$ decreases – the new distribution stochastically dominates the old one.[8] Some of the remaining villagers will also migrate, causing others to be more relatively deprived, until eventually only those whose income is highest are left.

It is instructive to examine, once again, whether the outcome is Pareto optimal. For those who ultimately remain in the village, relative deprivation remains intact at the zero level. As to the migrants, if their urban-secured income is higher than their pre-migration village income, then, compared with the base-line situation – that which prevailed in the village at the time of their departure – they are less relatively deprived. If, by village standards, their urban income is sufficiently high, they will endure less relative deprivation in comparing their lot with any village distribution.

It is a little more difficult to determine the relative deprivation consequences for the receiving urban community. If, relative to the urban population, the number of incoming migrants is an insignificant proportion, nothing will change in terms of relative deprivation. If this is not the case (migration is significant), it is useful to distinguish between two extreme possibilities: (a) Migrants secure an income at the lowest end of the urban income distribution. No urban person is in the position of comparing himself with more people with incomes higher than his own, and everyone finds that the *proportion* of people with incomes higher than his has *declined*. Hence, for every urban person, relative deprivation is lower. (b) The income distribution of the migrants matches that of the urban population (thus the average urban income remains intact). In this case, any urban person will find that his relative deprivation has not changed as the *proportion* of urban residents whose income is higher than his remains the same. To obtain this result, note that

$$RD(z) = \int_z^{z^h} [1 - F(x)]dx = \mu[1 - \phi(z)] - z[1 - F(z)]$$

where $z$ is the income of an urban person, $\mu$ is the urban average income, and $\phi(z)$ is the proportion of total urban income received by all urban persons whose income is less than or equal to $z$.[9] It is easily seen that $z$, $\mu$, $\phi(z)$, and $F(z)$ do not change. Hence the relative deprivation of any urban income recipient does not change either.

4

So far we have examined the consequences for societal relative deprivation of rural-to-urban migration motivated by personal relative deprivation. It is instructive to explore the relative deprivation consequences for society in the particularly important case when rural-to-urban migration is induced by the desire of families to improve their *absolute* income position *per se*.

We start by looking at the distributional characteristics of the modal rural-to-urban migration – migration by a young family member. The impact of such migration on the inequality of income distribution by size depends crucially on the choice of the basic income-receiving unit. The adopted choice criterion must be sensitive enough to grasp the type and nature of rural-to-urban migration and should fully reflect the identity of the decision-making unit with respect to income plans – both acquisition and disposition. Furthermore, in adopting any procedure it is crucial to maintain consistency between the definition of the income unit and the type of income covered by the procedure. When, as in the modal case, the *family* is the locus of major decisions on income (including the means of obtaining it – among other things through rural-to-urban migration of one of its members),[10] neither the household nor the individual is the relevant income-receiving unit. Thus, choice of a multi-person urban household in which the migrant happens to be staying (common residence, sharing housekeeping, common eating arrangements) appends the migrant to a family with which his economic ties are short lived, in whose income decisions he does not really participate, and by whose income decisions he is not really affected.

Considerations of a similar nature render it equally inappropriate to refer to the individual rural-to-urban migrant family member as an independent income-receiving unit. Although he lives separately from his family, he does participate in his family's common decisions (which affect him too), he is involved in familial pooling of resources and income, especially pooling aimed at facilitating his migration, he is responsible for substantial net urban-to-rural remittances,[11] and he maintains a close overall (at least in the medium run) bond with his family. Clearly, if separate households form a cluster of sufficiently close common interest that makes for joint economic decisions concerning acquisition and disposition of income, that cluster should constitute the income distribution unit. All this implies that it makes little analytical sense to refer to the migrant as an independent income-receiving unit and that in any meaningful evaluation both his and his family's incomes should be combined. The implication of this observation for a distribution-welfare analysis is that, at least for a considerable period of time, an *a priori* classification is in order (that is, the criterion for defining income as rural or urban should depend on the recipient's initial location, and not on his current one, or for that matter on the locality in which that income was actually generated); the income-receiving unit to which all incomes are attributed must be the rural-based family *including* its "urban extension," the migrant member.

Designate the urban and rural sectoral uniform wage rates by $W^u$ and $W^r$ respectively, and the respective labor force shares by $f^u$ and $f^r$ where $f^u + f^r = 1$. Assume that, following migration, some of the $f^r$ in the population receive a higher income than before, while the incomes of all the rest remain unchanged (thus the $f^r$ receive a larger share of total income). In terms of the Gini coefficient, a distributional improvement can be seen to apply as follows. If, through various sharing and filtering-down mechanisms, $W^r$ rises throughout, the Gini coefficient, which in the case of two homogeneous groups reduces to the difference between the rural population's share in the total population and the rural population's share in total income, registers a clear improvement:

$$G = f^r - \frac{f^r W^r}{f^r W^r + f^u W^u}$$

If $W^r$ rises, the numerator in the right-hand term increases by more than the denominator.

Does relative deprivation in society at large diminish also? Assume that *every* person's relative deprivation is given by

$$RD(y) = \int_y^{y^h} [1 - F(x)]dx$$

It is easily shown that the sum total of the relative deprivations defined as

$$TD = \int_0^{y^h} RD(y)f(y)dy$$

is $\mu G$, that is, the average income multiplied by the Gini coefficient.[12] It is generally impossible to determine analytically whether TD declines when $G$ is reduced through a rise in $\mu$, as this would clearly depend on the comparative proportionate changes taking place in $\mu$ and $G$. However, in the particular case examined here, TD definitely decreases. To obtain this result note that

$$\mu G = f^r(f^r W^r + f^u W^u) - f^r W^r$$

and therefore, by partial differentiation,

$$\frac{\partial(\mu G)}{\partial W^r} = f^r(f^r - 1) < 0$$

This is an interesting outcome: families whose migration decisions are motivated by maximization of utility from absolute income end up reducing total societal deprivation! Thus, although the explicit statistic that motivates migration is not relative deprivation, relative deprivation is nevertheless definitely reduced by migration.

5

In this chapter we have been concerned with presenting the relative deprivation approach to rural-to-urban migration in LDCs. The relative deprivation approach analyzes rural-to-urban migration as a response to measurable dissatisfaction within an origin reference group and as a means of reducing or eliminating such dissatisfaction. The analysis brings out distinct ways of capturing relative deprivation and outlines fairly general conditions under which rural-to-urban migration, motivated by a sense of individual relative deprivation, leads to a Pareto welfare improvement. Allowing for the possibility that rural-to-urban migration takes place in pursuit of pure absolute income maximization, we have also explored the effect of such behavior on societal relative deprivation. In the preceding section, a situation was examined in which this effect is favorable.

We end with three complementary remarks. First, we have developed the relative deprivation approach to rural-to-urban migration under an implicit "domain assumption":[13] income in its absolute form does not play a role. In some situations the desire to increase absolute income may play a weak role in determining migratory behavior and may have no detectable effect. Hence it can be ignored. In others it might be quite important. Then the assumption is perfectly legitimate as a heuristic device – "a way of simplifying the logical development of the theory." However, as such, its utilization has to be seen as the first stage in developing a precise migration theory, and there is therefore a natural need to illustrate what the next stage in such a process of "successive approximation" could look like – namely allowing for the possibility that income, as well as relative deprivation, are determinants of the migration decision.

If the well-being of an individual is determined by his income and his relative deprivation, we can postulate a utility function $U[y, \text{RD}(y)]$ with $U_1 > 0$, $U_{11} < 0$, $U_2 < 0$, $U_{22} > 0$. Thus, what we have is that there is diminishing utility of relative deprivation, but the marginal disutility is increasing in deprivation, for example. Given such a utility function, we can illustrate how a relative deprivation approach to rural-to-urban migration can be linked with an expected-income approach. Utilizing the

formulation of relative deprivation propounded in section 3, we find that
the utility of an individual in the rural sector, whose income is $y$, is

$$U\{y, \int_{y}^{y^h} [1 - F(x)]dx\}$$

The individual may compare this with the following. Assume a one-period
planning horizon and denote remunerations from employment in the urban
formal sector, the urban informal sector, and unemployment by $W$, $W'$,
and 0 respectively. (Individuals view $W$, $W'$ as parameters – they are
determined exogenously: $W$ is determined institutionally by minimum
wage legislation, customs and traditions, collective bargaining by powerful
unions, etc.; $W'$ is determined through a proportional or other monotonic
functional link to $W$ or through a linkage with urban subsistence conditions.) Employment prospects in the two urban sectors are given by
$0 < P < 1$ and $0 < P' < 1$. Given some additional simplifying assumptions (especially that failure to secure employment in one urban sector
does not, as such, lower the probability of success in securing employment
in another),[14] the urban utility is thus

$$PU\left\{W, \int_{W}^{y^h} [1 - F(x)]dx\right\} + P'U\left\{W', \int_{W'}^{y^h} [1 - F(x)]dx\right\}$$

A rural-to-urban migration equilibrium condition obtains when the latter
utility is equal to the rural sector utility as specified above. Since $W$, $W'$, $P$,
$P'$ are given, we need solve only for $F(\cdot)$. Denoting the solution by $F(y^*)$,
we obtain, given the functional forms of $F$ and $U$, the equilibrium income
$y^*$ and thereby characterization, in terms of income, of both migrants and
nonmigrants. Since the second argument in the utility function is a source
of dissatisfaction, we can characterize equilibrium through an equality
between (the utility from) rural income net of rural relative deprivation
and (the utility from) expected urban income net of rural relative deprivation associated with this income. Considering, for example, the original
expected income migration model (in which $P' = 0$) and an additive
separable utility function, the equilibrium rural income $y^*$ can be lower
than the urban actual wage $W$ but higher than the urban expected wage
$PW$, whereas $y^*$ net of the relative deprivation associated with $y^*$ is equal
to the expected urban wage net of the (probable) relative deprivation
associated with the urban actual wage.[15]

   Second, the conclusions reached in sections 2 and 3 need not be affected
by relaxing the assumption that the migrants' village of origin is a stable

and consistent reference group. As time goes by, it is possible that the migrants' degree of identification, allegiance, and social connectedness with their village will fade and that some urban community will "take over" as the reference group. We are not aware of a well-developed theory of how reference groups are formed (or dissolved), nor is such a direction of inquiry within the confines of the present chapter.

Suppose, however, that the urban community is decomposed into reference groups that, along with the village of origin, can be ranked by their average income. Assume, in order to simplify the argument, that the intra-group distributions are alike. Suppose further that some time after migration migrants refer not to their home village but to an urban group with an average income higher than the post-migration village average income. There is no *a priori* reason why such a shift need enhance their sense of relative deprivation. As time goes by, migrants' incomes rise as well (Stark, 1978). In terms of section 2, relative deprivation will be higher with the newly acquired urban reference group than with the forgone village reference group only if the migrants' higher income is lower than the average income of their urban reference group by *more* than their initial urban income was lower than the average income of their village. A similar argument applies if one urban reference group is replaced by another higher-ranked one. Two observations tend to negate the possibility of an increasing relative deprivation brought about through a reference group replacement process. First, the clustering in neighborhoods and the formation of associations which consist of fellow ex-villagers is a phenomenon discerned all around the world among rural-to-urban migrants, immigrants, and the like. Within such groups, the more established migrants of an earlier vintage are highly positioned. Second, enhanced relative deprivation could be converted into, and thus manifested through, radical political behavior. The evidence bearing on this issue has been examined elsewhere and it was concluded that "viewing the political profile of urban migrants as 'revolutionary' or 'radical' appears to be an illusion" (Stark, 1980a). This may indicate, even if indirectly and somewhat loosely, that the substitution of higher-ranked for lower-ranked reference groups does not necessarily give rise to enhanced relative deprivation.

Third, it seems to us that the relative deprivation approach to rural-to-urban migration warrants close confrontation with data and that it should be subjected to careful testing and systematic empirical verification. We are not aware of existing data sets to facilitate such an undertaking fully. Therefore, an implication for research design is that attempts should be made to shift away from exclusive interest in and collection of data bearing on the intersectoral wage differential (so often taken to be *the* explanatory variable of rural-to-urban migration in less developed countries) so as to generate data bearing on relative deprivation, for example the distribution of income by size at the village of origin, and on shrinkage of relative deprivation in association with migration. Such an endeavor will make it possible to test statistically the extent to which rural-to-urban migration is motivated by response to relative deprivation. If it is found to be significant, developments and policies affecting relative deprivation will also have to be assessed in terms of their derived impact on migration.

## Notes

Reprinted from *Economic Development and Cultural Change* 32, 1984. I am indebted to Michael Lipton, Jacob Paroush, Michael Roemer, Amartya Sen, Shlomo Yitzhaki, and the referees for helpful comments. This chapter was presented at the European Meeting of the Econometric Society, Dublin, September 5–9, 1982.

1   Relative deprivation has been used as an analytical device by sociologists, political scientists, and social psychologists in studying the relationship between social inequalities (in class, status, and power) and the grievances they cause (Runciman, 1966, and the references cited therein), but has not been explicitly applied to modeling migration.

2   The studies were drawn from a large collection of village studies gathered at the Institute of Development Studies at Sussex University as part of the Institute's Village Studies Programme.

3   Some recent statistical tests of the explanatory power of the intersectoral income differential have found that the elasticity of migration with respect to origin (village) income is surprisingly weak (Fields, 1982; Schultz, 1982). This, too, suggests that at the rural end a variable other than income *per se* could account for migratory behavior.

4   The assumption here is that a person's dissatisfaction is with his position in his group, not with this group's position in society. The group consists of those whose situation a person contrasts with his own. In this chapter, the common attribute which binds rural people into a reference group is their village affiliation. The implications stemming from a possible change of the reference group over time are briefly discussed in section 5.

5   Comparison with "the average" as a quantification of the magnitude of relative deprivation is not novel. For example, focusing on poverty, Townsend (1974) notes: "Poverty can be defined objectively and applied consistently only in terms of the concept of relative deprivation. . . . Individuals, families and groups in the population can be said to be in poverty when they lack the resources to obtain the types of diets, participate in the activities and have the living conditions and amenities which are customary, or are at least widely encouraged or approved, in the societies to which they belong. Their resources

are so seriously below those commanded by *the average* individual or family that they are, in effect, excluded from ordinary living patterns, customs and activities." (emphasis added).

6 On the urban employment experience of rural-to-urban migrants, see Stark (1978).

7 Sociologists have also attributed the self-sustaining nature of migrant flows and their persistence "after the economic incentives for physical displacement have all but disappeared" to the emergence of the social networks. These, they believe, account for "the anomaly of persistent migrant flows from some communities and not from others in the same region, despite *similar* economic conditions" (Portes, 1983; emphasis added). See also Lomnitz (1977). The argument in the text (a) does not consider such a process as an "anomaly," (b) does not concur with the opinion that "the economic incentives have all but disappeared," and (c) suggests an additional differentiating factor between origin communities which otherwise seem "similar" in their economic conditions – villages with a more unequal distribution of income by size also differ from those with more equal distribution because of the extent of the corresponding levels of relative deprivation that they generate with respect to the ensuing migration flows.

8 Those left in the village fall into two subgroups: those whose income is lower than $y$ (the income of the migrating villagers) and those whose income is higher than $y$. The former will surely feel more relatively deprived since the *proportion* of villagers whose income exceeds theirs is now larger. The relative deprivation of the latter group also increases – even though there is no change in the absolute number of higher-income recipients in the village – as the relative frequency of these people increases.

9 Utilizing Atkinson (1970) and Yitzhaki (1979),

$$RD(z) = \int_z^{z^h} [1 - F(x)]\, dx$$

$$= \int_0^{z^h} [1 - F(x)]\, dx - \int_0^z [1 - F(x)]\, dx$$

$$= \int_0^z F(x)\, dx - \int_0^{z^h} F(x)\, dx + \int_0^{z^h} dx - \int_0^z dx$$

$$= zF(z) - \mu\phi(z) - z^h F(z^h) + \mu\phi(z^h) + z^h - z$$

$$= \mu[1 - \phi(z)] - z[1 - F(z)]$$

since

$$\mu\phi(z) = zF(z) - \int_0^z F(x)\, dx \quad \text{and} \quad \phi(z^h) = F(z^h) = 1$$

10  There are strong empirical and theoretical grounds for this assumption. See, among others, Stark (1978).
11  Significant urban-to-rural remittances are one of the most important observed regularities of rural-to-urban migration in LDCs. See Stark (1978, ch. 3; 1980b).
12  By definition (Yitzhaki, 1979),

$$TD = \int_0^{y^h} RD(z)f(z)\, dz$$

From note 12 we know that

$$RD(z) = \mu[1 - \phi(z)] - z[1 - F(z)]$$

and from Atkinson (1970),

$$\mu G = \int_0^{y^h} [zF(z) - \mu\phi(z)]f(z)\, dz$$

Thus,

$$TD = \int_0^{y^h} \{\mu[1 - \phi(z)] - z[1 - F(z)]\}f(z)dz$$

$$= \int_0^{y^h} [zF(z) - \mu\phi(z)]f(z)dz + \int_0^{y^h} (\mu - z)f(z)dz$$

$$= \mu G + 0 = \mu G$$

13  "Domain assumption specifies the domain of applicability of the theory" (Musgrave, 1981).
14  For a fuller exposition of the labor market equilibrium conditions determining the intersectoral allocation of labor and the intra-urban allocation of rural migrant laborers between formal and informal employment see Stark (1982).
15  Note that in this extended framework relative deprivation is alleviated through migration only with probability less than unity. Therefore, not all who are relatively deprived will necessarily leave – those who are least averse to relative deprivation may not. The analysis offered in sections 2 and 3 can then be seen as a clue to who are the more averse to relative deprivation etc.

## References

Atkinson, A. B. (1970) "On the Measurement of Inequality." *Journal of Economic Theory* 2 (3): 244–63.

DaVanzo, Julie S. and Morrison, Peter A. (1981) "Return and Other Sequences of Migration in the United States." *Demography* 18 (1): 85–101.

Fields, Gary S. (1982) "Place-to-Place Migration in Colombia." *Economic Development and Cultural Change* 30 (3): 539–58.

Hey, John D. and Lambert, Peter J. (1980) "Relative Deprivation and the Gini Coefficient: Comment." *Quarterly Journal of Economics* 95 (3): 567–73.

Lomnitz, Larissa (1977) *Networks and Marginality: Life in a Mexican Shantytown.* New York: Academic Press.

Musgrave, Alan (1981) "'Unreal Assumptions' in Economic Theory: The F-Twist Untwisted." *Kyklos* 34 (3): 377–87.

Portes, Alejandro (1983) "International Labor Migration and National Development." In Mary Kritz (ed.), *U.S. Immigration and Refugee Policy.* Lexington, MA: Lexington Books.

Runciman, W. G. (1966) *Relative Deprivation and Social Justice: A Study of Attitudes to Social Inequality in Twentieth-Century England.* Berkeley, CA: University of California Press.

Schultz, T. Paul (1982) "Lifetime Migration Within Educational Strata in Venezuela: Estimates of a Logistic Model." *Economic Development and Cultural Change* 30 (3): 559–94.

Stark, Oded (1978) *Economic–Demographic Interactions in Agricultural Development: The Case of Rural-to-Urban Migration.* Rome: UN Food and Agriculture Organization.

—— (1980a) "On Slowing Metropolitan City Growth." *Population and Development Review* 6 (1): 95–102 (reprinted as ch. 20 in this volume).

—— (1980b) "On the Role of Urban-to-Rural Remittances in Rural Development." *Journal of Development Studies* 16 (3): 369–74 (reprinted as ch. 14 in this volume).

—— (1982) "On Modelling the Informal Sector." *World Development* 10 (5): 413–16.

Todaro, Michael P. (1969) "A Model of Labor Migration and Urban Unemployment in Less Developed Countries." *American Economic Review* 59 (1), 138–48.

—— (1980) "Internal Migration in Developing Countries: A Survey." In Richard A. Easterlin (ed.), *Population and Economic Change in Developing Countries.* Chicago, IL: University of Chicago Press for National Bureau of Economic Research.

Townsend, Peter (1974) "Poverty as Relative Deprivation: Resources and Style of Living." In Dorothy Wedderburn (ed.), *Poverty, Inequality and Class Structure.* Cambridge: Cambridge University Press.

Yitzhaki, Shlomo (1979) "Relative Deprivation and the Gini Coefficient." *Quarterly Journal of Economics* 93 (2): 321–4.

# 8

## Labor Migration as a Response to Relative Deprivation

### 1 Relative Deprivation: The Basic Approach

The theory of relative deprivation is a theory about the feelings raised by social inequalities. The original conceptualization of the theory appears in the famous three-volume research monograph *The American Soldier: Adjustment During Army Life* (Stouffer et al., 1949). The theory has been applied to several fields in order to model social behavior (see Crosby (1979) for an excellent review). However, as pointed out by Merton and Kitt (1950), the concept of relative deprivation is not formally defined in *The American Soldier*. Therefore it is not surprising that Crosby (1979) counts four versions of the theory and that in general there is no agreement on the exact meaning of the term "relative deprivation." In this chapter we follow the approach developed by Yitzhaki (1979, 1982) and Stark (1984a, b) which may be viewed as the economist's interpretation and quantification of the work of Runciman (1966). Runciman defines four conditions for an individual to feel relatively deprived: "We can roughly say that [a person] is relatively deprived of $X$ when (i) he does not have $X$, (ii) he sees some other person or persons (possibly including himself at some previous or future time) as having $X$ (whether or not that is or will be in fact the case), (iii) he wants $X$, and (iv) he sees it as feasible that he should have $X$" (Runciman, 1966, p. 10).

The relativity of the concept is due to (ii) and (iv). The feeling of deprivation is defined by (i) and (iii). Replacing (i) with (i′) "the person has $X$", where $X$ represents a bundle of commodities $x$, enables us to interpret (i′) as representing the utility or disutility derived from $x$, while (iii) eliminates disutility and thereby ensures utility. An individual's utility is a function of the commodities he has, whereas deprivation is the loss in forgone utility as a result of not having commodities. Obviously, having $x$

also means not having more than $x$ or being deprived of having more than $x$. Formally, if $u(x)$ is an index of the satisfaction from having $x$ then $-u(x)$ can serve as an index of the deprivation of having no more than $x$. Maximizing $u(x)$ subject to an income constraint yields the same result as minimizing deprivation $-u(x)$ subject to the same constraint. Hence we can argue that the deprivation concept and the utility concept are two sides of the same coin: whereas utility is defined on "having," deprivation is defined on "not having."

However, there are two major differences between a relative deprivation approach and the utility, or welfare function, approach. One, related to the relativity of the concept, emerges from the existence of reference groups in the society. How reference groups are formed and dissolved is a complicated issue that we hope to explore in the future. For the moment, we assume that the entire society constitutes the reference group and later on, when modeling migratory behavior, that society consists of two such groups. This assumption simplifies the presentation at the cost of ignoring an important dimension of the relative deprivation approach.

The other major difference between the relative deprivation approach and the welfare function approach relates to the marginal utility of income. Under the utility approach, the marginal utility of income is a function of income alone and hence does not depend on the income of others. Under the relative deprivation approach, each unit of income can be viewed as Runciman's $X$, and the feeling of deprivation which arises from not having the unit is an increasing function of the number of individuals in the reference group who have it.[1] Note, however, that envy or altruism are not postulated; what counts is how individuals evaluate what they have (satisfaction) and what they do not have (deprivation).

Assume a continuous income distribution. Then each income unit (Runciman's $X$) is represented by an income range $[y, y + \Delta y]$ where $\Delta y \rightarrow 0$. Let $F(y)$ be the cumulative distribution of income. Then $1 - F(y)$ is the percentage of individuals whose income is higher than $y$. Hence $1 - F(y)$ represents the percentage of individuals who have the commodities represented by the income range $[y, y + \Delta y]$ and the feeling of deprivation is an increasing function of the percentage of individuals who have income larger than $y$, that is, $1 - F(y)$.

Let $h[1 - F(y)]$ be the deprivation from not having $[y, y + \Delta y]$, where $h(0) = 0$ and $h' > 0$. Then an individual whose income is $y$ is deprived of all units of income above $y$. Thus we can write[2]

$$D(y) = \int_{y}^{\infty} h[1 - F(z)] \, dz \qquad (8.1)$$

In order to simplify the discussion, we shall assume for now a simple form of $h[1 - F(y)] = 1 - F(y)$. In section 3 we return to the more general form $h(\cdot)$.[3]

The deprivation function is defined on "not having." However, it might be more convenient to work with a concept defined on "having." It is fairly easy to obtain such a concept by adding up the marginal utilities of income on the range of income that the individual possesses. We call this function the satisfaction (gratification) function. Formally,

$$S(y) = \int_0^y h[1 - F(z)]\, dz \qquad (8.2)$$

which, given our assumption on the form of $h$, becomes

$$S(y) = \int_0^y [1 - F(z)]\, dz \qquad (8.3)$$

The satisfaction and deprivation functions complement each other in the following manner:

$$D(y) + S(y) = \mu \qquad (8.4)$$

where $\mu$ is mean income.[4] Hence in evaluating a change in the well-being of an individual in a *given* reference group, it does not matter which function is used. However, once we bring in migration, since the individual moves from one reference group to another, it may well happen that satisfaction and deprivation increase or decrease in tandem.

We now briefly note the main properties of the functions.

1  We have

$$\frac{\partial S}{\partial y} = [1 - F(y)] \geqslant 0 \qquad \frac{\partial^2 S}{\partial y^2} = - f(y) \leqslant 0$$

That is, the marginal satisfaction is nonnegative and nonincreasing. Intuitively, the individual will be more satisfied the more valued are the commodities he possesses. This value is an increasing function of $1 - F(y)$, the fraction of individuals in the reference group who possess these commodities. In a society in which possessing a car is uniformly desirable, having a car is more valuable to an individual when many individuals possess cars than when only a few do.

2 An increase in the income of a person who is poorer than the individual, such that the individual's rank remains intact, increases satisfaction but does not affect deprivation.

3 An increase in the income of someone richer than the individual does not affect the individual's satisfaction, but it increases his deprivation.

4 The deprivation of an individual can be written as the percentage of persons who are richer than the individual times their mean excess income, that is,

$$D(y) = [1 - F(y)] \, E(z - y|z > y)$$

where $z$ is the income of the richer persons.[5] Hence, for a given mean excess income of persons richer than the individual, the individual's deprivation is an increasing function of the percentage of such persons, and for a given percentage of persons richer than the individual, the individual's deprivation is higher the larger is their mean excess income.

5 The satisfaction of an individual can be written as[6]

$$S(y) = \mu\left\{\frac{\partial\phi(F)}{\partial F}[1 - F(y)] + \phi(F)\right\} \tag{8.5}$$

and his deprivation as

$$D(y) = \mu\left\{1 - \phi(F) - \frac{\partial\phi}{\partial F}[1 - F(y)]\right\} \tag{8.6}$$

where, as before, $F$ is the cumulative distribution function, that is, the rank of the individual in the society, $\phi(F)$ is the Lorenz curve, that is, the percentage of total income received by individuals with incomes lower than that of the individual and $\partial\phi/\partial F$ is the slope of the Lorenz curve. It is worth noting that $\partial\phi/\partial F = y/\mu$, that is, the income divided by the mean.

Using the absolute Lorenz curve,[7] that is, the Lorenz curve where incomes are *not* divided by mean income, enables us to portray $S(y)$ and $D(y)$ graphically as in figure 8.1. OAB is the absolute Lorenz curve. The curve passes through $(0, 0)$ and $(1,\mu)$; it is convex and its slope is equal to $y$. The line AC is tangent to the Lorenz curve at $F(y^*)$. Hence, BC is the deprivation of an individual with income $y^*$ whereas CD is his satisfaction. To obtain this note that $CE = y^*[1 - F(y^*)]$ and thus

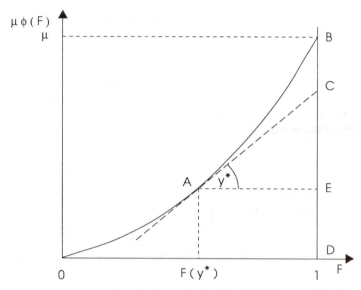

**Figure 8.1**    A diagrammatic presentation of deprivation and satisfaction

$CD = y^*[1 - F(y^*)] + \mu\phi[F(y^*)]$ which upon rearrangement gives (8.5). Equation (8.6) can be derived geometrically in a symmetrical manner.

## 2   Deprivation and Migration

An individual who feels deprived in his own community has an incentive to migrate. This incentive is inversely correlated with the possibilities for deprivation reduction through intra-community mobility. Of course, actual migration is a function of other considerations such as incurred costs, whether pecuniary or psychological, opportunities for migration, and attitudes toward risk (risk aversion). Our objective in this section is to examine the migration predictions of the pure relative deprivation theory. Since other variables are ignored, the discussion is restricted to whether a relative deprivation incentive to migrate exists and if so whether it is strong or weak. (We define these magnitudes below.) The predictions of the relative deprivation theory can be compared with the predictions of the utility theory, which are closely linked with those of the human capital approach. The prediction of the latter theory is fairly simple; an incentive to migrate exists if thereby expected lifetime income, appropriately discounted and netted, increases. Since the time dimension is fully and smoothly captured through the discounting procedure, there is no need to distinguish between short-run and long-run considerations.

However, in the case of a deprivation theory it is crucial to differentiate between the short run and the long run. In the short run, the migrating individual probably continues to associate himself with his origin reference group. In this case, an individual will have an incentive to migrate only if his income increases, a conclusion which replicates the prediction of the utility theory/human capital approach. In the long run, though, the migrating individual presumably associates with his new society, and refers to *it* as his new reference group.

In real life there is presumably a medium run in between, wherein the individual may associate himself simultaneously with two reference groups, although not necessarily attaching the same weight to each. The passage from the short run to the long run may indeed be characterized by a gradual reduction in the weight attached to the origin reference group and a corresponding increase in the weight attached to the reference group at destination. In this chapter we deal only with a situation in which migration is accompanied by a complete (perfect) substitution of the reference groups, that is, the long run. This is a departure from our focus in earlier work on relative deprivation and migration (Stark, 1984a, b).

Since the society a migrant leaves and the society he joins are different, it may happen that a migrating individual feels less deprived but also less satisfied in his new society or more satisfied yet more deprived. He feels more deprived if in the new society others have more goods than he does and more satisfied if he has more goods than before. Unless we explicitly model tastes, it is not clear which consideration dominates in such a case. We shall say that in situations of this type there is a weak incentive to migrate. That is, a weak incentive to migrate exists if by migrating the individual increases or decreases his satisfaction *and* deprivation at the same time. The implication of this condition is that it may then happen that some individuals will be motivated to migrate. We shall say that a strong incentive to migrate prevails if by migrating satisfaction increases *and* deprivation decreases. Then, migration is more likely, that is, likelier than when the incentive to migrate is weak.

Thus an individual who considers migrating from society A to society B has a strong incentive to migrate if $D_B < D_A$ and $S_B > S_A$ where $D$ and $S$ are deprivation and satisfaction respectively. It is assumed that both societies are large, so that the effect of migration by an individual on the distribution of income by size in both societies can be ignored.

Formally, a satisfaction incentive exists if

$$y_B(1 - F_B) + \mu_B\phi_B > y_A(1 - F_A) + \mu_A\phi_A \qquad (8.7)$$

and a deprivation incentive exists if

$$\mu_B(1 - \phi_B) - y_B(1 - F_B) < \mu_A(1 - \phi_A) - y_A(1 - F_A) \qquad (8.8)$$

Rearranging terms, the satisfaction condition for an incentive to migrate (the S condition hereafter) can be written as

$$y_B - y_A > \mu_B F_B \left[ \frac{y_B}{\mu_B} - \frac{\phi_B}{F_B} \right] - \mu_A F_A \left[ \frac{y_A}{\mu_A} - \frac{\phi_A}{F_A} \right] \qquad (8.7a)$$

and the deprivation condition (the D condition hereafter) as

$$y_B - y_A > (\mu_B - \mu_A) + \mu_B F_B \left[ \frac{y_B}{\mu_B} - \frac{\phi_B}{F_B} \right] - \mu_A F_A \left[ \frac{y_A}{\mu_A} - \frac{\phi_A}{F_A} \right]$$
$$(8.8a)$$

Note that the terms in square brackets are nonnegative. To see this, recall that $y/\mu$ is the slope of the Lorenz curve whereas $\phi/F$ is the slope of the line connecting the Lorenz curve to the origin. Since the Lorenz curve is convex, the nonnegativity is ensured. Consequently, it can easily be seen from (8.7a) and (8.8a) that if the social parameters are identical, that is, if $\mu_A = \mu_B$, $\phi_A = \phi_B$, and $F_A = F_B$, then the prediction of the deprivation theory will be identical with the prediction of the utility theory; in both cases $y_B > y_A$ is a sufficient condition for an incentive to migrate.

However, if the social parameters differ across societies then a prediction based on deprivation theory will be dependent on six parameters; of course not all of them are independent. To render the analysis tractable we shall thus initially restrict our attention to specific cases, where some of the parameters are given. As an aside we point out that if $\mu_A = \mu_B$, that is, if the two societies have the same mean income, then the S and D conditions are identical. However, if $\mu_B > \mu_A$ then fulfillment of the S condition is a necessary condition for the D condition to hold, whereas if $\mu_B < \mu_A$ then the D condition is a necessary condition for the S condition to hold.

### Migration of the Richest Person

For the richest person in society A, $\phi_A = F_A = 1$. Then the S condition (equation (8.7)) is

$$y_B(1 - F_B) + \mu_B \phi_B > \mu_A \qquad (8.9)$$

while the D condition (equation (8.8)) is

$$\mu_B(1 - \phi_B) - y_B(1 - F_B) < 0 \tag{8.10}$$

By using figure 8.1, it is easy to see that the D condition cannot be satisfied. On the other hand, the S condition is fulfilled if

$$y_B > \frac{\mu_A - \mu_B\phi_B}{1 - F_B} \tag{8.11}$$

However, if $\mu_A = \mu_B$, even the S condition cannot be fulfilled. To see this, replace $y^*$ by $y_B$ in figure 8.1. BE is $\mu - \mu\phi[F(y_B)]$ and AE is $1 - F(y_B)$. Since the absolute Lorenz curve is convex, its slope at A, which is $y_B$, is smaller than BE/AE. Therefore (8.11) is invalidated. Hence in this case the richest person in the society has no incentive to migrate. Intuitively, since relative deprivation is bounded from below by zero, the richest individual whose deprivation in A is zero cannot possibly reduce it through migration. Note, though, that if the society at destination is richer than the society at origin, that is, if $\mu_B > \mu_A$, and the individual is expected to be the richest individual in B, then, since (8.7) collapses to $\mu_B > \mu_A$, he can be said to have a strong incentive to migrate. (We say "can" since deprivation decreases only in the weak sense, that is, it remains unchanged.)

Thus, we conclude that in general the richest individual will not have a strong incentive to migrate but may have a weak incentive to migrate.

### Migration of the Poorest Person

For the poorest individual in A, $F_A = \phi_A = 0$. Hence the S condition is

$$y_B - y_A > \mu_B F_B \left[ \frac{y_B}{\mu_B} - \frac{\phi_B}{F_B} \right] \tag{8.12}$$

and the D condition is

$$y_B - y_A > (\mu_B - \mu_A) + \mu_B F_B \left[ \frac{y_B}{\mu_B} - \frac{\phi_B}{F_B} \right] \tag{8.13}$$

The right-hand side of (8.12) is nonnegative; hence the satisfaction condition is met if $y_B - y_A$ is sufficiently large. From the D condition we can conclude the following. If $\mu_B > \mu_A$ then the poorest individual has an incentive to migrate if $y_B$ is greater than $y_A$ by a large magnitude. Moreover, the richer (in terms of $\mu_B$) society B is, the greater the income increase would have to be to cause migration. On the other hand, if $\mu_B < \mu_A$, then the poorest individual in A may still have a weak incentive to migrate even if his income declines! A poor person may very well endure less deprivation if he were to leave a rich society and join a society where only a few persons possess goods which he does not possess. That we do not typically observe migratory moves of this kind must then have to do with the nonfulfillment of the S condition. Indeed, since the S condition cannot be fulfilled in this case, the overall condition for a strong migration incentive does not hold.

Consider now a situation wherein the income of the poorest individual in B is larger than it is in A, that is, $y_B > y_A$. Assume that conditions (8.12) and (8.13) hold. We now wish to check whether, under a specific shock to the parameters, conditions (8.12) and (8.13) hold *a fortiori*. We increase the individual's rank in B, that is, we assume that $F_B$ is larger. However, we keep $\mu_B$ and $\phi_B$ intact. Intuition might have led us to anticipate that the increase in rank will make (8.12) and (8.13) hold *a fortiori*. A higher rank is associated with a more appealing prospect. Apparently this is not the case. By inspecting (8.12) and (8.13) we note that, in each case, the right-hand side where $F_B$ enters multiplicatively is larger. This is portrayed with the help of figure 8.2. The absolute Lorenz curve in society B is OAC and the individual considered is at A. Since $\mu_B \phi_B$ is kept constant, then increasing

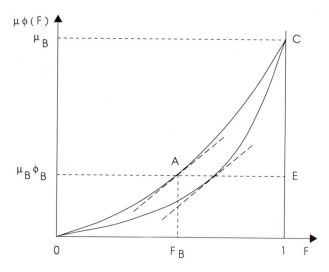

**Figure 8.2** Absolute Lorenz curves representation of the effect of migration on deprivation

$F_B$ means that the new absolute Lorenz curve must pass in the region AE. Since $y_B$ is the same, its slope when it intersects with AE is equal to the slope at A. Since $\mu_B$ is kept constant, the new curve must pass through C. Hence increasing $F_B$, keeping $\mu_B\phi_B$ constant, tends to make society B less egalitarian, causing the individual to feel more deprived (because the rich are richer) and less satisfied (because the poor are poorer).

Thus we conclude that the poorest individual may have a strong incentive to migrate and also a weak incentive to migrate.

### Migration of Other Individuals

As we have already pointed out, without restricting the social parameters it is hard to predict the implication of the relative deprivation approach for the incentive to migrate. However, the D and S functions are continuous. Therefore, if the S and D conditions are fulfilled for given incomes, they will be fulfilled in the neighborhood of these incomes. Since we have found that the incentive to migrate for the poorest individual in the society is greater than for the richest, we can conclude that the relative deprivation approach predicts that for a given income differential the poor have a higher incentive to migrate.

If we impose the restriction $F = F_A = F_B$, that is, we assume that the rank of the individual does not change, and assume also that $\phi_B = \phi_A = \phi$, then from (8.7a) the S condition becomes

$$y_B - y_A > \frac{\mu_A - \mu_B}{1 - F}\phi \tag{8.14}$$

while from (8.8a) the D condition is

$$y_B - y_A > \frac{(\mu_B - \mu_A)(1 - \phi)}{1 - F} \tag{8.15}$$

and, as can be seen from equation (8.14), the richer society B is, the larger is the incentive to migrate for a given difference in incomes. On the other hand, from equation (8.15), we note that the richer society B is, the larger the income difference $y_B - y_A$ would have to be in order to have a D incentive to migrate.

An interesting case arises when the individual will be the richest in B. In this case $\phi_B = F_B = 1$. The S condition is

$$\mu_B > y_A(1 - F_A) + \mu_A\phi_A \tag{8.16}$$

whereas the D condition is

$$0 < \mu_A(1 - \phi_A) - y_A(1 - F_A) \qquad (8.17)$$

The D condition is always fulfilled. Moreover, even the S condition may be fulfilled. This may hold even if $y_B < y_A$. Thus we can conclude that there is always a weak incentive for the second in line to move into a society in which he may be the top man and sometimes – and despite a decline in income – even a strong incentive exists (see also Frank 1984, 1985).

## 3 Deprivation and Migration: A Generalization

Hitherto we have employed a specific formulation of the theory of relative deprivation. Our main motivation in choosing the formulation has been to simplify the presentation. In this section we adopt a general formulation of the theory. In the preceding sections we have assumed that the intensity of deprivation of an individual is an increasing linear function of the number of individuals in the reference group who possess commodities that the individual does not have. Yet it is possible to argue that the intensity of deprivation is also determined by the utility function as this function weighs the importance of the commodities and that, rather than being linear in the number of individuals with higher income, deprivation is a monotonic increasing function of this number. We now incorporate these considerations, intimating as we do so that the implications of our approach for the incentive to migrate do not change in any qualitative way. However, the satisfaction and the deprivation incentives do change quantitatively, that is, they may become weaker or stronger, depending upon the utility function.

Assume that an individual who does not have the commodities represented by the income range $[y, y + \Delta y]$ feels deprived of the marginal utility $u'(y)$ and that the intensity of this feeling is, as before, an increasing function of the proportion of the individuals who are not deprived of this income range, that is, $1 - F(y)$.

The deprivation of an individual whose income is $y$ will be

$$D_u(y) = \int_y^\infty u'(z)[1 - F(z)]\, dz \qquad (8.18)$$

while the satisfaction will be given by

$$S_u(y) = \int_0^y u'(z)[1 - F(z)] \, dz \qquad (8.19)$$

For simplicity it is assumed that $u(0) = 0$. Then the sum of $D_u(y)$ and $S_u(y)$ is equal to the expected value $\mu_u$ of the utility function,[8] and the derivatives of $S(y)$ with respect to income have the same signs as before. The only property that requires modification concerns the relationship between $S_u(y)$ and $D_u(y)$ and the Lorenz curve. It can be shown that

$$S_u(y) = \mu_u \left\{ \frac{\partial \phi_u(F)}{\partial F} [1 - F(y)] + \phi_u(F) \right\} \qquad (8.20)$$

and

$$D_u(y) = \mu_u \left\{ 1 - \phi_u(F) - \frac{\partial \phi_u(F)}{\partial F} [1 - F(y)] \right\} \qquad (8.21)$$

where $\phi_u(F)$ is the cumulative percentage of $\mu_u$ that is derived from incomes lower than $y$, while $\partial \phi / \partial F$ is the slope of the curve.[9] Using the property $\partial \phi_u / \partial F = u(y)/\mu_u$ we can write the S and the D conditions as in (8.7a) and (8.8a) except that each $y$ is translated into $u(y)$ and $\phi$ and $\mu$ now carry the subscript $u$. Having defined the equivalent equations to (8.7a) and (8.8a), we can easily redo the preceding analysis with respect to migration. The qualitative conclusions do not change. For example, the richest person in the society may have only a weak incentive to migrate while the poorest person may have a weak incentive as well as a strong incentive. But, of course, both incentives now depend on the properties of the $u$ function as it affects the magnitudes of the parameters.

Assume, alternatively, that $h[1 - F(y)]$ is not linear. For example, let $h[1 - F(y)] = [1 - F(y)]^v$ where $v > 1$ is a given constant. Then the satisfaction function is given by

$$S(v, y) = \int_0^y [1 - F(z)]^v \, dz \qquad (8.22)$$

In this case, rather than portraying $S(y)$ and $D(y)$ using the absolute Lorenz curve (recall sections 1 and 2) we would need to utilize a weighted integration of the area below the Lorenz curve (as in Yitzhaki, 1983).

Taking the analysis one step further in the generalization ladder we can express the satisfaction function as

$$S_u(y) = \int_0^y u'(z)h[1 - F(z)] \, d(z) \qquad (8.23)$$

where $h' > 0$. Clearly, if $h(\cdot)$ converges to a constant, the satisfaction function collapses into the conventional utility function.


## 4 Concluding Comments

Students of migration have often failed to take note of the fact that the migration process is blurred by quite a lot of noise – as if the main "regular" phenomenon were accompanied by some "irregular" satellite phenomena. The latter have usually been accounted for by *ad hoc* explanations and described as anomalies. Migration in the "wrong" direction, in our terminology from A to B when $y_B < y_A$, cannot possibly be explained by those same variables accounting for migration in the "right" direction, that is, from A to B when $y_B > y_A$. Our approach has the valuable characteristic that not only does it add a layer of explanation to the main phenomenon but it also explains the accompanying phenomena and does so in a novel way.

For example, migration by retired persons, especially to communities characterized by a high ratio of retirees, might be construed as a strategic move aimed at preempting the likelihood of an increase in relative deprivation due to an anticipated continued growth in the income of the nonretirees (but not of the retirees) in the retirees' origin reference group. The relative deprivation approach may thus give rise to life-cycle-based migratory predictions.

Return by successful migrants which is, by definition, a form of migration is very often associated with a departure from a rich to a less rich society (economy). It appears as though maximum overall gains associated with migration accrue if, at appropriate points in time, *two* substitutions of reference groups take place: one is associated with the first move; the other accrues as a successful migrant decides to return when *rank-wise* his progress in the receiving community appears to grind to a halt.

Our analysis also has a bearing upon phenomena other than narrowly defined migration. For example, the third most senior executive in one corporation departs to become the chief executive officer in another corporation in a move which cannot possibly be sustained by considerations of income or income growth prospects.

We have seen that inequality *per se* has a bearing on migration propensities. The fad in empirical migration research of characterizing – hence ranking – sending and receiving societies (sectors) by their mean income alone may thus omit an important explanatory variable. Our theory gives rise to the belief that migration depends on the inequality in the distribution of income by size in the sending and receiving societies, that it is positively correlated with inequality in the society of origin, and that it is negatively correlated with inequality in the society of destination.

On the basis of our discussion in section 2 we may also note that the incentive to migrate is not a function of income levels but rather, and exclusively so, of income differentials. In order to verify this we may return to equation (8.3). Note that if we add a constant amount to the income of each and every individual, then satisfaction changes by exactly this constant whereas deprivation does not change at all. Hence, if we add the same constant amount to all incomes in A as well as in B, conditions (8.7)–(8.17) will remain exactly the same; absolute levels of income play no role at all. This cannot be said to hold under the utility–welfare function approach where, because of declining marginal utility, addition of a constant amount reduces the incentive to migrate throughout. Notice though that the conclusion pertaining to the robustness of conditions (8.7)–(8.17) may not hold once a $u$ function is introduced (as in section 3).

## Notes

Co-authored with Shlomo Yitzhaki. Reprinted from *Journal of Population Economics* 1, 1988. This is a revised version of Discussion Paper 20, Harvard University Migration and Development Program. We are indebted to an anonymous referee for helpful comments and suggestions.
1   Runciman uses the example of promotions and writes: "The more people a man sees promoted when he is not promoted himself, the more people he may compare himself with in a situation where the comparison will make him feel relatively deprived" (Runciman, 1966, p. 19).
2   For a detailed and explicit derivation of this equation from Runciman's axioms see Yitzhaki (1982).
3   The reader might question our definition of $D(y)$, pointing out that intuitively $1 - F(y)$ might do just as well. Unfortunately, such is not the case. If, for example, the income of an individual who is richer than our reference individual increases, $F(y)$ remains unchanged and so does $1 - F(y)$. Yet a proper measure

of relative deprivation should be sensitive to there now being more income units that the reference individual is deprived of. $D(y)$ as defined in (8.1) exhibits such sensitivity.

4   Proof: $S(y) + D(y) = \displaystyle\int_0^\infty [1 - F(z)]\, dz$

and by using integration by parts where $u = z$ and $v = 1 - F(z)$ we obtain

$$\int_0^\infty [1 - F(z)]\, dz = [1 - F(z)]z \Big|_0^\infty + \int_0^\infty zf(z)\, dz = \mu$$

5   Proof: Using integration by parts where

$$v(z) = 1 - F(z) \qquad v'(z) = - f(z) \qquad u(z) = z \qquad u'(z) = 1$$

and the property

$$\lim_{y \to \infty} [1 - F(y)] = 0$$

we obtain

$$D(y) = \int_y^\infty [1 - F(z)]\, dz = -[1 - F(y)]y + \int_y^\infty zf(z)\, dz$$

Using the conditional density function

$$f^*(z|z > y) = \frac{1}{1 - F(y)}\, f(z)$$

we insert $f(z)$ into the last integral to obtain the expression in property 4.

6   Proof: $S(y) = \displaystyle\int_0^y [1 - F(z)]\, dz$

and by using integration by parts

$$S(y) = y[1 - F(y)] - \int_0^y zf(z)\, dz = \mu \left( \frac{y}{\mu} \{1 - F(y) - \phi[F(y)]\} \right)$$

where $\phi$ is the Lorenz curve. Noting that $y/\mu = \partial\phi/\partial F$ completes the proof.

7   Shorrocks (1983) refers to the absolute Lorenz curve as the "generalized Lorenz curve."

8   Proof: $S_u(y) + D_u(y) = \displaystyle\int_0^\infty u'(z)[1 - F(z)] \, dz$

and using integration by parts we obtain

$$u(y)[1 - F(y)] \bigg|_0^\infty + \int_0^\infty u(z)f(z) \, dz = \mu_u + u(0)$$

Assuming that $u(0) = 0$ completes the proof.

9   Proof: $S_u(y) = \displaystyle\int_0^y u'(z)[1 - F(z)] \, dz$

which, using integration by parts, decomposes to

$$S_u(y) = u(y)[1 - F(y)] \bigg|_0^y + \int_0^y u(z)f(z) \, dz$$

$$= \mu_u \left[ \frac{u(y)}{\mu_u}[1 - F(y)] + \frac{1}{\mu_u} \int_0^y u(z)f(z) \, dz \right]$$

$$= \mu_u \left[ \frac{\partial \phi_u(F)}{\partial F}[1 - F(y)] + \phi_u(F) \right]$$

where

$$\phi_u(F) = \frac{1}{\mu_u} \int_0^y u(z)f(z) \, dz$$

is the percentage of $u$ derived from income lower than $y$. The derivative of $\phi_u(F)$ with respect to $F$ (the cumulative distribution of income) is obtained indirectly from

$$\frac{\partial \phi_u(F)}{\partial F} = \frac{\partial \phi_u/\partial y}{\partial F/\partial y} = \frac{u(y)f(y)}{\mu_u f(y)} = \frac{u(y)}{\mu_u}$$

# References

Crosby, F. (1979) "Relative Deprivation Revisited: A Response to Miller, Bolce, and Halligan." *American Political Science Review* 73 (1): 103–12.

Frank, R. H. (1984) "Are Workers Paid Their Marginal Products?" *American Economic Review* 74 (4): 549–71.

—— (1985) "The Demand for Unobservable and Other Nonpositional Goods." *American Economic Review* 75 (1): 101–16.

Merton, R. K. and Kitt, A. S. (1950) "Contributions to the Theory of Reference Group Behavior." In R. K. Merton and P. F. Lazarsfeld (eds), *Contributions in Social Research, Studies in the Scope and Method of "The American Soldier."* Glencoe, IL: Free Press, pp. 40–105.

Runciman, W. G. (1966) *Relative Deprivation and Social Justice: A Study of Attitudes to Social Inequality in Twentieth-Century England.* Berkeley, CA: University of California Press.

Shorrocks, A. F. (1983) "Ranking Income Distributions." *Economica* 50 (197): 3–17.

Stark, O. (1984a) "Rural-to-Urban Migration in LDCs: A Relative Deprivation Approach." *Economic Development and Cultural Change* 32(3): 475–86 (reprinted as ch.7 in this volume).

—— (1984b) "Discontinuity and the Theory of International Migration." *Kyklos* 37: 206–22.

Stouffer, S. A., Suchman, E. A., DeVinney, L. C., Star, S. A. and Williams, R. M., Jr (1949) *The American Soldier: Adjustment During Army Life.* Princeton, NJ: Princeton University Press.

Yitzhaki, S. (1979) "Relative Deprivation and the Gini Coefficient." *Quarterly Journal of Economics* 93: 321–4.

—— (1982) "Relative Deprivation and Economic Welfare." *European Economic Review* 17: 99–113.

—— (1983) "On an Extension of the Gini Inequality Index." *International Economic Review* 24: 617–28.

# 9

## Relative Deprivation and International Migration

Do intra-group comparisons affect perception, incentives, evaluation, and behavior? If relative magnitudes count, do they count enough to aid not only in understanding and in generating more accurate descriptions but also in facilitating prediction?

Suppose that there are two villages of households whose incomes are as follows: $A_1 = (20, 30, 40, 50, 60)$ and $A_2 = (20, 60, 65, 70, 75, 80)$. The configuration of these income distributions is such that an income of 60 places an $A_1$ household at the top of its village income distribution. By contrast, in $A_2$ this same absolute income places a household within one rank of the bottom of the income distribution.

Suppose that by reallocating some of its labor to international migration the household earning an income of 60 in each village can expect to receive a 20 percent (12 unit) increase in absolute income. An expected income model of migration would predict that the two households have the same propensity to participate in international migration. Assume, however, that the nature of the reallocation is such that when a household member is assigned to a foreign labor market the household together with that member continue to consider $A_1$ as the relevant reference distribution. (We shall discuss this assumption later.) If household utility is a function not only of absolute income but also of income position *vis-à-vis* other households in the village, then intuition could lead us to expect that the household in $A_2$ will have a stronger motivation to participate in migration than the one in $A_1$. That is, a given absolute income gain that confers a significant income position gain is worth more than the same absolute income gain that is not associated with an income position gain.

Suppose that, through migration of a family member, the total income of the family rises. Suppose also, however, that the migrant's income, which is fully pooled with the income of the rest of the family staying behind, is earned in an economy in which incomes are very much higher than those prevailing in the home village. If the migrant were to engage in income comparisons with members of the absorbing economy in a manner similar to that characterizing comparisons made by his family in the origin economy, and if the deprivation thereby experienced by the migrant is taken into consideration by the family, the family's income gain could be eroded by the migrant's enhanced deprivation.

Presumably families are aware of the risk that through a reference group substitution process they may fail to decrease the level of their relative deprivation (a concept formally defined in the next section) or to improve their level of relative satisfaction. Whereas migration within a country (particularly a culturally and socially homogeneous country) can generate alienation and increased relative deprivation through a smooth reference group substitution, international migration to an entirely different cultural and social milieu can carry with it built-in protection against such a substitution process and ensure that the original reference group continues to be the relevant reference group. By locating themselves in a host community distinct from their own, migrants are less likely to orient themselves to the host community than if they were to locate themselves in a "neighboring" host community. For a comparison to occur with the host community, some "minimal similarity" between the migrant and that community must be perceived. This becomes more likely when direct social interaction or sustained social relations persist. In some cases, the host community may consciously be selected to ensure estrangement, detachment, and social distance. Migrants may wish to guard against becoming oriented to the host community for fear that the secondary negative effects of a changing reference group might outweigh the primary positive effect of improving their position *vis-à-vis* the original reference group.[1] Thus international migration can enable households to exploit cultural and social discontinuity across international frontiers, capture this discontinuity, and transform international dissimilarities into a source of advantage.

## 1 Relative Deprivation: The "Cornerstone Equation" and the Migration Hypothesis

The theory of relative deprivation is concerned with the feelings raised by intra-group inequalities. The original conceptualization of the theory appears in the famous three-volume research monograph *The American Soldier: Adjustment During Army Life* (Stouffer et al., 1949). The theory has been applied to several fields to model social behavior (see Crosby

(1979) for an excellent review). As pointed out by Merton and Kitt (1950), however, the concept of relative deprivation is not formally defined in *The American Soldier*. Therefore it is not surprising that Crosby counted four versions of the theory and that in general there is no agreement on what is the exact meaning of the term "relative deprivation." In this chapter we follow the approach developed by Yitzhaki (1979, 1982), Stark (1984a, b), and Stark and Yitzhaki (1988), which can be viewed as the economist's interpretation and quantification of the work of Runciman (1966). Runciman defined four conditions for an individual to feel relatively deprived: "We can roughly say that [a person] is relatively deprived of $X$ when (i) he does not have $X$, (ii) he sees some other person or persons (possibly including himself at some previous or future time) as having $X$ (whether or not that is or will be in fact the case), (iii) he wants $X$, and (iv) he sees it as feasible that he should have $X$" (Runciman, 1966, p. 10).

The relativity of the concept comes from conditions (ii) and (iv). The feeling of deprivation is defined by conditions (i) and (iii). Replacing condition (i) with condition (i') – "the person has $X$," where $X$ represents a bundle of commodities $x$ – enables us to interpret condition (i') as representing the utility or disutility derived from $x$, while condition (iii) eliminates disutility and thereby ensures utility. An individual's utility is a function of the commodities he or she has, whereas deprivation is the loss in forgone utility as a result of not having commodities. Obviously, having $x$ also means not having more than $x$ or being deprived of having more than $x$. Formally, if $u(x)$ is an index of the satisfaction from having $x$, then $-u(x)$ can serve as an index of the deprivation from having no more than $x$. Maximizing $u(x)$ subject to an income constraint yields the same result as minimizing deprivation $-u(x)$ subject to the same constraint. Hence we can argue that the deprivation concept and the utility concept are two sides of the same coin: whereas utility is defined on "having," deprivation is defined on "not having."

There are two major differences, however, between a relative deprivation approach and the utility, or the welfare function, approach. One, related to the relativity of the concept, emerges from the existence of reference groups in the society. As already pointed out, how reference groups are formed and dissolved is a complicated issue that we hope to explore in the future. For the rest of this chapter, we assume that the village of origin is the relevant reference group.

The other major difference between the relative deprivation approach and the welfare function approach relates to the marginal utility of income. Under the utility approach, the marginal utility of income is a function of income alone and hence does not depend on the income of others. Under the relative deprivation approach, each unit of income can be viewed as

Runciman's $X$, and the feeling of deprivation that arises from not having the unit is an increasing function of the number of individuals in the reference group who have it.[2] Note, however, that envy and altruism are not postulated; what counts is how individuals evaluate what they have (satisfaction) and what they do not have (deprivation).

Assume a continuous income distribution. Then each income unit (Runciman's $X$) is represented by an income range $[y, y + \Delta y]$, where $\Delta y \rightarrow 0$. Let $F(y)$ be the cumulative distribution of income. Then $1 - F(y)$ is the percentage of individuals who have the commodities represented by the income range $[y, y + \Delta y]$, and the feeling of deprivation is an increasing function of the percentage of individuals who have income larger than $y$, that is, $1 - F(y)$.

Let $h[1 - F(y)]$ be the deprivation from not having $[y, y + \Delta y]$, where $h(0) = 0$ and $h' > 0$. An individual whose income is $y$ is deprived of all units of income above $y$. Thus we can write[3]

$$RD(y) = \int_{y}^{\infty} h[1 - F(z)]\, dz \tag{9.1}$$

To simplify the discussion, we shall assume for now a simple form of $h[1 - F(y)] = 1 - F(y)$. The more general form $h(\cdot)$ is addressed elsewhere (Stark and Yitzhaki, 1988).[4]

This function is particularly useful because it lends itself to the following conversion. The deprivation of an individual is the percentage of persons richer than the individual times their mean excess income, that is,

$$RD(y) = [1 - F(y)]E(z - y | z > y) \tag{9.2}$$

where $z$ is the income of the richer persons (the proof is given in the appendix).

Equation (9.2) implies that, for a given mean excess income of persons richer than the individual, the individual's deprivation is an increasing function of the percentage of such persons, and, for a given percentage of persons richer than the individual, the individual's deprivation is higher the larger is their mean excess income.

The entire analysis carries through if "an individual" and "persons" are replaced by "a village household" and "village households" respectively. It helps to write equation (9.2) as

$$RD^i = AD(Y_i)P(Y_i) \tag{9.3}$$

where $Y_i$ is the income of household $i$, $AD(Y_i)$ is the mean excess income of households richer than household $i$, and $P(Y_i)$ is the proportion of households in the village richer than household $i$. The households are ranked by income from lowest to highest with $i = 1, \ldots, n$ such that 1 is the poorest household and $n$ is the richest. Clearly, *ceteris paribus*, a decline in the proportion of households richer than $i$ will reduce the relative deprivation of household $i$.

The relative deprivation hypothesis of international migration is that, controlling for households' expected income gains from migration, the decision by households to send migrants to foreign labor markets is influenced by their initial perceived relative deprivation within the reference group. Specifically, given a household's initial absolute income and its expected net income from migration, more relatively deprived households are more likely to send migrants to foreign labor markets than are less relatively deprived households.

Empirical work is necessary to disentangle the influences of expected income gains and initial relative deprivation on international migration. By including instruments for these two variables in a single migration decision model, it is possible empirically to isolate the influence of relative deprivation on migration decisions, provided that not all migration decision units are drawn from the same reference group. This ensures that a specific income is not associated with the same income positions and hence, in principle, can trigger different relative-deprivation-based responses. The relative deprivation model would predict that, once we control for expected income gains, households' initial relative deprivation will be directly related to their propensity to send migrants.

## 2  Evidence from Mexico

### Data

Data from a recent survey of rural Mexican households are used to explore empirically the roles of absolute income and relative deprivation in explaining Mexico–United States migration. The sample consists of 61 randomly selected households in two villages in the Pátzcuaro region of the state of Michoacán, Mexico, which were surveyed during the winter of 1983. The sample is distributed almost equally between the two villages (30 and 31 households). From these households we obtained data on 423 adults aged 13 years or older.[5] Data were collected on a set of characteristics of both individuals and their households that were deemed likely to influence the returns to households from Mexico–United States migration versus work in Mexico by household members. Data were also gathered on the allocation of each individual's labor to migration and nonmigration activities and on each individual's income contribution to the household during 1982. The latter include, for nonmigrants to the United States, contributions of income from household farm production (farming, handicrafts, fishing, livestock, commerce, etc.), village wage work, rental income, and internal labor migration.[6] Income contributions in the form of remittances from household members who migrated either within Mexico or to the United States are all net of reverse (household-to-migrant) flows and of direct migration costs. In the remainder of this chapter, "migrants" will refer to international migrants, defined as individuals who were observed working in the United States at any time during 1982. The shortest term of international migration in our sample is approximately three weeks. Persons classified as "nonmigrants" include those who remained in the village throughout the year and those who were observed as internal labor migrants.

Selected household and individual characteristics for the Mexico–United States migrant and nonmigrant subsamples are summarized in table 9.1. Definite patterns distinguish the two labor groups. On average, families of nonmigrants to the United States have eight adult members aged 13 years or above compared with 9.1 for Mexico–United States migrant families. Nonmigrant households have less land and fewer physical assets overall than migrant households. They are likely to have internal migration networks or family contacts at internal migrant destinations (primarily Mexico City), but they are far less likely than Mexico–United States migrant households to have US migration networks. Fewer than half of nonmigrants are male (44 percent). On average, nonmigrants are somewhat older than migrants (32 years compared with 29 years), have slightly more schooling (4.50 years compared with 4.06 years), and have little past Mexico–United States migration experience (0.8 years compared with 4.9 years) but more internal migration experience (1.3 years compared with 0.8 years).

One in six individuals in the sample was observed as a Mexico–United States labor migrant during 1982. In no case, however, did an entire household leave the village. Thus the households covered by the sample remained as stable and meaningful entities in their respective villages while individual household members participated in Mexico–United States migration, typically remitting part of their earnings to the household.

**Table 9.1**   Selected average 1982 household and individual
characteristics for Mexico–United States migrants and nonmigrants

| Characteristic | Nonmigrants and internal migrants | Mexico–US migrants |
|---|---|---|
| *Household* | | |
| Adult family size (13 years or older) | 7.98 | 9.11 |
| Landholdings (hectares) | 5.14 | 7.14 |
| Percentage with family contacts at internal migrant destinations | 0.73 | 0.57 |
| Percentage with family contacts at US destinations | 0.49 | 0.89 |
| Wealth (US$000) | 2.19 | 3.47 |
| | | |
| *Individual* | | |
| Sex (male = 1.0) | 0.44 | 0.63 |
| Age | 32.30 | 28.70 |
| Years of completed schooling | 4.50 | 4.06 |
| Years of internal migration experience | 1.32 | 0.79 |
| Years of US migration experience | 0.76 | 4.91 |
| Sample size | 353 | 70 |

Family contact can be a sibling, a parent, or the sibling of a parent. Wealth is the
total US dollar value of land, animals, and machinery.

## Estimation

A multivariate probit was used to estimate the probability that the labor
time of household members was allocated to Mexico–United States
migration work during 1982, versus the alternative of engaging exclusively
in labor activities in Mexico. The observations in the data set are
the allocations of the labor time of individual household members to
Mexico–United States migration and nonmigration work.[7] The dependent
variable takes on the value of 1 if person $j$ was observed as a Mexico–
United States migrant at any time during 1982 and 0 otherwise.

Contributions to household income by person $j$ as a worker in Mexico
are denoted $R_0^j$. Remittances, net of migration costs, by household

members who succeed in entering and finding work (usually illegally) in the United States are denoted $R_1^j$. The probability that person $j$ will succeed in entering and finding employment in the United States is denoted $p^j$. Expected remittances by household members who leave the village to work as Mexico–United States migrants are therefore $p^j R_1^j$. The expected net income gain $\Delta y$ to the household from sending person $j$ to the United States is $p^j R_1^j - R_0^j$.

Migrant remittances are a function of migrant earnings as well as of migrants' propensity to share these earnings with the village household. A comprehensive theory of remittances should thus refer both to the determinants of migrant earnings and to what factors shape migrants' incentives to remit earnings to the household. Although we recognize the complexity of migrants' motives to remit, a detailed theory of remittance behavior is beyond the scope of this chapter. (The interested reader may refer to recent work developing and testing alternative theories of migrant remittance behavior (Lucas and Stark, 1985; Stark and Lucas, 1988).)

In our empirical analysis, we make the simplifying assumption that migrant remittances are positively related to migrant earnings. It should be stressed, however, that to the extent that variables affecting migrant earnings also influence remittance propensities, estimated coefficients on these variables in the remittance equation capture the net effect of the variables on earnings and remittance propensities. Let $X_1^j$ denote a vector of human capital and migration capital variables and other characteristics of person $j$ that "explain" his or her earnings as a Mexico–United States migrant worker and the propensity to share these earnings with the village household, such that $R_1^j = R_1(X_1^j)$. Analogously, for contributions by household members who do not migrate to the United States, let $R_0^j = R_0(X_0^j)$. Finally, let migration success probability $p^j$ be a function of variables $Z^j$. The complete migration model to be estimated consists of three equations: two equations for the expected returns to households from Mexico–United States migration and from nonmigration work by person $j$

$$\ln R_0^j = \alpha_0 + X_0^j \alpha_1 + v_0^j \qquad (9.4)$$

$$\ln R_1^j = \beta_0 + X_1^j \beta_1 + Z^j \beta_2 + v_1^j \qquad (9.5)$$

and a probit criterion equation for Mexico–United States migration

$$I^{*j} = \delta_0 + \delta_1 (\ln R_1^j - \ln R_0^j) + Z^j \delta_2 + \mathrm{RD}^j \delta_3 - \xi^j \qquad (9.6)$$

Household member $j$ is observed as an undocumented Mexico–United States migrant if $I^{*j} > 0$ and as a worker in Mexico otherwise. Equation (9.6) corresponds to the decision rule that states that person $j$ will be observed as a Mexico–United States migrant if the consequent expected change in absolute income given relative deprivation results in a positive utility gain for person $j$'s household.[8]

The explanatory variables $X_1$ and $X_0$ include the list of human capital variables typically found in studies of the earnings of different labor force groups (Mincer, 1974; Lee, 1978). These include age, sex, years of completed schooling, and work experience. This list is expanded and modified, however, to take account of earnings in migrant labor markets and to focus on migrant remittances. The explanatory variables include separate measures of prior experience as a migrant worker in the United States and in Mexico. To the extent that remittances are an increasing function of earnings, all other things being equal, we would expect the relationship of these variables to remittances to be similar to the effects commonly found in studies of earnings. For example, migration work experience is probably positively related to remittances – unless time away from the village reduces household members' motivation to remit and this effect dominates the positive effect of migrants' experience on earnings (Chiswick, 1978).

The effects of the explanatory variables on earnings will not generally be the same in all labor markets. For example, schooling is likely to have a positive effect on earnings and hence on income contributions in Mexico, particularly for internal migrants (Taylor, 1986). Its effect on Mexico–United States migrant remittances depends on the transferability of skills acquired through schooling across the border and the recognition and valuation of these skills by employers in the United States. In general, returns to schooling are expected to be small in the labor-intensive low-skill labor markets in which opportunities for undocumented immigrants are concentrated. A similar argument would hold for the effect of past work experience in Mexico on Mexico–United States migrant remittances. However, if skills acquired in the United States are transferable to Mexico, then US work experience may yield a positive return for workers in Mexico.

Both the $X_0$ and $X_1$ variables include individuals' status in the household as either a household head or nonhead. This, along with other variables, may influence individuals' propensity to share part of their earnings with their household of origin in Mexico. All else being equal, we would expect heads of households to have a stronger motivation to remit than other household members. Because of the important administrative role frequently played by household heads on the family farm, however, the opportunity cost of migration for these individuals may be large. Moreover, holders of *ejidos* (reform sector lands) are required to work their lands themselves or risk having them reallocated to other villagers.

Mexico–United States migration success probabilities $p^j$ are not observed in the data. However, two variables that are likely to have a major influence on these probabilities are observed: household migration capital, or contacts with family members in the United States, and individuals' US migration experience. These are included in the vector $Z^j$. Migration networks and experience can substantially improve the probability of successfully entering and finding work in the United States and avoiding apprehension by immigration authorities. Moreover, they can reduce and help finance migration costs. These variables may also influence migrants' earnings and their propensity to remit if they are successful in crossing the border and finding work in the United States. The latter effects can be isolated in a structural probit that controls for the effect of expected remittances on migration decisions.

An instrument $\overset{\sim}{Y}^{-j}$ for household income from sources besides person $j$ is also included to control for the effect of initial household absolute income on the motives for migration, interactions among household income decisions, and the household's ability and willingness to finance the initially relatively large costs of participating in illegal Mexico–United States migration in the absence of well-developed credit markets in rural Mexico. Migration costs include the cost of hiring *coyotes* (smugglers) to assist with the illegal border crossing. These averaged US$350 per migrant in 1982 for the households in the sample, representing a large investment in relation to average village incomes. The household income instrument is also included in the two income contribution equations to control for the possibility that propensities to contribute to village household income are responsive to household need. Derivation of this household income instrument is described in the appendix. A summary of variables included in the empirical analysis appears in table 9.2.

Instrumental variable techniques were used to obtain estimates of the expected net income gains to households from sending migrants to the United States and of the relative deprivation associated with nonmigration. These estimates correct for possible sample selectivity bias. As stated earlier, the household sample was drawn from two different villages. Thus two similar absolute incomes do not necessarily imply similar levels of relative deprivation, and absolute income and relative deprivation can be treated as independent variables.[9] The relative deprivation variable is the basis for empirically testing the relative deprivation hypothesis. Our presentation of the empirical findings will proceed in two parts: first, the

**Table 9.2** Definition of variables                                129

| Variable | Definition |
|---|---|
| Decision $I^{*j}$ | Mexico–US migrant in 1982: 0 if household member $j$ remained in Mexico throughout 1982; 1 if household member $j$ was observed as an undocumented migrant |
| **Income** | |
| $\hat{Y}^{-j}$ | Instrument for total household income from sources besides person $j$, (US$00) |
| $R_1(R_0)$ | Return to household income in 1982 from Mexico–US migration (work in Mexico) by person $j$ |
| $\Delta Y^j$ | Selectivity-corrected estimate of net income gain to the household from migration by person $j$ to the US |
| $RD^j$ | Estimated household relative deprivation in the absence of migration by household member $j$ |
| **Household** | |
| SIZE | Household size |
| LAND | Household landholdings (hectares) |
| ADULTS | Adult household size |
| ADLAND | ADULTS/LAND |
| PK | Total value of household's major physical assets (land, animals, and machinery) (US$000) |
| MEXNET | 1 if a close relative (sibling, parent, sibling of parent) of person $j$ was residing outside the village in Mexico at the start of 1982 0 otherwise |
| USNET | 1 if a close relative of person $j$ was residing in the US at the start of 1982 0 otherwise |
| **Individual** | |
| AGE | Age |
| SEX | 1 if male 0 if female |
| ED | Highest level of schooling completed |
| SEXAGE | SEX × AGE |
| HEAD | 1 if the person is a head of the village household 0 otherwise |
| MEXEX | Years of experience as an internal migrant prior to 1982 |
| USEX | Years of experience as a Mexico–US migrant prior to 1982 |

expected net income gains to households from sending migrants to the United States, and, second, the effect of expected income gains and relative deprivation on Mexico–United States migration decisions.

### Expected Net Gains to Households from Mexico–United States Migration

Estimates of expected net income gains to households in this sample from illegally sending migrants to the United States can be found in Taylor (1987). Our empirical work expands on this study by using the same estimation techniques together with instruments for other incomes in the respective village household income distributions to construct measures of households' relative deprivation in the absence of Mexico–United States migration (that is, households' initial relative deprivation). Because the present analysis makes use of estimates of the expected income gains from Mexico–United States migration and work in Mexico, we begin by summarizing the findings of the companion study.

The estimated coefficients of the Mexico–United States migrant remittances equation are presented on the left-hand side of table 9.3. The equation includes an inverse Mills ratio term to correct for possible sample selectivity bias. This correction is necessary because remittances are observed only for persons who migrate to the United States, and these persons are a self-selected sample of the village population. If villagers who are observed as Mexico–United States migrants are persons who are in the most favorable positions to contribute to their households' income by working in the United States, then their remittances will tend to overstate the true expected returns to Mexico–United States migration.

The findings on the left-hand side of table 9.3 do not provide evidence of a positive truncation effect for Mexico–United States migration (the selectivity parameter $\hat{\lambda}_{US}$ is insignificant).[10] They also show insignificant returns to schooling in the US labor markets in which opportunities for Mexico–United States migrants are concentrated and low returns to past work experience in urban Mexico for migrants in the United States. There is a significant positive relationship, however, between remittances and US work experience.

The findings for contributions by nonmigrants (table 9.3, right-hand side) reveal a different pattern. There is evidence that villagers who are in the best position to generate income for their households by working in Mexico are positively selected *not* to migrate to the United States. The returns to schooling are high in Mexican labor markets, and past US migration experience also appears to have a favorable impact on income

**Table 9.3** Estimates of household income contribution equations adjusted for selectivity bias

| Mexico–US migrant remittances (ln $R_1$) | | | Income contributions by workers in Mexico (ln $R_0$) | | |
|---|---|---|---|---|---|
| Variable | Coefficient | Standard error | Variable | Coefficient | Standard error |
| CONSTANT | 8.614 | 3.828** | ADLAND | −0.048 | 0.081 |
| ED | −0.086 | 0.125 | ED | 0.200 | 0.043** |
| AGE | −0.246 | 0.237 | AGE | 0.080 | 0.021** |
| AGE$^2$ | 0.001 | 0.004 | AGE$^2$ | −0.001 | 0.0003** |
| SEXAGE | 0.055 | 0.022** | SEXAGE | 0.050 | 0.008** |
| USEX | 0.190 | 0.101** | USEX | 0.117 | 0.057** |
| MEXEX | −0.033 | 0.113 | MEXEX | −0.019 | 0.037 |
| HEAD | 2.801 | 2.633 | HEAD | 2.456 | 0.428** |
| USNET | −1.967 | 1.279* | MEXNET | −0.280 | 0.287 |
| $\hat{Y}^{-j}$ | 0.042 | 0.031* | $\hat{Y}^{-j}$ | −0.033 | 0.013** |
| $\hat{\lambda}_{US}$ | 0.729 | 0.698 | $\hat{\lambda}_{MX}$ | 1.243 | 0.613** |

Log likelihood = −118.34
$\chi^2$(df) = 26.748 (10)
$\hat{\sigma}_1^2 = 4.12$
No. of observations = 59

Log likelihood = −792.32
$\chi^2$(df) = 179.84 (10)
$\hat{\sigma}_2^2 = 5.52$
No. of observations = 353

*Significant at below the 0.10 level.
**Significant at below the 0.05 level.

contributions by workers in Mexico – perhaps because skills acquired in the United States yield a positive return in Mexico.

Estimated coefficients from the two income contribution equations were used together with the explanatory variables $X_1$ and $X_0$ to estimate log contributions to household income for each person in the sample as a Mexico–United States migrant and as a worker in Mexico. The difference between these log contributions is the estimated net gain to the household from international migration by person $j$.

The level of household relative deprivation $RD^j$ associated with non-migration by person $j$ was estimated on the basis of expected contributions by person $j$ as a nonmigrant, the instrument $\hat{Y}^{-j}$ for household income from sources besides person $j$, and instruments for incomes of all other households in person $j$'s village. (The derivation of the household income instruments is given in the appendix.) These estimates provide all the information needed to use equation (9.3) to construct our measure of relative deprivation for the household in the absence of migration by person $j$. Note that, because our sample was drawn from two distinct village income distributions, the condition that the same absolute household incomes do not imply the same levels of relative deprivation is fully satisfied.

On average, estimated remittances by villagers who migrate to the United States, net of migration costs, are 2.9 times higher than the expected contributions to household income by these same individuals as nonmigrants. Mexico–United States migration therefore appears to be an effective mechanism for achieving income gains for the households that send migrants to the United States.

## Relative Deprivation and Migration Decisions

To test the relative deprivation hypothesis, predicted relative deprivation in the absence of migration was included, along with predicted absolute income gain, as an explanatory variable in the migration decision function. Although our theory predicts that relative deprivation will have an unambiguous positive effect on migration propensities, we recognize that in a real-world sense, at incomes very near or below subsistence level, relative income considerations may not matter as much as concern for mere survival. In addition, in the absence of smoothly functioning credit markets – a condition characteristic of village economies in less developed countries – households at very low income levels may be unable to afford to pursue migration, regardless of their perceived level of relative deprivation, especially if migration is costly and the initial risks associated with it are high. These considerations may erode the measured positive impact of relative deprivation on migration at the lowest income levels. To capture these potential nonlinearities, a quadratic initial relative deprivation term is also included in the migration decision model.

Structural probit estimates of the model are summarized in table 9.4. These estimates support the relative deprivation hypothesis. When we control for expected absolute income changes, the greater the household's initial relative deprivation is, the higher is the probability that the labor time of household members will be allocated to Mexico–United States migration. The exception occurs at the very bottom of the village income distributions, as evidenced by the significant negative coefficient on the relative-deprivation-squared term.[11]

**Table 9.4**   The Mexico–United States migration equation estimates
(structural form estimates)

| Variable | Coefficient | Standard error |
|---|---|---|
| CONSTANT | −11.990 | 3.086** |
| $\Delta Y$ | 0.490 | 0.286** |
| RD | 0.373 | 0.183** |
| $RD^2$ | −0.027 | 0.012** |
| $\hat{Y}^{-j}$ | 0.227 | 1.042 |
| $(\hat{Y}^{-j})^2$ | −0.061 | 0.179 |
| SIZE | 0.197 | 0.082** |
| MEXNET | 0.126 | 0.348 |
| USNET | 2.918 | 0.840** |
| AGE | 0.315 | 0.107** |
| $AGE^2$ | −0.004 | 0.001** |
| SEXAGE | 0.011 | 0.011 |
| HEAD | −3.518 | 0.949** |
| MEXEX | −0.256 | 0.093** |
| $MEXEX^2$ | 0.010 | 0.005** |
| USEX | 0.658 | 0.122** |
| $USEX^2$ | −0.036 | 0.009** |

Log likelihood = −60.059; $\chi^2(df)$ = 109.46 (16).
**Significant at below the 0.05 level.

Inclusion of the relative deprivation variable does not alter Taylor's (1987) finding that expected absolute income gains have a significant positive effect on Mexico–United States migration probabilities. These findings are consistent with comparative advantage in international migration: Mexico–United States migrants are persons who can provide their households with the largest net income gains by working in the United States. When the households' expected income in the absence of migration is translated into the associated relative deprivation, however, the latter has an independent effect on migration that is not predicted by expected income models of migration behavior.

The remaining coefficient estimates in the table suggest the robustness of our findings with respect to the definition of income variables. When we control for relative deprivation and the absolute income gains from migration, initial absolute income does not significantly affect migration decisions. Migration networks and experience (USNET and USEX), which are likely to affect positively migrants' probability of success in the United States, have a strong positive effect on migration probabilities. Given the high cost in US dollars of entering the United States, assistance from family contacts in the United States is the principal means of financing illegal Mexico–United States migration. This may explain the insignificance of the effect of initial absolute income $\hat{Y}^{-i}$ on Mexico–United States migration. Family contacts in the United States also encourage migration by reducing the psychological costs of working illegally in that country. Past migration experience to destinations in Mexico (MEXEX), in contrast, has a significant negative effect on Mexico–United States migration. Migrants are most likely to come from households with large numbers of adult family members (ADULTS), they are more likely to be male than female, and they are unlikely to be household heads. There is a significant inverted U-shaped relationship between age and Mexico–United States migration. This is consistent with a life-cycle pattern of migration (Cornelius, 1978). It is impossible, however, to separate life-cycle effects from cohort effects in these data. The negative coefficient on age squared reflects a tendency for older cohorts of migrants to resettle in Mexico, but it is not possible to ascertain on the basis of these data whether the migrants currently working in the United States will follow the resettlement pattern of their predecessors.

## 3  Conclusions

The findings in this chapter provide empirical support for the theory that relative deprivation plays a significant role in Mexico–United States migration decisions. Mexico–United States migration is an effective mechanism for achieving income gains by households that send migrants to the United States. In addition, when we control for absolute income gains, the probability that households participate in Mexico–United States migration is directly related to households' initial relative deprivation. Finally, our results indicate that households wisely choose as migrants to the United States those of their members who are most likely to provide the household with net income gains.

# Notes

Co-authored with J. Edward Taylor. Reprinted from *Demography* 26, 1989. This is Discussion Paper 36, Harvard University Migration and Development Program. We are indebted to Clifford C. Clogg, Gordon F. De Jong, Ann R. Miller, and several anonymous referees for very helpful comments and suggestions. The support of the Welfare and Human Resources Division, Population and Human Resources Department, World Bank is acknowledged with gratitude.

1 The Amba of East Africa worked for Europeans for a much lower wage than for employers from another tribe and were "quite willing to explain this state of affairs. They say that a European is on a much higher social plane, and therefore comparisons are out of the question. Europeans are so wealthy that an increase in their wealth makes no difference in the . . . standing" of the Amba relative to Europeans (quoted by Hyman and Singer, 1968). "Migration to the industrial community and the work performed there is purely instrumental: a means to gather income, income that can be taken back to [the migrant's] home community and used to fulfill or enhance his or her role within *that* social structure. From the perspective of the migrant, the work is essentially asocial: It is purely a means to an end" (Piore, 1979, p. 54).

2 Runciman used the example of promotions: "The more people a man sees promoted when he is not promoted himself, the more people he may compare himself with in a situation where the comparison will make him feel relatively deprived" (Runciman, 1966, p. 19).

3 For a detailed and explicit derivation of this equation from Runciman's axioms, see Yitzhaki (1982).

4 The reader might question our definition of $RD(y)$, pointing out that, intuitively, $1 - F(y)$ might do just as well. Unfortunately, this is not the case. If, for example, the income of an individual who is richer than our reference individual increases, $F(y)$ remains unchanged and so does $1 - F(y)$. Yet a proper measure of relative deprivation should be sensitive to there now being more income units of which the reference individual is deprived. $RD(y)$ as defined in equation (9.1) exhibits such sensitivity.

5 All interviews were conducted with at least one household head. In no case in this sample were both the male and female heads of the household absent at the time of the survey, and in the majority of the cases (58 out of 61), the male head of household was the primary respondent. The survey was timed to coincide with the season of lowest migrant labor demand in the United States. Data on household members who were outside the village at the time of the survey were provided by the remaining household members. This approach could be used because the focus of the survey was on the household and its returns from different labor allocations. Data were not needed on the earnings of household members who migrated or on other details concerning the absent migrants' work away from home.

6     Income contributions from household farm work are imputed on the basis of the number of days worked on the household farm valued at the prevailing agricultural wage in the village (this wage was substantially below the minimum agricultural wage in Mexico). Contributions by the owner (or *de facto* owner in the case of *ejidos* or reform sector lands) of the household farm also include farm profits. These are calculated as the difference between the gross value of farm output, evaluated at the average farm-gate sales price in the case of subsistence farming, and all direct costs plus invisible costs. Direct costs include the cost of all material inputs, hired physical capital inputs (mechanical services, animal services, land), and hired labor inputs. Invisible costs include the cost of imputed wages of unpaid family labor. Contributions also include rental income (land rents and payments received for capital services) and income from livestock (the net additions to animal stocks as well as sales of animals and animal products) received by owners of these capital goods from other households. Income contributions by household members working in handicrafts, wood gathering, fishing, and other household farm activities were calculated in a manner analogous to contributions from farm work.

7     Even though the use of a household decision framework obviously overlooks any autonomy of individuals in their labor allocations, we are convinced that to treat each migration decision as independent from a household decision problem would entail far more severe limiting assumptions than does simplifying the analysis to a household decision problem. As the empirical results presented later in this section demonstrate, socio-economic characteristics of households play a significant role alongside characteristics of individual household members in explaining migration behavior. In addition, economic ties between migrants and their households in the village tend to be very strong here as in other samples of rural households in less developed countries (Johnson and Whitelaw, 1974; Stark, 1978; Oberai and Singh, 1980; Lucas and Stark, 1985). One illustration of the economic ties between migrant and household is given by remittances. In the present sample, migrant remittances account for an average 36.5 percent of total household income.

8     The random error terms $v_0$, $v_1$, and $\xi$ are assumed to be independently normally distributed with zero means and variances $\sigma_1^2$, $\sigma_2^2$, and $\sigma_\xi^2$ respectively.

9     The correlation between absolute income and relative deprivation for the sample is $-0.41$.

10    The selectivity parameter, or inverse Mills ratio term, is derived (following Heckman, 1979) from a reduced-form probit in which the migration decision variable $I^*$ is regressed on the explanatory variables $Z$, $X_0$, and $X_1$ from equations (9.3)–(9.6) (see Taylor, 1987).

11    The quadratic term dominates the linear term in the 14 percent most relatively deprived cases in the sample.

## Appendix

*Proof of Equation (9.2)*

Using integration by parts, where $v(z) = 1 - F(z)$, $v'(z) = -f(z)$, $u(z) = z$, $u'(z) = 1$, and the property $\lim_{y \to \infty} [1 - F(y)] = 0$, we obtain

$$RD(y) = \int_y^\infty [1 - F(z)] \, dz = -[1 - F(y)]y + \int_y^\infty zf(z) \, dz$$

Using the conditional density function

$$f^*(z|z > y) = \frac{1}{1 - F(y)} f(z)$$

we insert $f(z)$ into the last integral to obtain equation (9.2).

*Derivation of the Instrument $\hat{Y}^{-j}$ for Household Income from Sources besides Person j*

The instrument $\hat{Y}^{-j}$ for total household income from sources besides person $j$ was constructed by regressing observed 1982 income from sources besides person $j$ on household holdings of income-producing assets at the start of the year and then using the estimated equation to predict household income from other sources for each person in the sample. The assets include the value PK of households' primary physical assets (land, animals, and machinery) in thousands, human capital assets (the number NADS of adults in the household and the number TED of household members with post-primary schooling), and household migration capital, represented by whether or not the household had a family contact in the United States (USNET = 1) or at an internal migrant destination (MEXNET = 1) at the start of 1982. The estimated income equation is

$$\hat{Y}^{-j} = 1376.8 + 0.29\text{PK} + 821.92\text{TED} - 96.275\text{NADS}$$
$$\phantom{\hat{Y}^{-j} = } (4.94) \quad (5.59) \qquad (8.87) \qquad (-1.98)$$

$$+ 558.08\text{USNET} - 397.96\text{MEXNET}$$
$$\phantom{+ } (2.81) \qquad\qquad (-1.85)$$

$$R^2 = 0.28$$

Numbers in parentheses are $t$-statistics.

*Estimation of Household Income Instruments*

Estimation of initial relative deprivation requires an estimate of the predicted 1982 income distribution of each of the two villages. For each household $n$ in the sample, an estimate of total household income $\hat{Y}$ was obtained from a regression of observed 1982 total household income on household holdings of income-producing assets at the start of the year. The assets include the value PK of households' primary physical capital assets (land and draft animals) in thousands, human capital assets (the number NADS of adults in the household and the number TED of household members with post-primary schooling), and migration capital, reflected by the number of household members who participated in internal migration (MEXMIG) and in Mexico–United States migration (USMIG) in the year prior to 1982. The estimated income equation is

$$\ln \hat{Y} = \underset{(27.2)}{7.17} + \underset{(2.19)}{0.13\text{PK}} + \underset{(2.53)}{0.26\text{TED}} - \underset{(-1.19)}{0.07\text{NADS}}$$

$$+ \underset{(2.26)}{0.59\text{USMIG}} - \underset{(-0.32)}{0.08\text{MEXMIG}}$$

$$R^2 = 0.32$$

$$N = 61.0$$

Numbers in parentheses are $t$-statistics.

## References

Chiswick, B. R. (1978) "The Effect of Americanization on the Earnings of Foreign-born Men." *Journal of Political Economy* 86: 897–921.

Cornelius, W. A. (1978) *Mexican Migration to the United States: Causes, Consequences and U.S. Responses*, Cambridge, MA: MIT Center for International Studies, Migration and Development Monograph c/78–9.

Crosby, F. (1979) "Relative Deprivation Revisited: A Response to Miller, Bolce, and Halligan." *American Political Science Review* 73: 103–12.

Heckman, J. J. (1979) "Sample Selection Bias as a Specification Error." *Econometrica* 47: 153–61.

Hyman, H. and Singer, E. (eds) (1968) *Readings in Reference Group Theory and Research*. New York: Free Press.

Johnson, G. E. and Whitelaw, W. E. (1974) "Urban–Rural Income Transfers in Kenya: An Estimated Remittances Function." *Economic Development and Cultural Change* 22: 473–9.

Lee, L. (1978) "Unionism and Wage Rates: A Simultaneous Equations Model with Qualitative and Limited Dependent Variables." *International Economic Review* 19: 415–33.

Lucas, R. E. B. and Stark, O. (1985) "Motivations to Remit: Evidence from Botswana." *Journal of Political Economy* 93: 901–18 (reprinted as ch. 16 in this volume).

Merton, R. K. and Kitt, A. S. (1950) "Contributions to the Theory of Reference Group Behavior." In R. K. Merton and P. F. Lazarsfeld (eds), *Contributions in Social Research, Studies in the Scope and Method of "The American Soldier."* Glencoe, IL: Free Press, pp. 40–105.

Mincer, J. (1974) *Schooling, Experience and Earnings.* New York: Columbia University Press.

Oberai, A. S. and Singh, H. K. M. (1980) "Migration, Remittances and Rural Development: Findings of a Case Study in the Indian Punjab." *International Labor Review* 119:229–41.

Piore, M. J. (1979) *Birds of Passage: Migrant Labor and Industrial Societies.* Cambridge: Cambridge University Press.

Runciman, W. G. (1966) *Relative Deprivation and Social Justice: A Study of Attitudes to Social Inequality in Twentieth-Century England.* Berkeley, CA: University of California Press.

Stark, O. (1978) *Economic–Demographic Interactions in Agricultural Development: The Case of Rural-to-Urban Migration.* Rome: UN Food and Agriculture Organization.

—— (1984a) "Rural-to-Urban Migration in LDCs: A Relative Deprivation Approach." *Economic Development and Cultural Change* 32: 475–86 (reprinted as ch.7 in this volume).

—— (1984b) "Discontinuity and the Theory of International Migration." *Kyklos* 37: 206–22.

—— and Lucas, R. E. B. (1988) "Migration, Remittances, and the Family." *Economic Development and Cultural Change* 36: 465–81 (reprinted as ch. 15 in this volume).

—— and Yitzhaki, S. (1988) "Labor Migration as a Response to Relative Deprivation." *Journal of Population Economics* 1: 57–70 (reprinted as ch. 8 in this volume).

Stouffer, S. A., Suchman, E. A., DeVinney, L. C., Star, S. A. and Williams, R. M., Jr (1949) *The American Soldier: Adjustment During Army Life.* Princeton, NJ: Princeton University Press.

Taylor, J. E. (1986) "Differential Migration, Networks, Information and Risk." In O. Stark (ed.), *Migration, Human Capital and Development.* Greenwich, CT: JAI Press, pp. 147–71.

—— (1987) "Undocumented Mexico–U.S. Migration and the Returns to Households in Rural Mexico." *American Journal of Agricultural Economics* 69: 626–38.

Yitzhaki, S. (1979) "Relative Deprivation and the Gini Coefficient." *Quarterly Journal of Economics* 93: 321–4.

—— (1982) "Relative Deprivation and Economic Welfare." *European Economic Review* 17:99–113.

# 10

## Migration Incentives, Migration Types: The Role of Relative Deprivation

Almost without exception, economic studies of labor migration in less developed countries (LDCs) focus on the potential contributions that migration may make to the *absolute* income of the relevant migration unit (the individual, the family, or the household). In contrast, Stark (1984) has hypothesized that rural-to-urban migration might be undertaken primarily to improve an individual's or a household's comparative income position with respect to that of other individuals or households in the relevant reference group (for example, the village).

In a recent study Stark and Taylor (1989) found empirical evidence that the initial relative deprivation of households in their village reference group plays a significant role in migration from Mexico to the United States. Controlling for initial absolute income and the expected income gains from migration, these authors showed that the propensity of households to participate in international migration is directly related to the households' initial relative deprivation.

In this chapter we expand this earlier work by addressing the role of absolute income versus relative deprivation incentives for internal and international migration for households in LDCs, taking into account continuities across some labor markets and discontinuities across others. The rationale for the analysis is threefold. First, there are fairly strong reasons to expect that the role of relative deprivation will differ between international migration and migration within a country, as we explain below. Second, sharp discontinuities in the returns to human capital between home and host country labor markets may affect the ability of households that differ in their human capital endowments to achieve gains in their income positions through international migration. Third, a relative deprivation approach to migration has important implications for development policy. For example, the effects of rural development policies on rural outmigration, as predicted by an expected income model, may be precisely opposite to those predicted by a relative deprivation model.

In section 1 of the chapter we outline the absolute income and relative deprivation models of migration and present an illustration of their divergent policy implications. We also consider the likely case in which the decision to migrate and the choice of migrant destination are influenced by both absolute income and relative deprivation objectives. In this case, income remittances from household members who migrate have a dual impact on the household's well-being: first, by contributing to its absolute income; second, by improving its income position relative to that of other village households. An attempt is made to identify distinct empirical implications of these two motives for migrating. In section 2 a migration decision model is estimated and is used to explore absolute and relative income motives for internal and international migration in a sample of rural Mexican households, as well as the extent to which the degree of discontinuity in labor markets shapes the choice of migrant destination.

## 1 Absolute and Relative Income Hypotheses of Migration

Empirical economic studies of migration are based on the general assumption that individuals migrate to maximize expected utility EU, which is typically defined on income $Y$ at the end of the relevant time period:

$$EU = EU(Y) \qquad (10.1)$$

where $U'(Y) > 0$. Let $Y_1$ denote income associated with migration, net of any implied moving costs, and let $Y_0$ denote income in the absence of migration. The absolute income hypothesis then states simply that a person will migrate if $EU(Y_1) > EU(Y_0)$. That is, an individual's labor is allocated to the labor market associated with the highest level of expected utility. A clearer picture of the economic determinants of migration can be gained when expected utility is replaced by its Taylor series approximation around the expected income EY (David, 1974):

$$EU(Y) = U(EY) + 0.5U''(EY)s^2 \qquad (10.2)$$

where $s^2$ is the variance of income $Y$ and $U''(EY)$ is the second derivative of utility evaluated at expected income EY. If decision-makers are risk neutral, that is, if $U''(EY)$ is zero, equation (10.2) reduces to the expected income hypothesis (see, for example, Todaro, 1969), which states that labor will be allocated to the destination that maximizes expected income. In contrast, if the migration decision-maker is risk averse, that is, $U''(EY) < 0$, then migration decisions are influenced by both the mean and the variability of income associated with alternative locations, as well as by the decision-maker's aversion to risk. In the case of risk aversion, the absolute income model predicts that an individual will migrate if the corresponding expected income gain outweighs any increase in income risk that may be associated with migration (Stark and Levhari, 1982).[1] Several studies provide empirical support for an absolute income motive for migration, with regard to both expected income (Yap, 1977; Todaro, 1980) and risk (Lucas and Stark, 1985; Taylor, 1986; Rosenzweig and Stark, 1989).

## A Relative Deprivation Hypothesis

In earlier papers (Stark, 1984; Stark and Taylor, 1989) it was hypothesized that household members undertake migration not necessarily to increase the household's absolute income but rather to improve the household's position (in terms of relative deprivation) with respect to a specific reference group. The case studied in those papers is of individuals who engage in migration to improve the income position of their households relative to that of all other households in the village.

Consider two villages of households whose incomes are as follows: $A_1 = (20, 30, 40, 50, 60)$ and $A_2 = (20, 37, 38, 39, 40, 41, 42, 43, 60)$. These two income distributions share the same average income (40) and cover the same income range (20, 60). However, whereas the five household incomes in $A_1$ are uniformly distributed over this range, seven of the nine incomes in $A_2$ are concentrated around the mean.

Suppose that by reallocating some of its labor to migration the household earning the average income in each village can enjoy a 20 percent (8 unit) increase in absolute income. For the household in $A_2$, this absolute income gain translates into a relative income gain of three ranks, enabling that household to move to within one rank of the top of its village income distribution. In contrast, the same absolute income gain leaves the $A_1$ household's rank unchanged. Assume that the nature of the reallocation is such that, when a household member is assigned to a different sector, the household together with that member continue to consider $A_i$ as the relevant reference distribution. (This assumption is discussed below in the context of international and internal migration.) If household utility is a function not only of absolute income but also of ranking in relation to other households in the village, then we would intuitively expect that the average household in $A_2$ will have a stronger motivation to participate in migration than the average household in $A_1$. That is, a given absolute income gain associated with an improvement in rank is worth more than an identical income gain without an improvement in rank.

Consider now the poorest households in $A_1$ and $A_2$. Suppose that each of these households can reap a 60 percent (12 unit) gain from migration by one of its members. This gain will not cause a rank change for the household in $A_2$, but the household in $A_1$ could escape from the very bottom of its village's income distribution through migration. Other things being equal, a given absolute income gain may be considered more valuable in the latter situation than in the former.

The two examples above have in common a correlation between rank within an income distribution and absolute income. However, we can easily consider rank gains that are not associated with income gains, or rank losses that are not associated with income losses. Consider two village household income distributions given by $B_1 = (30, 35, 40, 45, 50)$ and $B_2 = (30, 32, 34, 47, 62)$. For the household with income equal to 35, relocation from $B_1$ to $B_2$ would result in a rank gain that is not associated with an absolute income change. Intuition alone, however, may not provide clear-cut guidance on whether to expect this move to take place. Even though the change implies a higher rank in a new reference group having the same average income (after 35 is added to $B_2$, the average income in $B_2$ is 40), in a cardinal sense the new position may be perceived as inferior (if judged, for example, by the distance from the highest-income household: $62 - 35 > 50 - 35$). An ambiguity arises in this case because the simple rank measure is not sufficiently sensitive to all rank-related information. Hence there is a need to adopt a more complete measure of income ranking and relative deprivation. We shall draw here on an axiomatic foundation for an index of relative deprivation reported in related papers (Stark and Yitzhaki, 1988; Stark and Taylor, 1989).

Let $RD^i$ denote household $i$'s relative deprivation. Assume a continuous income distribution. Each income unit can then be represented by an income range $[x, x + \Delta x]$, where $\Delta x \rightarrow 0$. Let $F(x)$ be the cumulative distribution of income in a village. Then $1 - F(x)$ is the percentage of households whose income is higher than $x$. Hence $1 - F(x)$ represents the percentage of households that have incomes sufficient to obtain the commodities represented by the income range $[x, x + \Delta x]$. By hypothesis, the feeling of deprivation is an increasing function of the percentage of households with incomes larger than $x$. Let $g[1 - F(x)]$ be the deprivation from not having $[x, x + \Delta x]$, where $g(0) = 0$ and $g' > 0$. A household with income $x$ is deprived of all units of income above $x$. Thus, we can write the relative deprivation of household $i$, whose income is $y_i$, as

$$RD^i = \int_{y^i}^{y^h} g[1 - F(x)] \, dx \qquad (10.3)$$

where $y^h$ denotes the highest village income. To simplify the discussion, we shall assume a simple form of $g[1 - F(x)] = 1 - F(x)$. Subject to some algebraic manipulations, the expression on the right-hand side of equation (10.3) can be decomposed into the product of the mean excess income of households richer than the household with income $y^i$ and the proportion of households in the village that are richer than the household with income $y^i$. (For these procedures and an analysis of the more general form $g(\cdot)$, see Stark and Yitzhaki, 1988.) This interpretation nicely captures the point that, if all rankings are left intact, any increase in the income of a household richer than household $i$ will increase the relative deprivation of household $i$, whereas any rank gain by household $i$ (resulting in a decline of the proportion of households richer than $i$) will reduce the relative deprivation of household $i$. Given this interpretation, in the example above of household income distributions $B_1$ and $B_2$, the ambiguity associated with the relocation of the household with an income of 35 is not only better understood but is also resolved because the two effects are duly weighted (resulting, in the case of the example, in an increase of relative deprivation from 6.0 to 6.5).

The relative deprivation hypothesis is that migration will be observed if $EU(RD^i_1) > EU(RD^i_0)$, where $RD_1$ is the relative deprivation associated with migration and $RD_0$ is the relative deprivation in the absence of migration. Thus individuals or households below the upper end of the income distribution may decide to engage in migration on the assumption that they will thereby succeed in improving their positions in the village by securing an income higher than their initial income.

To illustrate some of the new policy implications of the relative deprivation approach to migration, we consider an extreme example. In a country consisting of a village and a town, the income of every village household is 100; in the town, it is 200. As the result of a certain development policy, the income of half the village households rises to 150. What are the likely migration implications? In a world motivated solely by income differentials, the incentives for village-to-town migration will have declined unequivocally: the propensity to migrate of those earning 150 has declined, whereas that of those earning 100 remains as before. In a world motivated solely by relative deprivation, the prediction is exactly the opposite. If the village is the relevant reference group for village households, before the change no household had any inducement to migrate, since the relative deprivation of each and every household was nil. After the change, however, half the village households – those which now experience relative deprivation (at the level of 25 units of income) – will have an incentive to migrate, whereas the incentive to migrate of the others (whose income is 150) will remain at zero.

When a household's utility is a function of both absolute income and relative deprivation arising from intra-group income comparisons, the effect of a policy change on the propensity to migrate from the village cannot be pre-signed because there are conflicting effects: the lower inducement to migrate of the households whose absolute incomes rise has to be weighed against the new inducement to migrate on the part of households whose relative incomes fall. The received theory, however, will admit only the former inducement and is completely blind to the latter. The relative deprivation theory of migration and the received theory of migration based on absolute income differentials generate conflicting predictions.

Suppose that a development agency is not indifferent to the migration implications of its policies and wishes to induce less migration, more migration, or keep migration at its existing level. If the relative deprivation theory of migration obtains, a new policy instrument is identified, and the policy mix will thereby change. For example, in an effort to stem rural-to-urban migration, equalization of the rural income distribution could be combined with, reinforced by, or substituted for the narrowing of town–village income differentials.

## An Integrated Approach

In real life it is likely that migration decisions are influenced by both absolute and relative income considerations. In this case utility is of the form

$$U = U(Y, \text{RD}) \tag{10.4}$$

where $\partial U/\partial Y > 0$ and $\partial U/\partial \text{RD} < 0$. The net utility gain from migration is given by the differential

$$\Delta_1 = U(Y_1, \text{RD}_1) - U(Y_0, \text{RD}_0) \tag{10.5}$$

This can be expressed as a function of $Y_0$, $\text{RD}_0$, and the net household income gain from migration (which we shall denote $W$) by replacing $\text{RD}_1$ with its Taylor series approximation around $Y_0$:

$$\Delta_1 = U(Y_0 + W, \text{RD}_0 + \text{RD}_0', W) - U(Y_0, \text{RD}_0)$$
$$= \theta(Y_0, \text{RD}_0, W) \tag{10.6}$$

where $RD_0'$ is the change in relative deprivation brought about by a small change in income at income level $Y_0$.

Assume for a moment that the relative deprivation function is stable in the face of migration by one or more household members; that is, the household including its migrants continues to view the village as its relevant reference group. In this case, any variable that enhances the net returns $W$ from migration can increase the household's incentive to participate in migration in two ways: first, by increasing absolute income $Y_1 = Y_0 + W$; second, by decreasing relative deprivation, since by construction $RD_0' < 0$. On the basis of this consideration, the effect of a household's income and relative deprivation levels in the absence of migration on its propensity to participate in migration is generally predictable. At low levels of income, incentives to engage in potentially income-enhancing migration may be strong. On the absolute income side, low village incomes presumably imply large income disparities between migration work and village work, and hence large potential net gains from migration. Low village incomes are also associated with high degrees of relative deprivation as defined in equation (10.3), and hence the incentive to reduce relative deprivation through migration may also be large for low-income households. Thus, other things being equal, both the absolute and relative income hypotheses would predict a greater desire to engage in migration among households or individuals at the lower end of the village income spectrum.

However, in the absence of smoothly functioning credit markets that give explicit preference to the poor – a condition characteristic of village economies in LDCs – households or individuals at very low levels of absolute income may be unable to engage in migration if migration is costly and the initial risks associated with it are high.[2] In addition, at incomes very near or below subsistence, relative income considerations are not likely to matter as much as concerns for mere survival. Thus, we would expect a small increase in income (and a small decrease in relative deprivation) to have a positive effect on migration from households at the very bottom of the village income distribution owing, first, to a loosening of capital constraints on migration and, second, to the increasing importance of relative deprivation considerations in these households' labor allocations. At higher income levels, in contrast, both the relative and absolute income hypotheses predict that increases in income will reduce the likelihood that households or individuals will engage in migration. It is therefore impossible on purely theoretical grounds to separate the effect of absolute income incentives from the effect of relative income incentives for migration, since, when credit markets are highly imperfect, absolute and relative income effects of changes in village incomes tend to move in tandem. Note that migration studies that ignore relative income effects may place undue significance on absolute income motives for migration.

### Reference Group Substitution, Labor Market Discontinuities, and Destination Choice

In a relative deprivation model of migration there is a risk that, through a reference group substitution of the host community for the village community, households may fail to decrease their relative deprivation – even if their relative incomes in terms of the village income distribution improve. That is, the household's relative deprivation function may not be stable in the face of migration by one or more household members. The household's well-being is an increasing function of the well-being of all its members, regardless of their location. Migration may be associated with a rise in a household's relative deprivation if the host community becomes the relevant reference group for either the migrant or, perhaps less likely, the household members who remain in the village.

In a recent study it was argued that international migration to an entirely different social and cultural milieu can carry with it built-in protection against such reference group substitution and can ensure that the original reference group continues to be the relevant one for the migrant and his or her household (Stark and Taylor, 1989). By locating themselves in a host community distinct from their own, migrants are less likely to orient themselves to the host community than if they were to locate themselves in a "neighboring" host community. For a comparison with the host community to occur, some "minimal similarity" between the migrant and that community must be perceived. This becomes more likely when direct social interaction or sustained social relations persist. In some cases, the host community may be intentionally selected to ensure estrangement, detachment, and social distance. Migrants may wish to guard against becoming oriented to the host community for fear that the secondary negative effects of a changing reference group might outweigh the primary positive effect of improving their position in relation to the original reference group. Thus international migration can enable households to exploit cultural and social discontinuity across international frontiers, capture this discontinuity, and transform international dissimilarities into a source of advantage. This consideration applies in particular to repetitive or temporary migration rather than to permanent once-and-for-all migration; in the recent study cited, migration was by and large of the former type.[3]

Indeed, households may behave strategically to preempt reference group substitution associated with migration of a long duration by given (that is, the same) household members. Household members might be shuffled between destination and home, replacing each other as migrants. Note that, by construction, the analysis in the present paper is of a short-run nature. Reference group association and household attachment could become endogenous processes conditional on relative performance in a set of reference groups. Households and individuals may substitute one reference group for another to suppress the dissatisfaction arising from a high level of a group-specific relative deprivation. Such a substitution typically involves locational *and* mental migration and is bound to be time consuming.

In contrast with international migration, migration within a country is more likely to generate alienation and increased relative deprivation through a smooth reference group substitution, particularly when the country is socially and culturally homogeneous. These considerations suggest that the role of relative deprivation in internal migration may be quite different from the role of relative deprivation in international migration, owing to social and cultural discontinuities across international borders.

Indeed, the full logic of this argument could lead to a puzzling neutrality result. Consider a household that experiences intra-village relative deprivation while, at the same time, facing a positive urban-to-rural income differential for one of its members. Should that household member engage in rural-to-urban migration, his increased alienation arising from a reference group substitution could offset any absolute income gain. The village household may recognize that the migrant member would need to "tax" his higher urban income to compensate for a rising relative deprivation, thereby leaving little for urban-to-rural remittances. In this case, a relatively deprived household would not engage in internal migration via one of its members, even though the associated expected absolute income differential is positive. Consequently, neither the estimated coefficient for relative deprivation nor that for absolute income may appear significant in an econometric migration model.

Discontinuities in labor markets across international frontiers may, however, temper the role of relative deprivation in migration decisions. Paramount among these are sharp differences in the returns to human capital. Education, skills, and work experience in the home country may enhance the returns to internal migration. But it is less clear to what degree these human capital assets are internationally transferable. When international migration takes the form of illegal entry into the host country, as is frequently the case with migration from rural Mexico to the United States, the returns to human capital in host country labor markets may be minimal (Taylor, 1987).

Empirical work is therefore needed to pursue further an analysis of explanations for internal and international migration motivated by absolute versus relative income considerations. By including both absolute income and relative deprivation variables in a single-household model of internal and international migration decisions, it is possible to isolate empirically the differential influence of relative deprivation on these two types of migration, provided that not all migration decision units are drawn from the same reference group. Estimated absolute household income if a household member does not migrate can be used to control for the effects of both the motivations to migrate and the capital constraints associated with absolute income in the migration equation. Controlling for the initial absolute income of households and for their human capital, the integrated model would predict that the initial relative deprivation of households will have a positive influence on the propensity to send migrants to destinations where the potential returns to migration are large enough to alter significantly the relative income positions in the village and where the risk of reference group substitution is small.

## 2 Evidence from Mexico

### Data

Data from a survey of rural Mexican households were used to test for the effects of absolute income and relative deprivation on migration both to Mexican destinations and to the United States. The sample consists of 61 randomly selected households surveyed in the Pátzcuaro region of the state of Michoacán, Mexico, during the winter of 1983. From these households we obtained data on 423 adults who were 13 years of age or older. Data were collected for a set of characteristics – of both the individuals themselves and their households – that are likely to influence the returns to households from migration versus nonmigration work by household members. Data were also collected on the allocation of each individual's labor to migration and nonmigration activities and on each individual's income contribution to the household during 1982. The latter include, for nonmigrants, contributions of income from household farm production (farming, handicrafts, fishing, livestock, commerce, and the like), village wage work, and rental income.[4] Income contributions in the form of remittances from household members who migrated, either within Mexico or to the United States, are all net of reverse (household-to-migrant) flows and of direct migration costs. A "migrant" is defined as an individual who left the village at any time during 1982 for the purpose of working. The shortest term of migration in the sample was approximately three weeks. Nonmigrants include individuals who remained in the village throughout the year, as well as a small group of secondary and post-secondary students who studied outside the village but did not participate in migrant *labor* activities. (The empirical results are not significantly altered if students are excluded entirely from the sample.)

Selected characteristics of the households of nonmigrants, internal migrants, and Mexico–United States migrants, together with individual characteristics of the migrant and nonmigrant subsamples, are summarized in table 10.1. (In no case in the sample was a person both an internal and a Mexico–United States migrant in 1982.) Distinct patterns characterize the households of the three labor groups. Families of nonmigrants, on average, are relatively small, with 7.8 adult members (13 years or older) compared with 8.5 and 9.1 respectively for internal migrant and Mexico–United States migrant families. Nonmigrant households have less land and fewer physical assets overall than do migrant households. They are likely to have internal migration networks, or family contacts at internal migrant destinations, but are far less likely to have networks for US migration. Fewer than half the nonmigrants are male (43 percent). On average, nonmigrants are somewhat older than migrants (33 years, compared with 28–29 years for the two migrant groups), have little schooling (3.9 years), and have little past internal and Mexico–United States migration experience (0.32 years and 0.76 years respectively).

Internal migrants are distinguished from the other two labor groups by their high schooling levels (6.5 years) and their past internal migration experience (4.8 years). Eighty percent of all internal migrants come from households with family contacts at internal migrant destinations. Overwhelmingly, internal migrants from the households in this sample migrate to Mexico City. The main exceptions are some villagers with secondary or post-secondary schooling who migrate into government teaching jobs scattered around rural Mexico. Mexico–United States migrants are predominantly male (63 percent) and uneducated (4.1 years) but have considerable past US migration experience (4.9 years). Their households are above average in terms of adult family size (9.1), landholdings (7.1 hectares), physical capital wealth ($3500 in 1982 dollars), and the probability of having family contacts in the United States (0.89).

More than a third of all individuals in the sample were labor migrants during 1982. In no case, however, did an entire household leave the village. Thus, the households covered by the sample remained as stable and meaningful entities in their respective villages while individual household members participated in labor migration, typically remitting part of

**Table 10.1**   Selected household and individual characteristics, 1982

|  | Nonmigrants | Internal migrants | Mexico–US migrants |
|---|---|---|---|
| *Household characteristics* | | | |
| Adult family size | | | |
| (13 years or older) | 7.84 | 8.47 | 9.11 |
| Landholdings (in hectares) | 4.75 | 6.48 | 7.14 |
| Percentage with family contacts (sibling, parent, sibling of parent) with internal migrant destinations | 0.71 | 0.80 | 0.57 |
| Percentage with family contacts (sibling, parent, sibling of parent) at US destinations | 0.50 | 0.44 | 0.89 |
| Wealth (total value of land, animals, and machinery) (1982 $US000) | 2.11 | 2.47 | 3.47 |
| *Individual characteristics* | | | |
| Sex (male = 1.0) | 0.43 | 0.49 | 0.63 |
| Age | 33.40 | 28.48 | 28.70 |
| Years of schooling completed | 3.93 | 6.50 | 4.06 |
| Years of internal migration experience | 0.32 | 4.75 | 0.79 |
| Years of US migration experience | 0.76 | 0.74 | 4.91 |
| Sample size | 273 | 80 | 70 |

their earnings to the household. Each observation in the sample represents a separate allocation of household labor time.[5]

### Estimation

A procedure to test the relative deprivation hypothesis presented earlier in this chapter requires, as indicated by equation (10.6), estimation of the effects on households' internal and Mexican–United States migration decisions of initial absolute income, initial relative deprivation, and factors expected to influence the net returns to households from undertaking migration.

A multinomial logit procedure was used to estimate the probabilities that an individual participated in internal migration or Mexico–United States migration work during 1982, versus the alternative of engaging exclusively in activities other than labor migration.

Let $X_d$ be a vector of characteristics of the household member and his or her household that are likely to influence the net income gain to the household from allocating the member's time to migrant destination $d$, such that this gain can be represented as $W_d = f_d(X_d)$. Thus the household's income if the member migrates to destination $d$ can be written as $Y_d = Y_0 + W_d = Y_0 + f_d(X_d)$, where $Y_0$ is the household's income in the absence of migration by the member. For $d = 1$ (internal migration) and $d = 2$ (Mexico–United States migration), the vector $X_d$ includes the household member's sex, age, education, status as household head or not, and migration work experience. These variables can influence household members' earnings as migrants in different labor markets as well as migrants' motivations to remit part of these earnings to the household. The vector $X_d$, $d = 1, 2$, also includes household migration networks or contacts with relatives at prospective migrant destinations, which can reduce the costs and risks associated with labor migration (especially those of illegal Mexico–United States migration), and household wealth, which can affect the household's willingness to participate in risky migration activities and its ability to secure financing for these activities. The net gains from migration are also a function of the income that household members would contribute to the household as nonmigrants. Thus $X_d$ also contains variables that affect the returns to the member's labor in the village. These include the individual characteristics mentioned above plus household adult labor available to assume household farm duties and household landholdings, which may be an indication of the demand for labor on the household farm, especially where limited land rental markets exist, as in *ejido* (land reform) areas of Mexico. Assuming that households allocate their members' time so as to maximise utility, the member will be observed as a migrant worker at destination $d^*$ with a probability of

$$P(d^*) = \text{Prob}[U(Y_{d^*}, \text{RD}_{d^*}) > U(Y_0, \text{RD}_0) \text{ and}$$
$$U(Y_{d^*}, \text{RD}_{d^*}) > U(Y_{d'}, \text{RD}_{d'})]$$

where $d'$ denotes the "migration route not taken."

Replacing $U(Y_{d^*}, \text{RD}_{d^*})$ and $U(Y_{d'}, \text{RD}_{d'})$ by their Taylor series approximations around $Y_0$, as in equation (10.6), we obtain

$$P(d^*) = \text{Prob}(\Delta_{d^*,0} > 0 \text{ and } \Delta_{d^*,d'} > 0)$$

where

$$\Delta_{d^*,0} = U(Y_0 + W_{d^*}, \text{RD}_0 + \text{RD}_0'W_{d^*}) - U(Y_0, \text{RD}_0)$$

and

$$\Delta_{d^*,d'} = U(Y_0 + W_{d^*}, \text{RD}_0 + \text{RD}_0'W_{d^*}) \\ - U(Y_0 + W_{d'}, \text{RD}_0 + \text{RD}_0'W_{d'})$$

Substituting $f_d(X_d)$ for $W_d$, $d = d^*$, $d'$, the probability that the member is assigned to migrant destination $d^*$ becomes

$$P(d^*) = \phi(Y_0, \text{RD}_0, X)$$

where $X$ is a vector containing the variables in $X_{d^*}$ and $X_{d'}$.

Let $Z$ denote a $1 \times K$ vector whose components $z_k$ are the explanatory variables $\hat{Y}_0$, $\text{RD}_0$, and $X$ (where $\hat{Y}_0$ is the household's estimated income if the household member does not migrate and $\text{RD}_0$ is the household's estimated level of relative deprivation associated with this income). The logit equations are given by

$$P(d^*) = \frac{\exp(Z\beta_{d^*})}{1 + \sum_{d=1}^{2} \exp(Z\beta_d)} \qquad (10.7)$$

for migration types $d^* = 1$ (internal migration) and $d^* = 2$ (Mexico–United States migration), where $\beta_d$ is a $K \times 1$ vector whose components $b_{d,k}$ are the coefficients on characteristic $k$ that correspond to migrant labor destination $d$. The logit reference category is nonmigration. The logit probability of nonmigration is $P(0) = 1/[1 + \sum_{d=1}^{2} \exp(Z\beta_d)]$.

Instrumental variable techniques were used to obtain estimates of household income in the absence of migration by a household member and of the level of relative deprivation associated with different income levels. These techniques are described in the appendix. The household sample was drawn from two villages. Thus, two similar absolute incomes do not necessarily imply similar levels of relative deprivation, and absolute income and relative deprivation can be treated as independent.[6] These absolute income and relative deprivation variables, together with a quadratic transformation of each, are the basis for testing the relative and absolute income hypotheses empirically. The quadratic variables are included in the empirical analysis to capture potential nonlinearities created by credit constraints (in the case of absolute income) and subsistence concerns (in the case of relative deprivation), as discussed previously. Definitions of the variables used in the logit analysis appear in table 10.2.

Strong dissimilarities between labor markets imply substantial differences in the returns to human capital for migrant workers. Although migration to a foreign labor market tends to minimize the added relative deprivation to which the household is exposed, there is evidence that returns to human capital are low in the labor-intensive low-skill sectors in which opportunities for undocumented migrants in the United States are concentrated (Taylor, 1987; Stark and Taylor, 1989). In addition, skills acquired through work experience in Mexico may not be readily transferable to the United States. Thus, in choosing between international and internal migration, households may be confronted with a tradeoff between the risk of increased relative deprivation (through a smooth reference group substitution) yet high returns to human capital in the case of internal migration, and a low return to human capital yet low risk of increased relative deprivation in the case of migration to the United States. Should we therefore expect households to sort themselves out such that those with high relative deprivation and low skills engage in international migration, whereas those with lower relative deprivation and high skills resort to internal migration?

In light of the postulated tradeoff, it is not clear *a priori* how differences in relative deprivation, on the one hand, and human capital of household members, on the other, will jointly influence the allocation of household labor between internal and international migration when investment in human capital is taken as exogenous.

## Logit Findings

The estimated coefficients in the decision model corresponding to each of the two migration labor categories are reported in table 10.3. Standard errors appear in parentheses below each estimated coefficient. The coefficient on variable $k$ for category $d$ corresponds to the effect of variable $k$ on the probability that a person migrated to place $d$ versus the probability that he or she did not participate in any form of labor migration.

**Table 10.2**   Definition of variables (time period 1982)

---

*Decision variable*
d             = 1 if the individual did not participate in labor migration
              = 2 if the individual was an internal migrant
              = 3 if the individual migrated to the United States

*Income variables*
Y             = instrument for total household income without migration
                  by household member $j$ (in US$000) (see appendix)
YSQ           = Y squared
RD            = instrument for relative deprivation associated with Y (in
                  US$000) (see appendix)
RDSQ          = RD squared

*Household characteristics*
SIZE          = household size
LAND          = household landholdings (in hectares)
ADULTS        = number of adult household members in the village
WEALTH        = total value of household's major physical assets (land,
                  animals, and machinery) (in US$000)
MEXNET        = 1 if a close relative (sibling, parent, sibling of parent) of
                  person $j$ was residing outside the village in Mexico at the
                  start of 1982
                0 otherwise
USNET         = 1 if a close relative (sibling, parent, sibling of parent) of
                  person $j$ was residing in the United States at the start of
                  1982
                0 otherwise

*Individual characteristics*
SEX           = 1 if male
                0 if female
AGE           = age
AGESQ         = age squared
ED            = highest level of schooling completed
HEAD          = 1 if the individual is a household head
                0 otherwise
MEXEX         = years of experience as an internal migrant
USEX          = years of experience as a Mexico–US migrant

---

**Table 10.3** Logit results

| | Estimated coefficient | |
| --- | --- | --- |
| Variable | Internal migration | Mexico–US migration |
| INTERCEPT | −10.309** | −16.491** |
| | (2.81) | (3.77) |
| SIZE | 0.089 | 0.063 |
| | (0.13) | (0.16) |
| LAND | 0.017 | −0.067 |
| | (0.06) | (0.06) |
| ADULTS | 0.130 | 0.422** |
| | (0.19) | (0.23) |
| Y | 0.440 | 2.501* |
| | (1.36) | (1.90) |
| YSQ | −0.074 | −0.400* |
| | (0.21) | (0.30) |
| RD | 0.109 | 0.571** |
| | (0.21) | (0.28) |
| RDSQ | 0.004 | −0.039** |
| | (0.01) | (0.02) |
| WEALTH | 0.027 | 0.185 |
| | (0.24) | (0.22) |
| MEXNET | 0.374 | −0.021 |
| | (0.52) | (0.55) |
| USNET | −0.315 | 1.993** |
| | (0.56) | (0.79) |
| SEX | 0.186 | 0.602* |
| | (0.36) | (0.43) |
| AGE | 0.348** | 0.552** |
| | (0.11) | (0.14) |
| AGESQ | −0.006** | −0.009** |
| | (0.002) | (0.002) |
| ED | 0.266** | −0.129* |
| | (0.06) | (0.09) |
| HEAD | 0.067 | −3.129** |
| | (0.82) | (1.09) |
| MEXEX | 0.467** | 0.144* |
| | (0.08) | (0.11) |
| USEX | 0.141* | 0.487** |
| | (0.10) | (0.09) |

Log likelihood = −194.22; standard errors appear in parentheses.
*Significance at below the 0.10 level.
**Significance at below the 0.05 level.

When interpreting these results, note that an insignificant coefficient with respect to a specific migration category does not imply that the corresponding variable does not affect the probability that an individual will be observed in that category. By equation (10.7), each probability depends on *all* the coefficients in the table. A variable that has a significant effect on one migration probability has at least an indirect effect on the other probabilities, since by construction the probabilities of the three destination choices must sum to unity.

In section 1 we argued that absolute income may have a positive effect on migration from poor village households when migration is costly, credit markets are imperfect, and households therefore must self-finance migration costs. Our empirical findings confirm this expectation. The logit estimation yields a positive coefficient on absolute income and a negative coefficient on absolute income squared for Mexico–United States migration, both significant at below the 0.10 level. US migration costs for the households in our sample include the costs of hiring *coyotes*, or smugglers, to assist with a risky illegal border crossing. These costs averaged US$350 per migrant in 1982, representing a large "sunk cost" relative to average village incomes. By comparison, internal migration entails low costs and little risk. The negative coefficient on income squared indicates that the probability of Mexico–United States migration declines at the highest income levels.

When all other variables in table 10.3 and also the effect of absolute income on international migration are controlled for, income does not have a significant *direct* effect on internal migration. It does, however, have a negative indirect effect on internal migration through its positive effect on international migration.

Like absolute income, relative deprivation (RD in table 10.3) has a significant impact on migration to US destinations but does not have a significant (direct) effect on internal migration. With everything else in the logit equation held constant, relatively deprived households are more likely to participate in Mexico–United States migration than are less relatively deprived households. The coefficient on RD of 0.57 for Mexico–United States migration is significant at below the 0.05 level, indicating an important role for relative income motives in Mexico–United States migration.

The influence of relative deprivation on international migration is not the same at all points in the village income spectrum. Relative income motives for Mexico–United States migration are lower in the most relatively deprived households. The negative coefficient on the square of relative deprivation (RDSQ) is significant at the 0.05 level for Mexico–United States migration. This result is consistent with the hypothesis, put forward in section 1, that subsistence concerns tend to dampen relative income considerations in the poorest village households.[7]

The findings suggest that the income neutrality result of relative deprivation theory, posited in the last subsection of section 1 above, may hold in the case of internal migration for the households in this sample. If the perceived risk of a reference group substitution through internal migration is high, then internal migration ceases to be an effective means for achieving relative deprivation gains for households in the village. If the household perceives that the cost of reducing the migrant's sense of relative deprivation in the city is high, then internal migration may also cease to be viewed as an effective device for village households to achieve absolute income gains, even if there is a positive urban–rural income differential. This interesting possibility is ruled out by conventional absolute income models of migration.

The remaining variables in the decision model are included for their hypothesized influence on the returns to migration versus nonmigration activities and on the motivation of household members to contribute all or part of their earnings to their respective households. We would expect migrating household members to be those whose attributes are most likely to be associated with high differentials in returns to the household from migration versus nonmigration activities. In addition, certain household characteristics are likely to have an important effect on both the probability of migration and the choice of migrant destination.

The logit analysis reveals striking differences between migrants and nonmigrants as well as between the two groups of migrants. On average, migrants tend to be male, 20–30 years of age, not heads of households, and to possess past migration experience. However, two of these variables affect the migrant categories in very different ways. Although males are significantly more likely than females to participate in Mexico–United States migration, sex plays an insignificant role in explaining internal migration. Household heads, in contrast, are very unlikely to engage in international migration but are no less likely to be internal migrants than are those who are not heads of households. The latter result no doubt reflects differences in opportunity costs between internal and international migration for household heads. For heads of households, administrative responsibilities on the family farm and other obligations in the village generally preclude migration to the United States, which typically entails a large commitment of both time and capital. Household members' schooling (ED) has a significant positive effect on the probability of internal migration but is negatively related to Mexico–United States migration. Not surprisingly, better educated villagers are much more likely to migrate to destinations in Mexico, where returns to schooling are likely to be high, than to low-skill undocumented immigrant labor markets in the United States.

Household members' experience as migrants in the United States and their experience as migrants in Mexico have a positive association with the probability of migration to *both* destinations. However, the estimated coefficient on US migration experience in the US migration equation (0.487, significant at below the 0.05 level) is more than three times the coefficient on US experience in the Mexico migration equation (0.141, significant at the 0.10 level). Similarly, although experience as an internal migrant is positively related to both types of migration, it has a larger and more significant effect on internal migration than on international migration. On the one hand, these findings suggest that migration experience has a general positive effect on migration propensities and that some migration work experience may be transferable across migrant destinations. On the other hand, they indicate that destination-specific migration experience plays a powerful role in shaping migration decisions. These general and destination-specific migration experience effects are analogous to the differential effects of general training and firm-specific training in employment and earnings studies.

Several other variables in table 10.3 stand out as significantly influencing migration decisions. Mexico–United States migrants tend to originate from households with other adult members in the village (ADULTS in the table) who can assume the household farm duties of those who migrate. In addition, households with kinship networks in place in the United States (USNET) are significantly more likely to send additional members to the United States. The particularly large and significant coefficient on USNET for the Mexico–United States migration category reflects the important role that kinship contacts play in international migration where risks are highest, labor market information is most costly and scarce, and the penalty for failure (that is, lost time and capital) is most severe. Internal migration networks (MEXNET), in contrast, do not significantly affect internal migration. This reflects the relative ease with which individuals in this sample can migrate and re-migrate internally (that is, take corrective action in case of a failure).

### 3  Conclusions

The findings from Mexico reported in this chapter provide evidence that, if absolute income is controlled for, relatively deprived households are more likely to engage in international migration than are households more favorably situated in their village's income distribution. In contrast, the findings suggest an interesting "income neutrality" result, unique to relative deprivation theory, in the case of internal migration. The perceived risk of a reference group substitution through internal migration is likely to be high. In this case, rural-to-urban migration may cease to be an effective vehicle for achieving either relative or absolute income gains for village households. This possibility is ruled out by conventional absolute income models of migration. The empirical finding that both relative deprivation and absolute income are significant in explaining international migration but have no significant (direct) effects on internal migration from the households in our sample is consistent with this "income neutrality" hypothesis. The results for Mexico–United States migration support the relative deprivation hypothesis in the case where a reference group substitution is less likely.

Choice of migrant destination is also influenced by the differential returns to human capital in internal and foreign labor markets. Our econometric results suggest that, independent of relative deprivation considerations, households wisely pair their members with the labor markets in which the returns to their human capital are likely to be greatest.

This analysis leads to several new policy implications. Contrary to the assumption that all types of migration can be attributed to the same explanatory variables, our results suggest that (at least in the context studied) a specific type of migration constitutes a response to a specific configuration of variables. Thus a distribution-neutral development policy that shifts a village income distribution to the right would reduce the incentive to engage in internal migration for all but the richest households (that is, in the present case, by relieving credit constraints on international migration). Conversely a distribution-biased policy leading to a more equal income distribution (for example, provision of stronger support for the poorest households) could tip a migration balance from international migration to internal migration.

The possibility that different variables may be the cause of different types of migration could lead to the paradoxical result that interference – say, to stem migration – will result in its rise. Raising the incomes of highly relatively deprived households in a poor village may reduce these households' relative deprivation incentive to engage in international migration but, in the presence of imperfect credit markets, may also unleash their hitherto constrained propensity to engage in such migration.

Finally, *if* the disutility from relative deprivation and the migration response to it are an increasing function of own (absolute) income, a "relative deprivation paradox of migration" may operate: economic development that does not redress intra-village income inequalities (that is, a distribution-neutral rise in income) will be associated with *more* international migration.

## Appendix

Estimation of equation (10.7) in the text requires measures, for each household member $j$, of the predicted household income $Y_0^j$ in the absence of migration by the household member and of the level $RD_0^j$ of relative deprivation associated with this predicted income. In this appendix we outline the method used to obtain, first, an instrument $\hat{Y}_0^j$ for household income in the absence of migration by person $j$ and, second, an instrument $\widehat{RD}_0^j$ for relative deprivation associated with this income.

### Household Income without Migration by Person j

A household's predicted income $\hat{Y}_0^j$ in the absence of migration by household member $j$ is the sum of predicted income $\hat{Y}^{-j}$ from other sources and the expected contribution $\hat{W}_0^j$ by the household member as a nonmigrant. Estimates of household income (from sources other than person $j$) were obtained by regressing observed 1982 income from sources other than person $j$ on household assets at the start of 1982. The estimated equation is

$$\hat{Y}^{-j} = 1376.8 + 0.29A + 821.92\text{TED} - 96.29\text{NADS}$$
$$(4.94) \quad (5.59) \quad\quad (8.87) \quad\quad\quad (-1.98)$$

$$+ 558.08\text{USNET} - 397.96\text{MEXNET} \tag{10.A1}$$
$$(2.81) \quad\quad\quad (-1.85)$$

$$R^2 = 0.28 \quad\quad N = 423$$

where $A$ is the value of households' primary physical capital assets (land and animals) in thousands of US dollars; NADS and TED are human capital assets (the number of adults in the household and the number of household members with post-primary schooling respectively); and MEXMIG and USMIG denote migration capital (the number of household members who participated in internal migration and in Mexico–United States migration respectively in the year before 1982).

Numbers in parentheses are *t*-statistics. Migration capital is included in equation (10.A1) for its impact on contributions to household income by family members other than member *j*.

Household member *j*'s predicted contribution to household income as a nonmigrant was estimated by regressing observed 1982 contributions by nonmigrants on a set of personal and household variables likely to influence earnings in the village as well as the willingness of nonmigrants to share these earnings with the household. Contributions by nonmigrants were observed only for individuals who did not migrate during the year. An inverse Mills ratio (LAMBDA) was included in the equation for contributions by nonmigrants to adjust for potential sample selection bias (Heckman, 1979; Greene, 1981). It was obtained from a reduced-form probit for nonmigration by using the explanatory variables in equation (10.A1) and the household and individual characteristics variables in table 10.1. The estimated equation for contributions by nonmigrants is

$$\hat{W}_0^j = -0.63 + 1.87\text{SEX} + 0.11\text{AGE} - 0.001\text{AGESQ} + 2.08\text{HEAD}$$
$$\quad\ (0.90)\quad\ (6.29)\qquad (2.29)\qquad\quad (-2.39)\qquad\qquad (3.86)$$

$$+ 0.21\text{MEXEX} + 0.22\text{USEX} - 1.30\text{LAMBDA}$$
$$\quad\ (1.87)\qquad\qquad (3.47)\qquad\ (-2.19) \qquad\qquad\qquad (10.\text{A2})$$

$$R^2 = 0.44 \qquad N = 273$$

where the numbers in parentheses are *t*-statistics. The variables as they appear in equation (10.A2), with the exception of LAMBDA, are defined in table 10.2. The instrument for household income in the absence of migration is given by $\hat{Y}_0^j = \hat{Y}^{-j} + \hat{W}_0^j$.

## Relative Deprivation without Migration by Person j

Estimation of a household's relative deprivation in the absence of migration by person *j* ($\text{RD}_0^j$) is complicated by the fact that relative deprivation is a function not only of the income of person *j*'s household but also of the incomes of all other households in person *j*'s village (equation (10.3)). We constructed an instrument for $\text{RD}_0^j$ by first estimating the income $\hat{Y}$ of each household in the village sample and then using this estimated income distribution to estimate the level of a household's relative deprivation associated with nonmigration by person *j*.

Estimates of total household income $\hat{Y}$ were obtained by regressing observed 1982 total household income on household holdings of income-producing assets at the start of the year and then using the estimated equation to predict 1982 income for each household represented in the sample. The estimated income equation is

$$\text{LN}(\hat{Y}) = 7.17 + 0.13A + 0.26\text{TED} - 0.07\text{NADS}$$
$$\qquad\quad (27.2)\ \ (2.19)\qquad (2.53)\qquad (-1.19)$$

$$+ 0.59\text{USMIG} - 0.08\text{MEXMIG} \qquad (10.\text{A}3)$$
$$(2.26) \qquad\qquad (-0.32)$$

$$R^2 = 0.32 \qquad N = 61$$

Variables are as defined for equation (10.A1). Numbers in parentheses are *t*-statistics.

Using the discrete form of equation (10.3), we can easily calculate households' predicted relative deprivation without migration by person $j$ from $\hat{Y}_0^j$ and the predicted total incomes $\hat{Y}$ of all other households in the corresponding village:

$$\widehat{\text{RD}}_0^j = \sum_{\hat{Y}_0^j}^{\hat{Y}^h} [1 - F(x)] \Delta x \qquad (10.\text{A}4)$$

where $\hat{Y}^h$ is the highest predicted total household income in the village and, for a given income $x_i$, $\Delta x_i = x_{i+1} - x_i$.

## Notes

Co-authored with J. Edward Taylor. This is a thoroughly revised version of Discussion Paper 45, Harvard University Migration and Development Program. Two anonymous referees provided very helpful comments and suggestions. The support of the Alfred P. Sloan Foundation; the Commission for the Study of International Migration and Cooperative Economic Development; the Welfare and Human Resources Division, Population and Human Resources Department, the World Bank; and the David Horowitz Institute for the Research of Developing Countries is acknowledged with gratitude.

1   Stark and Levhari (1982) suggest theoretical conditions under which migration can represent a risk-*reducing* strategy for rural households in LDCs. In this case, migration can be an optimal strategy even if expected income as a result of migration is not greater than expected rural income. For additional analysis, see Katz and Stark (1986); for empirical support, see Lucas and Stark (1985) and Rosenzweig and Stark (1989).

2   Borrowing against future earnings expected to arise from present investment in human capital is difficult even in developed countries, although the difficulty is eased somewhat by the availability of physical (nonhuman capital) assets that act as collateral. Such perfection of credit markets, limited as it is, does not typically apply to the poor in LDCs.

3   Note that there need not be a corresponding relation between absence of remittances and reference group substitution. For example, seasonal migrants who return home repeatedly may not need recourse to remittances to have their

households of origin partake in the income earned at the destination of migration. Conversely, migrants who do remit may do so even though their village of origin does not constitute (part of) their reference group, as is the case when remittance flows are part of mutually beneficial risk-sharing implicit contractual arrangements. See Stark and Lucas (1988).

4   Income contributions from household farm work were imputed on the basis of the number of days worked on the household farm, valued at the prevailing agricultural wage in the village (this wage was substantially below the minimum agricultural wage in Mexico). Contributions by the owner (or *de facto* owner in the case of *ejidos* or reform sector lands) of the household farm also include farm profits. These were calculated as the difference between the gross value of farm output, evaluated at the average farm-gate sales price in the case of subsistence farming, and all direct costs plus invisible costs. Direct costs include the cost of all material inputs, hired physical capital inputs (mechanical services, animal services, land), and hired labor inputs. Invisible costs include the cost of imputed wages of unpaid family labor. Contributions also include rental income (land rents and payments received for capital services) and income from livestock (the net additions to animal stocks as well as sales of animals and animal products) received by owners of these capital goods from other households. Income contributions by household members working in handicrafts, wood gathering, fishing, and other household farm activities were calculated in a manner analogous to contributions from farming work. Data on household members who were outside the village at the time of the survey were provided by the remaining household members. This approach could be used because the focus of the survey was on the household and its returns from different labor allocations. Data were not needed on the earnings of household members who migrated or on other details concerning the absent migrants' work away from home.

5   While the use of a household decision framework obviously overlooks any autonomy of individuals in their labor allocations, we believe that to treat each migration decision as independent of a household decision problem would entail far more severe limiting assumptions than does simplifying the analysis to a household decision problem. As the empirical results presented later in this section demonstrate, socio-economic characteristics of households play a significant role in addition to characteristics of individual household members in explaining migration behavior. Moreover, economic ties between migrants and their households in the village tend to be very strong here, as in other samples of rural households in LDCs. An illustration of economic ties between migrant and household is given by remittances. For all households in the present sample, migrant remittances account for an average 36.5 percent of total household income; every household that participated in labor migration received remittances; and nearly 90 percent of all migrants remitted.

6   The correlation between absolute income and relative deprivation for the sample is $-0.41$. This low correlation indicates sharp differences between the income distributions of the two villages.

7   Note that, even if subsistence concerns in poor households are captured by absolute income, we would nevertheless expect RD to lose its positive effect on migration probabilities in these households if relative income objectives are unimportant next to survival objectives. In the present sample, a marginal increase in RD ceases to have a positive effect on migration probabilities in the 14 percent of the sample that constituted the most relatively deprived households.

# References

David, P. A. (1974) "Fortune, Risk, and the Microeconomics of Migration." In P. A. David and M. W. Reder (eds), *Nations and Households in Economic Growth*. New York: Academic Press.

Greene, W. H. (1981) "Sample Selection Bias as a Specification Error: Comment." *Econometrica* 49 (3): 795–8.

Heckman, J. J. (1979) "Sample Selection Bias as a Specification Error." *Econometrica* 47 (1): 153–62.

Katz, E. and Stark, O. (1986) "Labor Migration and Risk Aversion in LDCs." *Journal of Labor Economics* 4 (1): 134–49 (reprinted as ch. 5 in this volume).

Lucas, R. E. B. and Stark, O. (1985) "Motivations to Remit: Evidence from Botswana." *Journal of Political Economy* 93 (5): 901–18 (reprinted as ch. 16 in this volume).

Rosenzweig, M. R. and Stark, O. (1989) "Consumption Smoothing, Migration, and Marriage: Evidence from Rural India." *Journal of Political Economy* 97 (4): 905–26 (reprinted as ch. 6 in this volume).

Stark, O. (1984) "Rural-to-Urban Migration in LDCs: A Relative Deprivation Approach." *Economic Development and Cultural Change* 32 (3): 475–86 (reprinted as ch. 7 in this volume).

—— and Levhari, D. (1982) "On Migration and Risk in LDCs." *Economic Development and Cultural Change* 31 (1): 191–6 (reprinted as ch. 4 in this volume).

—— and Lucas, R. E. B. (1988) "Migration, Remittances, and the Family." *Economic Development and Cultural Change* 36 (3): 465–81 (reprinted as ch. 15 in this volume).

—— and Taylor, J. E. (1989) "Relative Deprivation and International Migration." *Demography* 26 (1): 1–14 (reprinted as ch. 9 in this volume).

—— and Yitzhaki, S. (1988) "Labor Migration as a Response to Relative Deprivation." *Journal of Population Economics* 1 (1): 57–70 (reprinted as ch. 8 in this volume).

Taylor, J. E. (1986) "Differential Migration, Networks, Information and Risk." In O. Stark (ed.), *Migration, Human Capital and Development*. Greenwich, CT: JAI Press: 147–71.

—— (1987) "Undocumented Mexico–U.S. Migration and the Returns to House-holds in Rural Mexico." *American Journal of Agricultural Economics* 69: 626–38.

Todaro, M. P. (1969) "A Model of Labor Migration and Urban Unemployment in Less Developed Countries." *American Economic Review* 59 (1): 138–48.

—— (1980) "International Migration in Developing Countries: A Survey." In R. A. Easterlin (ed.), *Population and Economic Change in Developing Countries*. Chicago, IL: University of Chicago Press for National Bureau of Economic Research.

Yap, L. (1977) "The Attraction of Cities: A Review of the Migration Literature." *Journal of Development Economics* 4: 239–64.

# Part IV

## Labor Migration under Alternative Informational Regimes

# 11

## International Labor Migration under Alternative Informational Regimes: A Diagrammatic Analysis

### 1 Introduction

The explanatory role of informational asymmetry in labor market phenomena appears to have attracted a great deal of attention. Some researchers have even suggested that informational asymmetry is the major feature of employment arrangements and the nature of worker–firm relations (Hall and Lazear, 1984). Most research in this area and in particular work on implicit labor contracts has tended to place more of the relevant information in the hands of employers. Relatively little research has come to grips with bilateral limitations on information and hardly any attention at all has been paid to situations in which *workers* possess more information than employers.

At the same time work on international labor migration has continued to attribute the movement of labor to the persistence of international wage differentials with little reference to informational problems. (See, for example, various papers in the May 1983 special issue of the *Journal of International Economics* on "International Factor Mobility: A Symposium.") Yet information about labor skills and labor remuneration does not freely and costlessly cross international boundaries. Although it would have been natural to study the connection between international migration and informational asymmetry, realizing that the movement of workers across labor markets is bound to be associated with information asymmetries, little such research has been pursued. In a simple fashion, we set out in this chapter to model the interaction between international labor migration and asymmetric information when workers possess, at least for a while, more information than some of their employers.

The model concedes that economic agents come to markets with diverse information that is not publicly available (Radner, 1982). However, it assumes that the agents whose information is superior in some crucial respect may be the workers whereas, initially at least, the relatively ignorant agents are certain employers. Conventional wisdom could have led us to expect that, just as informed employers exploit superior information to *their* advantage by way of reducing wages (for example, below the value of marginal product) or level of employment, so do workers in a context such as ours exploit the relative ignorance of some employers to obtain higher wages than a symmetric information regime will sustain (and higher, too, than the value of their marginal product). One of the most surprising results of our study is that in many circumstances things do not turn out quite that way; in comparison with a symmetric information regime, the presence of informational asymmetry eliminates rather than furthers international migration by certain skill categories of workers. Another surprising result is that although it may seem reasonable to expect that, if workers possess more information than their employers, they will be able to turn this informational asymmetry to their own advantage, our study does not necessarily support this view. Frequently, the workers derive benefits from informational asymmetry regarding their skills – not from employers, but from each other. As we shall see below, this is a natural result of the "rational expectations" assumption that employers pay fair wages on average.

The true state of nature in our model is a worker's own skill level which is accurately observed by a worker himself but not by all potential employers. A worker who has an incentive not to announce his true skill level will tend deliberately to choose a market or an employer with whom the state of ignorance can be transformed into a source of advantage. The worker thus wishes to discriminate between distinguishable markets (in our study, countries) in a somewhat similar fashion to a monopolist who exercises price discrimination. For this worker, inter-market wage differentials are *contingent upon* asymmetric information. Migration from one labor market to another may thus be pursued in order to realize the full value of differential information. As we shall find out below, what could work *against* such a plan is the simultaneous action by other workers whose skills differ from each other.

We maintain that it is reasonable to assume that, in the general course of events, accurate information – either adverse or favorable – increases with the length of time over which observations are made. This seems to hold especially with respect to people and their productivity. Information about the true productivity of a worker will thus be relatively plentiful to observers – employers – in the country and labor market in which the worker has lived and worked most of his or her life and, at least initially, limited to nonobserving employers in another country.

Recent exploratory work has already demonstrated that information asymmetry is likely to be of considerable importance in the analysis of patterns of international labor migration (see Kwok and Leland, 1982; Katz and Stark, 1984, 1986; Stark, 1984). In this chapter we consider in some depth the fuller implications of asymmetric information, as introduced above, for the patterns of international migration of labor.

The plan of the rest of this chapter is as follows. In section 2 we present our basic model and derive the likely migratory patterns under public or symmetric (full) information. In section 3 we consider the effect of asymmetric information on migratory patterns within the context of our basic model. In section 4 we examine the impact of allowing employers, after a while, to identify individual workers' true productivities. In section 5 we set out our main conclusions and outline some directions along which future research in this area may prove fruitful.

## 2 The Basic Model Under Full Information

Throughout this chapter use is made of a simple diagram (initially developed by Katz and Stark (1984)). To derive this diagram, two countries are considered: a rich country R and a poor country P. In a given occupation the net wages for a worker with skill level $\theta$ are $W_R(\theta)$ and $W_P(\theta)$ in the rich and poor country respectively.[1] To reflect the fact that R is rich and P is poor, it is assumed that $W_R(\theta) > W_P(\theta)$ for all $\theta$.[2]

In addition, given that P workers are likely to have a preference for P life-style because of cultural factors, family relationships, etc., it is assumed that P workers apply a discount factor to R wages when comparing them with P wages. Thus, when making the migration decision, they compare $kW_R(\theta)$ with $W_P(\theta)$ where $k < 1$. A P worker migrates from P to R if

$$kW_R(\theta) > W_P(\theta) \tag{11.1}$$

Assume further that the $W_R(\theta)$ and $W_P(\theta)$ functions are linear[3] in $\theta$ so that

$$W_R(\theta) = r_0 + r\theta \qquad r_0 > 0, r > 0 \tag{11.2}$$

$$W_P(\theta) = p_0 + p\theta \qquad p_0 > 0, p > 0 \tag{11.3}$$

and, reflecting the relative richness of R, $(r_0 - p_0) + (r - p)\theta > 0$ for all $\theta$. Also, without loss of generality, let $\theta$ be defined upon the closed interval $[0, 1]$ and let the distribution of P workers on $\theta$ be $F_P(\theta)$; we thus have the skill levels distributed continuously on $[0, 1]$.

Given the above assumptions and allowing the skill level of each worker to be identifiable without cost in both P and R, that is, skill information is fully public and symmetric, we obtain the following outcomes.

In figure 11.1(a) it is clear that workers of all skill levels in the occupation will migrate from P to R. This is because the discounted rich country's wages $kW_R(\theta)$ are higher than $W_P(\theta)$ for all $\theta$. In the case described in figure 11.1(b) it is clear that workers in the skill interval $[0, \theta^*]$ will migrate and that higher-skill workers will remain in P. In figure 11.1(c) the opposite occurs and workers in the $[\theta^*, 1]$ skill range migrate, whereas lower-skill workers do not. Finally, figure 11.1(d) depicts the case wherein the discount factor applied by P workers to R wages is sufficiently large to dissuade any P workers from migrating.

## 3 The Basic Model Under Asymmetric Information[4]

Let us now assume that the skill of each potential migrant is known in P, where he has been observed for some time, but is unknown in R. Each worker knows his or her $\theta$, but the employers at R cannot observe this $\theta$. Also, let us exclude the possibility that migrants invest in devices which might identify their skill level to R employers.

Faced with a group of workers where the individual productivity of each worker is unknown to him, the wage offered by the employer will be the same for all such workers and will be related to the average product of all members of the group. Let us assume that the actual individual wage offered is *equal* to the average product of the group[5] and that wage offers are known to all workers.

It transpires that the nature of our results on the effects of asymmetric information on migration patterns depends crucially on the sign of $kW_R(0) - W_P(0)$. We therefore divide our treatment of asymmetric information into two parts: in the first part we assume that $kW_R(0) > W_P(0)$ and in the second part we assume that $kW_R(0) \leq W_P(0)$.

Assuming that $kW_R(0) - W_P(0) > 0$ implies that P workers of skill level 0 will migrate regardless of whether information is symmetric or asymmetric. To see this, note that if we define the average R wage of a group of P workers whose skill levels lie in the interval $[0, \theta^*]$ as $\overline{W}_R(\theta^*)$, then

$$\overline{W}_R(\theta^*)|_{\theta^*=0} = W_R(\theta)|_{\theta=0} \qquad (11.4)$$

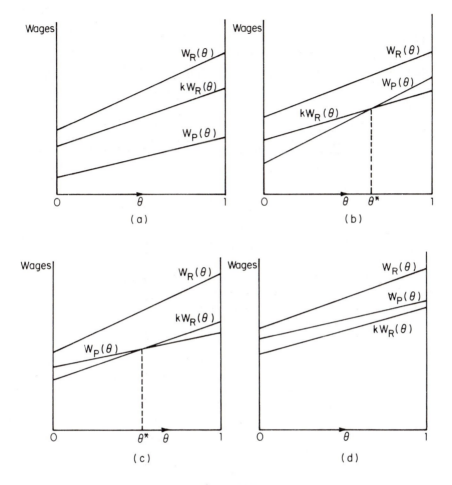

**Figure 11.1**

The actual equation for $W_R(\theta^*)$ is given by

$$\overline{W}_R(\theta^*) = \int_0^{\theta^*} W_R(\theta)F_P(\theta) \, d\theta \bigg/ \int_0^{\theta^*} F_P(\theta) \, d\theta \qquad (11.5)$$

so that if, for example, we assume that P workers are uniformly distributed along [0, 1] we know, by using (11.2), that

$$\overline{W}_R(\theta^*) = r_0 + \frac{r}{2} \theta^* \qquad (11.6)$$

In any event, it is clear from (11.4) and (11.5) that the $\overline{W}_R(\theta^*)$ curve will be below the $W_R(\theta)$ curve everywhere except at $\theta = 0$ where the two curves will coincide, and thus the condition $kW_R(\theta) - W_P(\theta) > 0$ and $k\overline{W}_R(\theta^*) - W_P(\theta) > 0$ is identical at $\theta^* = \theta = 0$ so that this sufficient condition for workers of skill level 0 to migrate is the same, regardless of the information scenario (symmetric with $kW_R(\theta)$, or asymmetric with $k\overline{W}_R(\theta^*)$).

The three possible categories of outcomes of asymmetric information for the assumption that $kW_R(0) - W_P(0) > 0$ are illustrated in figure 11.2.

In figure 11.2(a) the $kW_R(\theta)$ curve lies everywhere above the $W_P(\theta)$ curve. Hence in the presence of symmetric information all skill levels would migrate from P to R. In the presence of asymmetric information, however, the only workers who migrate are in the $[0, \theta_1]$ interval. Hence the fact of asymmetric information has reduced the amount of migration and further has reduced the skill level of those who migrate, that is, it has reduced migration from the top, saving P its most skilled workers, those in the $[\theta_1, 1]$ interval.

In figure 11.2(b) the existence of symmetric information would have led workers in the $[0, \theta_1]$ range to migrate. The presence of asymmetric information, however, is once again seen to reduce both the quantity and the quality of migrants since it eliminates the migration of $[\theta_2, \theta_1]$ skill levels.

Finally, in figure 11.2(c) the migration outcome is unaffected by the informational scenario; in this case, workers of all skill levels would migrate under either symmetric or asymmetric information since both $kW_R(\theta)$ and $k\overline{W}_R(\theta^*)$ lie everywhere above $W_P(\theta)$.

In the case where $kW_R(0) > W_P(0)$, therefore, asymmetric information will tend to reduce both the quality and quantity of migrants except where it has no effect at all.

Let us now turn to the case where $kW_R(0) \leq W_P(0)$. As we shall see shortly, this case is more difficult to handle than the previous one, and outcomes tend to be more dramatic. The point is illustrated in figure 11.3.

In this case, the use of the $k\overline{W}_R(\theta^*)$ curve is incorrect. This is because migration will now start from $\theta = 1$ and not $\theta = 0$. Thus we have drawn the $k\hat{W}_R(\theta^*)$ curve which represents the (discounted) average wage paid to workers when the group of workers contains the $[\theta^*, 1]$ skill interval, that is, it is the *average wage taken from the top*.

The equation for the $\hat{W}_R(\theta^*)$ curve is given by

$$\hat{W}_R(\theta^*) = \int_{\theta^*}^{1} W_R(\theta)F_P(\theta)\,d\theta \bigg/ \int_{\theta^*}^{1} F_P(\theta)\,d\theta \qquad (11.7)$$

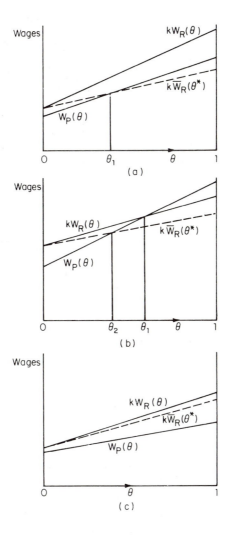

**Figure 11.2**

so that if, for example, we assume that P workers are uniformly distributed along [0, 1] we see by using (11.2) that[6]

$$\hat{W}_R(\theta^*) = r_0 + r\,\frac{1 + \theta^*}{2} \tag{11.8}$$

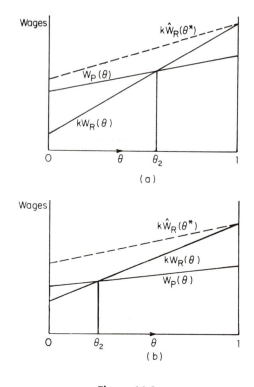

**Figure 11.3**

To obtain results using the $k\hat{W}_R(\theta^*)$ curve consider initially figure 11.3(a): the lowest point on the $k\hat{W}_R(\theta^*)$ curve (and this is the discounted wage each migrant would obtain if everyone migrated) is below the top point of the $W_P(\theta)$ curve, that is, $k\hat{W}_R(0) < W_P(1)$. Hence top-skilled workers will not migrate. This, in turn, implies that the $k\hat{W}_R(\theta^*)$ should be lower, since it is now defined on some interval $[\theta^*, \theta^{**}]$ where $\theta^{**} < 1$. This process goes on and it ends at the equilibrium point where no one migrates. The proof of this result is relegated to the appendix. Notice that the equilibrium concept we have in mind here is along the lines of a Stackelberg equilibrium rather than a Nash equilibrium. A good way of thinking about the equilibrium is to conceptualize it as a "reactive equilibrium." We say that a "reactive equilibrium" exists when agents take into account the responses of others while considering new actions. Essentially, the high-skill worker recognizes the clear incentive of lower-skill workers to react to his migration and hence is deterred from choosing migration (consult Miyazaki, 1977; Wilson, 1977; Riley, 1979).

Turning now to figure 11.3(b), it is clear that in the presence of symmetric information migration will be in the $[\theta_2, 1]$ skill range. To see what happens in the absence of symmetric information, note that at its lowest point, that is, at $\theta = 0$, $k\hat{W}_R(\theta^*)$ exceeds $W_P(1)$. Hence, in this case, the top-skilled migrants will still find it beneficial to migrate, and equilibrium will be established when all skill levels migrate.[7]

The above discussion has shown that the effect of asymmetric information on migration patterns is asymmetric. If, in the absence of informational asymmetry, low-skilled workers find it beneficial to migrate (that is, if $kW_R(0) - W_P(0) > 0$) then asymmetric information will tend to reduce both the quality and the quantity of migrants and may allow for an interior outcome wherein some, but not all, potential migrants actually migrate. If, however, low-skilled workers do not find it beneficial to migrate in the absence of information asymmetry (that is, if $kW_R(0) - W_P(0) < 0$), then information asymmetry will cause either all or none of the workers in the occupation concerned to migrate. Interior outcomes are thus ruled out.

## 4  Reinstating Symmetric Information by Discovery

In this section we consider the effect on the migration pattern of the possibility that, after spending some time in R, migrants' true skill levels will be discovered through observation by R employers. Early periods of employment thus act as a screening device.

To do this we need to define a new curve which will describe the relation between skill level and anticipated (discounted) wages in R. The way in which this curve is derived is as follows.

In figure 11.4 let $kW_R(\theta)$ and $k\overline{W}_R(\theta^*)$ be defined as above. Depending on the length of time that a person can work without his or her skill being discovered and on the length of his or her working life once this discovery has been made, it is possible to draw a curve such as $kW_R^D(\tilde{\theta})$ which tells us what the lifetime location discounted and time discounted income of a worker with skill level $\tilde{\theta}$ will be *when workers of skill $\tilde{\theta}$ are the highest level of skill actually migrating*.

The equation of $W_R^D(\tilde{\theta})$ will be given by

$$W_R^D(\tilde{\theta}) = \frac{\alpha\overline{W}_R(\tilde{\theta}) + \beta W_R(\tilde{\theta})}{\alpha + \beta} \tag{11.9}$$

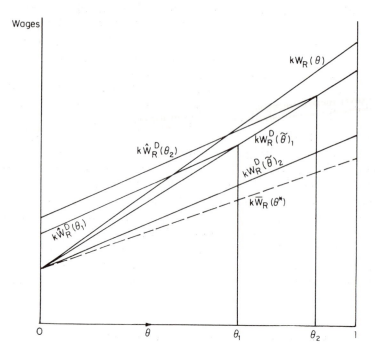

**Figure 11.4**

where $\alpha$ and $\beta$ are the weights attached to the pre-discovery and post-discovery time periods respectively. Hence, if we assume that P workers are uniformly distributed on [0, 1] and maintain our linearity assumption, we know from (11.2) and (11.6) that

$$W_R^D(\tilde{\theta}) = r_0 + \frac{r(\alpha + 2\beta)}{2(\alpha + \beta)}\,\tilde{\theta} \qquad (11.10)$$

Thus $kW_R^D(\tilde{\theta})_1$ and $kW_R^D(\tilde{\theta})_2$ are such curves, where $kW_R^D(\tilde{\theta})_2$ represents a situation wherein discovery is relatively slow so that the curve is near the $k\overline{W}_R(\theta^*)$ curve and $kW_R^D(\tilde{\theta})_1$ represents a situation wherein discovery is relatively fast (or working life after discovery is relatively long) so that the curve is nearer the $kW_R(\theta)$ curve which reflects true skill levels.

However, the story is rather more complex than a $kW_R^D(\tilde{\theta})$ curve appears to imply. This is because, if, for example, the top skill level migrating is $\theta_1$, only *that* skill level will be on $kW_R^D(\tilde{\theta})_1$. All other migrating workers will be on a curve reflecting a weighted average of $k\overline{W}_R(\theta_1)$ and their own specific value of $kW_R(\theta)$.

Thus, if $kW_R^D(\tilde{\theta})_1$ in figure 11.4 is the relevant curve and the top migrating skill level is $\theta_1$, the relevant benefits curve for migrants is $k\hat{W}_R^D(\theta_1)$, whereas if the top migrating skill level is $\theta_2$ the relevant benefits curve for migrants is $k\hat{W}_R^D(\theta)_2$. Clearly, the complexity of the analysis is due to the fact that to each point on the $kW_R^D(\tilde{\theta})_1$ curve there corresponds a different $k\hat{W}_R^D(\theta)$ curve.

The general equation of $\hat{W}_R^D(\theta)$ will be given by

$$\hat{W}_R^D(\theta) = \frac{\alpha\overline{W}_R(\tilde{\theta}) + \beta W_R(\theta)}{\alpha + \beta} \tag{11.11}$$

where $\alpha$ and $\beta$ are as defined above and $\tilde{\theta}$ is the highest skill level migrating. Hence if P workers are uniformly distributed on $[0, 1]$, using (11.2) and (11.6) yields

$$\hat{W}_R^D(\theta) = r_0 + \frac{r(\alpha + 2\beta)}{2(\alpha + \beta)}\theta + \frac{\alpha r}{2(\alpha + \beta)}(\tilde{\theta} - \theta) \tag{11.12}$$

To see the outcome of all this for the migration pattern, in figure 11.5 we combine the curves derived in figure 11.4 with the $W_P(\theta)$ curve.

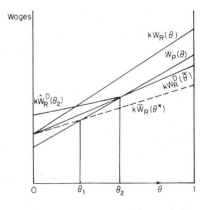

**Figure 11.5**

Clearly, with symmetric information, since $kW_R(\theta) > W_P(\theta)$ for all $\theta$, the situation depicted in figure 11.5 would lead to all skill levels migrating. Once asymmetric information is introduced, however, it is clear that $k\overline{W}_R(\theta^*) > W_P(\theta)$ only within the range $[0, \theta_1]$, so that only workers in this interval of skill levels migrate. Then, upon introducing the $kW_R^D(\tilde{\theta})$ curve, reflecting eventual discovery of the true skills of workers, it is clear that the migrants will now be in the $[0, \theta_2]$ range.

It is interesting to note that the actual benefits curve for workers in the $[0, \theta_2]$ range, once $\theta_2$ has been established as the top skill level migrating, is $k\hat{W}_R^D(\theta_2)$. Since $k\hat{W}_R^D(\theta_2) > k\overline{W}_R(\theta^*)$ for the range $[0, \theta_2]$, this suggests that the fact of eventual discovery not only increases the quantity and quality of migration but also *raises the benefits to the lowest-skill workers*. This would at first sight appear counter-intuitive since one would have thought that eventual discovery would lower the benefits to those that have most to hide – the workers with very low skill levels. This does not happen in our case since the workers with higher skill levels attracted by eventual discovery provide a benefit to low-skill workers by raising their pre-discovery wages. In our case this outweighs the cost of eventual discovery to low-skill workers.

We should warn the reader, however, that the case discussed above is only an example. For instance, if we reverse the assumption that $kW_R(0) > W_P(0)$, the results will alter drastically.

## 5  Conclusions

We shall now summarize our main results. International migration under asymmetric information usually differs from international migration under symmetric information, often quite dramatically so and in ways which are counter-intuitive. Since in real life information is indeed asymmetric it is somewhat surprising that the study of international migration has by and large proceeded without explicit recognition of the effects of informational asymmetry.

We have shown that when migration is desirable at the lowest skill level, that is, if the (discounted) wage differential is positive for the lowest skill level, the introduction of asymmetric information results in a reduction of the quality and quantity of international migration or has no effect at all. When migration is not desirable at the lowest skill level, that is, if the (discounted) differential is not positive at the lowest skill level, the introduction of asymmetric information may result in either migration by all or migration by none.

Allowing employers to discover, after a while, the true productivity of individual migrant workers, we obtain the somewhat surprising result that (under a reasonable set of assumptions) eventual discovery may increase the quantity and quality of migration *and* also increase the wage enjoyed by the low-quality migrants. Eventual discovery serves to mitigate the impact of group averaging that deters migration by the high-skill workers. Owing to migration of some such workers, the pre-discovery wage of the low-skill workers rises, in our case sufficiently to outweigh the effect of the future wage decline due to discovery.

Our work can be extended in a number of interesting directions. For example, allowing for risk aversion on the part of employers may alter the nature of the results by making the wage offered to a group of migrants dependent not only on their mean skill level but also on the spread of skills among workers. In turn, making employers risk averse may give them some motivation to invest in an early (or immediate) skill-determining device, an action which may alter the whole nature of the equilibrium. Another interesting extension would be the modeling of a bilateral asymmetric information scenario, wherein information is in part private to the workers and in part private to the employers. Patterns of investment in location-specific *vis-à-vis* transferable human capital are clearly affected by the opening of international migration. But we may also need to study investments by the high skilled to reduce cost and lag of precise discovery, and subsequent upward revision of wages, and investment by the low skilled to reduce ease of discovery and subsequent downward revision of wages. Can high-skilled workers who may wish to prevent "contamination" of the pool of migrants by low-skilled migrants bribe the latter so as to have them stay put, and then migrate, obtain higher wages, and still be better off? A step further may be taken by modeling more fully dynamic effects, for example, the implications of the process of migration for a poor country's wage schedule. In addition, allowing for the transformation of a poor country curve into a relevant rich country curve *vis-à-vis* a third poor(er) country may also warrant study. It would be interesting to study the dynamics of allowing workers to quit an employer at the end of the first period and move to another in an attempt to prolong the pre-discovery period. Also, it may be worthwhile characterizing the income distribution and welfare implications of our analysis for all groups of agents and countries involved in international migration under asymmetric information. In ongoing work we attempt to study these directions.

Finally, we should like to draw attention to the fact that the assumptions we have used are somewhat limiting: wages in both sending and receiving countries are exogenously given for every skill level and migrants do not face the prospect of unemployment. In addition, no provision was made for direct government intervention through immigration control in the receiving country. There are therefore neither economic nor political checks to counter international migration. Not surprisingly, the model shows that in certain cases all workers in a given occupation will migrate. One advantage of this approach is that it allows us to separate out clearly the damping and amplifying effects of informational asymmetry. Yet the usefulness of the model depends on whether in actual life economic or political checks operate. If political checks dominate, the model is relevant to show what could happen if governments do not interfere. However, if economic checks are also in operation, they would have to be built into the model by internalizing wages in both countries and/or by letting unemployment act as a buffer.

## Appendix

Figure 11.3(a) states that

$$k\hat{W}_R(\theta^*)|_{\theta^*=0} < W_P(\theta)_{\theta=1} \qquad (11.A1)$$

that is,

$$k\left(r_0 + r\frac{1 + \theta^*}{2}\right)\Bigg|_{\theta^*=0} < p_0 + p\theta|_{\theta=1}$$

or

$$k\left(r_0 + \frac{r}{2}\right) < p_0 + p$$

Hence

$$kr_0 - p_0 < p - \frac{kr}{2} \qquad (11.A2)$$

Figure 11.3(a) also states that

$$kr_0 < p_0 \qquad (11.A3)$$

The argument is that in this case (that is, the case depicted in figure 11.3(a)) no one will migrate from P to R.

## Proof

As can immediately be seen from the figure, if everyone migrates to R, the top-skilled workers will be better off by "returning" to P. Hence they will not be included in the pool of migrants. We then have to define $\hat{W}_R(\theta^*)$ on a new interval which *excludes* the top-skilled range. Say then that the top 10 percent "return." Hence

$$\hat{W}_R(\theta^*) = \int_{\theta^*}^{0.9} W_R(\theta) F_P(\theta) \, d\theta \bigg/ \int_{\theta^*}^{0.9} F_P(\theta) \, d\theta$$

$$= \int_{\theta^*}^{0.9} (r_0 + r\theta) \, d\theta \bigg/ \int_{\theta^*}^{0.9} d\theta$$

$$= \frac{[r_0\theta + (r\theta^2/2)]|_{\theta^*}^{0.9}}{\theta|_{\theta^*}^{0.9}}$$

$$= \frac{r_0(0.9 - \theta^*) + (r/2)(0.9^2 - \theta^{*2})}{0.9 - \theta^*}$$

$$= r_0 + \frac{r}{2}(0.9 + \theta^*)$$

Therefore, for the interval $[\theta^*, 0.9]$,

$$k\hat{W}_R(\theta^*) = kr_0 + \frac{kr}{2}(0.9 + \theta^*) \tag{11.A4}$$

Migration to R will *not* be undertaken by the *now* top-skilled workers if the right-hand side of (11.A4) is less than $p_0 + 0.9p$ – the wage they could alternatively receive by staying behind in P.

Thus, to verify our prediction, we need to check

$$kr_0 + \frac{kr}{2}(0.9 + \theta^*) \overset{?}{<} p_0 + 0.9p$$

or, since $\theta^* = 0$,

$$kr_0 - p_0 \overset{?}{<} 0.9\left(p - \frac{kr}{2}\right)$$

$$\frac{kr_0 - p_0}{0.9} \overset{?}{<} p - \frac{kr}{2} \tag{11.A5}$$

The numerator on the left-hand side of (11.A5) is negative (recall (11.A3)). Divided by a $\theta^{**} < 1$, it is a larger negative number. The right-hand side is exactly the right-hand side of (11.A2) which, as we already know from (11.A2), is larger than $kr_0 - p_0$ and hence, *a fortiori*, is larger than the left-hand side of (11.A5).

We can repeat the procedure for each and every $\theta^{**} < 1$, that is, for any interval $[\theta^*, \theta^{**}]$. Hence the argument is proved.

## Notes

Co-authored with Eliakim Katz. Reprinted from *European Economic Review* 33, 1989. This chapter is a revised and shortened version of Discussion Paper 1051, Harvard Institute of Economic Research, and Discussion Paper 8, Harvard University Migration and Development Program. Helpful comments on earlier versions of this chapter were made by Herbert Glejser and an anonymous referee as well as by participants in the December 1984 Joint Meeting of the Econometric Society and the American Economic Association and in seminars held at Ben-Gurion University, Brown University, Chr. Michelsen Institute, Columbia University, Florida International University, Harvard University, Institute of Developing Economies–Tokyo, McGill University, Nagoya University of Commerce and Business Administration, Technion–Israel Institute of Technology, The Johns Hopkins University, The Norwegian School of Economics and Business Administration, The Population Council, University of Barcelona, University of Colorado, University of Minnesota, and University of Toronto.

1   We assume throughout that the wages in both R and P are dependent only upon a worker's skill level and not upon the excess supply of or demand for labor. In this we follow the similar assumption made in the optimal tax literature.

2   This may, for example, result from a higher capital-to-labor ratio in R.

3   In this chapter we employ only linear functions to denote the relation between $\theta$ and $W$. This can be justified in two ways. First, our analysis could be construed as referring only to "a window" in the skills range within which poor country workers are indistinguishable from each other in the rich country. To the extent that this window is small, linear approximations are clearly legitimate. Second, the adoption of linear forms facilitates use of a highly intuitive diagrammatic approach.

4   The seminal contributions relevant to our analysis are Akerlof (1970) and the adaptation of his model by Hirshleifer and Riley (1979).

5   If employers are risk neutral and production functions are linear in skills, the employer does not suffer from his ignorance of the true skill level of each

worker, so that paying the average product per worker will be the competitive outcome. These assumptions of risk neutrality and linearity in production are the commonly accepted assumptions in the screening literature (see, for example, Stiglitz, 1975). Nonetheless, it may be of interest to examine wage schemes that are dependent on both the mean and the spread of the skill levels of individual workers.

6   Of course, the average wage for the entire skill range under (11.6) with $\theta^* = 1$ is exactly the same as the average wage for the entire skill range under (11.8) with $\theta^* = 0$.

7   This should not be interpreted as all members of the occupation but rather those within the "window" referred to above.

## References

Akerlof, George A. (1970) "The Market for 'Lemons': Qualitative Uncertainty and the Market Mechanism." *Quarterly Journal of Economics* 84: 488–500.

Hall, Robert E. and Lazear, Edward P. (1984) "The Excess Sensitivity of Layoffs and Quits to Demand." *Journal of Labor Economics* 2: 233–57.

Hirshleifer, Jack and Riley, John G. (1979) "The Analytics of Uncertainty and Information – An Expository Survey." *Journal of Economic Literature* 17: 1375–421.

Katz, Eliakim and Stark, Oded (1984) "Migration and Asymmetric Information: Comment." *American Economic Review* 74: 533–4.

—— and —— (1986) "Labor Mobility under Asymmetric Information with Moving and Signalling Costs." *Economics Letters* 21: 89–94.

Kwok, Viem and Leland, Hayne (1982) "An Economic Model of the Brain Drain." *American Economic Review* 72: 91–100.

Miyazaki, Hajime (1977) "The Rat Race and Internal Labor Markets." *Bell Journal of Economics* 8: 394–418.

Radner, Roy (1982) "The Role of Private Information in Markets and Other Organizations." In Werner Hildenbrand (ed.), *Advances in Economic Theory*. New York: Cambridge University Press, pp. 99–120.

Riley, John G. (1979) "Informational Equilibrium." *Econometrica* 47: 331–59.

Stark, Oded (1984) "Discontinuity and the Theory of International Migration." *Kyklos* 37: 206–22.

Stiglitz, Joseph E. (1975) "The Theory of 'Screening' Education, and the Distribution of Income." *American Economic Review* 65: 283–300.

Wilson, Charles (1977) "A Model of Insurance Markets with Incomplete Information." *Journal of Economic Theory* 16: 167–207.

# 12

## International Labor Migration under Alternative Informational Regimes: Supplement to Chapter 11

It is possible to extend the basic model of labor migration under asymmetric information (chapter 11, section 3) in several directions. For example, the model can be applied to a case where signaling is allowed or to a case where there are three countries or more. The rationale for using specific wage functions (chapter 11, section 2) and the general equilibrium property of the basic asymmetric information model (chapter 11, section 3) can also be discussed. The following sections take up these four issues in turn.

### 1 The Basic Model of Labor Migration under Asymmetric Information with Signaling

Assume now that migrants can invest in a signaling device such as an examination or professional qualifications. Several such devices may exist and each may bring about a different equilibrium. Given that our main aim here is not to extend the now prolific signaling literature but rather to indicate how the existence of signaling devices may alter migration patterns, we focus on a single type of signaling device. Thus our results should be taken as reflecting only one of many possible outcomes and revealing some of the richness of this vein for research.[1]

Specifically, let us assume that there exists a signaling device that enables a worker's skill level to be completely identified, that is, the device is such that the private information is completely revealed. A signaling game where this condition holds is called a separating equilibrium game.

Here, the "separation" that arises is that, upon signaling, the signaling migrants dissociate themselves from the group of migrants whose *individual* skill levels are not known to the employers in the rich country R. We shall also assume that the cost of the device does not vary with skill level[2] and that workers must bear the cost of this device – probably investing in it before leaving the poor country P. (For example, all workers can take an accurate pre-employment test at a fixed cost.) Also, we shall assume a positive and increasing post-discounted wage differential, that is, that $kW_R(1) - W_P(1) > kW_R(0) - W_P(0)$ and that $k\overline{W}_R(\theta^*)$ intersects $W_P(\theta)$ at $0 < \theta_1 < 1$. Notice that, for a worker who invests in the device and migrates, $kW_R(\theta)$ rather than $k\overline{W}_R(\theta^*)$ is relevant. A worker's choice to invest or not to invest in the device is made after the employers' skill–wage function is known.

The outcomes of this combination of assumptions are illustrated in figure 12.1. Note, first, that under asymmetric information migration will be in the $[0, \theta_1]$ interval.

Clearly, if the cost of the signaling device is greater than AB (maximum difference between $kW_R(\theta)$ and $W_P(\theta)$), none of the potential migrants will find it beneficial to invest in the device. The equilibrium will therefore be the same as that obtained in the absence of the device.

If, however, the cost of the device is smaller than AB two outcomes are possible. To see this, first let the cost of the device be AE (>CD) in figure 12.1(a). The net (discounted) income to those who invest in the device and become migrants is given by the line FE, which is parallel to $kW_R(\theta)$. Will the pattern of migration change? Clearly, for workers with skill levels below $\theta_2$ it does not pay to invest in the device since they are better off on $W_P(\theta)$ than on FE. For skill levels above $\theta_2$, however, it does pay to invest in the device since for them FE exceeds the alternative – namely, $W_P(\theta)$. Workers in the $[0, \theta_1]$ interval are unaffected by the availability of the device and migrate as before.

Hence in the case illustrated in figure 12.1(a) the equilibrium is given as follows: workers in the $[0, \theta_1]$ interval migrate without investing in the device; workers in the $[\theta_1, \theta_2]$ interval do not migrate; workers in the $[\theta_2, 1]$ interval invest in the signaling device and migrate. We have thus obtained a novel and interesting theoretical explanation for the often observed U-shaped pattern of migration.

Turning now to the case where the cost of the signaling device is lower than CD, we observe the situation depicted in figure 12.1(b). Clearly, it pays all workers in the $[\theta_2, 1]$ range to invest in the signaling device. For lower skill levels, however, it does not pay to invest in signaling since FE is below $k\overline{W}_R(\theta^*)$ in the $[0, \theta_2]$ range. The equilibrium in this case occurs

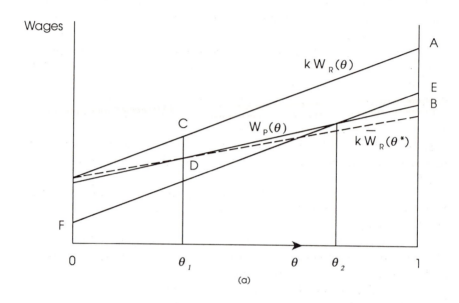

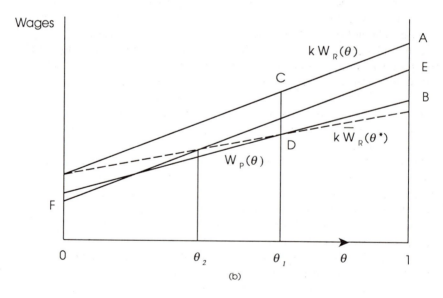

**Figure 12.1**

when all members of the occupation migrate – those in the $[0, \theta_2]$ range do so without investing in the signaling device, and those in the $[\theta_2, 1]$ range do so while investing in the signaling device.

## 2 The Basic Model of Labor Migration under Asymmetric Information with Three or More Countries

Physical and other characteristics of migrants from one country are often similar to the physical characteristics of migrants from another country. As a result, employers in the rich receiving country will frequently view all migrants from certain countries as coming from the same group. These migrants will impose externalities upon one another, and changes in exogenous variables in country $P_1$, via their effect on the migration pattern from $P_1$, will affect the migration pattern from country $P_2$.

The number of scenarios possible within the three-country context is, of course, considerable, and it is beyond the scope of this section to examine them all. Hence, we content ourselves by considering one example of the interaction of a three-country model with asymmetric information.

Let us assume that there are two poor countries, $P_1$ and $P_2$, which are initially identical in all respects. Their $W_P(\theta)$ is the same, the $k$ value of their workers is the same, and the distribution of their workers along $[0, 1]$ is the same. This initial position is described by $kW_R(\theta)$, $k\overline{W}_R(\theta^*)$, and $W_P(\theta)$ in figure 12.2 where these functions are as defined in chapter 11 (although it should be noted that here $k\overline{W}_R(\theta^*)$ is the joint curve for the two poor countries). The initial asymmetric information equilibrium is thus achieved at $\theta_1$, where skills $[0, \theta_1]$ migrate and skills $[\theta_1, 1]$ do not.

Assume now that matters in country $P_1$ improve politically or culturally such that the $k$ value for $P_1$ declines. Circumstances in $P_2$ are assumed to remain unaltered. The $kW_R(\theta)$ and the $k\overline{W}_R(\theta^*)$ curves for country $P_1$ shift downward. Thus there emerges a new lower joint average curve that is denoted by $k^*\overline{W}_R^*(\theta^*)$ in figure 12.2 (and, in turn, derives from $k^*W_R(\theta)$). It follows immediately that the workers reaching R after the change will be in the $[0, \theta_2]$ interval rather than in $[0, \theta_1]$ as previously.

The political change in $P_1$ thus has an effect on the migration pattern from $P_2$. Indeed, the effect is rather contrary to conventional logic: if migration from one country declines, we would expect migration from another country to substitute for that decline. Here, however, the decline in migration from one country reduces migration from the other. The reason for this is of course the special assumptions used in our model. In

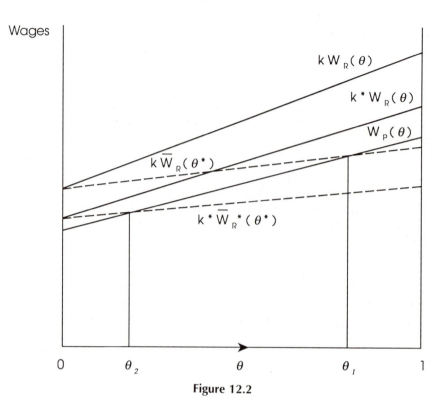

**Figure 12.2**

our model, each poor country is too small to affect the price of labor in the rich country. Hence, the decline in migration from $P_1$ leaves the $W_R(\theta)$ unaltered and thus does not, *per se*, encourage migration from $P_2$. In contrast, even though migration is too small to affect the general wages of labor in R, it does affect the wages paid to migrants via alteration of the composition of the group of migrants. The decline in the mean quality of migrants to R, resulting from the change in $P_1$, reduces the wage paid to all migrants and thus reduces migration from $P_2$.

Note finally the somewhat curious case that if *all* migration from $P_1$ ceases (rather than some), migration from $P_2$ remains unchanged since the average quality of workers migrating will be unchanged.

## 3 Derivation of the Wage Functions

It can be shown that equations (11.2) and (11.3) in chapter 11 are reduced equilibrium forms: in each equation the left-hand side is the equilibrium wage, whereas the right-hand side is the productivity of a worker with skill level $\theta$. Linearity of productivity and invariance of the wage function $W_i(\theta)$, $i = R, P$, to the number of migrants jointly imply the following function.

Let the (per laborer) production function of workers of skill level $\theta$ be $f_R(\theta) = r_0 + r\theta$ (the argument is developed for R; an identical argument applies to P). When a firm employs $L(\theta)$ workers of skill level $\theta$, the firm's production function is

$$\Sigma f_R(\theta)L(\theta) = \Sigma(r_0 + r\theta)L(\theta)$$

which exhibits additive separability and constant returns to scale in the number of workers hired. The marginal productivity function is

$$\text{MPL}_R[\theta, L(\theta)] = \frac{\partial\Sigma f_R(\theta)L(\theta)}{\partial L(\theta)} = r_0 + r\theta$$

Since the marginal productivity function is independent of the number of workers hired, we can write it as $\text{MPL}_R(\theta)$, that is, drop $L(\theta)$. In a competitive labor market (with perfect information) wage $W_R(\theta)$ is equal to marginal productivity $\text{MPL}_R(\theta)$ or $W_R(\theta) = r_0 + r\theta$. Thus, since we indeed assume competitive labor markets and linear production functions, equations (11.2) and (11.3) of chapter 11 follow.

## 4 The Notion of Equilibrium in the Basic Model of Labor Migration under Asymmetric Information

In this section we demonstrate that the equilibrium in the basic asymmetric information model arising from workers' incentive to migrate given the $k\overline{W}_R(\theta^*)$ function is compatible with, indeed also ensues from, the other side of the market, namely, the behavior of firms in the destination R. To see this, note the following.

We assume that firms in R are identical so that there is a unique equilibrium wage. Under perfect competition, the profits of a firm in R are, drawing on our discussion in the preceding section,

$$\Pi = \Sigma f_R(\theta) L(\theta) - \Sigma W_R(\theta) L(\theta) = \Sigma[f_R(\theta) - W_R(\theta)] L(\theta)$$
$$= \Sigma[\mathrm{MPL}_R(\theta) - W_R(\theta)] L(\theta)$$

To calculate the profits of a representative firm in R under asymmetric information, let $W$ be its offer wage. Then all workers whose skill levels are $\theta$ such that $\mathrm{MPL}_P(\theta) < kW$ will migrate. Let $\Theta(W) = \{\theta | \mathrm{MPL}_P(\theta) < kW\}$, that is, the set of all skill types that migrate given $W$. Let $\mathrm{MPL}_R(W) = \int \mathrm{MPL}_R(\theta) \, dF$ where $F$ is the cumulative distribution function of $\theta$ and the integration is over the set $\Theta(W)$. Since $\mathrm{MPL}_R(W)$ is the average marginal product, we can now write the firm's profits as follows: $\Pi(W, L) = [\mathrm{MPL}_R(W) - W] L$. Of course, the firm will go bankrupt unless $W < \mathrm{MPL}_R(W)$. Yet if $W < \mathrm{MPL}_R(W)$, the firm earns strictly positive profits. This induces other firms to offer slightly higher $W$. Competition among firms in $R$ will adjust $W$ until the maximum $\Pi$ in $R$ is zero. That is, in equilibrium, $W = \mathrm{MPL}_R(W)$. The tacit assumption is thus competitiveness in the form of free entry and exit of firms in R.

The zero profit condition can be rewritten as $kW = k\mathrm{MPL}_R(W)$. Therefore, the equilibrium set of migrants to R, given $W$, is $\Theta^*(W) = \{\theta | \mathrm{MPL}_P(\theta) < k\mathrm{MPL}_R(W)\}$. In chapter 11, section 3, the claim was made that equilibrium is established when $W_P(\theta) = \mathrm{MPL}_P(\theta)$ intersects (is equal to) $k\overline{W}_R(\theta^*)$ which is $k$ times the wage paid to each member of a group of migrants when the highest skill level migrating is $\theta^*$. Since, under competitive equilibrium, this wage is equal to $k\mathrm{MPL}_R(W)$ in the equilibrium set of migrants $\Theta^*(W)$, the claim made in chapter 11, section 3, rests not only upon the equilibrium that arises from migrants' utility maximization but also from the equilibrium due to firms' (employers') profit maximization.

**Notes**

1   See also Katz and Stark (1986) and Katz and Stark (1987).
2   A natural extension might be to assume lower signaling costs for higher levels of $\theta$.

## References

Katz, Eliakim and Stark, Oded (1986) "Labor Migration under Asymmetric Information with Moving and Signalling Costs." *Economics Letters* 21: 89–94.
—— and—— (1987) "Migration, Information and the Costs and Benefits of Signalling." *Regional Science and Urban Economics* 17: 323–31.

# 13

# International Migration under Asymmetric Information

The notion that the labor market is often characterized by asymmetric information – workers or the firm (or both) have information to which the other party is not privy – is by now well accepted. Indeed, some researchers have even gone as far as to suggest that informational asymmetry is the major feature of labor employment arrangements and the nature of worker–firm relations (Hall and Lazear, 1984).

Perhaps the most natural application of the informational asymmetry concept is to situations where (at least initially) employers do not know the productivity level of individual employees. Two such contexts come readily to mind. First, when workers are young and hence relatively unknown to any firm, no firm has as yet good information pertaining to their individual productivity. Second, when markets are isolated in the sense that information does not ordinarily flow across them (or does not flow costlessly and freely), a firm (or firms) in one market may possess information on individual worker productivity – for example, such information may be revealed to the firm over time as a by-product of its normal monitoring and coordinating activities – but this information is firm- or market-specific.

Obviously, when labor markets are in two different countries the idea of such information asymmetry is particularly appealing. It is from these considerations that the main impetus for our study arises. The patterns of labor migration under asymmetric information seem likely to differ from the patterns of labor migration under symmetric information. Indeed, our analysis suggests that the differences may be substantial: it can generate results which differ from traditional models of labor mobility, in some cases dramatically so. The present chapter thus takes us a step beyond the early contributions to this topic by Kwok and Leland (1982), Katz and Stark (1984, 1986), and Stark (1984). It should be noted, however, that what we offer here is not an attempt to put forward a definitive theory of migration under informational asymmetries. Rather, what we try to do is to show how migration under such conditions may give rise to interesting and plausible migratory patterns.

In the following sections we spell out our assumptions in full and present our main results. In section 1 we present our basic model of labor mobility under asymmetric information. Two devices might work to reinstate informational symmetry: signaling, which is costly, and revelation of true productivity through observation, which is time consuming. We deal with these two mechanisms and the ensuing migration implications in sections 2 and 3 respectively. In section 4 we report our main conclusions and outline some directions along which future research in this area may be of interest.

## 1 Asymmetric Information: The Basic Model

Assume a world consisting of two countries: a rich country R and a poor country P. In a given occupation let the net wages for a worker with skill level $S$ be $W_R(S)$ and $W_P(S)$ in the rich country and the poor country respectively[1] (such that $\partial W_P/\partial S > 0$, $\partial W_R/\partial S > 0$). To reflect the fact that R is rich and P is poor, it is assumed that $W_R(S) > W_P(S)$ for all $S$.[2] Also, without loss of generality, let $S$ be defined upon the closed internal $[0, 1]$ and let the density function of P workers on $S$ be $F(S)$.

In addition, given that P workers are likely to have a preference for P life-style because of cultural factors, family relationships, etc., it is assumed that P workers apply a discount factor to R wages when comparing them with P wages. Thus, when making the migration decision, they compare $kW_R(S)$ with $W_P(S)$ where $0 < k < 1$. A P worker will therefore migrate from P to R if

$$kW_R(S) > W_P(S) \qquad (13.1)$$

Clearly, without further restrictions on $W_R(S)$ and $W_P(S)$, there may be several values of $S$ for which $kW_R(S) - W_P(S) = 0$. Hence, as illustrated in figure 13.1, there may be several distinct skill groups along the skill axis. Thus, in figure 13.1, the workers in skill intervals $0S_1$, $S_2S_3$, $S_41$ migrate, whereas those in the complementary intervals do not. We shall refer to a case in which there are at least three distinct groups (for example, along the $S$ axis, migrating, nonmigrating, migrating) – a situation which can only occur if at least one of the $W_P(S)$ and $W_R(S)$ functions is nonlinear in $S$ – as the nonconvex case. Similarly, we shall refer to the type of case in which there are only two or less distinct groups as the convex case.

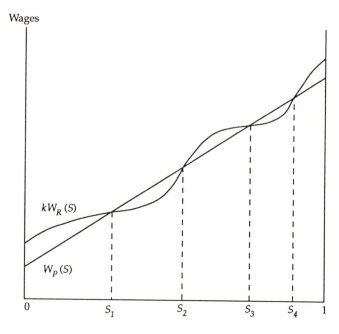

**Figure 13.1**

Let us now assume that the skill of each potential migrant is known in P, where he or she has been observed for many years, but is unknown in R. Also, let us exclude for the moment the possibilities that either migrants or employers can invest in devices which may identify the worker's true skill level or that true skill is revealed over time.

Faced with a group of workers where the individual productivity of each worker is unknown to him or her, the wage offered by the employer will be the same for all such workers and will be related to the average product of all members of the group. Let us assume that the actual individual wage offered is *equal* to the average product of the group[3] and that wage offers are known to all workers.

Hence, denoting by $\overline{W}$ the wage payable in the rich country to a migrant of unknown skill level and assuming $n$ distinct *migrating* groups, $\overline{W}$ is given by

$$\overline{W} = \sum_{i=1}^{n} \int_{\underline{S}^i}^{\overline{S}^i} W_R(S)\,F(S)\,\mathrm{d}S \Big/ \sum_{i=1}^{n} \int_{\underline{S}^i}^{\overline{S}^i} F(S)\,\mathrm{d}S \qquad (13.2)$$

where $\underline{S}^i$ and $\bar{S}^i$ are respectively the lowest and highest skill levels migrating in group $i$, where $i$ is one of the continuous groups migrating and the skill level increases with $i$ (note that $0 < \underline{S}^1 < \bar{S}^n < 1$ for a nonempty migrating set). It follows immediately that $\bar{W} < W_R(\bar{S}^n)$.

Using these assumptions we establish our first main result.

## Theorem 1

*Under asymmetric information if the top skill level migrating is $\bar{S}^n$ then any skill level $S^*$ where $S^* < \bar{S}^n$ will also migrate.*

PROOF   Consider any $S^*$ such that $S^* < \bar{S}^n$. Now, since by assumption $\bar{S}^n$ migrates, then

$$k\bar{W} > W_P(\bar{S}^n) \tag{13.3}$$

Also, since $S^* < \bar{S}^n$ then $W_P(S^*) < W_P(\bar{S}^n)$ and hence $k\bar{W} > W_P(S^*)$ so that $S^*$ skill levels also migrate.

The implications of this theorem are that, under asymmetric information, everyone with a skill level less than or equal to $\bar{S}^n$ migrates, so that all workers in the interval $[0, \bar{S}^n]$ migrate. Note the contrast with the case of full information, as depicted in figure 13.1, where the migration pattern could be nonconvex. Thus, under asymmetric information, the wage payable to all migrating workers in R is

$$\bar{W} = \int_0^{\bar{S}} W_R(S)\,F(S)\,\mathrm{d}S \Big/ \int_0^{\bar{S}} F(S)\,\mathrm{d}S \tag{13.4}$$

where $\bar{S}$ is the top skill level migrating. Thus $\bar{W}$ can be written as $\bar{W}(\bar{S})$.

We now have a characterization of the migration pattern under asymmetric information and can therefore proceed to establish the main differences between migration patterns under alternative informational regimes.

## Theorem 2

*The top skill level migrating under symmetric information will never be lower and may be higher than the top skill level migrating under asymmetric information.*

PROOF   Let the top skill level workers migrating under asymmetric information be $S^*$. Then, clearly, $k\overline{W}_R(S^*) \geq W_P(S^*)$. But $kW_R(S^*) \geq k\overline{W}_R(S^*)$ so that, if $S^*$ migrate under asymmetric information, they will definitely migrate under symmetric information. Indeed, if $0 < S^* < 1$, then $k\overline{W}_R(S^*) = W_P(S^*)$ and $W_R(S^*) > \overline{W}_R(S^*)$ so that by continuity the top skill level migrating under symmetric information will exceed $S^*$.

Clearly, this theorem is very reminiscent of the result obtained by Akerlof (1970) concerning the effect of asymmetric information on reducing the quality of second-hand cars that reach the market, and our intellectual debt to Akerlof's work should be emphasized.[4]

Finally, in this section we can establish the result that, if $kW_R(0) > W_P(0)$, then workers with the lowest skill levels migrate regardless of the informational regime. This follows from the fact that $k\overline{W}_R(0) = kW_R(0)$ so that if $kW_R(0) > W_P(0)$ then $k\overline{W}_R(0) > W_P(0)$ and hence 0 skill-level workers always migrate.

The intuition of this is that for the lowest skill workers who find it attractive to migrate from P to R under symmetric information, the introduction of informational asymmetry cannot reduce their R wage so that their decision to migrate is invariant to the informational regime.

## 2 The Basic Model under Asymmetric Information with Signaling

Assume now that migrants can invest in a signaling device such as an examination or professional qualifications. Several such devices may exist and each may bring about a different equilibrium. However, given that our main aim here is not to extend the now prolific signaling literature, but rather to indicate how the existence of a signaling device might affect migratory patterns, we focus on a single type of signaling device. Thus our results should be taken as reflecting only one of many possible outcomes and revealing some of the richness of this research direction.

Specifically, let us assume that there exists a signaling device which enables a worker's skill level to be completely identified. We shall also assume that the cost of the device is a constant $C$ which does not vary with skill level and that workers must bear the cost of this device – probably having to invest in it before leaving P. (For example, all workers can take an accurate pre-employment test at a fixed cost.) Also, we shall assume a positive and nondecreasing discounted wage differential, that is, that $kW_R(S) - W_P(S)$ is nondecreasing in $S$. Notice that, for a worker who invests in the device and migrates, $kW_R(S)$ rather than $k\overline{W}_R(\overline{S})$ is relevant. A worker's choice of whether or not to invest in the device is made after the employers' skill–wage demand for labor function is known.

Using the above assumptions we establish the following theorem.

**Theorem 3**

*Given asymmetric information, then, if $kW_R(S) - W_P(S)$ is nondecreasing in S and a signaling device costing C is available, and if migrating workers with skill level $S^{**}$ invest in the signaling device, all migrating workers with a skill level $S \geq S^{**}$ will also invest in the device.*

PROOF   If a worker of skill level $S^{**}$ finds it beneficial to invest in the signaling device, then, since $kW_R - W_P$ is increasing in S so that the net benefit to the device increases with S, all workers with $S \geq S^{**}$ will also invest in the device.

One direct implication of this theorem is that if ayone at all finds it worthwhile to migrate and invest in the signaling device, those with skill level $S = 1$ will definitely do so. Hence top-skill individuals are the most likely to signal.

A second implication of the theorem is that a migration pattern may emerge where the least skilled migrate without signaling, the next skill group does not migrate, and there is a higher group still that migrates with a signal. Since this possibility is of considerable interest it may be useful to illustrate this potential situation by way of a numerical example.

Assume that there are only three distinct skill groups, I, II, and III. The wages payable to these skill groups in R and P are given in table 13.1 as are the proportions of these skill groups in the population of potential migrants. In addition let the discount factor attached to R wages by P workers be 0.6 and let the signaling device cost £1.8.

Consider initially the situation in the absence of a signaling device. If the top migrating group is I, the wage payable to migrants in R will be 2 so that, since $k\overline{W}_R = 0.6 \times 2 = 1.2 > W_P(I) = 1$, group I will migrate. If, on the other hand, group II were the top migrating group, it is easily calculated that the wage payable to migrants in R would be 4, which after discounting would be insufficient to induce group II to migrate, so that this cannot be an equilibrium. A similar calculation shows that group III will not migrate. Hence under asymmetric information only group I migrates.

Now introduce the signaling device at a cost of 1.8. Clearly group I will not purchase it since it obtains its true wage, that is, 2, without it. Group II will also not purchase it *and* will not migrate since if it does purchase it and

**Table 13.1**

|  | Skill group | | |
| --- | :---: | :---: | :---: |
|  | *I* | *II* | *III* |
| $W_P$ (£) | 1 | 3 | 10 |
| $W_R$ (£) | 2 | 6 | 20 |
| Proportion in population | 3/10 | 3/10 | 4/10 |

migrates it will have $kW_R(\text{II}) - C = 0.6 \times 6 - 1.8 = 1.8$ as compared with 3 if it stays put. Finally, group III will purchase it and migrate since if it does it receives $kW_R(\text{III}) - C = 0.6 \times 20 - 1.8 = 10.2$ as opposed to the 10 it receives if it stays at home.

This then provides a possible information-based explanation for the frequently observed U-shaped pattern of migration by skill.

### 3 Reinstating Symmetric Information by Discovery

In this section we consider the effect on the migration pattern of the possibility that, after spending some time in R, migrants' true skill levels will be discovered through observation by R employers. Early periods of employment thus act as a screening device. In this case we have the following result which is essentially an application of theorem 2.

**Theorem 4**

*Under eventual discovery of true skill level, the top skill level migrating will not be lower and may be higher than in the absence of eventual discovery.*

PROOF    Let the top skill level migrating under asymmetric information be $S^*$. Let the weights attached to pre-discovery and post-discovery earnings be $\alpha$ and $1 - \alpha$ ($0 < \alpha < 1$) respectively. Then, since $W_R(S^*) \geq \overline{W}_R(S^*)$,

$$\alpha\overline{W}_R(S^*) + (1 - \alpha)W_R(S^*) \geq \overline{W}_R(S^*)$$

so that the top migrating skill under asymmetric information will definitely migrate with eventual discovery. Indeed, if $0 < S^* < 1$, then $kW_R(S^*) > k\overline{W}_R(S^*) = W_P(S^*)$ and by continuity the top skill level migrating will rise.

In addition the following result is obtained.

**Theorem 5**

*The welfare of lower-skill workers may be higher under eventual discovery than in its absence.*

PROOF   We prove the existence of this possibility by providing a numerical example. Once again we assume three distinct skill groups. The relevant data regarding these groups is given in table 13.2. In addition we assume that $k = 0.6$.

In the absence of eventual discovery, it is easily confirmed that the equilibrium migration pattern is for groups I and II to migrate with $k\overline{W}_R(\text{II}) = 0.6 \times 5.43 = 3.26 > W_P(\text{II}) = 3$. Group III will not migrate. If it did, $\overline{W}_R$ would be 14.9 which is insufficient after discounting to induce migration by group III.

Now, let eventual discovery of the skills take place in R and assume that this occurs after a period of time such that the appropriate weighting factors $\alpha$ and $1 - \alpha$ for wages earned before and after discovery respectively are 0.5 each. Consider what happens to group III. As before, its earnings for the asymmetric information period are $\overline{W}_R(\text{III}) = 14.9$. Its post-discovery earnings are, of course, 20. Hence its appropriate average earnings are $0.5 \times 14.9 + 0.5 \times 20 = 17.45$ which, applying the location discount factor $k$, yields $10.47 > W_P(\text{III}) = 10$. Hence in the presence of eventual discovery, as described above, group III migrates.

**Table 13.2**

|  | Skill group | | |
|---|---|---|---|
|  | *I* | *II* | *III* |
| $W_P$ (£) | 1 | 3 | 10 |
| $W_R$ (£) | 2 | 6 | 20 |
| Proportion in population | 1/20 | 6/20 | 13/20 |

Consider now what this does for groups I and II. For group I the pre-discovery R wage is 14.9. Hence its average wage is $0.5 \times 2 + 0.5 \times 14.9 = 8.45$, so that group I's location-discounted wage is $0.6 \times 8.45 = 5.07$, which exceeds its benefit under no discovery, which was 3.26. Group II, of course, does better: its average wage is $0.5 \times 6 + 0.5 \times 14.9 = 10.45$, which after the location discount yields $0.6 \times 10.45 = 6.27$, which also exceeds the no discovery equilibrium wage of 3.26.

Eventual discovery may thus benefit low-skill workers.

This result is at first sight counter-intuitive since one would have thought that eventual discovery will lower the benefits to those who have most to hide, namely the workers with low skill levels. However, this does not happen in our case since the workers with higher skill levels attracted by eventual discovery provide a benefit to low-skill workers by raising their pre-discovery wages. This outweighs the cost of eventual discovery to the low-skill workers.

## 4 Conclusions

In this chapter we have established several possible results on the effects of asymmetric information on migration, where the nature of the asymmetry is that foreign employers are less well informed than the migrant workers about the workers' skills. Asymmetric information may change the distribution of migrant groups in the population qualitatively as well as quantitatively, and it will tend to reduce the skill level of migrants. Devices which tend to restore information symmetry can have quite important effects on the migration pattern. One effect may be to induce migration by high-skill groups as well as by the low skilled, with middle-skill groups not migrating. The restoration of information symmetry may also have the counter-intuitive effect of raising the welfare of low-skill workers.

Our analysis can be extended in a number of interesting directions. For example, allowing for risk aversion on the part of employers may alter the nature of the results by making the wage offered to a group of migrants dependent not only on their mean skill level but also on the spread of skills among workers. In turn, employers' risk aversion may give *them* some motivation to invest in an early (or immediate) skill-determining device, an action which may alter the nature of the equilibrium. Another interesting extension would be to model a bilateral asymmetric information scenario, in which information is in part private to the workers and in part private to the employers.

Patterns of investment in location-specific *vis-à-vis* transferable human capital are clearly affected by the opening of international migration. Further, investments by the high skilled to reduce cost and lag of precise discovery, and subsequent upward revision of wages, and investment by the low skilled to reduce ease of discovery, and subsequent downward revision of (average) wages, may also need to be studied. The dynamics of allowing workers to quit an employer at the end of the first period and move to another in an attempt to prolong the pre-discovery period would also be of interest.

Furthermore, it should be noted that our model has several applications beyond the context of international migration. For example, it is pertinent to analyses of rural-to-rural migration,[5] rural-to-urban migration, inter-regional migration, and return migration (which may, for example, be explained by a decline in the initial informational advantages of low-skilled workers). Our model also pertains to general labor market mobility, for example, occupational change, quitting one firm and joining another, etc. We hope to present some results on these topics in future work.

Finally, a word of warning. Our model has abstracted from the dynamics of social attitudes and government policies toward migration when confronted with actual migration. These dynamics may be of great importance in the overall migration picture and should at a later stage be incorporated into the theory if it is to be used for formulating policy.

## Notes

Co-authored with Eliakim Katz. Reprinted from *The Economic Journal* 97, 1987. This chapter is a revised version of Discussion Paper 27, Harvard University Migration and Development Program. We are indebted to referees and in particular to associate editors of *The Economic Journal* for exceptionally helpful comments and suggestions.

1   To make the analysis tractable we assume throughout that the wages in both R and P are dependent only upon a worker's skill level. In this we follow the similar assumption made in the optimal income tax literature.
2   This may result from, for example, a higher capital-to-labor ratio in R.
3   If employers are risk neutral and production functions are linear in skills, the employer does not suffer from his ignorance of the true skill level of each worker, so that paying the average product per worker will be the competitive

outcome. These assumptions of risk neutrality and linearity in production are the commonly accepted assumptions in the screening literature (see, for example, Stiglitz, 1975). Nonetheless, it may be of interest to examine wage schemes that are dependent on both the mean and the spread of the skill levels of individual workers.

4  See also the work by Hirshleifer and Riley (1979).

5  It appears that in rural India some farmhands continuously shift from one village to another rather than back and forth within a specific well-defined group of villages. These "permanently mobile" are very low productivity workers who secure the average rural wage upon arrival at a village but, once their true productivity is revealed, they face the prospect of a lower wage. Apparently to avoid this they move to a new village, and so on.

## References

Akerlof, G. A. (1970) "The Market for 'Lemons': Qualitative Uncertainty and the Market Mechanism." *Quarterly Journal of Economics* 84: 488–500.

Hall, R. and Lazear, E. P. (1984) "The Excess Sensitivity of Layoffs and Quits to Demand." *Journal of Labor Economics* 2: 233–57.

Hirshleifer, J. and Riley, J. G. (1979) "The Analytics of Uncertainty and Information – An Expository Survey." *Journal of Economic Literature* 17: 1375–421.

Katz, E. and Stark, O. (1984) "Migration and Asymmetric Information: Comment." *American Economic Review* 74: 533–4.

—— and —— (1986) "Labor Mobility under Asymmetric Information with Moving and Signalling Costs." *Economics Letters* 21: 89–94.

Kwok, V. and Leland, H. (1982) "An Economic Model of the Brain Drain." *American Economic Review* 72: 91–100.

Stark, O. (1984) "Discontinuity and the Theory of International Migration." *Kyklos* 37: 206–22.

Stiglitz, J. E. (1975) "The Theory of 'Screening' Education, and the Distribution of Income." *American Economic Review* 65: 283–300.

# Part V

*Migrants' Remittances: Motives, Consequences, and Inequality Implications*

# 14

## On the Role of Urban-to-Rural Remittances in Rural Development

### 1 Introduction

In a recent paper Rempel and Lobdell (1978) (henceforth RL) set out to examine the "recent argument by several authors" that urban-to-rural remittances "represent a significant means for removing supply constraints to improved agriculture". RL "examine critically the available evidence on the rural impact of remittances" and put forward some analysis of their own. Utilizing both, they conclude their contribution by rejecting the "several authors' recent arguments," assessing pessimistically "the role remittances have played and are likely to play in the realization of rural development in low income countries."

RL refer explicitly only to two authors – Griffin and Stark. Since Griffin's argument, quoted by RL, is due to Stark (Griffin, 1976, note 28) (and since, in any case, Griffin refers to emigration and international remittances and not to migration and urban-to-rural remittances – the subject matter of RL's paper) it remains to be checked whether RL's contribution draws on a reasonable comprehension of what they have termed "Stark's contention." Our basic propositions are briefly outlined in section 2. It is consequently shown in section 3 that RL did not fully come to grips with our argument and that, in particular, much of the evidence they have harnessed to refute, as they put it, "Stark's claim" has been entrusted with more than it can deliver. Hence, RL's bleak view of the developmental usefulness of remittances appears to constitute more an impression than an informed judgment based on hard facts. A useful correlate of the analysis is the generation of some critical features of *optimal* evidence bearing on the roles of rural-to-urban migration and urban-to-rural remittances in rural development which, to a large extent, will have to differ from the currently accessible evidence. These features should be transformed into compelling guidelines when future surveys and data collection endeavors are planned and designed.

## 2 A New Approach to Rural-to-Urban Migration – an Outline

Our postulations concerning the role of urban-to-rural remittances in agricultural development stem from a new theoretical approach to rural-to-urban migration.[1] At the core of this approach lies the utility-maximizing family in its specific agricultural context.

Consider a family enterprise which is an agricultural producer on its smallholding. During the specific time span of its life-cycle relating to the earlier phases of its existence, the family observes a continuous reduction in its welfare as measured in "net utility" terms. The reduction is due to two "compositional changes": first, given the family size, there is a change in its age structure resulting in greater food requirements; secondly, family size itself changes over time as additional children are brought into the world. These changes can be translated into utility–disutility terms, leading to the result indicated above and generating an incentive to alter production technology, the intensity of which continuously increases.

However, the alteration of technology is hindered by (a) the characteristic features of the new technology itself and (b) the characteristics of the institutional and noninstitutional "surplus risk state" confronting the small farmer's family.

Of the factors characterizing the new technology, the more crucial ones are its surplus requirement and its (subjective) risk-increasing nature. (Both factors are usefully illustrated by the transition from traditional varieties to high-yielding varieties.) As to the features of the "surplus risk state," the absence of smoothly functioning market structures and appropriate institutional (as well as noninstitutional) facilities – notably credit and insurance arrangements – implies that the internal constraints arising from the prevalence of production risks and aversion to them, and the low level of (absolute and relative) surplus, cannot be alleviated through the (highly fragmented) markets. On the other hand, the small farmer's family possesses no surplus (or in insufficient volume) and no capacity for engagement in sufficient self-insurance; with the family initially endowed with the "cruel parameter" of only a smallholding, with average capacity to generate surplus being directly proportional to on-the-farm production but inversely proportional to the (standardized) number of consuming family members, the prevailing surplus and the expected surplus are likely to be low.

It is worth noting that with surplus insufficiency and risk averseness prevailing simultaneously, their joint impact is greater than the "sum" of each impact when exerted separately. This results from, and implies, the prevalence of a positive interaction between surplus insufficiency and averseness to risk. On the one hand, the degree of risk aversion is related directly to the degree of surplus insufficiency: a larger surplus diminishes the degree of risk aversion paired with a given risky prospect. On the other hand, a higher degree of risk aversion paired with a given risky prospect (that is, a prospect which requires a given surplus) magnifies the overall surplus requirements since, given the assumed absence of insurance markets, part of the surplus has to be destined as an insurance fund.

The easing of the surplus and risk constraints becomes a crucial condition for carrying out the desired technological change. It is rural-to-urban migration of a family member (that is, a son or daughter[2]) that, by bypassing the credit and insurance markets (with their bias against small farmers), facilitates the change. Migration succeeds in accomplishing this via its dual role in the accumulation of surplus (acting as an intermediate investment[3]) and, through diversification of income sources, in the control over the level of risk.

### 3 The Role of Remittances – Interpretation of Theory and Utilization of Evidence

From the point of view of the question at hand, the implication of the new theoretical approach is manifold. First, it is evidently clear that urban-to-rural remittances cannot capture the total effect that rural-to-urban migration bears on rural development. RL might have appropriately interpreted our argument to imply that *rural-to-urban migration* represents "a significant means for removing supply constraints to improved productivity in agriculture." However, to interpret the approach to imply that our contention is that "*urban-to-rural remittances* represent a significant means for removing supply constraints to improved productivity in agriculture" is logically false.

Second, urban-to-rural remittances cannot be assumed to account for the total accumulation of surplus consequent upon migration. If we designate the migrant's urban real income – net of nonoptional urban-incurred costs – by $F_U$, his pre-migration farm output by $F_R$, and his consumption level, which is assumed constant over sectors, by $F_C$, and consider the family inclusive of its urban member, surplus is accumulated *on the family farm* when $F_U > F_R$ and $F_U$, $F_R < F_C$; some farm-generated income which would have had to be spent feeding the migrant family member had he stayed on the farm is now "freed." Likewise if $F_U = F_C > F_R$.

Hence, in principle, a "farm-produced" surplus *and* an "urban-produced" surplus account in different situations with differing weights for the total accumulation of surplus consequent upon migration. The urban component, largely[4] revealed through urban-to-rural remittances, may thus assume weights ranging from zero to unity, with a zero weight *not* necessarily implying a zero total.[5]

Although urban-to-rural remittances cannot account for the impact of rural-to-urban migration on agricultural development (the first point above) or for its total surplus accumulation effect (the second point), it is important to attempt to quantify these remittances. If, for example, remittances constitute a large share of total familial resources, their potential (though, as yet, unproven) impact on technological change in agricultural production will be greater than if they are proportionately small.

However, two serious problems are inherent in the usage and interpretation of existing evidence. The first problem stems from the intertemporal changes in the magnitude of the urban-to-rural remittances flow. The second arises from the prevalence of a counter-flow. Referring first to the latter, it is often found that, even though the family lacks sufficient surplus to facilitate technological change in agricultural production, it does possess some surplus.[6] This surplus is earmarked to support the migrant member during the initial period of his stay in the urban sector and is evidenced in the prevalence of rural-to-urban remittances. Such remittances may constitute a once-and-for-all transfer but may also assume the nature of a flow. A study based on a sample drawn from a distribution of migrants by duration of stay which is skewed to the left is likely to find a low *average* net transfer per the reference period of time, say a given month, even though the transfer per an "established migrant" of urban-to-rural remittances may be quite high for the same period.

The first problem mentioned above stems from the nonuniform pattern of the (gross) urban-to-rural flow. The magnitude of a transfer at a given point in time is a function of a number of variables such as duration of stay in the urban sector, employment status and job seniority, the intensity and nature of kinship ties, cohesion and social control, and age (both of the migrant and of the head of the family) – all being, in turn, functions of time themselves. Thus, since time is of crucial importance in estimating any flow magnitude, the estimated remittances, for a given population of migrants, will vary widely depending on the vintage distribution of the migrants who happen to constitute the sample. Likewise, similar populations of migrants will produce differing estimates solely because of their differing vintage composition.[7] Even though it is clear, from a statistical point of view, how this flaw can be avoided (that is, through proper stratification), the main task is to secure an appropriate cross-section data set which can be transformed into a "time series flow"; the only way to gauge the total effect of urban-to-rural remittances on the "resource constraint" is to calculate the difference between two integrals, one under the declining rural-to-urban remittances curve and the other under the rising – and subsequently falling – urban-to-rural curve.

Unfortunately, with the exception of only a handful of cases, existing migration surveys were not undertaken with the purpose in mind of estimating remittances. Consequently, in view of the aforementioned points, prevailing evidence is usually biased and must therefore be handled with great caution.

A further caveat which must be kept in mind concerns the issue of the usage to which remittances are being put. Almost invariably, the questionnaire survey is the tool that has been employed to examine this issue. As it happens, this is a dubious device even if the relevant questions are put not to the migrant family member (which, nonetheless, is frequently the case), who is ill-positioned to inform a researcher that, say, a technological change has taken place at rural-end production, but to the migrant's family who stays behind in the rural sector.

The general deficiency of the questionnaire tool stems from the difficulty in interpreting the replies obtained. The specific deficiency of virtually all past questionnaires – the source of the findings of the surveys quoted by RL – is that none of the more appropriate questions was asked.

The former deficiency is due to asymmetry. That remittances were used, say, to purchase inputs embodying the new technology does prove that they are utilized to facilitate technological change. However, because of fungibility, observing that *remittances* were not directly used to facilitate such an end does not entail that they cannot be credited with responsibility for such a result. If there is evidence that technological change in agricultural production followed, with a lag, the event of rural-to-urban migration by a family member and that urban-to-rural remittances were transferred, the consequent release of other sources from the necessity of meeting pressing uses, facilitated by the flow of remittances, may have generated the transformation; although remittances are not a direct input in the process, they are a catalyst without which it could not have come about.

Moreover, remittances may have been responsible for this very same transformation in a manner which is even more indirect. In section 2 we referred to the risk and credit constraints impinging on technological change in agricultural production on the family farm. Considering, for example, the latter of these two constraints, it has been argued that the probable structure of the credit markets is such that the small farmer has no effective access to institutional or noninstitutional credit supply – a state of affairs that he can hardly expect to see changed. However, the situation concerning access to education for his children is totally different. Access to (some) universal education, which to a large extent is financed by governmental subsidies and not directly by those small farmers whose children are enrolled, is significantly easier and definitely more equal. Thus the small farmer's entrance into the market in which he is less discriminated against can be viewed as a surrogate to participation in the market into which entrance is effectively barred. Building on the expectation of a high cross rate of return to the joint decisions to educate, say, the maturing son and then "expel" him to the urban sector, migration and the education preceding it thus substitute for the credit deficency, the alleviation of which is mandatory in facilitating the technological change on the family farm.

Some familial surplus (which falls short of the "sufficient surplus") may be earmarked for the minimal finance of this education. In those cases where some education is incurred in the urban sector, such support may even assume the form of rural-to-urban transfer of remittances, precisely in the same way that, as mentioned earlier, "partial surplus" is utilized to enhance the migrant member's success in the urban labor market. The implication of this situation is that only a long-term view of objectives and means of furthering them can ensure against committing the fallacy of accusing migration and education of sucking surplus out of the rural sector or, as RL put it, of "diverting funds which would normally have been used for farm improvement."

The second specific deficiency of the questionnaire tool relates to the point made in the last but two paragraph. If a rupee of remittances frees a locally earned rupee, it is useless to ask only "what did you do with the money sent by your son?" If the mere fact that a rupee has been remitted signals to the risk-averse diversification-conscious farmer prevalence of an independent source of income, he may consequently adopt the (subjectively) riskier technology. If an elaborate, carefully prepared questionnaire cannot fully detect these and similar scenarios, the conclusion must be that an alternative methodology is required. Scrutinizing intensely two groups of small farmers similar in all respects but differing in their resource constraint and/or demographic composition and in that families belonging to one of them have expelled migrants to the urban sector whereas families belonging to the other did not could serve as such an alternative. This alternative control group methodology could best be exercised longitudinally. Given a usual budgetary constraint, this may necessitate a smaller-scale study – a price that is well worth paying.

The concluding comments of this chapter concern, first, the meaning of development and, last, the power of extrapolation.

Not only did RL interpret too restrictively the role of urban-to-rural remittances in "rural development," but they also appear to have assigned too narrow an interpretation to rural development and development at large. This may account for a total disregard of other roles of urban-to-rural remittances.

Should an economy achieving income growth of its lowest-income groups – even if the overall growth of its income is negligible – be classified as an economy which has failed to develop? If rural-to-urban migration results merely in a more equal distribution of income by size, should it not be regarded as conducive to "development"?

Consider an economy in which two-thirds to three-fourths of the poorest families, the bulk of which are small self-employed farmers, are located in the rural sector: the intra-rural income distribution is relatively more equal than the intra-urban income distribution; rural-to-urban migration is dominated by members of small-farmer families who are not concentrated in the upper range of the rural distribution of income by size. In such an economy, a transfer of income from a less equal segment of the income distribution (urban) to a lower more equal segment of the distribution (rural), directed not to the upper group in the latter but to the small farmers, is most probably equality increasing overall.

The informed reader may have sensed that the first part of the last paragraph depicts a typical rural-to-urban migration in a less developed country scenario. The second part accounts for the hypothesized impact of a typical urban-to-rural transfer of remittances. Theoretical reasoning provides support for this hypothesis (Stark, 1978, ch. IV). Evidence is, to say the least, sketchy. Yet a study (Knowles and Anker, 1977) based on a comprehensive data set drawn from Kenya, the very country on which RL base much of their argument, conclusively shows that, as a result of an urban-to-rural transfer of remittances, both the intersectoral and the overall degree of income inequality, as measured by the Gini coefficient, declined.[8]

The ease with which RL seem to have extrapolated into a likely future poor role what, to them, is a so far evidently unfavorable role of remittances must also be sanctioned.

There is no reason at all why remittances (and migration at large) should not be manipulated to become a vehicle of rural prosperity even if they were not conducive to agricultural development in the past. This *may* require some – yet minimal – institutional intervention. It is not difficult to envisage a system of incentives that will induce migrants to remit more and their rural families to utilize what they receive more productively. (Special remittance bank accounts, and matching grants or loans to be extended on the disbursement of receipts of remittances toward introduction of new technologies may constitute elements in such a system.)

By now there is sufficient evidence to suggest that rural-to-urban migration and urban-to-rural remittances can and have actually been used to transform agricultural modes of production (Stark, 1978, ch. III). What a constructive approach should do is attempt to analyze *why* in other cases urban-to-rural remittances have been – if indeed they were – less instrumental in agricultural development. Utilizing the moral of this analysis and drawing upon the encouraging experience, the challenge is to devise a system of the type just proposed.

**Notes**

Reprinted from *Journal of Development Studies* 16, 1980. I am indebted to the David Horowitz Institute for the Research of Developing Countries, Tel-Aviv University, for financial support and to Moises Syrquin and Adrian Ziderman for helpful comments.

1  For a detailed exposition see Stark (1978, ch. II).
2  For a discussion concerning the selection of the family migrant member see Stark (1978, ch. II).
3  In-between technological investment, which has a certain lumpiness, and investment in financial assets which has a low (or even negative) return.
4  "Largely" – since it is well documented that some proportion of the migrant's urban income, though saved and placed at the rural family's disposal, is *not* remitted but transferred via other means and in various forms, other than money.
5  In line with just one basic postulation of the approach presented in section 2, namely, the objective being maximization of total familial utility including the migrant member, the urban weight is bound to be positive provided that some additional fairly general postulations are specified. Assume, further, that all marginal utilities are positive and diminishing and that the pre-migration intra-family distribution of incomes is optimal. Then, if the post-migration income of the migrant is greater than his pre-migration income (with other members' incomes not increasing) urban-to-rural transfer of income must follow.
6  A great many and possibly most of the "relevant technological transformations" of recent times depend on new factors and inputs – elements in which the

technological change is "embodied." This in itself, independent of the factor of complementarity, creates strong discrete needs for "sufficient surplus" and produces a new pattern of technological change which differs from a "traditional technological change" – a continuous technological change involving gradual increments to the quantities of existing factors which is facilitated, in turn, by a continuous if sporadic accumulation of surplus.

7   This trait is bound to generate apparently contradictory results as given explanatory variables, utilized in different regression equations, appear with statistically significant, yet oppositely signed, coefficients.

8   In the study explicit reference is made to the intersectoral degree of inequality. Since, following the urban-to-rural transfer of remittances, the intra-urban Gini coefficient increases, and since the intra-rural coefficient declines by less than the overall coefficient declines, it follows, from a simple decomposition of the Gini coefficient, that the intersectoral coefficient must also decline after the urban-to-rural transfer.

## References

Griffin, Keith (1976) "On the Emigration of the Peasantry." *World Development* 4 (5): 353–61.

Knowles, James C. and Anker, Richard (1977) "An Analysis of Income Transfers in a Developing Country: The Case of Kenya." World Employment Programme, Population and Employment Project, Population and Employment Paper 59. Geneva: International Labour Office.

Rempel, Henry and Lobdell, Richard (1978) "The Role of Urban-to-Rural Remittances in Rural Development." *Journal of Development Studies* 14 (3): 324–41.

Stark, Oded (1978) *Economic–Demographic Interaction in Agricultural Development: The Case of Rural-to-Urban Migration.* Rome: UN Food and Agriculture Organization.

# 15

## Migration, Remittances, and the Family

### 1 Introduction

The importance of remittances in the development process is due to a number of factors: first, the scale and pace of rural-to-urban migration; second, the magnitude of urban-to-rural remittances (urban-to-rural remittances are usually transferred over quite a considerable period of time and amount to 10–30 percent of migrants' income (Stark, 1978, ch. III, and references cited therein)); third, the widespread interest in transfers of incomes and in mechanisms that generate changes in the distribution of income; fourth, the impact of remittances on the resource constraint in the economy at large where savings are suboptimal and, in particular, in the agricultural sector, especially with respect to technological change in agricultural production (Oberai and Manmohan Singh, 1980; Stark, 1980; Lucas, 1986); fifth, the role of children as migrants enhancing returns to the bearing and rearing of children (Stark, 1981; Katz and Stark, 1985, 1986).

Despite these factors, no comprehensive theory of urban-to-rural remittances exists. The need for at least some analytical clues regarding observed phenomena has been met partly by a number of recent studies that provide useful descriptive evidence and regression analyses (for example, Knowles and Anker, 1981). However, these endeavors fall short of a complete theory generating testable hypotheses. We have no rigorously derived answers to basic questions such as the following. Why do migrants remit? Why do some migrants remit much more than others? Why do some migrants remit for a long period of time, and others for a relatively short one? Why do remitting migrants stop remitting?

The theory developed below views remittances as part of, or one clause in, a migrant family's self-enforcing cooperative contractual arrangement. Indeed, the act of migration itself is an element in this contractual arrangement. In order to understand urban-to-rural remittances, it is necessary to understand the migrant–family contract and its properties. In section 2 the migrant–family contractual arrangement is taken as given, and the main interest is in issues of self-enforcement. The topic of what determines the precise contractual arrangement that the parties eventually strike and, in particular, what determines its provision of remittances is taken up in section 3. Tests on several specific implications are presented in section 4, using household survey data from Botswana. Concluding remarks are offered in section 5.

## 2 Rural-to-Urban Migration and Urban-to-Rural Remittances as Elements in a Self-Enforcing Cooperative Contractual Arrangement

The relation between the modal rural-to-urban migrating unit in less developed countries (LDCs) – a young single family member – and the rest of his family are modeled through a cooperative contractual arrangement. The migrant and the family enter into a voluntary contractual arrangement with each other because they expect to be better off with the contractual arrangement than without it.[1] Furthermore, the migrant expects to be better off by covering a given set of transactions or contingencies through an agreement with his family rather than with a third party, and likewise from the family's point of view. Although the term "contract" is applied here to such understandings, this is not meant necessarily to imply any explicit form or even terms; indeed, a less formal understanding may well be strengthened precisely by retaining greater flexibility.

Since the assumption here is that such a contractual arrangement covers a series of transactions that stretch over time, the migrant or the family may find it worthwhile to breach the contractual arrangement after it has run its course for some time. In principle, two mechanisms can deter violation: (a) an institution other than the two parties to the agreement, for example the legal powers of the state; (b) a calculation that the loss (for example, due to reprisal) entailed by such a breach outweighs the benefits. We shall rule out the first deterring device for the problem at hand and identify conditions under which, at any point in time, a migrant–family contractual arrangement will be self-enforcing.

Each party is assumed to face an income–time profile such that a higher risk has to be incurred first, whereas the increased benefit accrues subsequently. Each party can adopt an income-generating expected-income-increasing technology but is deterred from doing so by the high degree of the initial subjective risk associated with the generation of income through that technology. Thus each party is assumed to be risk averse.

Consider the migrant. On migrating, risks are very high at first: entry attempts into high-paying sectors may fail, entry into low-paying sectors, which may be relatively easy, entails high probability of discontinuity of employment because of the high sensitivity of these sectors to market fluctuations, and of course there is the distinct possibility of involuntary unemployment. However, as the migrant establishes himself, obtains more secure employment, and accumulates location-specific capital, the risks associated with urban employment and future urban earnings typically diminish.[2] Next, consider the family. We assume that its desire to adopt a new production technology in agriculture (high-yield varieties, for example) is strong but that the high-risk content of this technology acts as a deterrent. To facilitate technological transformation, it is thus necessary to resolve the familial aversion to the risk inherent in pursuing an initially risk-increasing strategy.

Assume that urban and rural incomes do not move in tandem, and that both the head of the family and the migrant are unable (sufficiently) to self-insure, cannot make insurance type arrangements with a third party, and, in particular, cannot insure against the increased risk in the marketplace. Provision of the required insurance may be impossible if markets are incomplete or the transaction costs of purchasing any insurance on the open market may be prohibitive. It is beyond the scope of the present chapter to explore the reasons why insurance markets for particular risks do not come into existence, but it is likely that the very nature of the particular risks described here (association with future earnings) contributes to this paucity.[3]

Given this assumption, can the parties turn to each other and act, in turn, as insurer and insuree? Consider the following arrangement. In the period immediately following migration, the migrant – the insuree – receives a less variable set of outcomes; the head of the family, who acts as the insurer, receives a somewhat more variable set of outcomes (in comparison with what each party would have received in the absence of such an exchange). In the next period, when the migrant has established himself in the urban sector, he acts as insurer. The head of the family – now the insuree – introduces technological change on the family farm, which is a risk-increasing venture but, because the migrant is acting as the insurer, the head of the family receives a less variable set of net outcomes. The parties can have identical attitudes toward risk, but, because of the difference in their time profile of risks, their behavior is analogous to what it would have been had they differed in their attitudes toward risk. Thus, in the period following migration, the head of the family may offer to pay the migrant a certain amount, often revealed through rural-to-urban remittances, under certain conditions (the event of unemployment). In return, once established, the migrant accepts a lower expected payoff because of his remitting to his family in the rural sector. Urban-to-rural remittances can thus be interpreted as delayed payment of a premium for the insurance taken up by the migrant in the first period and/or as a transfer of the insurance payment to the head of the family once the rural unfavorable state of nature has occurred.

Whereas none of the parties would have been able to bear the risk of failure alone, the exchange of risks permits the parties to engage in activities that are highly risky in the short run. These activities would not have been undertaken otherwise. Although each party has first to incur the higher risk in order to be able to reap increased benefit in the future, it incurs the higher risk while the other party is in a relatively less risky state. This is what we have in mind when we refer to a mutually advantageous cooperative agreement.

Note that this example illustrates the unusual flexibility and resourcefulness of the family unit – not only in overcoming market deficiencies but also in overcoming inherent scale deficiencies. The family whose capacity to spread risks is constrained by its limited *size* enlarges scale via broadening the relevant *space*; inability to realize scale economies is thus ameliorated via ability to realize space or scope economies. Migration of a family member facilitates effective pooling of risks and insurance in alleviating the size constraint and gaining access to independence of risks.[4]

An obvious difficulty in this example has to do with adherence. Once reached, will the contractual arrangement be binding? Will it be worthwhile to one party to deviate from a contractual arrangement even if the other party immediately detects the violation, interprets it as a fundamental breach, and terminates the agreement, inflicting a cost on the violator? In our example, after being supported by his family while pursuing the short-run risky urban employment strategy and succeeding, the migrant may decide to retain all urban-earned income and withdraw his commitment to act as a reliable insurer. Will he?

Since our interest in this chapter is whether the migrant will fulfill the remittances provision of the contractual arrangement, we shall try to identify conditions under which he will find it advantageous to adhere to his commitments. The argument that the family will find adherence a rewarding strategy is symmetrical.

A migrant will violate his agreement at any moment only if his discounted net expected benefits from the arrangement are negative. If we assume that the family would have discontinued the arrangement prior to this if they did not consider themselves net gainers, then violation of the agreement by the migrant would clearly impose a loss on the family.

But part of the benefits perceived by the migrant may stem from his altruism toward his family. Thus, avoiding imposing a cost on the family may benefit the migrant and encourage continuation of the arrangement. Hence altruism may either reinforce an already self-enforcing contractual arrangement or may be the *sine qua non* of the agreement.[5]

This is a convenient point for a moment's reflection. When the nature of the transactions that the parties wish to enter into is such that intertemporal transfers and intertemporal contracts must be involved, the parties will be duly concerned about the issue of enforcement. This concern would lead to preference for a partner with whom a contract will be (more) self-enforceable. Both migrant and family are endowed with a highly specific asset: mutual altruism. The value of this asset is realized when they trade with each other, but would be lost if they were to enter into an exchange relationship with a third party. As it enforces a self-enforcing contractual arrangement, altruism reduces the need for costly contractual safeguards. Other things being equal, it thus renders a migrant–family contractual arrangement more cost efficient than alternative contractual arrangements. In creating an effect similar to trust or loyalty, altruism assists the parties in solving problems that emerge when legally enforced property rights and contingent contracts cannot be written (Breton and Wintrobe, 1982).

However, since both migrant and family gain more from a lower-transaction-costs contractual arrangement with each other than from one with a third party, they should be willing to give more to each other than to a third party. Hence the migrant furnishes his family with more remittances, the family furnishes the migrant with more insurance and so forth. Thus, in terms of our trade-in-risks example, we now clearly see that the migrant and the family have an incentive to turn to each other even when the set of alternative parties is not empty. By entering into an exchange agreement with each other, they are relatively assured about fulfillment of the provisions of this exchange.

Now that we have noted the reinforcing effect of altruism, we can briefly check how crucial it is in generating the continuity properties of the exchange relation and how stable it is as an intertemporal self-enforcing device.

We have not yet said much about the nature of altruism. It is perhaps reasonable to assume that, in general, altruism will wane through time. This waning of the migrant's altruistic motive would then tend to weaken the self-enforcing property of the migrant–family contractual arrangement. However, since, as in our example, the value of the insurance benefits to the family may rise over time, the altruism-generated reinforcement mechanism may not break down even if the altruism weight itself declines.

### 3 Striking the Migrant–Family Contractual Arrangement

Beyond any altruistic concerns, there are a number of reasons why the migrant may derive utility from an arrangement with his family. First, though immune to the vagaries of weather that strongly affect agriculture, urban labor markets are often subject to upheavals brought about by economic cycles. Some urban subsectors (for example, construction) are more vulnerable than others. It is fairly likely that for quite a long period of time the migrant will belong to these, rather than to more secure subsectors. Familial support when the downswing hits hard could be quite important. Family insurance provided intertemporally is an invaluable hedge against the not too steady, sometimes even turbulent, urban labor markets. Moreover, the migrant may wish to reduce his vulnerability through enhanced labor mobility that could involve voluntary layoff, intensive job search, and lapse in employment. Engagement in such an attempt may crucially depend on tacit or explicit familial support.

Second, there are numerous indications that, for quite a long period of time after moving to the urban sector, migrants retain a strong degree of identification, allegiance, and social connectedness with their village of origin.[6] Their social status and prestige depend on their standing in their home village, over which a migrant's family exercises great power. It may even hold a natural monopoly position in determining the migrant's standing. This empowers the family to provide or deny the migrant an asset, albeit an intangible one.

Third, the family – or, more precisely, the head of the family – usually keeps tight control over its rural property. Bequests are normally deferred to a very late stage in life. The deed to the family land is usually not passed on before the head of the family dies or becomes too old to support himself. Claims by a migrant to family property rights are more likely when the family farm is subjected to technological advance that, as intimated in the example in section 2, may have been facilitated by the migrant himself.

We thus see how the family may continue to be a source of economic security, emotional satisfaction, and tangible assets to the migrant long past his departure for the urban sector. In addition, the migrant is often supported by his family during his formal education, perhaps both before and after leaving home. Again, this undertaking can be seen as a component in an intertemporal understanding: the family makes the initial sacrifice; the migrant benefits from augmented subsequent earnings; the family is recompensed through remittances.

Hence, there is a set of reasons why the migrant may, in principle, be willing to commit himself to the transfer of remittances. But it is the fact that the sequencing of net gains to migrant and family may thus oscillate intertemporally which provides for self-enforcement even beyond altruistic concerns. Indeed, the sequencing of certain events may well be viewed as endogenous to the enforcement of the long-term understanding.

For example, with respect to disposition of family property, the head of the family has the last word – he controls the last action taken in a temporal sequence. Realizing that the head of the family will react at a later stage, the migrant will be induced to condition his prior behavior. In a different context, a similar point has been made by Becker (1976, 1977, 1981) and Hirshleifer (1977). However, what they both capture may be a necessary but not a sufficient condition. For suppose that the migrant knows with certainty when the head of the family will die and that bequests, assumed throughout to be conditioned on behavior, are made by the head of the family immediately before his death. The migrant may decide not to remit until a short while prior to that date and only then make up for his "rotten" behavior. The threat of reprisal under full certainty concerning the timing of bequests cannot then guarantee that the desired conduct will occur in the preferred time periods. What may help to ensure such conduct is if the migrant does not know in advance when bequests are going to be made. In every period there is a positive probability that the decisions concerning bequests will be made in the subsequent period. Therefore, in terms of the contractual arrangement reached between himself and his family, in each and every moment in time the migrant is bound to be "in the black."[7]

In principle, several contractual arrangements could be Pareto efficient; that is, neither of the parties is worse off and at least one of them is better off with the contractual arrangement than without it. How then do the migrant and family agree on one particular arrangement?

The choice between the many feasible equilibrium points is a matter of bargaining between the migrant and the family. The parties use their bargaining power in pursuit of their self-interests. There is absolutely no contradiction between this and our mutual altruism assumption of section 2. Each party prefers the contractual arrangement that best suits its interests, which include anything, both selfish and altruistic, to which its utility function assigns positive utility. This implies that in some sense the outcome of the bargaining process is a reflection of the relative bargaining powers of the parties.

The bargaining power of each party depends, in turn, on the utility with which it can provide the other, on the cost that it will incur in providing this utility, and on its willingness to risk a conflict. This ties in nicely with our trade-in-risks example. If the migrant considers his entry into the urban labor market highly risky, he would attach a high value to the family-provided insurance and would be less willing to risk conflict with, or more willing to make concessions to, the family. Similarly, if the subjective risk that the family associates with a new technology is high, the family would be willing to go quite a long way in appeasing the migrant in order to gain his agreement to act as insurer.

It is now easy to see how this approach furnishes predictions about remittances. Since the outcome – the contractual arrangement that the parties strike – reflects their bargaining powers, variables enhancing the bargaining power of the family or weakening that of the migrant will positively influence the magnitude of migrant-to-family remittances, and variables enhancing the bargaining power of the migrant or weakening that of the family will affect them negatively. Highly valued family property, unstable urban labor markets, capital markets requiring reliance on the family to finance education, and close social cohesion illustrate the former. Tight rural insurance (financial) markets, strong dependence of the new agricultural technology on specific and indivisible investments, and high subjective and objective risk associated with the new technology illustrate the latter.

### 4 Empirical Illustrations from Botswana

In this section, some empirical illustrations of selected aspects of hypothesized intertemporal understandings sustained between the migrant and the family group are provided. In particular, evidence relating to the notions of coinsurance, repayment of schooling costs, and behavior conditioned by a concern to inherit is presented. The data are from the National Migration Survey (NMS) conducted in Botswana in 1978–9.[8]

The remittances examined are amounts received in cash and kind at rural homes from each adult reported absent from that home. Each observation is one adult with a total of 3179 adults in the sample. In each of the following regressions, the dependent variable is the logarithm of monthly remittances measured in pula averaged over the number of rounds in which the person was absent.[9] If no remittances occurred, the dependent variable is set equal to zero.

## Results on Repayment of School Costs

To test whether remittances are part of an intertemporal understanding to recompense the family for initial sacrifices during the migrant's schooling, it is essential to distinguish groups for whom the family has made such sacrifices. This distinction cannot be made definitively from the NMS data or, indeed, from most household surveys. However, groups for whom the costs of schooling are more likely to have been borne by the migrant's family can be defined. In the present context, the more likely group is assumed to consist of children of the household head (or his or her spouse), grandchildren, and nieces and nephews, as opposed to all others (parents, grandparents, uncles and aunts, brothers and sisters, cousins, sons and daughters-in-law, unrelated individuals, the household head himself or herself, etc.). In table 15.1 the former group is labeled "own young," and the remainder "others." The $t$-statistics for a zero null hypothesis appear in parentheses beneath estimated coefficients. The first four columns report results for all absentees, no matter whether in urban or rural areas; the last four columns are for urban absentees only.

Remittances do tend to rise with the level of education in most cases in table 15.1.[10] However, this is not surprising, for wages also rise with education. This is certainly not sufficient by itself to support a hypothesis of repaying school costs, though elsewhere it has been taken to be so (Johnson and Whitelaw, 1974; Rempel and Lobdell, 1978). The appropriate test is, rather, whether the coefficient on schooling is greater among own young than among others. For female absentees, both urban and overall, this difference is indeed positive in table 15.1, and a hypothesis of no difference is rejected at a 10 percent significance level, but for males the difference is indistinguishable from zero. At least for females, there is thus significant support for a hypothesis that the family invests in the education of its own young in return for an implicit understanding of subsequent remittance.

Moreover, among females the significant parabolic profile of remittances with years transpired since leaving school might suggest an ending to an agreement to repay. But, in fact, this is implausible. The turning point of the estimated parabola comes only 30–35 years after leaving school, and the turning point is almost identical for own young and others. Nor, if the equation is extended to include an interaction between years of school and time lapsed since school, does any obvious interaction or shift in turning point emerge.

It remains quite plausible that the family does educate its girls, in particular, with an understanding that the family will subsequently be

**Table 15.1** Repayment of schooling costs

| | All absentees | | | | Urban absentees only | | | |
| | Male | | Female | | Male | | Female | |
| | Own young | Others | Own young | Others | Own young | Others | Own young | Others |
|---|---|---|---|---|---|---|---|---|
| Intercept | -0.228 | -0.272 | -1.113 | -0.750 | -0.032 | -0.483 | -0.974 | -0.336 |
| | (0.78) | (0.40) | (3.04) | (1.28) | (0.09) | (0.51) | (2.22) | (0.35) |
| Years of schooling | 0.071 | 0.112 | 0.114 | 0.039 | 0.012 | 0.075 | 0.126 | 0.033 |
| | (4.26) | (3.26) | (5.06) | (0.97) | (0.41) | (0.96) | (3.01) | (0.34) |
| Years since leaving school | 0.022 | 0.071 | 0.088 | 0.099 | 0.021 | 0.079 | 0.091 | 0.082 |
| | (1.05) | (1.63) | (2.85) | (2.53) | (0.75) | (1.29) | (2.21) | (1.20) |
| Years since leaving school squared | -0.0003 | -0.0008 | -0.0014 | -0.0017 | -0.0003 | -0.0007 | -0.0013 | -0.0013 |
| | (0.73) | (0.99) | (1.83) | (2.39) | (0.50) | (0.66) | (1.28) | (0.99) |
| Statistical hazard rate | 27.3 | 34.2 | 28.5 | 2.02 | 66.4 | -13.8 | 11.3 | -5.5 |
| | (2.21) | (1.01) | (1.53) | (0.06) | (2.53) | (0.15) | (0.26) | (0.05) |
| $R^2$ | 0.08 | 0.09 | 0.14 | 0.08 | 0.05 | 0.09 | 0.13 | 0.19 |
| F-statistic | 12.6 | 5.1 | 12.4 | 1.7 | 5.3 | 2.3 | 7.0 | 1.4 |
| No. of observations | 594 | 220 | 303 | 82 | 379 | 99 | 195 | 27 |

Dependent variable is the logarithm of monthly remittances (truncated at zero); own young are children of the household head or his or her spouse; others are everyone else. *t*-statistics for a zero null hypothesis are in parentheses.

recompensed. However, there is no clear evidence to suggest a time profile or deadline on such arrangements.

### Aspiration to Inherit

Inheritance customs and laws among the Batswana are neither universal nor immutable. Practices vary from tribe to tribe and within a given tribe. Indeed, a statistical study of inheritance, whether in Botswana or elsewhere, truly requires a specialized survey, if only to record the existence of and links with children who are no longer members of the head's household.

Nonetheless, some limited suggestive evidence can be obtained from the NMS. On average, sons are more likely to inherit than daughters or other household members, though their inheritance is not assured. It may therefore be asked of the data whether sons (and their spouses) remit more to families with greater amounts of inheritable wealth and whether this differs from practices of daughters (and their spouses) and of others.

This question is explored in table 15.2. Cattle are the dominant form of inheritable wealth in Botswana. All land (other than towns and freehold farms) is common property of the tribes and is assigned traditionally in *kgotla* (the tribal council) and now by land boards.

In the regressions of table 15.2, a dummy variable is included for whether the household has a cattle herd of more than 20 beasts.[11] Both overall and from urban areas only, sons do remit more to families with larger herds; the effect passes a 7 percent significance test. Neither daughters nor "others" remit significantly more to families with larger herds. Moreover, the size of the coefficient on the cattle ownership dummy is larger for sons than for either daughters or "others," and the differential with daughters' behavior is significant at a 5 percent level though the comparison with others is statistically weaker. Together, these results suggest a particular concern of sons to remit to families with large herds, which is consistent with a strategy to maintain favor in inheritance.

No significant pattern of remittance with respect to age of the household head is found, nor, in an extension of the regressions in table 15.2, is a significant interaction between age of head and number of cattle discerned. If remittance is to curry favor, it seems that this must be independent of the head's age. This would be consistent with the fact that some cattle are often dispensed long before the head can reasonably expect to die while others are kept as a bequest: it may be essential to sustain favor continuously under such circumstances as discussed in section 3.

**Table 15.2** Aspiration to inherit

| | All absentees | | | | Urban absentees only | | | |
|---|---|---|---|---|---|---|---|---|
| | Head and spouse | Sons and spouses | Daughters and spouses | Others | Head and spouse | Sons and spouses | Daughters and spouses | Others |
| Intercept | 0.094 (0.73) | −0.295 (2.65) | −0.004 (0.04) | −0.001 (0.01) | 0.145 (0.53) | −0.311 (1.71) | 0.095 (0.58) | 0.061 (0.40) |
| Log absentee's wage ($l\omega$): | | | | | | | | |
| $0 < l\omega \leq 3$ | 0.160 (0.61) | 0.182 (0.82) | 0.307 (3.64) | 0.134 (1.28) | 1.541 (1.73) | 0.398 (1.17) | 0.442 (3.27) | 0.053 (0.24) |
| $3 < l\omega \leq 4$ | 1.063 (7.61) | 0.415 (5.51) | 0.604 (7.60) | 0.336 (4.84) | 1.456 (3.68) | 0.501 (3.48) | 0.672 (5.04) | 0.445 (2.92) |
| $4 < l\omega$ | 1.625 (10.98) | 0.775 (9.83) | 1.138 (10.40) | 0.753 (7.84) | 1.379 (4.19) | 0.706 (5.01) | 1.233 (6.70) | 0.702 (4.24) |
| Spouse | −0.143 (1.40) | 0.015 (0.16) | −0.274 (1.31) | — | −0.433 (1.35) | 0.026 (0.14) | −0.168 (0.33) | — |

(Table continues on the following page)

**Table 15.2** Aspiration to inherit (continued)

| | All absentees | | | | Urban absentees only | | | |
|---|---|---|---|---|---|---|---|---|
| | Head and spouse | Sons and spouses | Daughters and spouses | Others | Head and spouse | Sons and spouses | Daughters and spouses | Others |
| No. of cattle owned > 20 | 0.146 | 0.146 | −0.148 | 0.079 | 0.374 | 0.195 | −0.123 | 0.114 |
| | (1.61) | (2.32) | (2.28) | (1.40) | (1.26) | (1.81) | (1.04) | (0.81) |
| Head age | | | | | | | | |
| 46–60 | 0.073 | 0.120 | 0.052 | 0.024 | 0.076 | 0.203 | 0.071 | 0.174 |
| | (0.76) | (1.39) | (0.62) | (0.31) | (0.28) | (1.35) | (0.47) | (1.06) |
| 61+ | −0.034 | −0.037 | 0.010 | −0.032 | 0.202 | −0.033 | −0.064 | −0.101 |
| | (0.23) | (0.45) | (0.12) | (0.54) | (0.41) | (0.22) | (0.43) | (0.74) |
| Statistical hazard rate | 0.366 | 28.6 | 12.3 | 4.79 | 5.69 | 48.2 | 4.84 | 8.41 |
| | (0.03) | (4.47) | (1.68) | (0.77) | (0.11) | (3.78) | (0.25) | (0.52) |
| $R^2$ | 0.33 | 0.17 | 0.22 | 0.14 | 0.32 | 0.15 | 0.20 | 0.14 |
| F-statistic | 28.3 | 24.3 | 22.5 | 13.0 | 6.4 | 10.0 | 8.7 | 4.3 |
| No. of observations | 472 | 977 | 652 | 564 | 117 | 462 | 290 | 192 |

The dependent variable is the logarithm of monthly remittances (truncated at zero). t-statistics are in parentheses.

## Response to Drought

The year of the survey, 1978–9, happened to be a year of serious drought. Droughts are frequent in Botswana and can be devastating, such as the great drought of the mid-1960s. However, Botswana covers a large area, equal to that of Texas or France, and the incidence of drought is not uniform: some areas even receive above-normal precipitation during years of drought.

For most of the village areas sampled in the NMS, rainfall for the year 1978–9 is also recorded. An index of drought can then be defined for each village area, so that a higher value of the index indicates greater severity of drought. In table 15.3, this index is included in remittance equations. In this case, only urban absentees are analyzed, for two reasons: (a) for the household to spread risks, it may well be wiser to send migrants to town (or to South Africa, if possible) rather than elsewhere within the rural sector, where outcomes are probably more highly positively correlated; (b) the extent of drought in each absentee's rural destination is not known.[12]

In the first equation in table 15.3 drought is estimated to be significantly positively associated with the amount remitted: the worse the drought, the more is remitted. However, such a result is also consistent with a pure altruism theory: drought lowers income, and ensuing remittance may simply reflect the desire of the migrant to alleviate special hardships imposed on the family.

However, in the remaining two regressions in table 15.3 such a pure altruism interpretation is denied. The second equation adds two variables: logarithm of number of cattle owned (set equal to zero for no cattle) and the interaction of that logarithm with a drought index. The third equation adds two more: the logarithm of number of crop acres "possessed" and its interaction with drought. The existence of drought conditions and the possession of more cattle or more crop land have nothing to do with stimulating greater remittances *per se*; the interactions of drought with these drought-sensitive assets do. Families that are at risk of losing cattle unless feed and water rights can be purchased and those who are at risk because they customarily rely on crops for more of their sustenance receive greater remittances during the drought. This is precisely the response one would expect if households allocate members to urban migration in order to insure against adopting risky asset portfolios at home.

This is not to deny a role for altruism, for table 15.3 also shows that, given the degree of drought and assets at risk, more is received from close kin (defined as the immediate family – head, spouse, and own children).

230

**Table 15.3**  Responses to drought

| | Urban absentees only | | |
| --- | --- | --- | --- |
| | *(1)* | *(2)* | *(3)* |
| Intercept | −0.292 | −0.241 | −0.202 |
| | (2.96) | (2.06) | (1.61) |
| Log absentee's wage (*lω*): | | | |
| 0 < *lω* ≤ 3 | 0.365 | 0.364 | 0.358 |
| | (3.12) | (3.17) | (3.12) |
| 3 < *lω* ≤ 4 | 0.559 | 0.572 | 0.570 |
| | (6.76) | (7.01) | (6.99) |
| 4 < *lω* | 0.803 | 0.823 | 0.819 |
| | (8.82) | (9.21) | (9.16) |
| Close kin of household | 0.129 | 0.123 | 0.119 |
| | (1.72) | (1.67) | (1.61) |
| Duration of absence | 0.187 | 0.165 | 0.169 |
| | (2.13) | (1.91) | (1.96) |
| Duration squared | −0.022 | −0.020 | −0.021 |
| | (2.28) | (2.09) | (2.15) |
| Current drought index | 0.485 | 0.267 | 0.044 |
| | (3.41) | (1.14) | (0.17) |
| Log cattle | — | −0.023 | −0.017 |
| | | (0.79) | (0.56) |
| Drought × log cattle | — | 0.174 | 0.130 |
| | | (1.99) | (1.44) |
| Log crop acres | — | — | −0.028 |
| | | | (0.78) |
| Drought × log acres | — | — | 0.224 |
| | | | (2.00) |
| Statistical hazard rate | 34.3 | 27.5 | 27.2 |
| | (3.79) | (3.02) | (2.99) |
| $R^2$ | 0.16 | 0.17 | 0.17 |
| *F*-statistic | 24.4 | 20.4 | 17.5 |
| No. of observations | 1,051 | 1,036 | 1,036 |

The dependent variable is the logarithm of monthly remittance (truncated at zero). *t*-statistics are in parentheses.

That such closer members care helps to make them more responsible and more reliable coinsurers, as outlined in section 2.

The duration-of-absence terms (measured in months/100) in table 15.3 indicate that remittances at first rise and then subsequently decline with time away. However, as with schooling, the implied turning point is again some 30 years. For all practical purposes, the pattern is one of dwindling rise rather than decline in remittance with time. It seems that those who continue to be regarded as members of their original household are robust remitters. Indeed, robustness and sustained acceptance as a member are probably simultaneously determined: those who wish to maintain a link with home continue to remit.

## 5 Concluding Remarks

The thesis of this chapter is that remittances can be seen as one component of a longer-term understanding between a migrant and his or her family, an understanding that may involve many aspects including education of the migrant, migration itself, coinsurance, and inheritance. The family group as a whole can potentially gain from such arrangements, though the distribution of gains between migrants and home may be a matter for bargaining, and each may be the net beneficiary at different phases. Indeed, it is precisely this sequencing of gains that helps to render an understanding self-enforcing in addition to any feelings of mutual altruism. Thus the empirical illustrations from Botswana indicate that, having been educated by the family, the migrant gains from higher wages but is then expected to repay them; the family gains assurance in undertaking riskier agricultural activities, knowing that the migrant will support them during drought; sons remit in the hope of maintaining favor in ultimate inheritance.

The efficiency of an intra-familial implicit contract comes partly from the fact that much of it has to do with unwritten understandings about the obligations of the two parties, and it is probably true that mutual familiarity will support, enhance, and ease these understandings.

Migration can thus be fruitfully viewed as an intertemporal proposition generating streams of various benefits to both migrants and their families, rather than an *ad hoc* once-and-for-all adjustment to an intersectoral wage differential so often taken to be *the* explanatory variable of rural-to-urban migration in LDCs. We are accustomed to viewing migration as an indication that the family splits apart as the young move away and dissociate themselves from familial and traditional bondage, regardless of the negative externalities thus imposed on their families. Our work instead emphasizes the efficiency, flexibility, and what we might call the dynamic comparative advantage of the family. It also shifts the focus of migration theory from individual independence to mutual interdependence.

**Notes**

Co-authored with Robert E. B. Lucas. Reprinted from *Economic Development and Cultural Change* 36, 1988. This is Discussion Paper 28, Harvard University Migration and Development Program. We have benefited from and gratefully acknowledge discussions with William Alonso, Robert Aumann, Zvi Griliches, Tamara Hareven, Michael Intriligator, Simon Kuznets, Jacob Mincer, Jacob Paroush, Pauline Peters, Jennifer Roback, Reinhard Selten, Julian Simon, and Edward Wilson. Parts and earlier versions of this chapter were presented at the 1982 Annual Meeting of the Population Association of America, San Diego, the 1982 European Meeting of the Econometric Society, Dublin, the 1982 Joint Meeting of the Econometric Society and the American Economic Association, New York, the 1985 Annual Meeting of the Population Association of America, Boston, and at seminars held at Brown University, Harvard University, and Johns Hopkins University. Helpful comments were made by participants in these meetings and seminars. D. Gale Johnson and an anonymous referee provided valuable advice and suggestions for improving an earlier version of the chapter.

1  In some contexts, precisely who constitutes the family unit is not immediately obvious. Complex household arrangements that have different composition and decision-making structures for different kinds of decisions may well prevail. Coalition formation and composition with respect to control of specific resources cannot then be assumed away. The approach adopted here is guided by analytic convenience: simplifying the analysis into a two-person game. The reader should note, however, that we can sustain the approach in the text by assuming endogenous formation of a coalition: the family members excluding the migrant decide to act together, as one unit, relative to the migrant. The head of the family then assumes the role of a "representative agent." The decision is fueled by the expectation that, by committing themselves to act together rather than separately, the members are in a much better position when bargaining with the migrant on how to divide the amount made available through pursuance of the migrant–family contractual arrangement (see Hart and Kurz, 1983).

2  This stylized version of how migrants enter the urban economy is assumed to hold irrespective of whether "formal" employment or "informal" employment is preferred (see Stark, 1982).

3  Incompleteness of futures markets implies that economic agents are typically "unable to realize on the current set of markets the full potential value of

[their] future economic wealth" (Radner, 1982). Migration can be seen to constitute a particular form of investment in human capital. It is usually impossible to trade this type of capital even in competitive markets.

4  Here we differ from Pollak (1985) who, because he does not consider migration, naturally attributes to the small size of the family a critical technical disadvantage in familial insurance provision capacity.

5  On the great multitude of altruistic equilibria in the repeated economy and attempts to narrow down the set of these equilibria, see Kurz (1978).

6  See, for example, Gugler and Flanagan (1978) and De Jong and Gardner (1981). This property is analytically exploited by Stark (1984).

7  Michael Intriligator (personal communication, September 1982) has suggested that a strong demonstration effect could account for "proper" behavior by the migrant. A migrant may be aware that his children are likelier to adhere to a contractual arrangement with him if they observe him adhering to a contractual arrangement with his own father. The migrant would thus be induced to behave accordingly. Imitation and recurrent behavior are often critical elements in the formation of preferences and the evolutionary emergence of social norms of conduct.

8  For more details on the survey and data, see *National Migration Study* (1983) and Lucas and Stark (1985).

9  At the time of the survey, the pula was worth US$1.20. The survey comprised four rounds of interviews, one every three months for a year, revisiting all dwellings in each round. In the regressions, a statistical hazard rate is added as an explanatory variable. This is a correction factor for sample selection and is estimated from the probability of being an absentee (or urban absentee when considered separately) in the sample, given sex, years of schooling, age and age squared, whether head of household, and number of consumer units in the household. Since this hazard rate correction is purely a statistical adjustment, no economic interpretation of the associated coefficient need be offered here. It may be noted, however, that despite the statistical significance of the coefficients on the statistical hazard rate measure, whether this correction is made or not makes essentially no difference to estimates of other coefficients. Although the regression results here are presented as separate nonnested tests for purposes of exposition, each of the tests reported also holds if a combined equation is estimated.

10  Missing data, and particularly missing data on education of migrants, reduces the sample size to 1199, or some 38 percent of the total in table 15.1, compared with a response rate of 84 percent in table 15.2.

11  A herd of 20 beasts is often adopted as a significant dividing line in Botswana. A common argument for this particular break point is that some eight beasts are required for ploughing and a total herd of 20 is necessary to assure eight adult ploughing animals. Other variables included in the regressions of table 15.2 but not discussed in the text include three dummy variables respectively set equal to 1 if the logarithm of the absentee's wage is positive but less than or equal to 3, greater than 3 but less than or equal to 4, greater than 4. The omitted category is therefore those with no earnings. Clearly, the results show

that remittances rise with migrants' earnings, though not necessarily in a fashion that would be strictly linear in logarithm of the wage. In addition, a dummy variable set equal to 1 for a spouse, within each group, and 0 otherwise, is included in table 15.2. This measure is inserted to see whether behavior, for example of daughters-in-law, is significantly different from that of their husbands, but in general this proves not to be the case.

12   Moreover, the sexes are combined in table 15.3. There is no inherent reason to anticipate different risk strategies with respect to male and female members (whereas, *a priori*, this was untrue for opportunity cost of schooling in table 15.1). In fact, if separate male–female regressions are estimated for the drought model, coefficients are not significantly different between sexes.

## References

Becker, Gary S. (1976) "Altruism, Egoism, and Genetic Fitness: Economics and Sociobiology." *Journal of Economic Literature* 14 (3): 817–26.
—— (1977) "Reply to Hirshleifer and Tullock." *Journal of Economic Literature* 15 (2), 506–7.
—— (1981) "Altruism in the Family and Selfishness in the Market Place." *Economica* 48 (1), 1–15.
Breton, Albert and Wintrobe, Ronald (1982) *The Logic of Bureaucratic Conduct: An Economic Analysis of Competition, Exchange, and Efficiency in Private and Public Organizations.* Cambridge: Cambridge University Press.
De Jong, Gordon F. and Gardner, Robert W. (eds) (1981) *Migration Decision Making.* New York: Pergamon Press.
Gugler, Joseph and Flanagan, William G. (1978) *Urbanization and Social Change in West Africa.* Cambridge: Cambridge University Press.
Hart, Sergiu and Kurz, Mordecai (1983) "Endogenous Formation of Coalitions." *Econometrica* 51: 1047–64.
Hirshleifer, Jack (1977) "Shakespeare vs. Becker on Altruism: The Importance of Having the Last Word." *Journal of Economic Literature* 15 (2): 500–2.
Johnson, G. E. and Whitelaw, W. E. (1974) "Urban–Rural Income Transfers in Kenya: An Estimated-Remittances Function." *Economic Development and Cultural Change* 22: 473–9.
Katz, Eliakim and Stark, Oded (1985) "Desired Fertility and Migration in LDCs: Signing the Connection." *Proceedings of the General Conference, Florence, 1985.* Liège: International Union for the Scientific Study of Population.
—— and —— (1986) "On Fertility, Migration and Remittances in LDCs." *World Development* 14 (1): 133–5.
Knowles, James C. and Anker, Richard (1981) "An Analysis of Income Transfers in a Developing Country: The Case of Kenya." *Journal of Development Economics* 8: 205–26.

Kurz, Mordecai (1978) "Altruism as an Outcome of Social Interaction." *American Economic Review* 68 (2): 216–22.

Lucas, Robert E. B. (1986) "Emigration, Employment and Accumulation: The Miners of Southern Africa." In Oded Stark (ed.), *Migration, Human Capital and Development*. Greenwich, CT: JAI Press.

—— and Stark, Oded (1985) "Motivations to Remit: Evidence from Botswana." *Journal of Political Economy* 93 (5): 901–18 (reprinted as ch. 16 in this volume).

National Migration Study (1983) *Proceedings of the Conference held in Gaborone, Botswana, December 1982.*

Oberai, A. S. and Manmohan Singh, H. K. (1980) "Migration, Remittances and Rural Development." *International Labour Review* 119 (2): 229–41.

Pollak, Robert A. (1985) "A Transaction Cost Approach to Families and Households." *Journal of Economic Literature* 23 (2): 581–608.

Radner, Roy (1982) "The Role of Private Information in Markets and Other Organizations." In Werner Hildenbrand (ed.), *Advances in Economic Theory*. New York: Cambridge University Press, pp. 97–120.

Rempel, H. and Lobdell, R. A. (1978) "The Role of Urban-to-Rural Remittances in Rural Development." *Journal of Development Studies* 14: 324–41.

Stark, Oded (1978) *Economic–Demographic Interactions in Agricultural Development: The Case of Rural-to-Urban Migration*. Rome: UN Food and Agriculture Organization.

—— (1980) "On the Role of Urban-to-Rural Remittances in Rural Development." *Journal of Development Studies* 16 (3): 369–74 (reprinted as ch. 14 in this volume).

—— (1981) "The Asset Demand for Children During Agricultural Modernization." *Population and Development Review* 7 (4): 671–5.

—— (1982) "On Modelling the Informal Sector," *World Development* 10 (5): 413–6.

—— (1984) "Rural-to-Urban Migration in LDCs: A Relative Deprivation Approach." *Economic Development and Cultural Change* 32 (3): 475–86 (reprinted as ch. 7 in this volume).

# 16

# Motivations to Remit: Evidence from Botswana

In examining determinants of fertility, marriage, and divorce, economists have begun to address questions of household composition more traditionally posed by anthropologists and sociologists. Yet although membership in the household has now been exposed to econometric analysis, the unit of study is almost always the household as a cohabiting group, eating from a common pot. The recent literature on bequests does extend the familial context beyond that of the nuclear household to encompass intergenerational links for purposes of risk sharing, attention for the elderly, or storage of asset-specific knowledge (Kotlikoff and Spivak, 1981; Rosenzweig and Wolpin, 1983; Bernheim et al., 1984). But not only intergenerational issues warrant consideration of a broader family, for in many societies intra-familial remittances are observed on a substantial scale. At least for certain economic dimensions, it seems the unit of analysis may appropriately be extended spatially across households as well as intergenerationally.

In spite of the potential importance of remitting as a private mechanism of income redistribution between persons and across sectors, permitting, for example, consumption in excess of locally generated incomes or granting access to an additional source of capital funds, no comprehensive theory of remittances exists. Moreover, there is surprisingly little statistical evidence on the motives for remitting, and the few studies that have appeared are not couched in terms of testable hypotheses derived from a theoretical framework (Mohammad et al., 1973; Johnson and Whitelaw, 1974; Rempel and Lobdell, 1978; Knowles and Anker, 1981).

Certainly the most obvious motive for remitting is pure altruism – the care of a migrant for those left behind. Indeed, this appears to be the single notion underlying much of the remittance literature. But household arrangements, particularly within an extended family, may be considerably more complex than such a simple form would suggest. The first part of section 1 sketches a theory of pure altruism, while the second subsection develops a polar opposite: remittance motivated entirely by pure self-interest. Yet no doubt the world is more balanced. The last subsection therefore offers an account of tempered altruism or enlightened self-interest. This views remittances as part of, or one clause in, a self-enforcing contractual arrangement between migrant and family. The underlying idea is that for the household as a whole it may be a Pareto-superior strategy to have members migrate elsewhere, either as a means of risk sharing or as an investment in access to higher earnings streams. Remittances may then be seen as a device for redistributing gains, with relative shares determined in an implicit arrangement struck between the migrant and remaining family. The migrant adheres to the contractual arrangement so long as it is in his or her interest to do so. This interest may be either altruistic or more self-seeking, such as concern for inheritance or the right to return home ultimately in dignity. Remitting may thus cease either if the arrangement is no longer self-enforcing or if the contractual terms themselves provide for cessation of transfers at a given point in time.

In evolving these ideas in section 1 an attempt is made to draw out certain empirical implications of the various elements. Section 2 then explores these implications in the context of a recent household survey conducted in Botswana, and section 3 closes the chapter with some more general reflections on the concept of a household and dual theories of development.

## 1 Theories of Remittance

### Pure Altruism

If one states only that a typical migrant enjoys remitting, no testable propositions emerge. However, more incisive results can be obtained from an altruistic model wherein the migrant derives utility $u_m$ from the utility of those left at home, and the latter utility is presumed to depend on per capita consumption $c_h$. For example, suppose the migrant maximizes his own utility with respect to the amount $r$ remitted:

$$u_m = u\left[ c_m(w - r), \sum_{h=1}^{n} a_h u(c_h) \right]$$ (16.1)

where $w$ is the migrant's wage, $c_m$ is his or her consumption, $a_h$ are altruism weights attached to various household members, and $n$ is the household size. Consumption per capita may further be assumed to increase with income per capita available at the home base and may also vary with household size if there are economies or diseconomies of scale in consumption:

$$c_h = c\left(y + \frac{r}{n}, n\right) \tag{16.2}$$

where $y$ is the income per capita at home before receipt of any remittances. Choosing a level of $r$ to maximize (16.1) subject to (16.2) provides[1]

$$r = r(w, y, n) \tag{16.3}$$

If the migrant indeed cares about his home family and if both his utility function (16.1) and the home family utility functions are well behaved, two properties of the remittance function (16.3) are predicted: $\partial r/\partial w > 0$ and $\partial r/\partial y < 0$. The sign of $\partial r/\partial n$ is unrestricted, however, depending on the presence of (dis)economies of scale in consumption, the rate of diminution in the marginal utility of home consumers, and whether specific preference exists for a subset of the home group.

### Pure Self-Interest

As a stark counterpoint, three reasons to remit are now considered, relying on purely selfish motivations and the absence of altruism by the migrant toward the family.

1   The first is the aspiration to inherit. If we assume that inheritance is conditioned on behavior, an avaricious migrant's motives for supporting his or her family, and particularly parents, may encompass the concern to maintain favor in the line of inheritance. If applicable, this should generally mean larger remittances the larger is the potential inheritance.

2   A second self-interest of the migrant in remitting home may be to invest in assets in the home area and ensure their careful maintenance. In this context, one's own family may be a particularly trustworthy agent both in selecting the specific item for purchase (land, cattle, etc.) and in maintaining the asset on the migrant's behalf. Altruism of the family toward the migrant may underlie or enhance such a trust.[2]

3   Third is the intent to return home, which may suffice to promote remittance for investment in fixed capital such as land, livestock, or a

house, in public assets to enhance prestige or political influence, and in what might be termed social assets – the relationships with family and friends. Yet the last of these serves to illustrate how inextricable are motives of altruism and self-interest. In the end one cannot probe whether the true motive is one of caring or of more selfishly wishing to enhance prestige by being perceived as caring.

### Tempered Altruism or Enlightened Self-Interest

Both pure altruism and pure self-interest alone may be inadequate explanations of the extent of remittance and its variability through time and across persons. In this section, an alternative theory is therefore outlined, viewing remittances as part of an intertemporal mutually beneficial contractual arrangement between migrant and home. This theory is not merely the intersection of pure altruism and pure self-interest but rather offers a quite separate set of hypotheses. We shall return to altruism and self-interest in accounting for enforcement of such mutual contracts.

Two components may underlie the arrangements to be considered: investment and risk. It is well known that urban migrants are, on average, better educated than those remaining in the rural sector. The initial costs of this education, and particularly subsistence support while not earning, are usually borne by the immediate family. Some authors have noted a positive association between the amount remitted and the education of the migrant and have interpreted this as repayment of the principal (plus interest) invested by the family (Johnson and Whitelaw, 1974; Rempel and Lobdell, 1978). It should be noted that such an argument does not necessarily require that a higher fraction of an enhanced educated migrant's wage be remitted; to reap a return on their investment, it is sufficient that the family's receipts rise with the education of the migrant. Yet such a positive association is hardly a discriminating test of this explanation. Thus wages are generally higher for educated migrants, and the altruism model also indicates a positive association between remittance and wage and hence education. A more discerning test can be proposed, however. The costs of educating certain members of the particular household (for example, children of the head) are far more likely to have been incurred by that household than are the costs for other members (daughters-in-law, sons-in-law, and even spouses). The investment argument would therefore predict that the effect of education on raising remittances should be greater among the former group than among the latter.[3]

We now turn to the second component that may underlie mutually beneficial informal contracts: in an economy where insurance and capital markets are highly incomplete, the act of migration may be seen as a diversification response in the presence of risk. Risks of crop failure, price fluctuations, insecurity of land tenancy, livestock diseases, and inadequate availability of agricultural wage work may each render the rural context quite precarious (Stark and Levhari, 1982). The household may elect to spread its risks by allocating some members to urban migration. Initial job search in town can, of course, also be risky, and even subsequent security of employment is not guaranteed (Harris and Sabot, 1982). However, provided that the vagaries of the rural and urban context are not highly positively correlated, it can be mutually beneficial to both migrant and family to enter a coinsurance contract. Remittances as claims would then flow to the family at times of crop failure and to the migrant during spells of unemployment. What will be the consequences of this for remittance patterns during unexceptional times? It would seem that this should depend on who is the net provider of insurance, relative risk preferences, and relative bargaining powers. As with many forms of insurance, an element of moral hazard may well emerge in such arrangements. Indeed, in instances when the household wishes, for example, to partake of a particularly risky strategy at home such as trying some new agricultural techniques, it may then pay to buy additional insurance and send more members to town.

Arrangements between migrant and family are voluntary and thus must be self-enforcing. Mutual altruism among close relations is the most obvious force in avoiding delinquency and presumably helps to explain why the family is the most frequent context of such arrangements. Such elements as those discussed in section 1 – an aspiration to inherit, convenience in rural investments, and the intent to return – mean that the migrant retains a vested interest in his origins beyond altruistic concerns. This interest increases the confidence of the family that the migrant will not default and hence encourages the prevalence of intra-familial cooperative contracts. Moreover, these elements of command of the family over its migrant members may contribute to determining the distribution of benefits. If the bargain struck between migrant and family as to the remittance pattern is affected by elements of family command over the migrant, a prediction emerges that is clearly contrary to the pure altruism story. Within a game-theoretic view, greater wealth of the family should increase its relative bargaining strength. Thus, whereas the pure altruism model predicts higher remittance to lower-income households, *ceteris paribus*, the reverse is implied by a bargaining model.

## 2  Evidence from Botswana

*Specification and Estimation*

To explore empirically some of the ideas evolved in the foregoing section, estimates of a rather complex remittance equation can now be reported. Each observation is an adult migrant from a particularly detailed household survey of migration conducted in Botswana: the National Migration Study of Botswana, 1978–9 (NMS).

The model is of the following form:

$$r = \beta_0 + \sum_{i=1}^{3} \omega_i w_i + \alpha_1 y + \alpha_2 n + \epsilon_1 e + \epsilon_2 ej$$

$$+ \kappa_1 k + \kappa_2 ks + \kappa_3 kp + \delta_1 d + \delta_2 b + \delta_3 bd + \delta_4 l + \delta_5 ld$$

$$+ \phi_1 f + \phi_2 h + \phi_3 v + \sum_{i=1}^{5} \tau_i t_i + \mu m \qquad (16.4)$$

where $r$ is the logarithm of monthly remittances in cash and kind, averaged over the number of survey rounds in which the person was absent, or zero if no remittances occurred, $w$ are dummies for ranges in monthly wages plus net self-employment earnings of the migrant, $y$ is the logarithm of the income generated by the home group per consumer unit, $n$ is the logarithm of the number of consumer units at home (adults = 1, and children = 0.5 weighted by frequency of presence at home over the survey rounds), $e$ is the number of years of education completed by the migrant, $j$ is a dummy equal to 1 if the migrant was a member of this household when young, $k$ is a dummy equal to 1 if the household owns more than 20 cattle, $s$ is a dummy equal to 1 for sons and daughters-in-law of the household, $p$ is a dummy equal to 1 for the head of the household and the head's spouse, $d$ is an index for ongoing local drought, $b$ is the logarithm of the number of cattle owned, $l$ is the logarithm of crop acres, $f$ is a dummy equal to 1 if female, $h$ is a dummy equal to 1 if head of household, $v$ is a dummy equal to 1 if child of head or of head's spouse, $t$ are break points in a piecewise linear function for duration of absence (years), and $m$ is the statistical hazard rate.

The reasons for adopting this specification, and in particular the various interaction terms, may best be discussed together with the results. More precise definitions of certain variables will be given in the text, and sample means and standard deviations of variables are tabulated in the appendix (table 16.A1).

Before actually turning to the results, two prior issues of estimation must be addressed. In the NMS, four interviews were conducted at each dwelling, one every three months, and each person reported absent on any occasion is included in the analysis as a potential remitter.[4] The absentees can be divided into three groups: those in town, those elsewhere in the rural sector (including the commercial freehold farms), and those in South Africa. The last group is omitted from the present study for two reasons: first, most Botswana citizens employed in South Africa are in mines, and miners send or bring money home both in the form of remittances and through a deferred pay scheme, but the NMS does not record the amounts of deferred pay; second, there is insufficient information about variation in earnings among the absent miners. Thus two issues of sample selection arise: the selection on who is absent from the home, and, within this group, who is in South Africa and hence excluded. Moreover, for reasons to be discussed later, separate estimates of equation (16.4) are undertaken for those absent in urban Botswana, adding a further selection criterion. To correct for potential sample selection bias, a hazard rate (assuming a normal distribution) is included in the remittance regressions. The hazard rates are calculated from the probability of sample entry, distinguishing overall and urban only, among all adults including those absent in South Africa, as predicted by a binomial logit equation specified as

$$z = \exp(\pi_0 + \pi_1 f + \pi_2 h + \pi_3 g + \pi_4 g^2 + \pi_5 e + \pi_6 n) \qquad (16.5)$$

where $z$ is the odds of being included in the remittance sample, $g$ is age, and other terms are as previously defined.

The second prior issue is that the NMS does not record earnings of any absentees. To circumvent this lacuna, earnings equations are estimated from NMS data on persons present in urban Botswana, the freehold farms, and the tribal areas (the residual rural sector). The estimates appear in the appendix (table 16.A2). Explanatory variables are confined to information known also about each absentee, so that absentees' earnings can be predicted if they are reported to be working. Earnings include both wages and net self-employment earnings.

*Results*

The estimated remittance equations for all absentees and urban absentees only are reported in table 16.1, with $t$-statistics for a zero null hypothesis in parentheses beneath each coefficient.[5]

In both contexts, remittances rise steadily with the earnings of the absentee. Although this result is certainly consistent with the properties of the simple pure altruism model (16.3), it is not a very discerning test. For example, ability to coinsure or signaling concern when aspiring to inherit would also imply rising remittance with earnings. But the kernel of the pure altruism model is the per capita income of the home group. Instead of being negative as the pure altruism model hypothesizes, the estimates tend to show a positive association between the amount remitted and per capita income of the household from other sources.[6] In a dynamic setting, one cannot rule out the possibility that past remittances, sent with altruistic intent, have helped to raise today's income. To disentangle satisfactorily such life-cycle models ideally requires longitudinal data. Nonetheless, these cross-sectional results do show that, at the particular time of the survey, absentees were not remitting more to support lower-income home groups out of any given level of earnings.

To test whether remittances are part of an intertemporal understanding to recompense the family for initial sacrifices during the migrant's schooling, it is essential to distinguish groups for whom the family has made such sacrifices. This distinction cannot be made definitively from the NMS data or indeed from most household surveys. But groups for whom the costs of schooling are more likely to have been borne by this specific family can be defined. In the present context, the more likely group, labeled "own young" in table 16.1, is assumed to consist of children of the household head, grandchildren, and nieces and nephews.[7] Both in the overall regression and for urban absentees only, the coefficient on years of schooling interacted with the dummy for own young tends to be positive, though confidence levels for these tests are not high. However, it was noted in section 1 that repayment of school costs does not require that a higher fraction of a given wage be remitted, but only that remittances rise with education by those in whom investments are made. If the overall equation of table 16.1 is therefore re-estimated omitting the wage class dummies, it appears that remittances not only rise significantly with years of schooling for all absentees but also rise significantly more (at a 93 percent confidence level) among the household's own young. Thus support is certainly lent to the notion that remittances are partially a result of an understanding to repay initial educational investments.

Inheritance customs and laws among the Batswana are neither universal nor immutable. Practices vary from tribe to tribe and within a given tribe.[8] Indeed, a statistical study of inheritance, whether in Botswana or elsewhere, truly requires a specialized survey if only to record the existence of and links with children who are no longer members of the head's household, having established their own home. Nonetheless, some limited

244

**Table 16.1**  Estimated remittance equations

| Variables | All absentees | Urban absentees only |
|---|---|---|
| Intercept | −0.514 | −0.560 |
| | (5.35) | (2.88) |
| Log absentee's wage (*lω*): | | |
| $\quad 0 < l\omega \leqslant 3$ | 0.251 | 0.409 |
| | (3.59) | (3.51) |
| $\quad 3 < l\omega \leqslant 4$ | 0.472 | 0.578 |
| | (10.20) | (6.50) |
| $\quad 4 < l\omega$ | 0.732 | 0.666 |
| | (11.53) | (5.61) |
| Log home income per consumer unit | 0.011 | 0.022 |
| | (1.11) | (1.24) |
| Log consumer units at home | 0.084 | 0.069 |
| | (2.42) | (1.01) |
| Years of schooling | −0.002 | −0.034 |
| | (0.23) | (1.62) |
| Years of schooling × own young | 0.014 | 0.015 |
| | (1.50) | (0.88) |
| No. of cattle owned > 20 | −0.054 | 0.061 |
| | (1.06) | (0.47) |
| No. of cattle owned > 20 × sons and their spouses | 0.154 | 0.228 |
| | (2.26) | (1.80) |
| No. of cattle owned > 20 × heads and spouses | 0.162 | 0.465 |
| | (1.85) | (1.93) |
| Drought | | 0.066 |
| | | (0.25) |
| Log cattle | | −0.071 |
| | | (1.75) |
| Log cattle × drought | | 0.165 |
| | | (1.83) |
| Log crop acres | | −0.011 |
| | | (0.32) |
| Log crop acres × drought | | 0.184 |
| | | (1.66) |
| Female | 0.141 | 0.166 |
| | (3.29) | (1.89) |

*(Table continues on the following page)*

**Table 16.1** Estimated remittance equations (*continued*)

| Variables | All absentees | Urban absentees only |
|---|---|---|
| Head of household | 0.498 | 0.801 |
| | (7.50) | (5.69) |
| Child of head | 0.011 | −0.024 |
| | (0.24) | (0.29) |
| Duration of absence: | | |
| 0.5 years | 0.155 | 0.117 |
| | (2.30) | (0.88) |
| 1 year | 0.211 | 0.139 |
| | (3.17) | (1.10) |
| 2 years | 0.334 | 0.209 |
| | (4.66) | (1.56) |
| 5 years | 0.530 | 0.475 |
| | (6.79) | (3.32) |
| 50 years | 0.056 | 0.061 |
| | (0.37) | (0.18) |
| Hazard rate | 15.4 | 59.2 |
| | (3.07) | (3.79) |
| $R^2$ | 0.22 | 0.21 |
| $F$-statistic | 37.3 | 11.4 |
| No. of observations | 2,531 | 1,027 |

suggestive evidence can be obtained from the NMS. On average, sons are more likely to inherit than daughters or other household members, though their inheritance is not assured. It may therefore be asked of the data whether sons (and their spouses) remit more to families with greater amounts of inheritable wealth and whether this differs from the practices of others. Cattle are the dominant form of inheritable wealth in Botswana. All land (other than towns and freehold farms) is common property of the tribes. In the regression of table 16.1, a dummy variable is included for whether the household has a cattle herd larger than 20 beasts.[9] Both overall and from urban areas only, sons do remit more to families with larger herds, with the effect passing a 2 percent and a 7 percent significance test respectively. However, if an additional term is inserted, interacting the dummy for more than 20 cattle with a dummy for daughters and their spouses, the associated coefficient proves to be weakly negative. Thus sons do behave significantly differently from daughters and from other relatives in remitting more to households with large herds, which is consistent with a strategy to maintain favor in inheritance.

However, it is also common for sons to keep their cattle with those of the household, and, in fact, the distinction is not always clear cut. Thus an alternative or additional motive for sons to remit to households with larger herds is for maintenance or indeed expansion of their herd. Whether the motive here is to inherit or to have the household care for and acquire cattle on behalf of the son (both arguments listed in the pure self-interest model in section 1) cannot be discerned. Indeed, it is not obvious that they are truly distinct arguments in this context unless the son is assured that the demarcation of his cattle will be rigidly maintained.

The view of remittances as part of a coinsurance contract indicates certain ideas that may also be explored empirically. During times of particular hardship in rural areas (such as that of drought in Botswana), this approach predicts that urban-to-rural remittances should increase as claims are made against the coinsurance arrangements. However, such a test is not definitive, for a pure altruism model has the same prediction as family income declines. A more discerning test is whether during times of crisis remittances are relatively higher to households possessing assets particularly sensitive to such incidents. During droughts are remittances to operators of cropland and owners of livestock greater than to other households?

The year of the NMS survey, 1978–9, happened to be one of substantial drought, though its severity varied from location to location. For each village sampled, the severity of drought is measured by an index defined as 1 − (actual rainfall/30 year average rainfall) for that location. In the urban absentee remittance equation in table 16.1 this index is included separately and also interacted with the logarithm of crop acres operated and of cattle owned. The reasons for confining this analysis to the urban case alone are two-fold: (a) for the household to spread risks, it may well be wiser to send migrants to town (or South Africa, if possible) rather than elsewhere within the rural sector, where outcomes are probably more highly posit-ively correlated; (b) the extent of drought in each absentee's rural destination is not known.

If the two interaction terms of drought with cattle and with land are omitted, the coefficient on the drought index alone proves significantly positive – the more severe the drought, the greater are remittances. But in the specification reported in table 16.1, with the interactions included, it is seen that the existence of drought conditions and the possession of more cattle or more cropland have nothing to do with stimulating greater remittances *per se*. The interactions of drought with these drought-sensitive assets do. Those families who are at risk of losing cattle unless feed and water rights can be purchased, and those who are at risk by virtue of normally relying on crops for more of their sustenance are the ones who receive greater remittances during the drought. This is precisely the response one would expect if households allocate members to urban migration in order to insure against adopting risky asset portfolios at home.[10]

Although some evidence is thus found to support such ideas as repayment of school costs, aspirations to inherit, and coinsurance, this is not to deny the importance of caring for one's family. Indeed, remittances by heads of households are substantially and significantly greater than those by other absentees, no doubt reflecting a sense of caring and responsibility on behalf of family heads. Interestingly, however, children of the head do not remit more than any other members of the household *ceteris paribus*, as indicated in table 16.1.

Last, the role of duration of absence may be mentioned. If out of sight, out of mind were the rule, one would expect remittances to fade with duration of absence. If repayment of school costs were the target, again remittances should ultimately cease. Indeed, the piecewise linear terms on duration of absence do suggest an ultimate diminution in remittance, but not within the first five years, during which remittances continue to rise.[11] It seems that those who continue to be identified as household members are very persistent remitters, and vice versa.

### 3 Concluding Remarks

Several elements in a theory of motivations to remit are outlined in this chapter; empirical implications are elicited and explored using evidence from Botswana. In contrast, the small number of prior statistical studies of remittance correlates have been primarily concerned with discerning patterns rather than developing an explicit behavioral model.

The single notion underlying most previous work is that migrants remit because they care for those left behind. Unless qualified, this idea has no empirical content. It does not begin to answer why some migrants remit more, why some remit for longer, or why some do not remit at all. Yet altruism as a motive may be refined, and a model of pure altruism was presented in section 1. But the evidence of section 2 does not lend support to one of the main components of such a model, that remittances should be greater to lower-income families, *ceteris paribus*. Altruism alone does not appear to be a sufficient explanation of the motivations to remit, at least not in Botswana.

But this does not deny that altruism may be an important or even critical component. Rather, the evidence in this chapter lends support to a more eclectic model, which is labeled tempered altruism or enlightened self-interest in section 1. This views the migrant and family as having an implicit understanding that is of mutual benefit. For the household as a whole, to allocate certain members as migrants may be a Pareto-superior strategy, and remittances are the mechanism for redistributing the gains. One major source for potential gain is risk spreading: the household buys insurance by placing members in markets whose outcomes are not highly positively correlated. Indeed, such risk spreading may permit or encourage greater risk taking by any one component of the household. Moral hazard is involved. Thus in Botswana, the greater is the degree of ongoing drought in the family's home area, the more remittances are observed passing from urban migrants. But this is not an act of relief motivated by simple altruism. Once the drought index is interacted with amounts of cattle and land possessed – assets at risk during drought – drought alone is not positively associated with remittance. Migrants act not to relieve all families in drought-stricken areas but to protect during the drought those families with more cattle. This is quite consistent with families reaching an understanding that urban members will provide insurance during drought, and this permits the household to pursue a riskier rural strategy.

A second source of potential gain to the overall household is derived from investing in the education of youngsters who then migrate to town to reap returns and remit to repay the family's outlay. To test this, it is insufficient merely to note that remittances rise (or even rise as a fraction of wage) with education, as previous studies have suggested. However, in section 2 a contrast was drawn between household members in whose education the family is more likely to invest compared with others. Evidence is found to suggest that the family's own youngsters do increase remittances more with education than do others, tending to confirm a repayment hypothesis.

But how can such understandings between migrant and family be enforced? For example, if schooling costs are incurred before migration, what incentive does the migrant have to remit subsequently? Three classes of self-seeking motives on behalf of the migrant are postulated: to aspire to an inheritance, to channel one's rural investments through the trustworthy family both as purchasing agent and for subsequent maintenance, and to retain the prospect of ultimately returning home with dignity. Again, the Botswana data are highly suggestive (though not definitive), showing sons remitting more to households with more cattle. Moreover, this effect is stronger among sons than among daughters or others. Sons are more likely to inherit, though certainly not necessarily so, and they need to maintain favor with the head of the household.

Yet self-seeking motives of the migrant do not complete the mechanisms of enforcing intertemporal arrangements. Indeed, nothing in the eclectic model so far explains why remittances are concentrated within the family or why the family should be the source of school investment and insurance. Altruism is a relatively family-specific asset. It is precisely the existence of intra-familial mutual care that encourages such arrangements to be confined within the family and helps to reinforce arrangements that are of mutual benefit. Both altruism and individual gain are components: altruism is tempered and self-interest is enlightened.

In many senses, this chapter can be seen as beginning to extend the recent intergenerational view of the household to a spatial dimension. But such an extension is not trivial. It has quite profound implications for many elements in conventional wisdom: the distribution of income across geographically extended households may bear little resemblance to the more conventionally measured distribution across dwellings, and neither is uniquely appropriate; high urban earnings create a labor aristocracy that must be re-evaluated if that aristocracy is part of a plebeian set of households; dualistic theories of development must be revised. Instead of an urban sector and a rural sector, each with its own populace benefiting from the sectoral-specific speeds of development, the family straddles the two. Classes cease to be only peasants and workers, and a hybrid peasant–worker group emerges. This perception is not new to anthropologists but has not previously been integrated with the economics of the household.

250

# Appendix

**Table 16.A1** Sample means

| Variables | All absentees | Urban absentees |
|---|---|---|
| $r$ = ln remittance | 0.38 | 0.59 |
| | (0.93) | (1.09) |
| $w$ = ln wage | 2.07 | 2.51 |
| | (2.05) | (1.94) |
| $y$ = ln home income | 2.78 | 2.78 |
| | (1.75) | (1.76) |
| $n$ = ln consumer units | 1.77 | 1.75 |
| | (0.51) | (0.48) |
| $e$ = schooling | 3.31 | 4.81 |
| | (3.54) | (3.59) |
| $j$ = own young | 0.66 | 0.75 |
| | (0.47) | (0.43) |
| $k$ = more than 20 cattle | 0.32 | 0.28 |
| | (0.47) | (0.45) |
| $s$ = sons and their spouses | 0.41 | 0.43 |
| | (0.49) | (0.50) |
| $p$ = heads and spouses | 0.16 | 0.11 |
| | (0.37) | (0.31) |
| $d$ = drought index | 0.29 | 0.23 |
| | (0.23) | (0.23) |
| $b$ = ln cattle | 2.26 | 2.15 |
| | (1.62) | (1.62) |
| $l$ = ln acres | 1.52 | 1.55 |
| | (1.29) | (1.27) |
| $f$ = female | 0.42 | 0.49 |
| | (0.43) | (0.50) |
| $h$ = head | 0.10 | 0.30 |
| | (0.08) | (0.27) |
| $v$ = child of head | 0.58 | 0.49 |
| | (0.66) | (0.47) |
| $t$ = years of absence | 0.37 | 1.30 |
| | (0.32) | (0.98) |

Standard deviations are in parentheses.

**Table 16.A2** Earnings equations

| | Urban areas | | Tribal areas | | Freehold farms | |
|---|---|---|---|---|---|---|
| | Male | Female | Male | Female | Male | Female |
| Intercept | 3.093 | 2.318 | 2.395 | 2.866 | 2.074 | 1.364 |
| | (15.81) | (8.83) | (8.66) | (10.62) | (5.59) | (2.09) |
| Years of schooling | 0.126 | 0.191 | 0.120 | 0.116 | 0.131 | 0.232 |
| | (11.82) | (12.66) | (5.36) | (5.38) | (3.89) | (3.51) |
| Post-school experience | 0.070 | 0.069 | 0.071 | 0.005 | 0.048 | 0.054 |
| | (6.96) | (4.17) | (4.26) | (0.30) | (2.22) | (1.46) |
| Experience squared | −0.00087 | −0.00097 | −0.00087 | 0.000 | −0.00045 | −0.00098 |
| | (5.39) | (2.96) | (3.50) | (0.08) | (1.53) | (1.82) |
| Self-employed | −0.849 | −1.238 | −1.068 | −1.418 | — | — |
| | (7.71) | (11.42) | (5.59) | (10.26) | | |
| $1/(1 + \text{years in town})$ | −1.064 | −1.607 | — | — | — | — |
| | (3.95) | (4.53) | | | | |
| $R^2$ | 0.35 | 0.54 | 0.24 | 0.34 | 0.17 | 0.38 |
| F-statistic | 51.8 | 93.3 | 17.7 | 45.1 | 5.9 | 6.6 |
| No. of observations | 492 | 397 | 226 | 347 | 91 | 35 |

**Notes**

Co-authored with Robert E. B. Lucas. Reprinted from *Journal of Political Economy* 93, 1985. Since this is a joint product, the authors would like to blame each other for all remaining errors. However, Jim Heckman and a referee did provide many helpful comments. This is a revised and shortened version of Discussion Paper 10, Harvard University Migration and Development Program.

1  Implicitly, this treats $w$ and $y$ as given. In particular, the migrant is assumed neither to work harder nor to accept worse working conditions with higher pay in order to remit, and no moral hazard is involved in the sense of the home group's reducing effort.

2  Two forms of investment are worth specific mention in this context. First, it is, of course, not uncommon for children to be left in the village, with both their formal education and their upbringing entrusted to family members with remittances intended to compensate for the costs. Second, remittances are often spent on religious structures or public works in the home area, partly to enhance the prestige of the migrant and his family. The migrant's own family may be immediate recipients of the remittances here, too, for they have a natural monopoly in determining the migrant's home village prestige.

3  Such investment arguments can be extended, for example, to include initial costs of relocation – both financial costs of transportation and of preliminary job search and psychological costs (Sjaastad, 1962). An investment model would suggest that the greater are any such initial costs imposed on the remaining family, the greater should be eventual remittances in repayment.

4  Absentees are defined to include all persons whom the head of the household regards as normally belonging to that *lolwapa* (home) who did not sleep there on the previous night. It is neither clearly relevant to distinguish temporary from long-term migrants nor simple as a practical matter. The Batswana are amazingly peripatetic: the margin between whether one is based at home and visiting elsewhere or vice versa is quite illusive. A man who has worked in town for 10 or 20 years will answer that he does not live there: he lives at "home" but stays in town. In the first round of interviews, spokespersons were also asked whether anyone besides absent members had remitted, but the number of positive responses was negligible and the module was dropped from subsequent rounds.

5  Only those adults ages 15–54 who are not in school or higher education are included. The upper age limit is imposed to concentrate on a working age group. In this sense, 54 is too young, but the next age group coded in the survey is open ended.

6  This result proves robust over a wide range of specifications, including forms in which land and cattle owned are omitted.

7  Uncles play an important role in Batswana kinship patterns. If nieces and nephews are reported as absent members of a household, their education quite

probably has been the responsibility of this household, and their own parents may well live with the household.

8  See Schapera (1938, especially pp. 214–38) and a more recent account by Roberts (1972).

9  A herd of 20 beasts is often adopted as a significant dividing line in Botswana. A common argument for this particular breakpoint is that some eight beasts are required for plowing and a total herd of 20 is necessary to assure eight adult plowing animals.

10  An alternative interpretation — that during drought members migrate to town in order to remit — can be ruled out. If the drought index is interacted with a dummy variable for having been in town six months or less, the estimated sign on the associated coefficient is negative. Remittances during drought thus come from those members already well placed in town.

11  It is interesting to compare the initial rising remittance profile with the estimated asymptotic rise in urban earnings. The urban coefficients in table 16.1 indicate a 7 percent rise in remittances as absence increases from one to two years and a further cumulative rise of 30 percent over the next three years. In both intervals the earnings equations in the appendix imply a rise in earnings of 19 percent for males and 31 percent for females. This suggests that the remittance profile rises less rapidly than that of earnings in the earlier period but that then the two approximately keep pace. During the initial very uncertain period the migrant is not expected to support the family, but once he or she is successfully settled, such an undertaking becomes apparent.

# References

Bernheim, B. Douglas, Shleifer, Andrei and Summers, Lawrence H. (1984) "Bequests as a Means of Payment." Working Paper 1303, National Bureau of Economic Research, Cambridge, MA.

Harris, John R., and Sabot, R. H. (1982) "Urban Unemployment in LDCs: Towards a More General Search Model." In R. H. Sabot (ed.), *Migration and the Labor Market in Developing Countries*. Boulder, CO: Westview.

Johnson, George E. and Whitelaw, W. E. (1974) "Urban–Rural Income Transfers in Kenya: An Estimated-Remittances Function." *Economic Development and Cultural Change* 22: 473–9.

Knowles, James C. and Anker, Richard (1981) "An Analysis of Income Transfers in a Developing Country: The Case of Kenya." *Journal of Development Economics* 8: 205–26.

Kotlikoff, Laurence J. and Spivak, Avia (1981) "The Family as an Incomplete Annuities Market." *Journal of Political Economy* 89: 372–91.

Mohammad, A., Butcher, Walter R. and Gotsch, C. H. (1973) "Temporary Migration of Workers and Return Flow of Remittances in Pakistan." Economic Development Report 234, Center for International Affairs, Harvard University.

Rempel, Henry and Lobdell, Richard A. (1978) "The Role of Urban-to-Rural Remittances in Rural Development." *Journal of Development Studies* 14: 324–41.

Roberts, Simon (1972) *Tswana Family Law*. London: Sweet and Maxwell.

Rosenzweig, Mark R. and Wolpin, Kenneth I. (1983) "Specific Experience, Household Structure and Intergenerational Transfers: Farm Family Land and Labor Arrangements in Developing Countries." Mimeo, University of Minnesota.

Schapera, Isaac (1938) *A Handbook of Tswana Law and Custom*. London: Oxford University Press.

Sjaastad, Larry A. (1962) "The Costs and Returns of Human Migration." *Journal of Political Economy* 70 (5): 80–93.

Stark, Oded and Levhari, David (1982) "On Migration and Risk in LDCs." *Economic Development and Cultural Change* 31: 191–6 (reprinted as ch. 4 in this volume).

# 17

## Remittances and Inequality

The impact of rural outmigration upon the distribution of household income by size in rural areas is central to the relationship between economic growth and equity in less developed countries (LDCs). As long as a large proportion of the population resides in rural areas, rural income inequalities must constitute an important source of overall income inequality. Therefore changes in rural income inequalities can have important implications for both social welfare and economic development. To the extent that rural incomes are lower than incomes in other sectors, concern for issues of poverty highlight the importance of the rural component of national income distribution. In addition, a deterioration in the national income distribution caused by an increase in inequalities at the low (that is, rural) end may have very different economic implications, particularly with regard to investment and consumption patterns, than a deterioration caused by either an increase in inequality at the high (that is, urban) end or a rise in inequality between sectors. A focus on the rural income distribution is also a prerequisite for understanding which households, at which segments of the rural income spectrum, would be most affected by changes in migration policy, migrant labor market conditions, or the rural employment and production environment.

Despite these considerations and the number of studies that they have generated, there is still no consensus about the general or typical effect of migration from rural areas on the distribution of rural income by size. Lipton (1977, 1980) has argued that rural outmigration is likely to lead to a worsening of village income distribution (and, implicitly, to a loss in rural welfare). His analysis of migrants' characteristics leads him to believe that migrants' absence from rural areas generates negative externalities of various types; these externalities are responsible for a worsening distribution. In Lipton's view, migrants' remittances do not compensate for this adverse impact because, in net terms, the remittances are either very small or go disproportionately to those who are better off. Stark (1978) and Stark and Yitzhaki (1982) present a case where the reverse result obtains. They emphasize equality-enhancing considerations associated with migration such as risk diversification, alleviation of credit constraints, and various sharing and filtering-down mechanisms pertaining to migrants' remittances. They also note that an increase in income inequalities does not necessarily imply a social welfare loss, and may be consistent with a situation that is preferred under both general social welfare and Pareto criteria.

Three major reasons appear to account for the opposing views regarding migration and the distribution of rural income: lack of techniques for properly assessing the contribution of outmigration to village income inequality, use of analytical frameworks which preclude unambiguous welfare judgments about changes in income distribution,[1] and lack of systematic empirical studies focusing on the appropriate income-earning entities.

In the present study a framework is proposed and techniques are developed for analyzing the role of net remittances in village income inequalities and village welfare, which in turn constitute important components of rural income inequalities and rural welfare.[2] While we are fully aware of the wide range of effects *other than remittances* which migration has upon village incomes and their distribution (see, for example, Stark, 1980), we confine the present study to the remittance element. Related work deals with other efffects, for example, the risk-reducing insurance-enhancing impacts of migration upon production and investment decisions (see Stark and Levhari, 1982; Taylor, 1986). The present study also redresses the paucity of empirical research in this area.

Our findings indicate that the distributional impact of migration *is not* the same for all types of migration or at all points in a village's migration history. Migration can be conceived of as a diffusion process (Stark and Bloom, 1985): the level of migration at any point in time is likely to be positively related to past migration by village members. The role of contacts at prospective migrant destinations in encouraging rural outmigration is well documented (see, for example, the survey by Todaro, 1980), and the differential impact of contacts at different prospective migrant destinations has also been explored (Taylor, 1986). At the beginning of a village's migration history, when few households have established contacts at a migration destination, the distribution of remittances is necessarily unequal. The role of remittances in the overall household income distribution at this initial stage depends upon the magnitude of remittances in relation to income from other sources, as well as upon the rankings in terms of total income of remittance-receiving households. When information is costly and scarce, migration is subject to a significant degree of uncertainty. The first households to adopt a migration "investment" are likely to be from the upper end of the village income distribution, since they are the ones best equipped to assume a high-risk high-return "investment." If remittances to these households are significant, they can have a notable negative effect on the village income distribution by size. However, villagers who have successfully migrated provide valuable information which alters the parameters characterizing the subjective distribution of returns to migration for *other* villagers. The early migrants may also provide direct assistance to new migrants which enables the latter to adopt a strategy resulting in a shift of the distribution of returns in their favor (Taylor, 1986). Thus, as the stock of village migrants grows at a particular location, so too does the propensity of migration by other villagers. The effect of remittances on inequalities over time depends critically on how migration-facilitating information and contacts become diffused through the village population. If contacts and information are not household specific, that is, if there is a tendency for them to spread across household units, then migration and receipt of remittances by households at the lower end of the income distribution is likely to occur. This would erode and possibly reverse any initially unfavorable effects of remittances on income inequality.

Analysis of remittances is a promising means of studying an important impact of migration upon rural income distribution. If remittances represent a very small part of income for village households, then the distribution of income by size will be altered by them only slightly. If, at the other extreme, remittances comprise a very large share of household income, then the distribution of remittances in large part will determine the distribution of village income. Most likely, perhaps, remittances may be sufficiently large not to be ignored, yet must be viewed in the context of other household income sources.

In this chapter numerical coefficients are assigned to the role of net remittances in village income inequality using household data from two Mexican villages. The data afford a unique opportunity to compare the effects of remittances from both internal and international migrants on income inequality in villages that are at different stages of their migration histories. One village has relatively little Mexico–United States migration experience and few Mexico–United States migrants per household, but possesses significant migration experience at Mexican destinations. The other village has a long history of migration into the undocumented labor markets of southern California.

The current study gives rise to some quite interesting policy considerations. If remittances do not have a neutral impact upon the distribution of income by size, a government with a stand in favor of reducing inequalities may wish to alter their magnitude. While political and institutional considerations may render interference amounting to a major alteration impractical, modifications at the margin are feasible. Implications for migration and rural development policy arise as well. For example, a change in United States–Mexico remittances might result from changes in US immigration laws. Agricultural price supports and subsidies can have not only a direct bearing on the nonremittance component of farm incomes, but also an indirect effect on the remittance component to the extent that they influence migration and remittance behavior. In addition, labor market policies which alter the earnings profile – and hence the potential remittances – of internal migrants are likely to affect the domestic remittance component of village incomes. The methodology developed and tested here deals precisely with these issues. It will be used to explore the effect of a small change in each income category, including remittances from both internal and Mexico–United States migrants, upon village indices of inequality.

The remainder of this chapter is organized as follows. In section 1 we present the framework which will be used to analyze the role of remittances in the distribution of village income. The effect of remittances upon income inequality as measured by the Gini index will be shown to depend upon three terms: the magnitude of remittances relative to total village income, the inequality of remittances, and the (Gini) correlation between remittances and total income. In section 2, Mexican village household data are utilized to derive Gini indices empirically and to highlight the role of remittances from both internal and international migrants in the level and distribution of village income. In section 3 we assess the effect of small changes in remittances upon rural income inequality and social welfare, and in section 4 we summarize our main findings and offer some conclusions.

## 1 Analytical Framework

Let $y_1, \ldots, y_K$ represent $K$ components of household income and let $y_0$ represent total household income such that $y_0 = \Sigma_{k=1}^{K} y_k$. Since the income-receiving unit of analysis in this chapter is the household, in the discussion that follows "income" will refer to household income, and "income component $k$" will refer to household income component $k$. The components of income may be positive (for example, migrant-to-household remittances, regular income) or negative (household-to-migrant remittances, taxes). We follow Stuart (1954) and, more recently, Pyatt et al. (1980) and Lerman and Yitzhaki (1985) by writing the Gini coefficient for village incomes as a function of the covariance between income and its cumulative distribution; that is,

$$G_0 = \frac{2 \, \text{cov}[y_0, F(y_0)]}{\mu_0} \tag{17.1}$$

where $G_0$ is the Gini coefficient of total village incomes, $\mu_0$ denotes village mean income, and $F(y_0)$ is the cumulative distribution of total incomes in the village. Utilizing the properties of the covariance, we can write equation (17.1) as

$$G_0 = \frac{2 \, \Sigma_{k=1}^{K} \, \text{cov}[y_k, F(y_0)]}{\mu_0} = \sum_{k=1}^{K} R_k G_k S_k \tag{17.2}$$

where $S_k$ is the share of the component $k$ of village incomes in total village income, that is, $S_k = \bar{y}_k / \bar{y}_0$, $G_k$ is the Gini index corresponding to the income component $k$, and

$$R_k = \frac{\text{cov}[y_k, F(y_0)]}{\text{cov}[y_k, F(y_k)]} \tag{17.3}$$

$R_k$ is the Gini correlation of component $k$ with total income.[3] As shown by Schechtman and Yitzhaki (1985), the properties of the Gini correlation are a mixture of the properties of the Pearson and Spearman correlation coefficients. In particular, note the following.

1 $-1 \leq R_k \leq 1$. $R_k$ is equal to zero if $y_k$ and $y_0$ are independent, and is equal to 1 ($-1$) if $y_k$ is an increasing (decreasing) function of total income. (This is similar to Spearman's rank correlation.)
2 If $y_k$ and $y_0$ are normally distributed variables, then $R_k = \rho$, where $\rho$ is Pearson's correlation coefficient.

Hence $R_k$ is appropriately termed the Gini correlation.
  Equation (17.2) enables us to decompose the role of remittances in inequality into three easily interpretable terms:

1 the magnitude of remittances relative to total income;
2 the inequality of remittances;
3 the correlation of remittances with total income.

Using this formulation, we can calculate the effect of a small percentage change in any one component on the Gini coefficient of total income. Taking household labor and production decisions as given, consider an exogenous change in each household's income component $j$ by a factor $e$, such that $y_j(e) = (1 + e)y_j$. Then[4]

$$\frac{\partial G_0}{\partial e} = S_j(R_j G_j - G_0) \qquad (17.4)$$

where $S_j$, $G_j$, $G_0$, and $R_j$ denote the $j$th income share, Gini coefficients, and Gini correlation before the marginal income change, respectively. Dividing by $G_0$ we obtain

$$\frac{\partial G_0/\partial e}{G_0} = \frac{S_j G_j R_j}{G_0} - S_j \qquad (17.5)$$

Equation (17.5) states that the relative effect of a marginal percentage change in component $j$ upon inequality equals the relative contribution of component $j$ to overall inequality minus the relative contribution to total income. It is easy to see that, as long as remittances play some role in village income, the following hold.

1  If the Gini correlation $R_j$ between remittances and total income is negative or zero, an increase in remittances necessarily *decreases* inequality.
2  If the Gini correlation is positive, then the impact on inequality depends on the sign of $R_j G_j - G_0$. A necessary condition for inequality to *increase* is that the inequality of remittances must exceed the inequality of total household income: $G_j > G_0$ (since $R_j \leqslant 1$).

Further insight into the meaning of equation (17.5) can be gained by rewriting it as[5]

$$\frac{\partial G_0/\partial e}{G_0} = MR - AR \qquad (17.6)$$

where MR is a weighted average of the marginal importance of income from source $j$ in households' total income, calculated over all possible pairs of households and weighted by income differences, and AR is the average importance of income from source $j$ in households' total income. Equation (17.6) states that the effect of a small percentage change in income from source $j$ on inequality depends on the difference between the importance of this income in households' total income at the margin and its average importance in households' total income.

The actual estimation of equations (17.2)–(17.6) is done by estimating the cumulative distribution by the rank divided by the number of observations and calculating the relevant covariances using the Times Series Processor.

## 2 Migration and Income Distribution in Two Mexican Villages

The stage is now set for empirically deriving decomposed Gini indices. This will be accomplished using data from two Mexican villages. Three components of village income and hence of income inequality are considered: remittances from internal migrants, remittances from international (Mexico–United States) migrants, and nonremittance income.

Data for constructing the decomposed Gini indices for the two villages were collected in a survey carried out in the Pátzcuaro region of the state of Michoacán, Mexico, approximately 2000 km south of the Mexico–Arizona border. The sample consists of 425 adults 13 years of age or older representing the total adult population in 61 households, approximately 10 percent of the total number of households in each village. Detailed data were collected on each individual's characteristics, labor allocations, and contributions to household income in 1982. Data were also gathered on income from household farm production (farming, handicrafts, fishing, livestock, commerce, etc.) and rental income.[6] Income contributions in the form of remittances from household members who migrated, either within Mexico or to the United States, are all net of reverse (household-to-migrant) flows and of direct migration costs. A "migrant" is defined as an individual who left the village at any time during 1982 for the purpose of working. The shortest term of migration in our sample is approximately three weeks.

Selected characteristics of households in the two village samples are summarized in table 17.1. Although the villages are only 2 km apart and are statistically similar in terms of family size, the differences in their migration patterns are significant. Only 26 percent of village 1 households had at least one family member working in the United States in 1982. In contrast, village 2 households show evidence of a long tradition of Mexico–United States migration. Seventy percent of households in this village had family members who were Mexico–United States migrants in 1982, and these households had an average of 2.8 Mexico–United States

**Table 17.1**  Selected 1982 household and migrant characteristics

| Household averages | Village 1 | Village 2 |
|---|---|---|
| Adult family size | 6.8 | 7.4 |
| Share of families with at least 1 Mexico–US migrant (%)** | 25.8 | 70.0 |
| Average number of Mexico–US migrants per Mexico–US migrant family** | 1.7 | 2.8 |
| Share of Mexico–US migrant remittances in total household income (%)** | 9.1 | 27.0 |
| Share of families with at least 1 internal migrant (%)* | 71.0 | 46.7 |
| Number of internal migrants per internal migrant family** | 1.9 | 2.8 |
| Share of internal migrant remittances in total household income (%) | 22.0 | 11.0 |
| | | |
| 1982 Mexico–US migrant averages | | |
| Average US experience**[a] | 2.4 | 5.6 |
| Share of year spent in United States (%)** | 65.8 | 95.8 |
| Sex (male = 100, female = 0)** | 92.9 | 55.4 |
| Age | 32.0 | 27.9 |
| Years of completed schooling | 4.2 | 4.0 |
| Remittances | 472.0 | 354.7 |
| | | |
| 1982 internal migrant averages | | |
| Internal migration experience*[a] | 3.6 | 6.0 |
| Share of year outside village (%) | 75.0 | 88.8 |
| Sex (male = 100, female = 0) | 54.8 | 42.1 |
| Age | 27.9 | 29.0 |
| Years of completed schooling | 6.7 | 6.3 |
| Remittances | 249.5 | 445.7 |

* Difference between villages is significant at the 0.10 level.
** Difference between villages is significant at the 0.05 level.
[a] Migration experience is measured as the number of years in a person's adult life in which he or she has spent all or part of the year as a labor migrant.

migrants each, compared with an average of 1.7 Mexico–United States migrants per household in village 1. As a result, Mexico–United States migrant remittances constituted a much larger share of total income in village 2 households (27 percent) than in village 1 households (9 percent). This difference is significant at the 0.005 level.

Differences in the roles played by Mexico–United States migration in the two villages are also evident in the experience and in certain personal characteristics of the migrants themselves. Mexico–United States migrants from village 2 are significantly more experienced in Mexico–United States migration than their village 1 counterparts, having worked in the United States in each of an average of 5.6 years of their adult life, compared with 2.4 years for village 1 Mexico–United States migrants. Village 2 Mexico–United States migrants also spent a larger share of the year in the United States during 1982 (96 percent compared with 66 percent for village 1). The average Mexico–United States migrant from village 1 is predominantly male; however, males are not significantly more likely to migrate to the United States than females in the village which is more experienced in Mexico–United States migration. Mexico–United States migrants in both villages are young, averaging 28–32 years of age, and they have little formal education, averaging slightly more than four years of completed schooling. Average 1982 remittances per Mexico–United States migrant to households in village 1 are somewhat higher than those to village 2 households (US$472 and US$355 respectively), but this difference is not statistically significant.

Internal migration plays an important role in labor allocations in both villages. A significantly larger share of households participates in internal migration in village 1 (71 percent) than in village 2 (46.7 percent). However, the average number of internal migrants per internal migrant family is significantly larger in village 2. Thus the difference between the shares of internal migrant remittances in households' total income in the two villages is not statistically significant. Village 2 internal migrants, like village 2 international migrants, are significantly more experienced than their village 1 counterparts. The average 1982 internal migrant from village 2 had migrated internally in six years of his or her adult life, compared with 3.6 years for village 1 internal migrants. Village 2 internal migrants spent an average of 89 percent of the year outside the village, compared with 75 percent for internal migrants from village 1. Internal migrants, like Mexico–United States migrants, are young, averaging 28–29 years of age. They are no more likely to be males than females in either village. They are significantly better schooled than their Mexico–United States counterparts, averaging at least some post-primary schooling. The average internal migrant contributed US$249 to village 1 households and US$446 to village

2 households; as with Mexico–United States migrant remittances, however, this difference is not statistically significant.

We now turn to an analysis of the composition of household income inequality in each of the two villages, and then explore the effect of small changes in the magnitude of income from each source upon the village income distributions.[7] The three terms comprising the effect on inequality as per equation (17.2) of (a) remittances, both internal and foreign, and (b) other household income were estimated for each of the two villages. All income denominated in Mexican currency was converted to US dollars using the average 1982 exchange rate of 55 pesos to the dollar.

### The Composition of Income Inequality

A decomposition of income inequality in the two villages is provided in table 17.2. The table presents an *ex post* "snapshot view" of the components of village income inequalities. The first column $S$ presents the share of each income source in the total income of each village. Nonremittance income comprises well over half of all income in the two villages (67 percent and 60 percent respectively). The contribution of migrant remittances to household income, however, is significant. It ranges from 33 percent of total income in the first village to 40 percent in the second.

The Gini coefficient $G$ in the first row for each village captures the distribution of village income by size if migrant remittances are ignored. By comparing these with the Gini coefficients corresponding to total income (bottom row for each village), we obtain a measure of the overall impact of remittances upon village income inequality. In each village, income inequalities decrease when migrant remittances are considered. The village 1 Gini coefficient drops 3 percentage points when migrant remittances are included (from 0.43 to 0.40), while the village 2 Gini coefficient declines 7 percentage points (from 0.53 to 0.46).

In the introduction we argued that the impact of migrant remittances upon income inequalities tends to become more favorable (or less unfavorable) as migration opportunities spread throughout the village. A comparison of the impact of overall remittances upon inequalities in the two villages provides support for such a relationship. The decline in inequality due to migrant remittances is higher in village 2, where the frequency of labor migration by persons 13 years of age and older is higher both in terms of the probability of migrating in 1982 (0.44, compared with 0.26 for village 1) and in terms of the average share of the year spent in migration (0.41, compared with 0.19 for village 1).

A richer analysis of the distributional impact of remittances as migration "spreads" across village households can be carried out by considering

**Table 17.2** Composition of 1982 village inequality

| Village and income source | Share in total household income (S) | Gini coefficient for income source (G) | Gini correlation with total income rankings (R) | Contribution to Gini coefficient of total income (SGR) | Percentage share in Gini of total income |
|---|---|---|---|---|---|
| Village 1 | | | | | |
| Nonremittance income | 0.67 | 0.43 | 0.84 | 0.24 | 59.9 |
| Domestic remittances | 0.17 | 0.71 | 0.33 | 0.04 | 10.2 |
| US–Mexico remittances | 0.16 | 0.90 | 0.86 | 0.12 | 29.9 |
| Total income | 1.00 | 0.40 | 1.00 | 0.40 | 100.0 |
| Village 2 | | | | | |
| Nonremittance income | 0.60 | 0.53 | 0.86 | 0.28 | 59.6 |
| Domestic remittances | 0.19 | 0.86 | 0.85 | 0.14 | 29.2 |
| US–Mexico remittances | 0.21 | 0.68 | 0.36 | 0.05 | 11.2 |
| Total income | 1.00 | 0.46 | 1.00 | 0.47 | 100.0 |

separately the effect of United States–Mexico remittances and internal remittances on income inequality. Income shares and Gini indices of inequality corresponding to the migration income components – domestic remittances and remittances by Mexico–United States migrants – appear in the columns labeled $S$ and $G$ respectively in table 17.2. In village 1, slightly more than half of all remittances originate from internal migrants, while in village 2 most remittances accrue from Mexico–United States migrants. The distribution of each type of migrant remittance is considerably more skewed than the distribution of nonremittance income in each of the two villages. However, the distributions vary considerably between villages. In village 1, where relatively few households send migrants to the United States, the distribution of remittances from Mexico–United States migrants is most highly skewed (Gini coefficient of 0.90). The distribution of remittances from internal migrants in this village is also unequal, though considerably less so than United States–Mexico remittances (0.71). In contrast, village 2 United States–Mexico remittances are more equally distributed than internal migrant remittances (Gini values of 0.68 and 0.86 respectively).

However, as equation (17.2) shows, the distribution of income from a particular source and the share of that source in total income reflect only part of the contribution of the income source to overall income inequality. The remaining contribution depends on where the recipients of different categories of income are located in the overall village income distribution. Column $R$ of table 17.2 presents the (Gini) correlations between each income category and total income. The variation in these correlations in the two villages is striking. In village 1, where United States–Mexico remittance inequality is high, these remittances are also highly correlated with total income ($R = 0.86$). Thus it is primarily households at the upper end of the income distribution that receive remittances from Mexico–United States migrants in this village. Internal migrant remittances, in contrast, have a low correlation with total income in village 1 (0.33), indicating that internal migration is widely accessible across income groups. The importance of the (Gini) correlation is evident when we compare the percentage contribution of each income category to village income inequality. Although the two types of remittances represent similar shares of total income in village 1, internal migrant remittances account for only a small part of total inequality (10.2 percent) compared with United States–Mexico remittances (29.9 percent).[8]

The story is entirely different for village 2, with its well-developed migrant networks to the United States. Here, not only are United States–Mexico remittances distributed more equally than internal migrant remittances, but their correlation with total income is small as well (0.36).

Apparently, even households at the lower end of the income spectrum in this village have obtained access to US labor markets. As a result, United States–Mexico remittances account for only 11.2 percent of total income inequality. Furthermore, remittances from internal migrants now play a relatively unequalizing role. Even though they are slightly more evenly distributed than United States–Mexico remittances, they are highly correlated with total income in this village. Thus internal migrant remittances contribute a relatively large amount to overall income inequality (29.2 percent). The apparent explanation for this finding is that internal migrant remittances contain a large returns-to-schooling component, and the distribution of education across income groups varies significantly between the two villages. Remittances by internal migrants with secondary and post-secondary schooling are more than five times greater, on average, than remittances by internal migrants with only primary schooling. This difference is significant at the 0.005 level. In contrast, rewards to schooling are small for Mexico–United States migrants who, typically, must work illegally in low-skill labor-intensive jobs. The latter is evidenced by the average education levels of Mexico–United States migrants reported in table 17.1, which are significantly lower than average schooling levels of internal migrants. In fact, of 34 migrants in the sample with post-primary schooling, only six were observed as Mexico–United States migrants in 1982, and these actually remitted less, on average, than less educated Mexico–United States migrants.

Because of the large returns-to-schooling component in internal migrant remittances, the distribution of education across household income groups has an important influence on the distribution of internal migrant remittances as well as on the latter's impact on income inequalities. In village 2, education is concentrated significantly in high-income households: the average income of households in which at least one family member has secondary or post-secondary schooling is 2.97 times that of less educated households, and this difference is significant at the 0.001 level. In contrast, there is no significant difference in income between educated and less educated households in village 1. The latter result is particularly strong when we consider the large returns to schooling that are included in the income of educated households. A still clearer picture of the differences in education distribution between the two villages can be gleaned by considering 1982 schooling investments. In village 2, where the distribution of schooling was already skewed in favor of high-income households, the latter were significantly more likely to send family members to secondary and post-secondary schools in 1982 than were households at lower income levels. The average income of village 2 households that supported secondary or post-secondary students in 1982 was 57.4 percent higher than the average income of households that did not invest in such schooling. In contrast, there was no statistically significant relationship between household income and schooling investments in village 1 households. It is likely that in village 2 the presence of attractive Mexico–United States migration opportunities, which increase the opportunity cost of sending a family member to school, discourage all but households with relatively high income from investing in schooling for family members. In village 1, however, the scarcity of Mexico–United States migration opportunities means that the opportunity cost of sending a child to school is relatively low. Thus, given the high joint return to schooling and internal migration, investment in schooling appears to be perceived by middle- and lower-income households in village 1 as a relatively effective vehicle for achieving long-term income gains.

## The Impact of Changes in Remittances on Inequality

In the preceding subsection we focused on the contribution of remittances to income inequalities. In this subsection we take the analysis a step further and ask what effect a small percentage change in specific categories of income would have on inequality in the two villages. Quite often, sober realism compels policy-makers to stop short of attempting to bring about dramatic changes.

The impact of a small change in each of the three income components in the two villages is given in table 17.3.[4] In each village a 1 percent increase in farm (nonremittance) income for all households reduces income inequalities, although the improvement is small in village 2 compared with village 1 (−0.006 percent and −0.07 percent respectively). The difference between the impacts of small changes in the remittance income components upon inequalities in the two villages is large. A 1 percent increase in remittances by Mexico–United States migrants *increases* inequalities in village 1 (by 0.14 percent) but *reduces* inequalities in village 2 (by −0.10 percent). Conversely, a 1 percent increase in remittances from *internal* migrants *reduces* inequalities in village 1 (by −0.07 percent) while *enhancing* inequalities in village 2 (by 0.11 percent). Thus the impact of marginal changes in remittances upon inequality as captured by the Gini coefficient is not unequivocal. It depends critically upon where the recipients of remittances are situated in an overall village income distribution, the share of remittances in village incomes, and the distribution of the remittances themselves. These considerations, in turn, are closely tied to the way in which opportunities for different types of migration are distributed across village households, as well as to the distribution of human capital (educa-

**Table 17.3** Effects of a 1 percent increase in household income from different sources on income inequalities

| Village and income source | Absolute change in Gini coefficient $(\times\ 10^{-3})$ | Percentage change in Gini coefficient |
|---|---|---|
| Village 1 | | |
| Nonremittance income | −0.28 | −0.07 |
| Domestic remittances | −0.29 | −0.07 |
| US–Mexico remittances | 0.57 | 0.14 |
| Village 2 | | |
| Nonremittance income | −0.03 | −0.01 |
| Domestic remittances | 0.50 | 0.11 |
| US–Mexico remittances | −0.48 | −0.10 |

tion and skills) which can significantly influence the distribution of remittances from particular destinations.

### 3 Remittances and Social Welfare

Changes in inequality do not have unambiguous implications with regard to social welfare. For example, a small increase in the income of any member of society, leaving all other members' incomes unchanged, may result in a worsening of inequalities, depending upon the recipient's initial relative income position. Yet, if we rule out envy as an argument in utility, this event is associated with an unambiguous welfare gain according to social welfare and Pareto criteria. In this section we ask what effect a small change in income from source $k$ (for example, remittances, or remittances from a particular destination) will have on social welfare in each of the two villages. A social welfare function for invoking direct welfare judgments in this type of situation has been proposed by Yitzhaki (1982) and Stark and Yitzhaki (1982). It is of the form

$$W = \bar{Y}(1 - G_0) \tag{17.7}$$

*Migrants' Remittances*

where $\overline{Y}$ is the mean village income. This function has the properties that either an increase in the income of any one member of society or a transfer of income from a rich person to a less rich person will result in an increase in $W$, independent of the shape of the initial income distribution. Using this measure of social welfare, we can assess the impact of a small percentage change in income from source $k$ on village welfare by taking the derivative of $W$ with respect to $e$ where, as before, the new income $y_k(e)$ from source $k$ is defined as $y_k(e) = (1 + e) y_k$, $e > 0$, and $y_k$ denotes actual income from source $k$. That is,

$$\frac{\partial W}{\partial e} = \frac{\partial \overline{Y}}{\partial e} (1 - G_0) - \overline{Y} \frac{\partial G_0}{\partial e} \tag{17.8}$$

The derivative of mean income with respect to $e$ is the mean income $\overline{Y}_k$ from source $k$, while the derivative of $G_0$ is given by equation (17.4). By substituting these derivatives into (17.8) and rearranging terms we obtain

$$\frac{\partial W}{\partial e} = \overline{Y}_k(1 - R_k G_k) \tag{17.9}$$

where $R_k$ is the Gini correlation of income from source $k$ with total income and $G_k$ is the Gini index of income component $k$. Equation (17.9) states that the effect on $W$ of a small percentage increase in $y_k$ consists of two components: a positive income effect equal to $\overline{Y}_k$, and a distributional effect $\overline{Y}_k R_k G_k$, whose sign depends on the effect of income from source $k$ on inequality which is given by the sign of $R_k$. Since $R_k$ and $G_k$ are less than 1, the income effect is always larger than the distributional effect. The intuitive explanation for this result is that the welfare function (17.7) increases if the income of one (or several) members of society increases leaving other incomes unchanged. The importance of the distributional effect is that it can significantly enhance or weaken the income effect.

Table 17.4 summarizes the net welfare changes in the two villages corresponding to a 1 percent change in each category of income. The welfare impacts vary greatly among income categories and between the two villages. The most dramatic improvements in welfare come as a result of an increase in nonremittance income (0.72 percent and 0.61 percent respectively for the two villages). Welfare gains from a marginal increase in remittances from internal migrants in village 1 and from Mexico–United States migrants in village 2 are also large (0.22 percent and 0.30 percent respectively). Smaller gains result from a marginal increase in remittances from Mexico–United States migrants in village 1 (0.06 percent) and from internal migrants in village 2 (0.09 percent).

**Table 17.4**  Village welfare effects of a 1 percent increase in household income from different sources

| Village and income source | Percentage change in Stark –Yitzhaki welfare index[a] |
|---|---|
| **Village 1** | |
| Nonremittance income | 0.72 |
| Domestic remittances | 0.22 |
| US–Mexico remittances | 0.06 |
| **Village 2** | |
| Nonremittance income | 0.61 |
| Domestic remittances | 0.09 |
| US–Mexico remittances | 0.30 |

[a] $\dfrac{\partial W/\partial e}{W} = S_k \dfrac{1 - R_k G_k}{1 - G_0}$

The figures reported in the table are derived by setting $e$ equal to 0.01.

The relative magnitudes of these welfare changes are not surprising in light of the findings reported in section 2. Increases in nonremittance income are negatively related to inequality, and this category occupies the largest share of total household income in both villages. Although changes in internal migrant remittances in village 1 and Mexico–United States migrant remittances in village 2 are also negatively related to inequality, these categories claim smaller shares of village income. The magnitude of their marginal effect on village welfare stems primarily from their role as income equalizers in the respective villages. Finally, we observed in table 17.3 that United States–Mexico remittances and internal migrant remittances have unfavorable distributional impacts on income in village 1 and village 2 respectively. This adverse distributional effect is just offset by the positive mean income effect, resulting in only a modest welfare gain in each case.

We are aware of the possibility that some of our welfare-oriented empirical results are likely to be quite sensitive to the choice of the welfare function. We believe that, in terms of both social welfare and Pareto-optimality considerations, the desirable properties of the welfare criterion used in the present study make this criterion a reasonable candidate for assessing the impacts of policy changes on village welfare. Moreover, of the six marginal welfare changes reported in table 17.4, four are consistent with quite a number of social welfare functions, that is, those changes for which income increases are both positively related to mean income and negatively related to inequality (Yitzhaki, 1983). With regard to the remaining two changes (United States–Mexico remittances in village 1 and internal migrant remittances in village 2), the impact upon welfare clearly depends on the weight attached to equity versus mean income considerations. It can be shown[10] that the welfare effect of an increase in Mexico–United States migrant remittances to village 1 and in internal migrant remittances to village 2 is positive as long as the weight attached to equity is no more than 4.3 times the weight attached to mean income, and negative for equity weights greater than 4.3. If, as pointed out above, envy is ruled out as an argument in the household utility function, the reasons for selecting such a large equity weight may not be too compelling.

## 4 Conclusions

The impact of migrant remittances on the rural income distribution by size appears to depend critically on a village's migration history and on the degree to which migration opportunities are diffused across village households. It also depends on the returns to human capital embodied in remittances, and the distribution of potentially remittance-enhancing skills and education. Our empirical findings demonstrate that in a village where many households contain internal migrants but few have experienced migration to the United States, remittances from Mexico–United States migrants have a profound unequalizing impact on village incomes, while remittances from internal migrants have a favorable effect on the village income distribution. In contrast, United States–Mexico remittances have an equalizing impact on incomes in a village with a long history of sending migrants to the United States and hence a more ready access to US labor markets. Remittances from internal migrants, however, embody a large returns-to-schooling component, and education is highly correlated with household income in village 2. Hence internal migrant remittances account for a comparatively large share of inequality in this village. Where returns to schooling constitute a large part of remittances, as in the case of internal migration, the influence of remittances on the village income distribution depends crucially on the distribution of human capital investments across household income groups.

The welfare implications of remittances depend on the weight attached to distributional versus mean income objectives. For the welfare function used in the present study, an unambiguous welfare gain is associated with both types of remittances in the two villages. Nevertheless, the unequalizing impact of United States–Mexico remittances in village 1 and internal migrant remittances in village 2 significantly dampen welfare gains associated with these income sources, while income-equalizing internal remittances in village 1 and Mexico–United States migrant remittances in village 2 are associated with considerably larger welfare gains. The high human capital content of internal migrant remittances, together with the high correlation between income and human capital investments in village 2, highlight the importance of the uses of remittances and other household income in shaping the future profile of household incomes. While in the short to medium run the distributional impact of migrant remittances is closely linked to the rate of diffusion of migration opportunities, the long-term effect of remittances on village income inequalities depends on how remittance-generated income gains are allocated among productive and nonproductive ends. Yet, in real life, the short run always matters. And, by definition, the long run is the integral of short runs.

## Appendix

### Derivation of Equation (17.4)

The purpose of this part of the appendix is to prove that the derivative of the overall Gini coefficient with respect to a uniform percentage change in income source $j$ is equation (17.4) in the text.

Let $G_0$ be the Gini coefficient before multiplying each household's income from source $j$ by $1 + e$, and let $G(e)$ be the Gini coefficient after the multiplication. From (17.2), we know that

$$G_0 = \sum_{k=1}^{K} S_k R_k G_k$$

The multiplication of income source $j$ by $1 + e$ does not affect $G_k$ ($k = 1, \ldots, K$). However, $R_k$ is a function of the ranks of total income. The rank function is not well defined for incomes that are equal. In order to avoid the problem created in this case, we assume that incomes vary slightly across households (aside from households whose income from source $j$ is zero). Then $R_k$ does not change for $k = 1, \ldots, K$. Hence

$$G(e) = \sum_{k=1}^{K} S_k(e) R_k G_k$$

By definition,

$$S_k(e) = \frac{\mu_k}{\Sigma_{k \neq j} \mu_k + (1 + e) \, \mu_j} = \frac{\mu_k}{\Sigma_{k=1}^{K} \mu_k + e\mu_j} \qquad \text{for } k \neq j$$

while for source $j$

$$S_j(e) = \frac{(1 + e) \, \mu_j}{\Sigma_{k=1}^{K} \mu_k + e\mu_j}$$

Let us now evaluate

$$G = G(e) - G_0$$

$$= \sum_{k=1}^{K} S_k(e) \, R_k G_k - \sum_{k=1}^{K} S_k R_k G_k$$

$$= \sum_{k=1}^{K} [S_k(e) - S_k] \, R_k G_k \qquad (17.A1)$$

For $k \neq j$,

$$S_k(e) - S_k = \frac{\mu_k}{\Sigma_{k=1}^{K} \mu_k + e\mu_j} - \frac{\mu_k}{\Sigma_{k=1}^{K} \mu_k}$$

This simplifies to

$$S_k(e) - S_k = \frac{-e S_k S_j}{1 + e S_j} \qquad (17.A2)$$

Now, for $k = j$,

$$S_j(e) - S_j = \frac{e S_j - e S_j^2}{1 + e S_j} \qquad (17.A3)$$

Substituting (17.A2) and (17.A3) into (17.A1), we have

$$G(e) - G_0 = \sum_{k=1}^{K} [S_k(e) - S_k] R_k G_k$$

$$= \sum_{k \neq j} \frac{-eS_k S_j}{1 + eS_j} R_k G_k + \frac{eS_j - eS_j^2}{1 + eS_j} R_j G_j$$

$$= \sum_{k=1}^{K} \frac{-eS_k S_j}{1 + eS_j} R_k G_k + \frac{eS_j}{1 + eS_j} R_j G_j \qquad (17.A4)$$

Using (17.A4), we can examine the derivative

$$\lim_{e \to 0} \frac{G(e) - G_0}{e} = -S_j \lim_{e \to 0} \sum_{k=1}^{K} \frac{S_k}{1 + eS_j} R_k G_k + \lim_{e \to 0} \frac{S_j}{1 + eS_j} R_j G_j$$

$$= -S_j \sum_{k=1}^{K} S_k R_k G_k + S_j R_j G_j$$

Hence

$$\frac{\partial G_0}{\partial e_j} = S_j (R_j G_j - G_0) \qquad (17.A5)$$

Subject to the required modification, equation (17.A5) appears in the text as equation (17.4). When a component is a decreasing function of total income, as for example with a progressive or proportional tax paid by all units, then as pointed out previously $R_j$ will equal $-1$, making the derivative (17.A5) negative.[11] When $y_j$ is constant across households, $R_j$ will be zero implying that the share of source $j$ in the total Gini coefficient is zero. In this case, as $y_j$ rises as a share of total income, overall inequality will fall.

## Derivation of Equation (17.6)

Let $y^1 < y^2 < \ldots < y^n$ be incomes ordered in increasing order and let $y_k(y_0^i)$ be income from source $k$ associated with income $y_0^i$. Note that the $y_k(y_0^i)$ are ordered according to $y_0^i$ and that $y_0^i = y_{-k}^i + y_k^i$, where $y_{-k}^i$ denotes income from sources other than $k$. Rewriting equation (17.5) in the text, we have

$$\frac{\partial G_0 / \partial e}{G_0} = \frac{S_k G_k R_k}{G_0} - S_k \qquad (17.A6)$$

where $e > 0$ is defined by $y_k(e) = (1 + e)\, y_k$. Using the definitions of $S_k$, $G_k$, and $R_k$, that is

$$S_k = \frac{\bar{y}_k}{\bar{y}_0}$$

$$G_k = \frac{2\,\text{cov}[y_k, F(y_k)]}{\bar{y}_k}$$

$$R_k = \frac{\text{cov}[y_k, F(y_0)]}{\text{cov}[y_k, F(y_k)]}$$

substituting into (17.A6), and rearranging, we obtain

$$\frac{\partial G_0/\partial e}{G_0} = \frac{\text{cov}[y_k, F(y_0)]}{\text{cov}[y_0, F(y_0)]} - \frac{\bar{y}_k}{\bar{y}_0} \tag{17.A7}$$

But

$$\text{cov}[y_k, F(y_0)] = \frac{1}{n(n-1)} \sum_{i=1}^{n} \left( i\,\frac{n+1}{2} \right) y_k(y_0^i)$$

$$= \frac{2}{n(n-1)} \sum_{i=1}^{n} \sum_{j=i+1}^{n} [y_k(y_0^i) - y_k(y_0^i)].$$

We can write $\text{cov}[y_0, F(y_0)]$ in a similar form. Substituting into (17.A7) we obtain

$$\frac{\partial G_0/\partial e}{G_0} = \sum_{i=1}^{n} \sum_{j=i+1}^{n} \frac{y_k(y_0^j) - y_k(y_0^i)}{y_0^j - y_0^i}\, w_{i,j} - \sum_{i=1}^{n} \frac{y_k(y_0^i)}{y_0^i}\, w_i \tag{17.A8}$$

where

$$w_{i,j} = \frac{y_0^j - y_0^i}{\sum_{i=1}^{n} \sum_{j=i+1}^{n} (y_0^j - y_0^i)}$$

$$w_i = \frac{y_0^i}{\sum_{i=1}^{n} y_0^i}$$

Let

$$\beta_{i,j} = \frac{y_k(y_0^j) - y_k(y_0^i)}{y_0^j - y_0^i}$$

Then $\beta_{i,j}$ is the marginal importance of income from source $k$ in total household income calculated using incomes $y_0^i$ and $y_0^j$. Its magnitude is $-1 \leq \beta_{i,j} \leq 1$. It is easy to check that it is equal to 1 if all the differences $y_0^j - y_0^i$ are composed of income from source $k$, it is equal to zero if $y_k(y_0^j) = y_k(y_0^i)$, and it is equal to $-1$ if $y_k(y_0^j) - y_k(y_0^i) = y_0^i - y_0^j$. Therefore the first term in (17.8) is the marginal importance of income from source $k$ in total household income weighted by income differences and calculated using all possible pairs of incomes. If we let $b_i = y_k(y_0^i)/y_0^i$, then $b_i$ is the share of income from source $k$ in the total income of household $i$, and the second term is an average of this share across households weighted by household incomes.

## Notes

Co-authored with J. Edward Taylor and Shlomo Yitzhaki. Reprinted from *The Economic Journal* 96, 1986. This chapter is a revised version of Discussion Paper 16, Harvard University Migration and Development Program. It was presented at the Fifth World Congress of the Econometric Society, Cambridge, Massachusetts, August 17–24, 1985. We are indebted to an associate editor of *The Economic Journal*, to Charles H. Feinstein, to an anonymous referee, and to Michael Lipton whose most helpful comments and advice have facilitated improvements of earlier versions of this chapter.
1   However, Stark and Yitzhaki (1982) have proposed a social welfare measure with desirable properties for assessing the effect of changes in income and inequality on social welfare.
2   In this study we focus on the impact of migrant remittances on income inequalities at the margin, and the role of remittances in overall inequality when migration decisions are taken as given. We do not, therefore, attempt to assess the whole impact of migration (through remittances and other means) on the village income distribution. Such a task would require estimating migration and remittance functions (including within-village remittance functions) in order to predict what migrants' income contributions would have been had they not migrated – adjusting, of course, for sample selection. While we are aware of the usefulness of such an exercise, we have chosen to limit our current scope in order not to add additional complications to an already somewhat complex analysis.
3   Note that $R_k$ is a correlation coefficient between two variables $y_k$ and $y_0$. For simplicity, we have omitted the subscript zero.

4  See the appendix for the derivation of equation (17.4).

5  See the appendix for the derivation of equation (17.6).

6  Agricultural income is calculated as the total value of crops produced minus the cost of all material inputs, physical capital inputs (mechanical services, animal services, land), and hired labor inputs. Rental income includes land rents and payments for capital services received by the household. Income from livestock includes the value of net additions to animal stocks as well as sales of animals and animal products. Net revenues from handicrafts, wood gathering, fishing, and other household farm activities is calculated in a manner analogous to agricultural income.

7  Although the computations that follow are based on income per household, at a referee's request we also experimented with using a measure of per capita household income (household income divided by the number of household members 13 years of age or older who spent any part of the year "at home"). There was no change worth noting, however, in any aspect of our results. This illustrates the robustness of the analysis with respect to the choice of income-receiving unit.

8  The finding that migrant remittances account for a positive share of total inequality in the two villages is perfectly consistent with our earlier finding that remittances on the whole reduced income inequalities. When mixed with nonremittance income, total remittances dilute the inequalities associated with the former. Yet, unless the correlation between remittances and household total income is negative, remittances must account for a nonnegative share of total income inequality. This is analogous to a simple chemical experiment in which a highly concentrated solution is mixed with a less (but still positively) concentrated one. The resulting mixture is less concentrated than the original, but there is no doubt that the added solution is responsible for part of the concentration of this final mix.

9  The derivatives reported in table 17.3 represent the *initial* impact of changes in income from particular sources upon village income inequalities, that is, before any possible adjustments in household labor and production plans in response to these income changes occur. If labor and production decisions adjust to a marginal change in income from a particular source, the magnitude of $\partial G_0/\partial e$ might be affected somewhat; however, we consider it unlikely that the *sign* of this derivative would be altered. In fact, if part of income gains are invested in productivity-enhancing income-generating activities, the secondary effects of income changes would tend to strengthen the conclusions drawn below. For some evidence in support of this possibility, see Lucas and Stark (1985). In this case, the results reported below would represent the minimum impact of marginal percentage income changes on inequality. Only in the extreme case where total household income *declines* in response to a marginal increase in income from a particular source would the signs of our results be altered.

10  If we let $\alpha$ represent the weight attached to equity versus mean income, the welfare function (17.7) becomes

$$W = \overline{Y}(1 - \alpha G_v)$$

The percentage change in $W$ with respect to a marginal change in $e_k$ is now

$$\frac{\partial W/\partial e_k}{W} = S_k \frac{1 - \alpha R_k G_k}{1 - \alpha G_0}$$

Setting this equal to zero, we can solve for the level of $\hat{\alpha}$ for which a change in $e_k$ begins to have a nonpositive impact on welfare: $\hat{\alpha} = 1/R_k G_k$. Substituting the values of $R_k$ and $G_k$ corresponding to United States–Mexico remittances in village 1 and domestic remittances in village 2, we find that the values of $\hat{\alpha}$ for the two villages are 4.3 and 4.1 respectively.

11  Although the absolute value of taxes rises with income, viewing taxes as negative income leads to a negative correlation between taxes and total income.

**References**

Lerman, R. and Yitzhaki, S. (1985) "Income Inequality Effects by Income Source: A New Approach and Applications to the United States." *Review of Economics and Statistics* 67 (1): 151–6.

Lipton, M. (1977) *Why Poor People Stay Poor: A Study of Urban Bias in World Development*. London: Temple Smith.

—— (1980) "Migration from Rural Areas of Poor Countries: The Impact on Rural Productivity and Income Distribution." *World Development* 8 (1): 1–24.

Lucas, R. E. B. and Stark, O. (1985) "Motivations to Remit: Evidence from Botswana." *Journal of Political Economy* 93 (5): 901–18 (reprinted as ch. 16 in this volume).

Pyatt, G., Chen, C. and Fei, J. (1980) "The Distribution of Income by Factor Components." *Quarterly Journal of Economics* 95 (3): 451–73.

Schechtman, E. and Yitzhaki, S. (1985) "A Measure of Association Based on Gini's Mean Difference." Working Paper 8503, Center for Agricultural Economic Research, Hebrew University.

Stark, O. (1978) *Economic–Demographic Interaction in the Course of Agricultural Development: The Case of Rural-to-Urban Migration*. Rome: UN Food and Agriculture Organization.

—— (1980) "On the Role of Urban-to-Rural Remittances in Rural Development." *Journal of Development Studies* 16 (3): 369–74 (reprinted as ch. 14 in this volume).

—— and Bloom, D. (1985) "The New Economics of Labor Migration." *American Economic Review* 75: 173–8 (reprinted as ch. 2 in this volume).

—— and Levhari, D. (1982) "On Migration and Risk in LDCs." *Economic Development and Cultural Change* 31: 191–6 (reprinted as ch. 4 in this volume).

—— and Yitzhaki, S. (1982) "Migration, Growth, Distribution, and Welfare." *Economics Letters* 10: 243–9 (reprinted as ch.21 in this volume).

Stuart, A. (1954) "The Correlation Between Variate-Values and Ranks in Samples from a Continuous Distribution." *British Journal of Statistical Psychology* 7: 37–44.

Taylor, J. E. (1986) "Differential Migration, Networks, Information and Risk." In Oded Stark (ed.), *Migration, Human Capital and Development*. Greenwich, CT: JAI Press.

Todaro, M. (1980) "International Migration in Developing Countries: A Survey." In Richard A. Easterlin (ed.), *Population and Economic Change in Developing Countries*. Chicago, IL: University of Chicago Press for National Bureau of Economic Research.

Yitzhaki, S. (1982) "Stochastic Dominance, Mean Variance, and Gini's Mean Difference." *American Economic Review* 72: 178–85.

—— (1983) "On an Extension of the Gini Inequality Index." *International Economic Review* 24 (3): 617–28.

# 18

# Migration, Remittances, and Inequality: A Sensitivity Analysis using the Extended Gini Index

## 1 Introduction

The role of rural-to-urban migration in the process of urbanization and economic growth in less developed countries (LDCs) has sparked a debate on the consequences for income distribution and welfare in the rural sending areas (Lipton, 1977, 1980; Stark, 1978; Stark and Yitzhaki, 1982; Stark et al., 1986). This debate is prompted by several considerations: the large contribution of rural inequalities to overall income inequality in LDCs, the rural component of national poverty, and the varying impacts of development processes and policies on different segments of the rural income spectrum. In addition, the economic implications of a small change in the national income distribution occurring at the low (rural) end may be very different from the implications of a small change occurring at the urban end of the distribution, particularly with regard to investment and consumption patterns.

The full impact of migration on a village's income distribution is multi-faceted and complex, and many components of this impact may not be quantifiable. For example, estimates of the migrants' net contributions to household income need to take account of the full opportunity cost of migration, including income that migrants would have contributed to their households had they not migrated. Migrants' net contributions to household income are a subset of the overall impact of migration on the household's resources and opportunities. For example, migration affects the household's income risk (Lucas and Stark, 1985), the household's production and investment decisions (Stark and Levhari, 1982), the household's rank (Stark and Taylor, 1986), and so on. Remittances may also favorably affect the distribution of income via a filtering-down effect, for example, if they result in an increased demand for the products and services of the poorest households within the village.

Diverging views concerning the effect of outmigration on the distribution of income by size in rural sending areas and on rural welfare reflect assumptions about both short-term and long-term externalities associated with migrants' departure from their villages, the size of migrant remittances, and the position of migrant-sending households in the rural income distribution. They also reflect value judgments, in particular the weight attached to distributional versus mean income objectives and the weight attached to incomes of households at different points in the income distribution when calculating indices of inequality.

Whereas migrants' net remittances are not likely to represent the full effect of migration on village income inequalities, they constitute perhaps the most important direct impact of migration on village household incomes, are relatively easily measured, and are a logical and useful starting point for understanding the distributional consequences of migration for migrant-sending areas. In an earlier paper (Stark et al., 1986) we proposed a framework and developed techniques for analyzing the impact of migrant net remittances upon the distribution of household income by size, and consequently on economic welfare in migrant-sending communities. Gini decompositions and household data were used to assign numerical coefficients to the impact of net remittances from Mexico–United States migrants and from internal migrants on income inequality in two Mexican villages. Our findings suggest that the distributional impact of migrants' remittances is favorable overall but differs for different types of migration and for different periods in a village's migration history. This impact depends critically on the degree to which migration opportunities become diffused through the village population, on the returns to human capital embedded in remittances, and on the distribution of potentially remittance-enhancing skills and education across households.

How robust are these findings to the implicit – but nonetheless specific – distributional weights inherent in calculating the standard Gini index? For example, would a shift in weights entail a reversal of our conclusion that migrants' remittances have an equalizing impact upon the distribution of income by size in the village of origin? In this chapter we go a step beyond our earlier findings by exploring their sensitivity to different value judgments when measuring inequality. This is achieved through the use of the extended Gini inequality index (Yitzhaki, 1983; Lerman and Yitzhaki, 1985). In section 2 we describe the properties of the extended Gini index, of which the standard Gini index is a special case. In section 3 we examine the sensitivity of results obtained in our earlier work to the weights attached to incomes at different points in the village income distribution. Conclusions are presented in section 4.

## 2 The Properties of the Extended Gini Index

Let $v$ be an "equity weight" parameter ranging from 1 to infinity. The extended Gini index of a variable $Y$ is defined as

$$G_Y(v) = -\frac{v \operatorname{cov}\{Y, [1 - F(Y)]^{v-1}\}}{\overline{Y}} \qquad (18.1)$$

where $\overline{Y}$ is the mean of $Y$. In the special case where $v = 2$, (18.1) gives the standard Gini index:

$$G_Y(2) = -\frac{2 \operatorname{cov}\{Y, [1 - F(Y)]\}}{\overline{Y}}$$

$$= \frac{2 \operatorname{cov}[Y, F(Y)]}{\overline{Y}}$$

The extended Gini index is similar to Atkinson's (1970) index of inequality. The parameter $v$ in the extended Gini index plays a role similar to that of $\epsilon$ in Atkinson's index. The exact weighting scheme for each $v$ is investigated by Yitzhaki (1983). For our purposes, it is worth noting the following cases. As $v \to \infty$, the index $G_Y(v)$ reflects the Rawlsian criterion. That is, if $Y$ is household income, we evaluate inequality as though we were interested in maximizing the income of the poorest household in the society. As $v \to 1$ we obtain an inequality index in which there is no concern about inequality at all. Graphically, the difference between the Gini index and the extended Gini index is that, while the Gini index represents the area between the Lorenz curve and the 45° line, the extended Gini index assigns different weights to different portions of this area. These weights depend on $v$. A larger value of $v$ implies a larger weight on incomes at the bottom of the income distribution, and vice versa.

The decomposition of the extended Gini index is similar to the decomposition of the standard Gini index presented by Lerman and Yitzhaki (1985) and Stark et al. (1986). Let $Y = \Sigma_k x_k$, where $x_k$ denotes component $k$ of household income. Then the decomposed extended Gini index is

$$G_Y(v) = \sum_k S_k R(k, v) G(k, v)$$

where

$$G(k, v) = -\frac{v \, \text{cov}\{x_k, [1 - F(x_k)]^{v-1}\}}{\bar{x}_k}$$

is the extended Gini index corresponding to income component $k$, $0 < G(k, v) < 1$; $S_k = \bar{x}_k / \bar{Y}$ is the share of income from source $k$ in total household income, and

$$R(k, v) = \frac{\text{cov}\{x_k, [1 - F(Y)]^{v-1}\}}{\text{cov}\{x_k, [1 - F(x_k)]^{v-1}\}}$$

denotes the extended Gini correlation coefficient. The extended Gini correlation coefficient is a correlation coefficient between income from source $k$ and household rankings in terms of total income. Its properties include the following:

1  $-1 < R(k, v) < 1$, where $R(k, v) = 1$ $(-1)$ for all $v > 1$ if $x_k$ is a monotonic increasing (decreasing) function of $Y$;
2  $R(k, v) = 0$ for all $v$ if $x_k$ and $Y$ (in the general case) are independent or if $x_k$ is a constant;
3  $R(k, v) = \rho_k$, where $\rho_k$ is Pearson's correlation coefficient, if $Y$ and $x_k$ are normally distributed (a proof is provided in the appendix).

Extended Gini indices cannot be meaningfully compared for different equity weights $v$, just as absolute values of different welfare functions cannot be meaningfully compared. However, the percentage contributions of different income sources to total income inequality can be compared for different equity weights. In addition, the three properties of the extended Gini correlation listed above enable us to compare extended Gini correlations for different values of $v$. If the extended Gini correlation decreases (increases) as $v$ increases, this reveals that the correlation between income from source $k$ and total income is lower (higher) at the lower end of the income distribution. Extended Gini correlations together with relative contributions of different income sources to income inequality for different equity weights are the focus of the sensitivity analysis which follows.

## 3 Sensitivity Analysis

In our earlier study we used the decomposed standard Gini index $G_Y(2)$ to examine the contribution of Mexico–United States migrant remittances, of internal migrant remittances, and of nonremittance income to income inequalities in two Mexican villages. The data afford a unique opportunity to compare the effects of remittances from both internal and international migrants on income inequality in villages with different degrees of migration experience. Since we shall use our earlier findings as a benchmark for our current inquiry we shall first briefly describe the villages and offer a summary of these findings.

Data for constructing the extended Gini indices were collected in 1983 in two villages in the Pátzcuaro region of the state of Michoacán, Mexico, approximately 2000 km south of the Mexico–Arizona border. The survey sample consists of 425 adults 13 years of age or older representing the total adult population in 61 randomly chosen households, or approximately 10 percent of the total number of households in each village. In no case in our sample had an entire household left the village. The households in the sample follow a migration strategy that is reminiscent of rural-to-urban migration in many LDCs (Stark, 1978): presumably in line with comparative advantage considerations, some sons and daughters migrate, remitting part of their earnings to the village household, while their parents typically remain in the village, tending to domestic affairs and managing the household farm. In some cases heads of household worked for a short term as internal migrants. However, they rarely participated in Mexico–United States migration, which generally requires a large commitment of capital and time away from the village, thereby effectively precluding raising crops in Mexico.

Although the villages we studied are only 2 km apart and are statistically similar in several respects, for example in terms of family size, the differences in their migration patterns are striking. Only 26 percent of village 1 households had at least one family member working in the United States in 1982. In contrast, village 2 households show evidence of a long tradition of Mexico–United States migration. Seventy percent of households in this village had family members who were Mexico–United States migrants in 1982, and these households had an average of 2.8 Mexico–United States migrants each, compared with an average of just 1.7 per household in village 1. As a result, Mexico–United States migrant remittances constituted a much larger share of total income in village 2 households (27 percent) than in village 1 households (9 percent). This difference is significant at the 0.005 level.

Internal migration plays an important role in labor allocations in both villages. A significantly larger share of households participate in internal migration in village 1 (71 percent) than in village 2 (46.7 percent), but the average number of internal migrants per internal migrant household is significantly larger in village 2. As a result, the difference between the shares of internal migrant remittances in households' total income in the two villages is not statistically significant.

In the discussion that follows our interest is in examining the effect of migrants' net remittances on inequality in what is essentially the short run.[1] That is, given nonremittance income, we ask what will be the effect of a given increase in remittances on inequality. Of course, as already noted in the introduction, the short- and long-term impacts of migration on village income inequality, both as measured by the standard Gini index and as measured by the extended Gini index, may be influenced by factors other than net remittances. A change in the sign of our findings will result only if these factors are very significant *and* their distributional effects run in a direction that is contrary to the direction of the effects of net remittances. At this point, we can see no empirical basis for such a possibility. Finally, we recognize the caveat that the magnitude and impact of migrant remittances may also differ depending upon the location-specific attributes of the village, especially, in our case, proximity to the Mexico–United States border. Distance from the border can influence villagers' information about US labor markets and the costs and risks of Mexico–United States migration, and thus the capacity to engage in international migration and the likelihood of success of such activity.

### Extended Gini Decompositions of Village Income Inequality

The rows labeled $S$ in panels A and B of table 18.1 show the share of each income source in the total income of each village. Nonremittance income comprises well over half of all income in the two villages (67 percent and 60 percent respectively). The contribution of migrant remittances to household income is also significant, however. It ranges from 33 percent of total income in the first village to 40 percent in the second.

The rows labeled $SRG/G_Y$ in the table show the percentage contributions of nonremittance income, internal migrant remittances, and remittances from Mexico–United States migrants to total income inequality in each village, for different equity weights. These are calculated using equation (18.1).

The results illustrate the robustness of the general findings in our earlier paper with respect to value judgments concerning inequality. In village 1, where many households contain internal migrants but few have experience in migrating to the United States, remittances from Mexico–United States migrants represent a relatively large share of overall income inequality, while remittances from internal migrants account for a much smaller part of total inequality. The reverse is true for village 2, with its extensive migration networks to the United States and hence more ready access to US labor markets. Here, however, remittances from internal migrants represent a comparatively large share of inequalities in village 2. One plausible explanation for this finding is that in this village internal migrant remittances contain a large returns-to-schooling component, and education is concentrated significantly in high-income households (Stark et al., 1986). These findings hold for all equity weights appearing in the table.

However, these findings appear to be quite sensitive to the weights attached to different points in the village income distribution.

In both villages, nonremittance income represents a fairly constant share of overall income inequality as $v$ increases from 1.5 to 4.0. The percentage contribution of nonremittance income to inequality rises from 59 to 62 percent in village 1 and declines from 61 to 58 percent in village 2 as $v$ goes from 1.5 to 4.0. Thus the percentage contribution of nonremittance income to income inequalities is not very sensitive to the weight attached to incomes at the lower end of the village income distribution.

Obviously, this also applies to the proportionate contribution of remittance income. However, as regards the foreign or domestic origin of remittances, in village 2, where Mexico–United States migrant remittances represent a relatively small share of income inequalities, this share is a positive function of $v$. That is, the more weight we give to households at the lower end of the village 2 income distribution, the greater is the percentage contribution of Mexico–United States migrant remittances to income inequality. The share of inequality attributable to Mexico–United States migrant remittances rises more than 100 percent over the range of weights considered, from 8 percent for $v = 1.5$ (a weight slightly favoring inequality) to 17 percent for $v = 4.0$ (a weight strongly favoring households at the bottom of the income distribution). The explanation for this result can be found in the extended Gini correlation coefficients, which appear in the row labeled $R$. These more than double, from 0.25 to 0.58, over the range of $v$ considered. Although Mexico–United States migrant remittance income is not limited to households at the top of the village 2 income distribution, high-paying Mexico–United States migration opportunities do not appear to be accessible to the poorest village 2 households.

**Table 18.1** Extended Gini decompositions of village income for different equity weights[a]

| | Equity weights | | | | |
|---|---|---|---|---|---|
| | $v = 1.5$ | $v = 2.0$ | $v = 2.5$ | $v = 3.0$ | $v = 4.0$ |
| **A  Village 1** | | | | | |
| Nonremittance income | | | | | |
| $S$ | 0.67 | | | | |
| $R$ | 0.85 | 0.84 | 0.84 | 0.84 | 0.85 |
| $SRG/G_Y$ | 0.59 | 0.60 | 0.60 | 0.61 | 0.62 |
| $(\partial G_Y/\partial e)/G_Y$ | −0.08 | −0.07 | −0.06 | −0.06 | −0.05 |
| | | | | | |
| Internal migrant remittances | | | | | |
| $S$ | 0.17 | | | | |
| $R$ | 0.26 | 0.33 | 0.37 | 0.41 | 0.45 |
| $SRG/G_Y$ | 0.08 | 0.10 | 0.11 | 0.12 | 0.13 |
| $(\partial G_Y/\partial e)/G_Y$ | −0.10 | −0.07 | −0.06 | −0.05 | −0.05 |
| | | | | | |
| Mexico–US migrant remittances | | | | | |
| $S$ | 0.16 | | | | |
| $R$ | 0.85 | 0.86 | 0.87 | 0.89 | 0.92 |
| $SRG/G_Y$ | 0.33 | 0.30 | 0.28 | 0.27 | 0.25 |
| $(\partial G_Y/\partial e)/G_Y$ | 0.17 | 0.14 | 0.12 | 0.11 | 0.09 |
| | | | | | |
| **B  Village 2** | | | | | |
| Nonremittance income | | | | | |
| $S$ | 0.60 | | | | |
| $R$ | 0.85 | 0.87 | 0.88 | 0.89 | 0.89 |
| $SRG/G_Y$ | 0.61 | 0.60 | 0.59 | 0.59 | 0.58 |
| $(\partial G_Y/\partial e)/G_Y$ | 0.01 | −0.01 | −0.01 | −0.01 | −0.02 |
| | | | | | |
| Internal migrant remittances | | | | | |
| $S$ | 0.18 | | | | |
| $R$ | 0.82 | 0.85 | 0.88 | 0.90 | 0.92 |
| $SRG/G_Y$ | 0.31 | 0.29 | 0.28 | 0.26 | 0.25 |
| $(\partial G_Y/\partial e)/G_Y$ | 0.12 | 0.11 | 0.09 | 0.08 | 0.06 |

*(Table continues on the following page)*

**Table 18.1** Extended Gini decompositions of village income for different equity weights[a] (*continued*)

|  | Equity weights | | | | |
| --- | --- | --- | --- | --- | --- |
|  | v = 1.5 | v = 2.0 | v = 2.5 | v = 3.0 | v = 4.0 |
| Mexico–US migrant remittances | | | | | |
| S | 0.21 | | | | |
| R | 0.25 | 0.36 | 0.44 | 0.50 | 0.58 |
| $SRG/G_Y$ | 0.08 | 0.11 | 0.13 | 0.15 | 0.17 |
| $(\partial G_Y/\partial e)/G_Y$ | −0.13 | −0.10 | −0.08 | −0.07 | −0.05 |

[a]Extended Gini indices for different income components are not compared in the table, as this would be tantamount to comparing absolute values of different social welfare functions. Readers who are interested in computing Gini indices for different income components can do so from the values for $SRG/G_Y$ reported in the table, using the following extended Ginis of total income for the two villages.

|  | $G_Y(1.5)$ | $G_Y(2.0)$ | $G_Y(2.5)$ | $G_Y(3.0)$ | $G_Y(4.0)$ |
| --- | --- | --- | --- | --- | --- |
| Village 1 | 0.27 | 0.40 | 0.48 | 0.53 | 0.59 |
| Village 2 | 0.30 | 0.46 | 0.56 | 0.63 | 0.71 |

Even in a highly experienced Mexico–United States migrant village, migration to the United States is essentially a middle-class phenomenon.

This result is consistent with the findings of other studies that Mexico–United States migrants in general do not originate from households at the very top or the very bottom of the rural income distribution (Cross and Sandos, 1981, p. 76; Stark and Taylor, 1986; Taylor, 1987). Households at the top of their village income distribution in general have weak motives for sending migrants to the United States compared with households at the bottom and middle of the income distribution. The former typically enjoy both income-earning opportunities and social status without having to incur the material and psychological costs associated with sending family members, usually clandestinely, into an unfamiliar foreign labor market. At the other income extreme, while the poorest rural households might stand to benefit significantly from high-paying Mexico–United States migrant jobs, they often lack the resources and economic security to finance and bear the risk of sending members illegally across international frontiers. Members of these households are more likely to supplement their families' income through seasonal migration within Mexico, often returning home to assist in major agricultural tasks on the family farm.

Although remittances from internal migrants comprise a relatively large share of inequality in village 2, this share declines somewhat as more weight is attached to incomes in the poorest households. This relative decline in the contribution of internal migrant remittances to inequality is due largely to the rapid rise in the contribution of Mexico–United States migrant remittances to inequality. The extended Gini correlation between internal migrant remittances and total income, which is very high overall, actually increases (from 0.82 to 0.92) as $v$ goes from 1.5 to 4.0. This reflects the extent to which high-income households in this village, with their relatively large endowment of human capital, reap high returns from internal migration.

The contributions of migrant remittances to inequality are somewhat less sensitive to changes in equity weights in village 1. However, the percentage contribution of internal migrant remittances, while small overall, increases by nearly two-thirds (from 8 to 13 percent) as $v$ ranges from 1.5 to 4.0. The extended Gini correlation between internal migrant remittances and total income increases from 0.26 to 0.45 over the range of equity weights. Although internal migrant remittances play a small role in village 1 income inequalities, it appears that the *highest-paying* internal migrant jobs are more available to middle-income households than to households at the bottom of the village income distribution. The increased share of income inequality attributable to internal migrant remittances in village 1 is mirrored by a slight drop in the relative contribution to inequality of remittances from Mexico–United States migrants.

### Impacts of Changes in Remittances on Income Inequalities

The effect of a small percentage change in income from a particular source on the extended Gini index of inequality can be calculated using the decomposition formula given by (18.1). Taking household labor and production decisions as given, consider an exogenous change in each household's income component $j$ by a factor $e$, such that $y_j(e) = (1 + e)y_j$. Then[2]

$$\frac{\partial G_Y(v)}{\partial e} = S_j[R(j, v)G(j, v) - G_Y(v)] \qquad (18.2)$$

where $S_j$, $R(j, v)$, $G(j, v)$, and $G_Y(v)$ denote respectively the $j$th income share, the extended Gini correlation, and the extended Gini coefficients prior to the marginal income change. Dividing throughout by $G_Y(v)$ we obtain

$$\frac{\partial G_Y(v)/\partial e}{G_Y(v)} = \frac{S_j R(j, v) G(j, v)}{G_Y(v)} - S_j \qquad (18.3)$$

Equation (18.3) states that the relative effect of a marginal percentage change in income component *j* upon the extended Gini index of inequality equals the relative contribution of component *j* to overall inequality minus the relative contribution of this component to total income.

In our earlier study we calculated the derivatives (18.3) for each income source in the two villages on the basis of the standard Gini index ($v = 2$). These, together with the derivatives for the other four equity weights, appear in the last row for each income source in the table. In each village, a 1 percent increase in nonremittance income for all households reduces income inequality for every value of $v$, with one exception: inequality increases slightly in village 2 if the importance of incomes at the bottom of the distribution is discounted heavily ($v = 1.5$). In this case, nonremittance income is highly correlated with total income, and this correlation is highest at the top of the village income distribution. Thus a small increase in income from this source exerts an adverse effect on equality when incomes in the poorest households are discounted.

The calculations for both types of remittance income reported in the table confirm our general findings based on the standard Gini index. Differences between the two villages with respect to the impacts of small changes in the remittance components upon inequality are striking. A 1 percent increase in remittances by Mexico–United States migrants *increases* inequalities in village 1 but *reduces* inequalities in village 2 for every value of $v$. A 1 percent increase in remittances from *internal* migrants, on the other hand, *reduces* inequalities in village 1 while *sharpening* inequalities in village 2 for every value of $v$.

As before, however, the strength of these results is sensitive to value judgments underlying the extended Gini calculations. The more weight that we attach to incomes of the poorest households, the smaller is the improvement in village 2 income inequalities that results from a 1 percent increase in remittances from Mexico–United States migrants. The latter drops from 0.13 percent when little weight is attached to the incomes of the poorest households to just 0.05 percent when a large weight is attached to the lower end of the village income distribution. Conversely, while a 1 percent increase in internal migrant remittances sharpens income inequalities in village 2, this adverse effect declines as more weight is placed on the incomes of the poorest households. This decrease is from 0.12 percent for $v = 1.5$ to 0.06 percent for $v = 4.0$. The latter result might seem surprising in light of the increase in the extended Gini correlation for internal migrant remittances over the same range of $v$ in village 2. The explanation for this result can be found in the extended Gini correlation of Mexico–United

States migrant remittances in the village. It increases at such a rapid rate over the range of equity weights that a marginal increase in *internal* migrant remittances, which raises the share of internal migrant remittances in total household income (and hence lowers the share of Mexico–United States migrant remittances), has a progressively smaller adverse effect on village income inequality as more weight is attached to the poorest households.

In village 1, the favorable distributional effect of a small increase in internal migrant remittances drops from 0.10 percent to 0.05 percent when the equity weight increases from 1.5 to 4.0. The unfavorable effect of a 1 percent change in Mexico–United States migrant remittances in this village declines from 0.17 to 0.09 percent over the same range of equity weights.

Analysis of extended Gini derivatives demonstrates that the impact of marginal changes in remittances upon inequality is not unequivocal. It depends critically on where the recipients of remittances are situated in an overall village income distribution, on the share of remittances in village incomes, and on the distribution of remittances themselves. However, it also depends upon the weight attached to incomes at different points of the village income distribution. Although the sign of the extended Gini derivative differs from that of the standard Gini derivative in only one case shown in table 18.1, the equity weight used in the extended Gini calculations bears importantly on the magnitude of these derivatives for particular components of household income.

# 4 Conclusions

Our analyses of migration from and remittances into two Mexican villages provide evidence that the impact of migrant remittances on the rural income distribution by size depends critically on the degree to which migration opportunities of different types become diffused through a village population, as well as on the returns to human capital embedded in migrants' remittances and on the distribution of potentially remittance-enhancing skills and education across village households.

In this chapter we have used extended Gini decompositions to explore the sensitivity of several findings to different value judgments when constructing measures of inequality. The results illustrate the robustness of the main conclusions obtained in earlier work with respect to the weight attached to incomes at the bottom of the income distribution when calculating the extended Gini index. Nevertheless, at times the strength of the conclusions can be quite sensitive to value judgments concerning inequality. For example, our earlier study reveals that, in a village with considerable Mexico–United States migration experience, remittances from Mexico–United States migrants have a favorable effect on the village income distribution. However, the extended Gini analysis shows that this favorable impact diminishes as more weight is attached to incomes in the poorest households. It appears that, while remittances from Mexico–United States migrants have become generally accessible to this village's middle-income groups, barriers to high-paying Mexico–United States migration work exist for households at the bottom of the village income distribution. Remittances from internal migrants in this village have an adverse effect on inequality because the returns to schooling are large at internal migrant destinations and education in the village is concentrated in high-income households. However, in a village where many households contain internal migrants but few have US migration experience, remittances from internal migrants have an equalizing impact on village incomes. Nonetheless, the extended Gini analysis underscores the implications of the greater availability of the *highest-paying* internal migrant jobs to middle-income households than to households at the bottom of the village income distribution.

**Appendix**

In this appendix we derive the properties of the extended Gini correlation coefficient (EGCC). The EGCC for two random variables $x$ and $y$ is defined as

$$R(v) = \frac{\text{cov}\{y, [1 - F_x(x)]^{v-1}\}}{\text{cov}\{y, [1 - F_y(y)]^{v-1}\}}$$

where $F_x$ and $F_y$ are the cumulative distribution functions for $x$ and $y$ respectively and $v$ is a given parameter, with $v > 1$. For $v = 2$, the EGCC is equal to the Gini correlation coefficient. Like the Gini correlation, it is asymmetric in the variables.
   The properties of the EGCC are as follows.

1   If $x$ and $y$ are independent then, for all $v > 1$, $R(v) = 0$. This property follows from the proposition that functions of independent random variables are also independent.
2   If $x$ is a monotonic increasing (decreasing) transformation of $y$ then, for all $v > 1$, $R(v) = 1$ ($-1$). This property follows from the fact that if $x = g(y)$, where $g'(y) > 0$, then $F_x(x) = F_x[g(y)] = F_y(y)$. Moreover, an increasing monotonic transformation of $x$ does not affect $R(v)$. These properties render the EGCC similar to Spearman's correlation coefficient.
3   A linear increasing transformation of $y$ does not affect the EGCC. This property follows immediately from the properties of the covariance and is similar to the property of Pearson's correlation coefficient.

4   If $x$ and $y$ are normally distributed with the parameters $m_x$, $m_y$, $s_x$, $s_y$, and $r$, then, for all $v > 1$, $R(v) = r$.

*Proof*

The conditional expectation of $y$ with respect to $x$, given that both variables are normally distributed, is (see, for example, DeGroot, 1975, p. 250)

$$E(y|x) = m_y + \frac{rs_y(x - m_x)}{s_x}$$

Thus

$$\mathrm{cov}\{y, [1 - F_x(x)]^{v-1}\} = \mathrm{cov}\{[m_y + rs_y(x - m_x)/s_x], [1 - F_x(x)]^{v-1}\}$$

Utilizing the properties of the covariance, we can write

$$\mathrm{cov}\{y, [1 - F_x(x)]^{v-1}\} = rs_y \, \mathrm{cov}\{z, [1 - F_z(z)]^{v-1}\}$$

where $z$ is a standard normal variable with $s_z = 1$. To complete the proof all we have to do is write the denominator as a standard normal variable.

The differences among EGCCs are in the weight attached to the lower portion of the distribution relative to the higher portions. The higher $v$ is, the higher is the weight given to the correlation at the lower end of the distribution. In the extreme case where $v \to \infty$, the only correlation that matters is the correlation among the poorest (see Yitzhaki (1983) for a detailed description of the weighting scheme).

The properties that the EGCCs have the same range regardless of the value of $v$ and that they are equal in the case of the normal distribution enable us to compare EGCCs to check whether the correlation between the variables changes over the entire income distribution.

**Notes**

Co-authored with J. Edward Taylor and Shlomo Yitzhaki. Reprinted from *Journal of Development Economics* 28, 1988. This paper is a revised version of Discussion Paper 23, Harvard University Migration and Development Program. We are extremely grateful to an anonymous referee for helpful comments and advice.

1   The computations that follow are based on income per household. Calculations of standard Gini decompositions using a measure of per capita household income (household income divided by the number of household members 13 years of age or older who spent any part of the year "at home") produced no change worth noting.

2   In the derivation of equation (18.2) the derivative of the extended Gini index with respect to a small percentage change in income from a particular source is completely analogous to the derivative of the standard Gini index (that is, for $v = 2$). The latter can be found in Stark et al. (1986).

**References**

Atkinson, A. B. (1970) "On the Measurement of Inequality." *Journal of Economic Theory* 2: 244–63.

Cross, H. E. and Sandos, J. A. (1981) *Across the Border: Rural Development in Mexico and Recent Migration to the United States.* Institute of Governmental Studies, University of California, Berkeley, CA.

DeGroot, M. H. (1975) *Probability and Statistics.* Reading, MA: Addison-Wesley.

Lerman, R. and Yitzhaki, S. (1985) "Income Inequality Effects by Income Source: A New Approach and Applications to the United States." *Review of Economics and Statistics* 67 (1): 151–6.

Lipton, M. (1977) *Why Poor People Stay Poor: A Study of Urban Bias in World Development.* London: Temple Smith.

—— (1980) "Migration from Rural Areas of Poor Countries: The Impact on Rural Productivity and Income Distribution." *World Development* 8 (1): 1–24.

Lucas, R. E. B. and Stark, O. (1985) "Motivations to Remit: Evidence from Botswana." *Journal of Political Economy* 93 (5): 901–18 (reprinted as ch. 16 in this volume).

Stark, O. (1978) *Economic–Demographic Interaction in the Course of Agricultural Development: The Case of Rural-to-Urban Migration.* Rome: UN Food and Agriculture Organization.

—— and Levhari, D. (1982) "On Migration and Risk in LDCs." *Economic Development and Cultural Change* 31: 191–6 (reprinted as ch. 4 in this volume).

—— and Taylor, J. E. (1986) "Testing for Relative Deprivation: Mexican Labor Migration." Discussion Paper 26, Harvard University Migration and Development Program.

—— and Yitzhaki, S. (1982) "Migration, Growth, Distribution, and Welfare." *Economics Letters* 10: 243–9 (reprinted as ch. 21 in this volume).

—— Taylor, J. E. and Yitzhaki, S. (1986) "Remittances and Inequality." *Economic Journal* 96: 722–40 (reprinted as ch. 17 in this volume).

Taylor, J. E. (1987) "Undocumented Mexico–U.S. Migration and the Returns to Households in Rural Mexico." *American Journal of Agricultural Economics* 69 (3): 626–38.

Yitzhaki, S. (1983) "On an Extension of the Gini Inequality Index." *International Economic Review* 24 (3): 617–28.

# Part VI

*Planning with Migration*

# 19

# On the Optimal Choice of Capital Intensity in Less Developed Countries with Migration

## 1 Introduction

In Sen's (1968) illuminating work on the choice of capital intensity of investment in less developed countries (LDCs), migrants are treated in a rather peculiar manner. They are available in infinite quantity for employment in the urban ("advanced") sector at the going real wage rate; they produce nothing prior to their move; once employed in the urban sector and earning a wage $w$ they (and their families) save nothing – thus failing to contribute toward the accumulation of surplus which is critical for the achievement of future growth. With these "well-behaved" migrants, a powerful simple model is developed and a condition is derived ("condition 2") for the maximization of surplus.

By now, long after these assumptions were made and simplicity of exposition considerations notwithstanding, the assumptions are somewhat difficult to justify. Migration theory and evidence have developed sufficiently and become abundant enough to warrant an effort to remodel the choice of capital intensity problem without recourse to the behavioral characteristics of migrants as implied by Sen.

The purpose of this chapter is to do precisely that. In section 2 Sen's basic model is reconstructed so as to incorporate a migration function. A new condition for surplus maximization is derived. Its implication for the choice of capital intensity in comparison with that of the corresponding condition in the original basic model is examined. In section 3 we take up the social implication of saving by the migrants (including their families who remain behind in the rural sector) in an economy where the share of investment in the national output is below optimum. Again, a condition for surplus maximization is derived and is compared with the new condition developed in section 2. In section 4 we examine the labor market equilibrium condition utilized in sections 2 and 3 under risk aversion. It is shown, in the light of the familial decision-making process generating migration, that even if risk aversion is introduced the equilibrium condition holds.

A short appendix provides a check for the qualitative results obtained through comparisons made in sections 2 and 3.

## 2 The Basic Choice of Capital Intensity Model with Migration

In Sen's basic model the "family-based peasant sector" (henceforth referred to as the rural sector) is a reservoir of manpower and surplus in a process whereby production of machinery and consumption goods is initiated in the "advanced state-owned sector" (henceforth referred to as the urban sector). The latter sector consists of two departments – $i$ where capital goods are manufactured and $c$ where a single consumption good is produced. In addition to the migration-related assumptions already mentioned in section 1, a number of other simplifying assumptions are made, in particular that capital goods (which last forever) can be made by (the homogeneous) labor alone, and that the gestation period of the capital intensity chosen in department $i$ is precisely the same as that of the rejected intensity. (To simplify matters, the choice is narrowed down to one of only two possible capital intensities called "techniques" and defined as "the number of man-years required in department $i$ to make sufficient fixed capital to employ one man fully in department $c$.")

The story begins with the government "starting" the advanced urban sector by extracting "through taxation or other means" a surplus $S$ of the consumption good from the rural sector. $L_i = S/w$ laborers can thus be employed in department $i$, where $w$ is a constant (real) wage rate. Since every $a$ of these laborers produce enough machinery to employ one laborer in department $c$, where $a$ is the chosen capital intensity, total employment in this department is $L_c = S/wa$. If $P_c$ is the productivity of each of these laborers, total consumption-good production in department $c$ becomes $SP_c/wa$. With a wage bill of $(S/wa)w$, the total surplus of the consumption-good is $N = S(P_c - w)/wa$. If, however, the alternative technique is chosen, $a$ and $P_c$ are replaced by $a'$ and $P'_c$ so that the total surplus available for future investment is $N' = S(P'_c - w)/wa'$. Designating the alternative techniques as the (comparatively) high capital intensity technique (H) and the low capital intensity technique (L), and taking the primed and nonprimed notations to represent H and L respectively, the choice rule, when the object is to maximize surplus, is

$$\text{choose L if } N > N', \text{ choose H if } N < N'$$

That is,

$$\text{choose L if } \frac{P_c - w}{P'_c - w} > \frac{a}{a'}, \text{ choose H if } \frac{P_c - w}{P'_c - w} < \frac{a}{a'} \quad (19.1)$$

If some rural output is lost as a consequence of migrants leaving the rural sector to (hopefully) take up urban jobs, rural production of the consumption good, and hence the surplus extracted from the rural sector, will be smaller. To allow for this diminution it is assumed that the *net* surplus $\bar{S}$ extracted from the rural sector differs from the gross surplus $S$ by $m$MPL where MPL is the marginal product of each departing migrant and $m$ is the number of migrants, that is,[1]

$$\bar{S} = S - m\text{MPL} \quad (19.2)$$

Since $\bar{S} = S$ if MPL $= 0$, it immediately follows that Sen's is a special case.

In subsequent expressions, $\bar{S}$ substitutes for $S$, and therefore, if L is chosen,

$$N = \frac{\bar{S}(P_c - w)}{wa} \quad (19.3)$$

and if H is utilized

$$N' = \frac{\bar{S}'(P'_c - w)}{wa'} \quad (19.4)$$

To simplify matters (without in any way affecting the substance), it is assumed that all urban sector jobs are available at the same period of time. This amounts to assuming that production (of machinery) in department $i$ involves a negligible period of time so that the $L_c$ jobs are available as soon as the $L_i$ jobs are created.

Migration decisions are assumed to be taken by small-farmer families aiming at maximizing *family* utility (see section 4). Therefore the value of income forgone by the rural family when one of its members moves townward is the migrant's marginal product. To simplify further, it is assumed that MPL is the same for all migrants.

Given these postulations, the equilibrium condition in the labor market is taken to be[2]

$$\frac{L_i + L_c}{m} w = \text{MPL} \tag{19.5}$$

Therefore

$$\tilde{S} = S - (L_i + L_c)w \tag{19.6}$$

Since (under L) $L_i = \tilde{S}/w = a\tilde{S}/aw$ and $L_c = \tilde{S}/aw$, $(L_i + L_c)w = \tilde{S}(1 + a)/a$. Putting this into (19.6) and rearranging yields

$$\tilde{S} = S\frac{a}{2a + 1} \quad \text{and similarly} \quad \tilde{S}' = S\frac{a'}{2a' + 1} \tag{19.7}$$

with the accompanying property that

$$\frac{\partial \tilde{S}}{\partial a} = \frac{S}{(2a + 1)^2} > 0 \tag{19.8}[3]$$

The analogous expressions to (19.3) and (19.4) are, respectively,

$$N = \frac{(S - m\text{MPL})(P_c - w)}{wa} \tag{19.9}$$

and

$$N' = \frac{(S - m'\text{MPL})(P_c' - w)}{wa'} \tag{19.10}$$

The maximization of a surplus condition analogous to (19.1) is (making use of (19.2) and the abridged notation $\tilde{S}' = S - m'\text{MPL}$)

$$\text{choose L if} \quad \frac{\tilde{S}(P_c - w)}{\tilde{S}'(P_c' - w)} > \frac{a}{a'}$$

$$\text{choose H if} \quad \frac{\tilde{S}(P_c - w)}{\tilde{S}'(P_c' - w)} < \frac{a}{a'} \tag{19.11}$$

Since $a' > a$, $\bar{S}/\bar{S}' < 1$ because of (19.8). This means that, in comparison with (19.1), (19.11) advocates the choice of a relatively less labor intensive technique; the incidence of induced migration with a consequent loss of some rural output implies that the total surplus available for the next round of investment is at a maximum when a relatively capital intensive technique is chosen in the production of machinery in department $i$. The logic of this result is easily seen. Since under the modified model (due to (19.5)) more initially surplus-reducing laborers leave their sector than under the conditions of the basic model, a regulator must operate to ensure that (a) not *too* many depart, thus reducing the scale of the process which generates surplus for future growth, and (b) that a sufficiently high surplus, sufficient to compensate for the rural loss, is generated per a department $c$ employee. Given $S$, $w$, and MPL, such a role is fulfilled by a changing $a$, set at a higher level.

## 3 The Choice of Capital Intensity Model with Savings by Migrants

In formulating (19.9) migrants were assumed to contribute nothing to surplus accumulation by way of direct savings (that is, wages are totally consumed). Future investment is thus secured solely through the savings of the public authority that owns the means of production in the urban sector. These savings equal the part of the product that remains after paying wages to the laborers. Yet theory suggests that a fundamental objective leading to rural-to-urban migration is the generation of surplus and evidence confirms that, in general, migrants suceed (often quite dramatically) in pursuing this objective. (On both these points see section 4.)[4]

Equation (19.9) also abstracts from another consideration. It is likely that in an economy of the type dealt with here, where an industrialization effort has just been initiated, the share of investment in national output is suboptimal. A marginal unit of investment should thus be awarded a premium, reflecting its higher social value *vis-à-vis* consumption. One way of expressing the differential weighting is to multiply each extra unit of investment by $\alpha > 1$, thus magnifying it compared with consumption. (As is well known, taking $\alpha > 1$ amounts to arguing that the investment rate of discount is higher than the consumption rate of discount. Consequently, the marginal social value of investment is higher than its marginal social cost which, in turn, is the consumption forgone in undertaking the investment.)

To incorporate positive savings by employed migrants, $P_c - w$ in (19.3) (and (19.4)) is replaced by $P_c - \tau w$, where $\tau < 1$ is the fraction of $w$ which is consumed, which is the successful migrant's average propensity to consume (including that of his rural family).

To incorporate the investment premium, $\tilde{S}$ in (19.3) (and (19.4)) is replaced by $\alpha\tilde{S}$. Likewise, the fraction $P_c - \tau w$ of output per department $c$ laborer which is not consumed is replaced by $\alpha(P_c - \tau w)$.[5]

Putting together these bits and pieces, we obtain

$$N = \frac{\alpha^2(S - m\text{MPL})(P_c - \tau w)}{aw} \tag{19.12}$$

$$N' = \frac{\alpha^2(S - m'\text{MPL})(P'_c - \tau w)}{a'w} \tag{19.13}$$

which substitute for (19.9) and (19.10) respectively.

The maximization of surplus condition thus becomes

$$\text{choose L if } \quad \frac{\tilde{S}(P_c - \tau w)}{\tilde{S}'(P'_c - \tau w)} > \frac{a}{a'}$$

$$\text{choose H if } \quad \frac{\tilde{S}(P_c - \tau w)}{\tilde{S}'(P'_c - \tau w)} < \frac{a}{a'} \tag{19.14}$$

Since $P'_c > P_c$ and $\tau < 1$, $(P_c - \tau w)/(P'_c - \tau w) > (P_c - w)/(P'_c - w)$. This means that in comparison with (9.11), (19.14) advocates the choice of a relatively more labor intensive technique; part of the product per employee previously taken to constitute a consumption leakage, namely $w$, is now seen to contain the socially highly valued investment component. Use of labor is not as unwarranted as before, and therefore the case for choosing H is weaker than that established in section 2.

As to a comparison between (19.14) and (19.1), only very general observations can be made. For example, the lower is $\tau$ the greater is the edge of $(P_c - \tau w)/(P'_c - \tau w)$ in (19.14) over $(P_c - w)/(P'_c - w)$ in (19.1), and thus the higher is the likelihood that the positive "saving effect" of migration will outweigh its negative "surplus effect." The case for choosing a relatively labor intensive technique under (19.14) will consequently become stronger and, with sufficiently low $\tau$, even stronger than under (19.1).

## 4  The Labor Market Equilibrium Condition under Risk Aversion

In sections 2 and 3 use was made of equation (19.5) – an equilibrium condition in the labor market which, on the face of it, must represent "risk neutrality."

It has often been pointed out (for example, Sen, 1972, p. 498; Stiglitz, 1974, p. 204) that if concave utility maximization with its distaste of riskier situations is the name of the game, then (19.5) cannot represent the equilibrium solution of the labor market, since migration will cease at a lower level than $m$, say $m^*$, such that in equilibrium[6]

$$\frac{L_i + L_c}{m^*} w = \text{MPL} \qquad (19.15)$$

It is the purpose of this section to show that when migration is placed in its appropriate dynamic context and when the proper decision-making unit responsible for generating migration is accounted for, utility maximization and risk aversion entail equilibrium condition (19.5), *not* (19.15).

Consider a family enterprise which is an agricultural producer on its smallholding. During the specific time span of its life-cycle relating to the earlier phases of its existence, the family observes a continuous reduction in its welfare as measured in "net utility" terms. The reduction is due to two "compositional changes": first, given the family size, there is a change in its age structure resulting in greater food requirements; second, family size itself changes over time as additional children are brought into the world. These changes can be translated into utility–disutility terms, leading to the result indicated above and generating an incentive to alter production technology, the intensity of which continuously increases.

However, altering technology is hindered by (a) the characteristic features of the new technology itself and (b) the characteristics of the institutional and noninstitutional "surplus risk state" confronting the small farmer's family.

Of the factors characterizing the new technology, the most crucial are its surplus requirement and its (subjective) risk-increasing nature. (Both factors are usefully illustrated by the transition from traditional varieties to high-yielding varieties.) As to the features of the "surplus risk state," the absence of smoothly functioning market structures and appropriate institutional (as well as noninstitutional) facilities – notably credit and insurance arrangements – implies that the internal constraints arising from the prevalence of production risks and aversion to them, and the low level of (absolute and relative) surplus, cannot be alleviated through the (highly fragmented) markets. On the other hand, the small farmer's family possesses no surplus (or in insufficient volume) and no capacity for engagement in sufficient self-insurance; with the family initially endowed with the "cruel parameter" of only a smallholding, with average capacity to generate surplus being directly proportional to on the farm production but inversely proportional to the (standardized) number of consuming family members, the prevailing surplus and the expected surplus are likely to be low.

It is worth noting that, with surplus insufficiency and risk averseness prevailing simultaneously, their joint impact is greater than the "sum" of each impact when exerted separately. This results from and implies the prevalence of positive interaction between surplus insufficiency and averseness to risk. On the one hand, the degree of risk aversion is related directly to the degree of surplus insufficiency: a larger surplus diminishes the degree of risk aversion paired with a given risky prospect. On the other hand, a higher degree of risk aversion paired with a given risky prospect (that is, a prospect which requires a given surplus) magnifies the overall surplus requirements since – given the assumed absence of insurance markets – part of the surplus has to be destined as an insurance fund.

The easing of the surplus and risk constraints becomes a crucial condition for carrying out the desired technological change. It is rural-to-urban migration of a family member (that is, a son or a daughter)[7] that, by bypassing the credit and insurance markets (with their bias against small farmers), facilitates the change. Migration succeeds in accomplishing this via its dual role in the accumulation of surplus (acting as an intermediate investment)[8] and, through diversification of income sources, in its control over the level of risk.

Although the surplus factor provides a theoretical base for the postulation of saving by employed migrants (section 3), the particular interest of this section is the connection between the risk role of migration and the equilibrium condition in the labor market.

It is of no avail to the small farmer that *objectively* the higher risk entailed in pursuing the new technology is rewarded by higher expected output; it is his *subjective* risk that counts with him. If the small farmer were to be portrayed on a risk–expected return plane, a necessary condition for his moving upward from his present equilibrium position on a given efficiency frontier is that the risk involved in obtaining the higher expected return should exactly match his subjective preference represented by the frontier. (This, of course, assumes that all variables determining the location of the frontier do not change.) Although in figure 19.1 the new technology involves an initial[9] objective move from A to D, the small

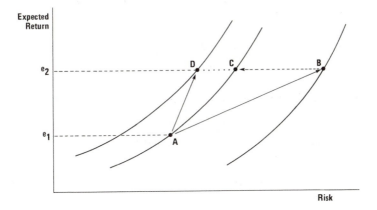

**Figure 19.1**

farmer considers his new (subjective) position to be represented by B, whereas, given $e_2$, what he is willing to bear is a move to C.

To avoid B and to locate on C, a simultaneous adoption of a risk-depressing strategy must accompany the introduction of the new technology. Such a strategy is the allocation of a maturing son's (or daughter's) labor to the urban sector. The rationale for such an allocation derives from a general diversification rule in a portfolio selection theory sense.[10]

Assume that at the initial technology adoption period the small farmer's evaluation is that the *expected* return to his son's engaging in urban employment is higher than the expected return he would have enjoyed had that son remained on the farm. Assume further that this son can either locate on the family farm in the rural sector *or* move to the urban sector, and that the distributions of employment returns in the two sectors are independent of one another and of the distribution of other return-generating familial activities. Under these conditions, it can be shown (see Stark, 1978, appendix 2) that, for a risk-prone *family*, the "portfolio" into which the *urban* sector employment "security" enters is the optimal portfolio.

The cardinal implication of this corollary for labor market behavior and for the equilibrium condition in this market is that rural-to-urban migration as an act of purchasing the "right security" in building up an optimal portfolio will proceed only if the urban expected labor return is higher than the rural return; this is so because, owing to risk aversion, such a "purchase" is mandatory. In terms of equation (19.5) *migration with risk aversion* occurs when

$$\frac{L_i + L_c}{m} w > \text{MPL}$$

and ceases – equilibrium obtains – when

$$\frac{L_i + L_c}{m} w = \text{MPL}$$

That is, (19.5) is maintained.

## Appendix

The qualitative results obtained by comparisons of (19.11) and (19.1), (19.14) and (19.11) (and (19.14) and (19.8)) are obtained here through derivation of the first-order conditions of the respective maximization problems. The degree of capital intensity is taken throughout to be a continuous variable.

In the first part of section 2 the problem is

$$\max_{a} N = \frac{S(P_c - w)}{wa}$$

The first-order condition is

$$\frac{S}{wa^2} \left[ \frac{\partial P_c}{\partial a} a - (P_c - w) \right] = 0$$

(with $\partial^2 P_c / \partial a^2 < 0$ ensuring that the second-order condition for maximization is satisfied). This yields

$$P_c = \frac{w}{1 - \eta} \qquad (19.\text{A}1)$$

where $\eta = (\partial P_c / \partial a)(a / P_c) < 1$ is the elasticity of labor productivity in department $c$ with respect to the capital intensity $a$ ($\eta$ could have been made explicit if the production function of the consumption good had been specified). Thus surplus for future investment is maximized when $a$ is chosen such that the consumption output per laborer equals the "effective wage rate" defined as the ratio between the real wage and 1 minus the elasticity of consumption output with respect to the capital intensity.

In the second part of section 2 the problem is

$$\max_{a} N = (S - m\text{MPL})\frac{P_c - w}{wa}$$

If we use (19.2) and (19.7), the first-order condition turns into

$$\frac{S}{w}\left[\frac{\partial P_c}{\partial a}(2a + 1) - 2(P_c - w)\right] = 0$$

This yields

$$P_c = \frac{w}{1 - \eta(1 + 1/2a)} \qquad (19.A2)$$

Comparison of (19.A2) with (19.A1) immediately shows that $P_c$ in (19.A2) must be larger; thus $a$ which solves (19.A2) is higher – hence the conclusion that the incidence of induced migration with a consequent loss of some rural output dictates the choice of a relatively capital intensive technique.

In section 3 the problem is

$$\max_{a} N = \alpha^2(S - m\text{MPL})\frac{P_c - \tau w}{wa}$$

Again, using (19.2) and (19.7) and rearranging, we obtain the first-order condition as

$$P_c = \frac{\tau w}{1 - \eta(1 + 1/2a)} \qquad (19.A3)$$

In comparing (19.A3) with (19.A2), $P_c$ in (19.A3) is smaller, requiring a lower $a$. Hence we conclude that, with the socially highly valued savings by migrants, a less capital intensive technique should be chosen.

The difficulty in comparing (19.14) with (19.1), mentioned in section 3, is verified by a comparison between (19.A3) and (19.A1). As both the numerator and the denominator in (19.A3) are smaller than in (19.A1), it is not possible, without some explicitness of the parameters, to draw any clear-cut conclusions.

**Notes**

Reprinted from *Journal of Development Economics* 9, 1981. This chapter was presented at the 4th World Congress of the Econometric Society, Aix-en-Provence, August 28–September 2, 1980.

1  If the gross surplus is reduced by some positive fraction $\beta$ of $m$MPL, equation (19.2) is replaced by $\tilde{S} = S - \beta m$MPL. For example, the government may "start" the advanced urban sector by imposing a per capita rural tax of $\beta$MPL. Migration then reduces total tax receipts – the gross surplus – by $\beta m$MPL.

2  One implication of (19.5) is that rural laborers drift into urban unemployment. This need not adversely affect the size of $\tilde{S}$ as two mechanisms are likely to operate: first, provision by the unemployed migrant's family of a "subsistence subsidy" which draws on the difference between his income while with his family and his marginal product; second, income sharing by the employed migrants with their unemployed fellow villagers. For evidence bearing on this point see Stark (1978, pp. 84–6).

3  $a$ is treated here as a continuous variable, although the range of technological possibilities is often not sufficiently dense or wide to justify this treatment.

4  For simplicity, the terms "savings" and "investment" are used interchangeably, "Keynesian problems of translating savings into productive investment" notwithstanding.

5  For every $P_c$ the public authority saves $P_c - w$, and the employed migrants save $(1 - \tau)w$. The social value of these savings is $\alpha(P_c - w) + \alpha(1 - \tau)w = \alpha(P_c - \tau w)$; it is assumed, while doing this, that it is appropriate to attach the same social weight $\alpha$ to a unit of private savings as to a unit of public savings.

6  To obtain (19.15) note that in utility terms the equilibrium condition is

$$\frac{L_i + L_c}{m} U(w) + \left(1 - \frac{L + L_c}{m}\right) U(0) = U(\text{MPL})$$

or

$$\frac{L_i + L_c}{m} U(w) = U(\text{MPL})$$

taking $U(0) = 0$. (Use of $U(0) = 0$ is appropriate since $U$ represents familial utility.) If $U$ is linear, then (19.5) is derived since

$$\frac{U(w)}{U(\text{MPL})} = \frac{w}{\text{MPL}}$$

If $U$ is concave,

$$\frac{U(w)}{U(\text{MPL})} < \frac{w}{\text{MPL}}$$

and therefore

$$\frac{L_i + L_c}{m} = \frac{U(\text{MPL})}{U(w)} > \frac{\text{MPL}}{w}$$

or

$$\frac{L_i + L_c}{m} w > \text{MPL}$$

7  For a discussion concerning the selection of the family migrant member see Stark (1978, ch. 2).
8  In-between technological investment, which has a certain lumpiness, and investment in financial assets, which has a low (or even negative) return.
9  Once the new technology is utilized, familiarity with it and experience in its application, apart from reducing the subjective risk, also ensures a greater expected return.
10  Other old forms of diversification have probably already been exhausted and may have proven (or will prove) incompatible with the new technology. New forms may either not be available or, if they are, provide relatively little diminution of risk. For further references to these points see Stark (1978, ch. 2).

# References

Sen, Amartya K. (1968) *Choice of Techniques: An Aspect of the Theory of Planned Economic Development*, 3rd edn. Oxford: Blackwell.
—— (1972) "Control Areas and Accounting Prices: An Approach to Economic Evaluation." *Economic Journal* 82(325s): 486–501.
Stark, Oded (1978) *Economic–Demographic Interactions in Agricultural Development: The Case of Rural-to-Urban Migration*. Rome:UN Food and Agricultural Organization.
Stiglitz, Joseph E. (1974) "Alternative Theories of Wage Determination and Unemployment in LDCs: The Labor Turnover Model." *Quarterly Journal of Economics* 88(2): 194–227.

# 20

# On Slowing Metropolitan City Growth

In an article published in the March 1979 *Population and Development Review*, Alan Simmons reviewed four policy approaches for slowing metropolitan growth in Asia (Simmons, 1979a). Noting that to date redistribution policies have shown modest or no impact, Simmons concluded that "each of the policies can be successful" but only provided that a number of specified conditions are fulfilled. In the June 1979 issue of the *Review*, Samuel Preston also discussed the desirability of reducing rates of urban growth and rural-to-urban migration and suggested policies and "palatable means" of reducing urban growth (Preston, 1979). In yet another article Paul Shaw proposed a strategy for controlling new housing construction as an effective means of influencing the direction of migration flows away from "problem urban centers." (Shaw, 1978). At a meeting held under the joint sponsorship of the UN Population Division and the UN Fund for Population Activities[1] papers were read advancing the cause and reviewing the results of specific interventionist policies directed at constraining or redirecting migration. Participants from a number of developing countries expressed, in writing and orally, a desire to see their governments pursue an effective vigorous "population redistribution policy" – the new code name for stemming the "drift of rural migrants into the large urban centers." Governments of most developing countries have themselves expressed great anxiety over the "present spatial distribution of their populations," implying, chiefly, the unacceptability of current rates of rural-to-urban migration (United Nations, 1979, especially ch. 9).

Thus there seems to be a rare convergence of real-world concern, professional interest, and research activity. The scene appears set for the experts to settle their quibbles and to advance, as quickly as possible, an agreed prescription that the action-prone impatient governments can eagerly and swiftly adopt.

Yet a major issue that confounds dispassionate observers is whether governments really want to stem the "tide of migrants to the cities." As the subsequent discussion makes clear, this question reflects uncertainty as to whether governments *can* intervene and has nothing to do with the related, yet clearly separate, concern of whether governments *should* intervene.

One indication of the ambivalence of governments' interventionist position is the weak correlation between their perceptions of the overall acceptability of the spatial distribution of their populations and their policies with respect to the basic trend in spatial redistribution from nonmetropolitan to metropolitan regions and from rural to urban centers.[2] Another possible symptom of the same ambivalence is the frequent ineffectiveness or, at best, very limited success of government policies aimed at substantially reducing rural-to-urban migration (Simmons 1979a, b). A third indication that governments do not really want to contain migration is the frequent (and increasing) incidence of accommodationist policies that "aspire to improve the lot of the migrants" (Laquian, 1979). Such policies (for example, sites and services projects, reception centers for new migrants) run counter to declared perceptions since, virtually by definition, they increase the attractiveness of the urban destination, often not so much by increasing expected income as by decreasing uncertainty (income variance). Accommodationist policies are thus conducive to rural-to-urban migration rather than being an added constraint upon it.

One possible explanation of why governments fail to intervene, or intervene ineffectively, is that they are wary of acting decisively until ongoing research has produced an agreed optimal strategy. However, for researchers to believe such an explanation is at best self-serving and at worst pure naiveté. Another possible explanation is that governments' poor performance in pursuing interventionist policies is due to the half-hearted application of measures; if intensively applied, success would have been more apparent. Yet, clearly, this explanation merely begs the question why full-fledged policy statements are applied half-heartedly.

In the following analysis, an alternative explanation is presented by way of an economic hypothesis that needs to be fully tested.[3]

## 1 An Economic Argument for Increased Rural-to-Urban Migration

Assume the following production relation:

$$Q = f(K, L) \tag{20.1}$$

where $Q$ is the value of urban output produced with capital input $K$ and labor input $L$. It is possible to express $Q$ as

$$Q = \pi + wL \qquad (20.2)$$

that is, the sum of profits $\pi$ and the wage bill $wL$, where $w$ is the wage paid per employee and $L$ is the number of employees. Hence

$$\pi = Q - wL \qquad (20.2')$$

Assume, initially, that only short-run current-period considerations matter. To gauge first the immediate impact, assume that $Q$ is given. Then, from (20.2'), prior to any adjustment, $\partial\pi/\partial w < 0$; that is, profits are higher when wages are lower. $Q$ will be adjusted beyond the immediate impact, but it is simple to show that the consequent change in profits will be positive; assuming that profit-earners are profit-maximizers and given that the immediate impact of lower wages is higher profits, pursuit of an adjustment must imply that it increases profits further.[4] Thus, other things being equal, profit-earners benefit from paying lower wages and can generally be assumed to favor them.

An undisputed consequence of a continuous rural-to-urban migration is the downward pressure that it exerts upon urban wages. Therefore, if government actions are influenced by profit-earners' interests, governments are unlikely to pursue antimigratory policies actively.[5]

Assume that the interests of profit-earners are coincident with those of the government but that output growth is the relevant consideration. Equation (20.2) can then be rewritten as

$$Q = c_2\pi + (1 - c_2)\pi + c_1wL + (1 - c_1)wL \qquad (20.3)$$

where $c_2$ and $c_1$ are the proportions consumed out of profits and wages respectively and therefore the complementary proportions are of the corresponding saving shares. Keynesian problems of translating savings into investment notwithstanding, future output directly depends on current savings. Since $c_2 \neq c_1$, the contribution of a unit of wage income to savings will differ from that of a unit of profit income; drawing on the well-documented finding that $c_2 < c_1$ (profit-earners are richer and better able to invest), a unit of profit income, in terms of growth, is more valuable than a unit of wage income. This can be demonstrated as follows. If it is assumed that the share of savings or investment in national output is suboptimal, a marginal unit of invesment should be awarded a premium, reflecting its higher social value *vis-à-vis* consumption. One way of expressing the differential weighting is to multiply each extra unit of investment by $\alpha > 1$, thus magnifying it compared with consumption. (As is well known, taking $\alpha > 1$ amounts to arguing that the investment rate of discount is higher than the consumption rate of discount. Consequently, the marginal social value of investment is higher than its marginal social cost, which, in turn, is the consumption forgone in undertaking the investment.) The total social value of the components of $Q$ listed in (20.3) is thus

$$V = c_2\pi + \alpha(1 - c_2)\pi + c_1 wL + \alpha(1 - c_1)wL \qquad (20.4)$$

Whereas a unit of profit income produces $1 - c_2$ investment units with a value of $\alpha(1 - c_2)$, a unit of wage income produces $1 - c_1$ investment units with a value of only $\alpha(1 - c_1) < \alpha(1 - c_2)$.

As already shown, rural-to-urban migration, with its consequent damping of urban wages, increases profits. Hence it leads to higher savings, investment, and output growth.[6] Either because of pure self-interest (a situation illustrated by equation (20.2)) or because of self-interest that may tally with a broader goal (as illustrated by equation (20.4)), profit-earners favor continuous migration, which, through its downward pressure on wages, increases their share of output.

## 2 The Convergence of Economic Advantage and Government Policy

Three closely related points have an obvious bearing on the foregoing argument. They are (a) the mechanism by which rural-to-urban migration depresses urban wages, (b) the mechanism by which the interests of profit-earners are transformed into government policy, and (c) the extent to which such interests override interests that may favor an antimigratory policy.

Under normal conditions, an increased supply of labor, unless outpaced by increased demand, will tend to depress wages or mitigate their rise. In the urban sector or in its capital intensive subsector, however, it is unrealistic to refer to a single and a fully variable wage. Nevertheless, the argument holds. It can be pointed out that, in precisely those establishments owned by large profit-earners, wages are rigid downward owing, for example, to the power of unions. But even in situations such as this, increased supply of migration-fed urban labor will tend to constrain the bargaining power of unionized labor and modify its wage claims because of (a) the threat of competition from abundant nonunionized labor, (b) the cheapness of urban manufactured goods and services produced with nonunionized labor in the urban "informal subsector" – goods and services that are heavily purchased by unionized labor – and (c) the fear of an increased practice by the large profit-earners of subcontracting to informal sector workshops and small-scale enterprises where wages are competitively determined. If large profit-earners are legally required to pay high wages, rather than being pressed to do so by unions' bargaining power, subcontracting becomes an excellent means around the legal constraint. An increased supply of rural-to-urban migrants thus renders wages lower than they otherwise would be.

Concerning the second point, a number of political configurations may account for the hypothesized convergence of government action and the interests of profit-earners. First, the profit-earners may themselves head the government. In Latin America and Southeast Asia, large industrialists often formally share power at various high levels of government. Second, even if they do not formally share power, profit-earners reside in cities where governments sit, decision-making is centralized, and power is concentrated. By regular and intensive contact with politicians and officials, profit-earners exercise influence and exert pressure to bias decisions in their favor. Even if the government decides to curtail migration drastically, profit-earners may wield sufficient power to neutralize policies designed to implement these decisions. Very often, the administrative function commands wide discretionary powers and considerable latitude and has a political will of its own. When such an administrative system is charged with policy implementation, profit-earners will bring pressure to bear on it to dilute actions that do not tally with their interests and to reinforce those that do. This pressure will probably succeed because the risk of falling out of favor with influential profit-earners outweighs the risk of being reprimanded for unsatisfactory performance. Finally, even if governments do not include profit-earners and are not subject to regular pressures by them to deliver benefits, they still further the interests of profit-earners on whose tacit or manifest support they crucially depend. Governments of all forms are careful to preserve their power base and do not require reminders when considering or attempting to execute policies to stem the rural-to-urban influx of labor.

The third point concerns the extent to which the desire to maximize profit income – hence to avoid constraining rural-to-urban migration – dominates other considerations that may call for action to depress migration. That such "economic" behavior influences political behavior is taken here as axiomatic. Indeed, influencing migration policy is not the only manifestation of political power being exercised by profit-earners to increase their profit share of output; power and influence are widely used to secure subsidies for various capital intensive, basically labor-replacing investments. In terms of equation (20.2) and given $Q$, this brings about an increase in $\pi$ through the lowering of $L$ and hence the wage bill.

Two possible consequences of rural-to-urban migration would be likely to encourage profit-earners to adopt an antimigratory stand: a rise in food prices and the growth of an urban revolutionary potential. Cheap food is a main concern of profit-earners. Compared with the alternative of high food prices, it ensures that urban laborers are well fed, productive, and moderate in their demands for wage increases. Rural-to-urban migration may adversely affect agricultural labor supply and production, thus pushing up food prices. The second consequence is the increase in the number of unemployed, underemployed, and low-paid urban laborers whose absolute or relative deprivation and frustration might be converted into political action, threatening the very political order that is crucial for smooth production and continued profits.

If substantiated, these concerns may pull the rug from under the argument that rural-to-urban migration increases profits. When closely examined, however, they appear more imaginary than real. Rural-to-urban migration may account for a large proportion of urban population growth (though for a lower proportion than natural increase, see Preston, 1979) but usually displaces only a meager proportion of the rural population. Hence, its adverse impact on agricultural labor supply is minute – even nil if an intra-familial compensatory adjustment to labor withdrawal takes place. Moreover, by easing the surplus and risk constraints that hinder technological change in agricultural production, rural-to-urban migration of labor acts as a catalyst for such a change via its dual role in the accumulation of surplus and, through diversification of income sources, in the control of the level of risk (Stark, 1978). In assuming such a role, rural-to-urban migration results, even if with some lag, in more and not less food being produced.

As to the second concern, viewing the political profile of urban migrants as "revolutionary" or "radical" appears to be an illusion. Time and again (Nelson, 1970; Cornelius, 1975; Dietz, 1975; Perlman, 1976; Kemper, 1977) migrants have been found to undergo quick political socialization, to be conservative in their political orientation, to be keen to ensure political stability,[7] and to be averse to confrontation and turmoil that may hurt them first and most. Their hostility toward threats to the existing order reflects a fear of the adverse personal consequences of a radical political change that outweighs the benefits, if any. The same aversion to risk that explains production behavior may also account for political behavior and the evaluation that the expected net benefit from manipulating the existing system is greater than the expected net benefit from threatening it.

Perhaps the very rural origin of the migrants and their pre-migration political socialization explain, at least partly, their conservative political conduct in the urban sector. Accustomed to a low-profile government, they have modest expectations of the government's ability to solve their urban problems, and disillusionment is thus limited.[8] Indeed, it is questionable whether the nature of the migrant's employment experience gives rise to a potential for politically disruptive behavior. Presumably, if the typical migrant were to secure employment for a considerable period of time and then lose it, he would become politically more nonconformist and disruptive than if he were unemployed for a time, yet anticipating future employment. Since evidence suggests that the urban migrant's typical employment experience is a relatively short spell of unemployment followed by a progressively improved employment status (Stark, 1978), the possibility of radical political behavior can generally be ruled out.

In addition, migrants' expectations are likely, at least during the initial years of urban residence, to be based on their *rural* experience. Thus, since a comparison of their lot, realized or anticipated, with that of their rural counterparts – or with their own prior to migration – does not generally give rise to dissatisfaction, ensuing resentment and frustration transformed into political radicalism are unlikely. As time goes by, the impact of migrants' rural origins or aspirations will probably fade, and urban-inspired norms will increasingly influence the shaping of aspirations. It is very doubtful, however, whether such a process will give rise to increasing dissatisfaction. For this to happen, migrants' new aspirations would have to rise faster than their economic achievements. Given the typical migrant's favorable urban employment and economic record, this seems unlikely. Finally, even if some dissatisfaction and frustration should arise, there are several reasons (including those mentioned earlier) why (a) they need not be converted into political action (no use of political means) or (b) they cannot be transformed into political radicalism (no use of destabilizing political means).[9]

Having established that the net interest of profit-earners is to further rural-to-urban migration, we conclude that the capacity of governments effectively to pursue migration policies aimed at "slowing metropolitan city growth" remains highly questionable. We suggest that this constrained capacity at least partly accounts for the discrepancy between governmental statements concerning the need to stem rural-to-urban migration and governments' low-key approach in carrying out such policies.

Is the outcome of the preceding analysis a reasoned despair regarding rapid metropolitan city growth in developing countries? Not really. We conclude by identifying a few points that have a bearing on whether and to what extent governments can pursue a policy of slowing rural-to-urban migration.

1   There is an intimate relationship between the feasibility of a policy to stem rural-to-urban migration and the maintenance of the political

power structure. The net interests of profit-earners must be reckoned with in devising a migration-related policy.

2   The work of the present author has led to the view that, as a general rule, the net social effect of rural-to-urban migration in developing countries is positive. This view bears on a question posed at the outset but excluded from the current analysis, namely, whether governments should pursue antimigratory policies. The argument advanced above suggests that political realism points in the same direction as economic analysis; in other words, the "cannot" tallies with the "should not."

3   If a serious attempt to stem rural-to-urban migration were to be undertaken, profit-earners would have to be bought off. The required "compensatory measures" might entail a high social cost – for example, heavy subsidization of labor-replacing capital intensive machinery – but they need not. Perhaps the most reasonable strategy would be to create an incentive cum subsidies system to encourage profit-earners to locate industry where the potential migrants are – a rural industrialization program.

## Notes

Reprinted from *Population and Development Review* 6, 1980. I am indebted to Jacob Paroush, Shlomo Yitzhaki, and Adrian Ziderman for helpful comments.

1   UN Population Division/UN Fund for Population Activities Workshop on Population Distribution Policies in Development Planning, Bangkok, Thailand, September 1979.

2   United Nations (1979, pp. 75–6). Although this finding relates to governments of developed and developing countries grouped together, a breakdown into these categories reveals that the pattern described in the text is a characteristic of each.

3   One caveat that has to be borne in mind is that what follows adopts the analog of a partial, rather than a general, equilibrium approach. Not all economically categorized groups whose interests are usually politically manifested (for example, unionized labor) are accounted for. The appeal of the hypothesized explanation may be weakened or strengthened depending on the net interest of each group and the weighted sum total of these net interests. Such complete analysis remains to be undertaken. (Interestingly, though, this might well *enforce* the validity of the suggested hypothesis. For example, if the net interest of unionized labor is to favor migration-stemming policies, the explanation of the observed behavior of governments as one that reflects the net interest of profit-earners, which, in turn, is to refrain from pursuit of such policies, *gains* strength.)

4   Algebraically,

$$(\pi + \Delta\pi) - \pi = [Q + \Delta Q - (w + \Delta w)(L + \Delta L)] - (Q - wL)$$

Hence

$$\Delta\pi = \Delta Q - w\Delta L - \Delta wL - \Delta w\Delta L$$

Ignoring $\Delta w\Delta L$ and using (20.1), which, with no change in the capital stock, gives $\Delta Q = f_L \, \Delta L$,

$$\Delta\pi = f_L\Delta L - w\Delta L - \Delta wL = (f_L - w)\Delta L - \Delta wL$$

Since $f_L \geq w$, when wages are lower, that is, $\Delta w < 0$, profits are higher as $\Delta\pi > 0$.

5   Note that each increment in $L$ results in a *larger* increase in profit $\Delta\pi > 0$ consequent upon a given decrease in wages $\Delta w < 0$. (This can be seen immediately by inserting higher values of $L$ into the last equation in note 4). In a dynamic context, this implies that from the profit-earners' point of view the favorable impact of migration leads to further migration producing a *more* favorable impact – an ever-*increasing* interest in continued migration.

6   One usual concomitant of this growth is that workers in industry are progressively endowed with more and better equipment. This raises not only their marginal product – thus providing a powerful argument for wage increases – but also their bargaining power. The continued flow of migrants erodes this build-up of power.

7   If gains were already realized, such an approach is consistent with a desire to consolidate them.

8   The nature of these urban problems may also account for the political orientation of migrants. The type of demand may explain the way it is made. Local-level community type demands – for example, provision of water, electricity, and public transport, putting in streets, construction of a school, seeking regulation of lots and land titles – appear to be the primary candidates for conversion into political demands. Pursuit of such demands can hardly lead to an active disapproval of the existing system of government and politics. It is of particular interest to note here that a common finding of virtually all studies of migrant communities is the high propensity to attempt first to self-solve communal problems rather than to impose them upon the administration.

9   For a complementary analysis see Nelson (1970).

# References

Cornelius, Wayne, A. (1975) *Politics and the Migrant Poor in Mexico City.* Stanford, CA: Stanford University Press.

Dietz, Henry A. (1975) "Becoming a Poblador: Political Adjustment to the Urban Environment in Lima, Peru." Ph.D. Dissertation, Stanford University.

Kemper, Robert V. (1977) *Migration and Adaptation: Tzintzuntzan Peasants in Mexico City.* Beverly Hills, CA: Sage Publications.

Laquian, Aprodicio A. (1979) "Review and Evaluation of Accommodationist Policies in Population Redistribution." Presented at UN Population Division/UN Fund for Population Activities Workshop on Population Distribution Policies in Development Planning, Bangkok, September 1979.

Nelson, Joan (1970) "The Urban Poor: Disruption or Political Integration in Third World Cities." *World Politics* 22 (3): 393–414.

Perlman, Janice E. (1976) *The Myth of Marginality: Urban Poverty and Politics in Rio de Janeiro.* Berkeley, CA: University of California Press.

Preston, Samuel H. (1979) "Urban Growth in Developing Countries: A Demographic Reappraisal." *Population and Development Review* 5 (2): 195–215.

Shaw, R. Paul (1978) "On Modifying Metropolitan Migration." *Economic Development and Cultural Change* 26 (4): 677–92.

Simmons, Alan B. (1979a) "Slowing Metropolitan City Growth in Asia: Policies, Programs, and Results." *Population and Development Review* 5 (1): 87–104.

—— (1976b) "A Review and Evaluation of Attempts to Constrain Migration to Selected Urban Centers and Regions." Presented at UN Population Division/ UN Fund for Population Activities Workshop on Population Distribution Policies in Development Planning, Bangkok, September 1979.

Stark, Oded (1978) *Economic–Demographic Interactions in Agricultural Development: The Case of Rural-to-Urban Migration.* Rome: UN Food and Agriculture Organization.

United Nations (1979) *World Population Trends and Policies: 1977 Monitoring Report*, vol. 2. New York: United Nations.

# 21

## Migration, Growth, Distribution, and Welfare

In current less developed countries (LDCs) and in the past of present day developed countries (DCs), urbanization and the rural-to-urban migration which contributes to it have been fairly close correlates of economic growth. Since they have also been associated, over some domain, with adverse distributional effects as measured by *conventional* indices of inequality, the net welfare implications of the processes became a topic of intense interest and debate. Which development strategies and national policies avoid such repercussions? How could the adverse effects be averted? Much research effort has focused on an *empirically* developed relationship – the "Kuznets curve," the inverted U hypothesis that inequality first increases and then declines with growth.[1] There is extensive literature on how "unequal" and "unbalanced" and, consequently, "integrated" and "even" development and growth generate the Kuznets curve. The purpose of the following comments is to add analytical clarity to the discussion concerning the inverted U hypothesis and, more generally, to the study of the interactions between migration, growth, distribution, and welfare.

Consider the following situation. In a population in which everyone is equally poor, one person obtains a higher income. Ruling out envy as a source of welfare loss, one's natural reaction would be that something good has happened – poverty is a little less widespread. However, all indices of absolute or relative inequality – for example, the Gini index, the Kuznets index, the Theil index – register an increase whereas welfare registers an improvement. More generally, consider a population which consists of two homogeneous groups. Compare the following two states of nature: (a) the incomes of some of the poorer $f^t$ in the population ($f^t$ is the share of the poor in the total population) are raised while those of all the rest are left intact; (b) the incomes of none of the poorer $f^t$ in the population are raised and those of all the rest are also left intact. Both social welfare and Pareto criteria produce preference of (a) over (b).[2] However, conventional indices do not. Consider for example the Gini index. Clearly in case (a) the mean income is raised and the Lorenz curves intersect. This can also be easily seen mathematically: in this case the Gini index takes the form of the difference between the share of the poorer group in the population and the share out of the total income accruing to it. When both are smaller, the net effect cannot be determined analytically. Situations of this type have often been approached in despair. For example, Fields (1979, p. 331) argues that "when Lorenz curves cross, there is nothing to say" and Moreh (1981, p. 30) comments that "the ordering of the equality of income distributions" is possible only if "the Lorenz curves pertaining to the income distributions do not intersect." It seems to us that the breakdown of the Lorenz domination criterion should imply inadequacy of the criterion rather than incapacity to make distributional judgments. We should also like to emphasize that a distinction should be made between a situation whereby the mean incomes of the distributions under review are equal and a situation whereby the mean incomes are not equal. Whereas with respect to the former, concerns such as the ones quoted above are valid, with respect to the latter – for example, the case addressed in this chapter – they are not; a welfare ranking of the distributions *is* possible.[3]

We shall continue modeling the economy by dividing it into two homogeneous income groups. We shall designate the lower-income group the traditional/rural sector and the other the modern/urban sector and denote them by t and m respectively; hence, the respective population shares are $f^t$ and $f^m$ ($f^t + f^m = 1$) and the uniform sectoral incomes are $Y^t$ and $Y^m$. A rural-to-urban migration-fueled urban sector growth resulting in higher absolute income constitutes a specific illustration of state (a) above. How will this change be formally registered by conventional indices of inequality? Note that any such index $I = I(Y^m, f^m, Y^t, f^t)$ maintains (a) $I(Y^m, 0, Y^t, 1) = I(Y^m, 1, Y^t, 0) = 0$, that is, if all income-recipient units have the same income, the value of the index is zero, and (b) for any $0 < f^m < 1, I(Y^m, f^m, Y^t, f^t) > 0$, and $I$ is continuous in $f^m$. From (a) and (b) it immediately follows that $\partial I / \partial f^m > 0$ for low values of $f^m$ and $\partial I / \partial f^m < 0$ for high values of $f^m$.

Two conclusions follow: whereas in our abstract economy through rural-to-urban migration more and more people substitute $Y^m$ for $Y^t$ ($Y^m > Y^t$), a change which is *consistently* welfare-augmenting, our welfare judgment, if it were to be captured by $I$, would be *conditional*. Through a little algebraic manipulation we can obtain

$$G = f^t - \frac{f^t Y^t}{f^t Y^t + f^m Y^m} = \frac{f^t (1 - f^t)(Y^m - Y^t)}{Y^t + (1 - f^t)(Y^m - Y^t)}$$

and the point at which $G$ obtains a maximum is

$$f^{t^*} = \frac{Y^m - (Y^m Y^t)^{1/2}}{Y^m - Y^t}$$

Then if, for example, the uniform urban incomes are higher by 50 percent than the uniform rural incomes, rural-to-urban migration resulting in migrants' capturing the higher income will generate a more and more unequal distribution as measured by the Gini coefficient until 55 percent of the population remains in the rural areas. Past this point, *additional* rural-to-urban migration will result in reduced inequality. It is illogical to expect populations to urbanize by leaps and bounds; before 45 percent are in the urban sector, 44 percent would have to be there. And it would be odd, on distributional grounds, to advocate urbanization *past* the 55–45 percent rural–urban shares, but resent it otherwise. Second, the inverted U pattern of the inequality in the distribution of income by size is automatically generated by the axiomatic attributes of the indices measuring this inequality. Thus, *to the extent* that the simplifying conditions underlying our analysis are reproduced by the reality of LDCs, the Kuznets curve is a mathematical artifact; that income inequality first increases and then declines with growth is nothing more than a derivative of the attributes of the inequality indices. Viewed in this light, some of the debate surrounding the inverted U curve, for example, a recent exchange in the *Development Digest* as well as earlier work, is partly misplaced.[4]

The study of the relationship between migration-fueled urban growth and inequality in the distribution of income by size seems to be subject not only to a mathematical artifact but also, at least to some extent, to a statistical artifact. Income *earners* do not necessarily constitute the independent income *recipient* units whose income should be counted as inputs into the calculation of the relative inequality index, should one decide to employ such measure. There is a body of theory, and empirical evidence to support it (see Stark, 1978, 1981, 1982; Stark and Levhari, 1982), that as far as the identity of the decision-making unit with respect to income plans (both earning and disposition) is concerned, rural-to-urban migrants may not constitute a separate entity. In present day LDCs, the modal migrating unit is a young individual – a member of a family but *not* a family. However, the *family* is the locus of major decisions on income (including the means of obtaining it, among other things through rural-to-urban migration of one of its members). This also remains so for a considerable post-migration period. It follows that neither the household nor, for that matter, the individual, is the relevant income recipient unit. Thus choice of a multi-person urban household in which the migrant happens to be staying (common residence, housekeeping sharing) appends the migrant to a family with which his economic ties are short lived, in whose income decisions he does not really participate, and by whose income decisions he is not really affected. Considerations of a similar nature render it equally inappropriate to refer to the individual rural-to-urban migrant family member as an independent income recipient unit. Although living separately from his family, he does participate in the family's common decisions (which affect him also); he is involved in familial pooling of resources and income, especially pooling aimed at facilitating his migration and enhancing his success in the urban labor market; he is responsible for substantial urban-to-rural remittances and maintains a close overall intensive bond (at least in the medium run) with his family. All this implies that it makes little analytical sense to refer to the migrant as an independent income recipient unit; in any meaningful evaluation, both his and his family's incomes should be combined.

The implication of this observation for a distribution welfare analysis is that, *at least for a considerable period of time*, (a) an *a priori* classification is in order, that is, the criterion for defining income as rural or urban should depend on the recipient's initial location and not on his current one or, for that matter, on the locality in which that income has actually been generated, and (b) the income recipient unit to which all incomes are attributed has to be the rural-based family inclusive of its "urban extension" – the migrant member. Hence, even if a relative measure of inequality, for example, the Gini index, is used, inequality could be shown to continuously decrease; if through various sharing and filtering-down mechanisms incomes in the $t$ sector rise throughout,

$$G = f^t - \frac{f^t Y^t}{f^t Y^t + f^m Y^m}$$

unequivocally diminishes as the numerator in the right-hand term increases by more than the denominator. If the benefits of migration are not evenly distributed, that is, if only $0 < \lambda < 1$ of the $f^t$ enjoy a higher income $Y^{t'} > Y^t$, then $f^t$ receives a higher share of total income:

$$\frac{\lambda f^t Y^{t'} + (1 - \lambda)f^t Y^t}{\lambda f^t Y^{t'} + (1 - \lambda)f^t Y^t + f^m Y^m} > \frac{f^t Y^t}{f^t Y^t + f^m Y^m}$$

and, of course, a higher absolute income. The possible ambiguity stemming from the intersection of the Lorenz curves should only imply that usage of the Gini coefficient must not exceed its delivery boundaries. We thus return to the point that we have made earlier, namely that a welfare judgment can and should be made based on social welfare or Pareto criteria. Utilization of these measures thus results in a strict preference of the post-migration state.

To invoke direct welfare judgment pertaining to this situation a specific social welfare function will be utilized: $W = Y(1 - G)$, where $Y = f^m Y^m + f^t Y^t$. This function has the following properties.

1  An increase in the income of any member of the society will result in a higher value of $W$. This is consistent with both social welfare and Pareto criteria.
2  A transfer of income from a rich person to a poor person will result in a higher value of $W$. (This fulfills "the Dalton principle of transfer.")

As proved by Yitzhaki (1982), these two properties are independent of the distributions one begins with.

In our case, it can easily be shown that a necessary and sufficient condition for the post-migration distribution A to be preferred to the pre-migration distribution B is that

$$Y^A \geq Y^B \text{ and } W^A = Y^A(1 - G^A) > W^B = Y^B(1 - G^B)$$

Obviously, $Y^A > Y^B$. To see why $W^A > W^B$, note that through the use of our particular form of $G$ we obtain

$$W = (f^m)^2(Y^m - Y^t) + Y^t$$

For a given $Y^m$,

$$dW = 2f^m(Y^m - Y^t)\, df^m + [1 - (f^m)^2]\, dY^t$$

Since $f^m < 1$ and $Y^m > Y^t$, it is clear that with any $df^m > 0$ leading to $dY^t > 0$ welfare increases.

**Notes**

Co-authored with Shlomo Yitzhaki. Reprinted from *Economics Letters* 10, 1982.
1  We shall mention just a few of the many studies addressing this hypothesis: Kuznets (1955, 1963), Oshima (1962), Adelman and Morris (1973), Paukert

(1973), Chenery et al. (1974), Roberti (1974), Cline (1975), Robinson (1976), Frank and Webb (1977), Bacha (1979), and Fields (1979).

2   In using social welfare we employ the conventional assumption that the social welfare function is additive and well behaved.

3   On this point see Atkinson (1970).

4   See Donald (1981) and references in note 1.

**References**

Adelman, Irma and Morris, Cynthia Taft (1973) *Economic Growth and Social Equity in Developing Countries.* Stanford, CA: Stanford University Press.

Atkinson, Anthony B. (1970) "On the Measurement of Inequality." *Journal of Economic Theory* 2: 244–63.

Bacha, Edmar (1979) "The Kuznets Curve and Beyond: Growth and Changes in Inequalities." In Edmund Malinvaud (ed.), *Economic Growth and Resources,* vol. I, *The Major Issues. Proceedings of the Fifth World Congress of the International Economic Association, Tokyo.* New York: St Martin's Press.

Chenery, Hollis, Ahluwalia, Montek S., Bell, C. L. G., Duloy, John H. and Jolly, Richard (1974) *Redistribution with Growth.* New York: Oxford University Press.

Cline, William R. (1975) "Distribution and Development: A Survey of Literature." *Journal of Development Economics* 1:359–400.

Donald, Gordon (1981) "Some Trends in Thinking about Development in the 1970s as Reflected in the *Development Digest." Development Digest* 19: 125–8.

Fields, Gary S. (1979) "A Welfare Economic Approach to Growth and Distribution in the Dual Economy." *Quarterly Journal of Economics* 93: 325–53.

Frank, Charles R., Jr, and Richard C. Webb (eds) (1977) *Income Distribution and Growth in the Less Developed Countries.* Washington, DC: Brookings Institution.

Kuznets, Simon (1955) "Economic Growth and Income Inequality." *American Economic Review* 45: 1–28.

—— (1963) "Quantitative Aspects of the Economic Growth of Nations: VIII. Distribution of Income by Size." *Economic Development and Cultural Change* 11: 1–80.

Moreh, J. (1981) "Income Inequality and the Social Welfare Function." *Journal of Economic Studies* 8, 25–37.

Oshima, Harry T. (1962) "The International Comparison of Size Distribution of Family Incomes with Special Reference to Asia." *Review of Economics and Statistics* 44: 439–45.

Paukert, Felix (1973) "Income Distribution at Different Levels of Development: A Survey of Evidence." *International Labour Review* 108: 97–126.

Roberti, P. (1974) "Income Distribution: A Time-series and a Cross-section Study." *Economic Journal* 84: 629–38.

Robinson, Sherman (1976) "A Note on the U Hypothesis Relating Income Inequality and Economic Development." *American Economic Review* 66: 437–40.

Stark, Oded (1978) *Economic–Demographic Interactions in Agricultural Development: The Case of Rural-to-Urban Migration*. Rome: UN Food and Agriculture Organization.

—— (1981) "On the Optimal Choice of Capital Intensity in LDCs with Migration." *Journal of Development Economics* 9(1): 31–41 (reprinted as ch. 19 in this volume).

—— (1982) "Rural–Urban Migration and Surplus Labour: Reservations on Bhatia." *Oxford Economic Papers* 34(3): 569–73.

—— and Levhari, David (1982) "On Migration and Risk in LDCs." *Economic Development and Cultural Change* 31: 191–6 (reprinted as ch. 4 in this volume).

Yitzhaki, Shlomo (1982) "Stochastic Dominance, Mean Variance, and Gini's Mean Difference." *American Economic Review* 72(1): 178–85.

# 22

---

# Merging Populations, Stochastic Dominance, and Lorenz Curves

When influenza strikes a school community classes are often combined; substitute teachers may be called in. The progress of a battle may require that two platoons be placed under the command of one platoon commander. For the performance of certain operas two or more choirs are brought under the baton of one choir leader. And on several occasions recently, one airline has been acquired by another. Given some well-defined information about the relationship between the constituent populations, when can the teacher, the captain, the choir master, or the president of the new airline expect the new population to dominate, in some fundamental sense, the constituent populations?

## 1

Let us consider a population A characterized by the cumulative distribution function $F_A(y)$ where the values of $y$ are the incomes of members of A whose number $n_A$ is given and known. Suppose that there is also a population B characterized by the cumulative distribution function $F_B(y)$ where, again, the values of $y$ are the incomes of the given number of members denoted by $n_B$. Assume now that the two populations merge. We can think of several scenarios wherein such a process takes place: migration of population A into population B;[1] the addition of a new generation B to an existing population A. Defining $p = n_A/(n_A + n_B)$, we know that

$$F_C(y) = pF_A(y) + (1 - p)F_B(y) \tag{22.1}$$

where C is the combined population.

We utilize the Bergson–Samuelson welfare function to compare the mean welfare of population C with the mean welfare of population A. The following properties of the welfare function are assumed throughout: $W = \int u(y)f(y)\,\mathrm{d}y$ where $W$ is mean welfare; $u(y)$ is the utility derived from income $y$; $u' > 0$; and $u'' < 0$. Note that no assumption is made regarding the specific functional form of $u$. Given the above assumptions and properties we set out to establish a condition under which for every $u(y)$ the mean welfare of distribution (population) C is higher than the mean welfare of distribution (population) A. This is the basic methodological issue recently addressed by Lam (1986). In line with Atkinson (1970), the condition that we seek to establish falls in the domain of second-degree stochastic dominance. Thus we have first the following proposition.

**Proposition 1**

*Distribution C dominates distribution A if and only if distribution B dominates distribution A. (Here, as in the rest of the chapter, dominates stands for second-degree stochastic dominance.)*

PROOF   Following Hanoch and Levy (1969), Hadar and Russell (1969), and Rothschild and Stiglitz (1970), a necessary and sufficient condition for $F_C(y)$ to dominate $F_A(y)$ is

$$\int_{-\infty}^{y} F_C(x)\,\mathrm{d}x \leq \int_{-\infty}^{y} F_A(x)\,\mathrm{d}x \qquad \text{for all } y \qquad (22.2)$$

with at least strict inequality holding for some $y$. By substituting (22.1) into (22.2) we obtain

$$\int_{-\infty}^{y} [pF_A(x) + (1-p)\,F_B(x)]\,\mathrm{d}x \leq \int_{-\infty}^{y} F_A(x)\,\mathrm{d}x \qquad \text{for all } y$$

$$(22.3)$$

By simple algebra we obtain

$$\int_{-\infty}^{y} F_B(x)\,\mathrm{d}x \leq \int_{-\infty}^{y} F_A(x)\,\mathrm{d}x \qquad \text{for all } y$$

Note that the relative weights of the component populations are completely washed out. Thus, for example, the condition holds regardless of the relative size of the joining population B. Furthermore, $F_A(y)$ can be transformed into $F_C(y)$ via a process of additions and diminutions, for example, fertility and mortality or inmigration and outmigration in which case $F_B(y)$ constitutes the cumulative distribution of the changes.[2]

## 2

In this section we express the stochastic dominance criterion in terms of Lorenz curves. In order to do this we shall make use of the absolute Lorenz curve (or, using Shorrocks' (1983) terminology, the "generalized Lorenz curve") which is defined as the conventional Lorenz curve multiplied by the mean income. Denote by $L(F)$ the absolute Lorenz curve. We now have our next result.

**Proposition 2**

$L_C(F) \geq L_A(F)$ *for all F if and only if* $F_C(y)$ *dominates* $F_A(y)$.

PROOF   See Shorrocks (1983) or Yitzhaki and Olkin (1987, pp. 25–7).

Note that proposition 2 extends Atkinson's (1970) well-known theorem pertaining to the comparison of distributions with unequal means. Proposition 2, which states that

$$\mu_C \phi_C(F) \geq \mu_A \phi_A(F) \qquad \text{for all } 0 \leq F \leq 1 \tag{22.4}$$

where $\phi(F)$ is the Lorenz curve, immediately lends itself to several implications. First, since $\phi_C(1) = \phi_A(1) = 1$, a necessary condition for distribution C to dominate distribution A is that $\mu_C \geq \mu_A$. Second, if $\mu_C = \mu_A$ then a necessary and sufficient condition for distribution C to dominate distribution A is that $\phi_C(F) \geq \phi_A(F)$ for all F. This condition is the Lorenz intersection criterion. Yet if $\mu_C > \mu_A$, it is still possible to have the Lorenz curves intersect, while distribution C dominates distribution A.

For many years now the intersection of the Lorenz curves has been viewed with despair (see, for example, Lam (1986, section II) and Fields (1979) who remarks "when the Lorenz curves cross there is nothing to say" (p. 331)). In contrast, our proposition makes it possible for an intersection of the Lorenz curves to coexist, so to speak, with stochastic dominance, thereby facilitating a comparison. Moreover, even if the Lorenz curve of distribution C lies below the Lorenz curve of distribution A throughout, it is still possible for distribution C to dominate distribution A. For example, if A = {1, 2} and C = {1, 2, 9}, that is, the new entrant has income 9, the C Lorenz curve lies entirely under the A Lorenz curve yet distribution C dominates distribution A. If C = {1, 2, 2} then the C Lorenz curve intersects the A Lorenz curve yet distribution C again dominates distribution A. These examples serve to illustrate that, in a typical case wherein mean incomes are unequal, the Lorenz nonintersection is neither a necessary nor sufficient condition for stochastic dominance. Hence, accepting stochastic dominance as the appropriate criterion for comparing distributions and admitting that in real life equality of means is a rarity, we conclude that the widespread usage of the Lorenz curves intersection criterion should be abandoned in favor of the absolute curves intersection criterion. Of course, in situations where the concern is only with inequality, nonintersection of the Lorenz curves *is* a valid concern.


### 3


A difficulty associated with the stochastic dominance criterion is that it does not generate a complete ranking of distributions. Consequently we may be compelled to use necessary conditions rather than necessary and sufficient conditions. As shown by Yitzhaki (1982), necessary conditions for distribution C to dominate distribution A stochastically are as follows:

$$\mu_C \geqslant \mu_A \qquad\qquad (22.5a)$$

$$\mu_C(1 - G_C) \geqslant \mu_A(1 - G_A) \qquad\qquad (22.5b)$$

where $G$ is the Gini coefficient of inequality, and

$$\mu_C[1 - G_C(V)] \geqslant \mu_A[1 - G_A(V)] \qquad\qquad (22.5c)$$

where $G(V)$ is the extended Gini coefficient and $V > 1$ is a choice parameter[3] (see Yitzhaki, 1983). Clearly, distribution C can dominate distribution A even though $G_C(V)$ is greater than $G_A(V)$. For this to hold we require that the rate of increase of the means will be larger than the rate of decline in equality.

Finally we note that in order to check whether the necessary conditions for dominance of C over A hold we can utilize the results of section 2, thereby working with the parameters characterizing distributions A and B rather than A and C. Thus we can rewrite condition (22.5) by substituting B for C. Hence, for example, even if the mean income of a group of migrants is higher than the mean income of the absorbing population, the distribution of the composite population will not dominate the distribution of the initial absorbing population if the Gini coefficient of the migrants is sufficiently higher than the Gini coefficient of the absorbing population.

## Notes

Co-authored with Shlomo Yitzhaki. Reprinted from *Journal of Population Economics* 1, 1988. This is a revised version of Discussion Paper 29, Harvard University Migration and Development Program. We are indebted to Pierre Pestieau for helpful comments and suggestions.

1  We assume here that migrants can and do carry with them all their income-earning assets, human and nonhuman alike, and that at least for the period under review an increase in income neither motivates nor is entailed by migration.

2  However, in the event of deaths or outmigration which may outweigh births or inmigration respectively, the "surrogate density function" $f_B(y)$ which is essentially the appropriately weighted difference between two density functions, conventionally defined, namely of entries and exits, can be negative and hence $F_B(y) = \int_{-\infty}^{y} f_B(x)\,dx$ may not concur with the usual statistical definition of a cumulative distribution function.

3  Condition (22.5b) is a special case of condition (22.5c) wherein $V = 2$. Condition (22.5b) and, for that matter, condition (22.5c) immediately follow from proposition 2 by integrating (22.4) over [0,1]. Notice that (22.5c) embodies a necessary condition for stochastic dominance since

$$\mu[1 - G(V)] = \int_0^\infty [1 - F(y)]^V \, dy.$$

## References

Atkinson, A. B. (1970) "On the Measurement of Inequality." *Journal of Economic Theory* 2: 244–63.

Fields, G. S. (1979) "A Welfare Economic Approach to Growth and Distribution in the Dual Economy." *Quarterly Journal of Economics* 93: 325–53.

Hadar, J. and Russell, W. R. (1969) "Rules for Ordering Uncertain Prospects." *American Economic Review* 59: 25–34.

Hanoch, G. and Levy, H. (1969) "The Efficiency Analysis of Choices Involving Risk." *Review of Economic Studies* 36: 335–46.

Lam, D. (1986) "The Dynamics of Population Growth, Differential Fertility, and Inequality." *American Economic Review* 76(5): 1103–16.

Rothschild, M. and Stiglitz, J. E. (1970) "Increasing Risk: I. A Definition." *Journal of Economic Theory* 2: 225–43.

Shorrocks, A. F. (1983) "Ranking Income Distributions." *Economica* 50: 3–17.

Yitzhaki, S. (1982) "Stochastic Dominance, Mean Variance, and Gini's Mean Difference." *American Economic Review* 72: 178–85.

—— (1983) "On an Extension of the Gini Inequality Index." *International Economic Review* 24: 617–28.

—— and Olkin, I. (1987) "Concentration Curves." Technical Report 230, Department of Statistics, Stanford University.

# 23

## On Agglomeration Economies and Optimal Migration

### 1 Introduction

Hitherto, urban economics does not seem to have significantly contributed to migration economics, although there are reasons to believe that such a contribution can be made. As we demonstrate in this chapter, it is possible to utilize urban economics to identify socially optimal levels of urbanization and, by implication, optimal levels of rural-to-urban migration. Our analysis addresses the case where there is one urban center (region) in the economy.[1]

After identifying the reason that private actions do not add up to the social optimum, we offer an analysis of instruments which could confer efficiency gains by closing the gap(s) between the privately efficient and socially optimal urban concentrations. On the basis of theoretical considerations and permissible parameter values, for the log-linear case, we are able to rank these instruments and thereby suggest policy implications. The private decisions identified in this chapter are responsible for a smaller city size, or a smaller urban sector, than is socially optimal. We compare this outcome with another policy-related observation. A 1983 United Nations survey of 126 governments of less developed countries (LDCs) found that all but three small island nations did not consider the distribution of their populations "appropriate": more than three-quarters stated that they were pursuing policies to slow down or reverse internal migration, almost always rural-to-urban migration. These policies do not have a remarkable success record. Might this lack of success be due to the fact that, alongside the problems of congestion and pollution usually associated with rapid urban growth, there are, over a significant range, powerful agglomeration economies conferred by urban concentration? This may help to explain why policies aimed at stemming rural-to-urban migration have a dismal success record (Stark, 1980).

## 2 External Agglomeration Economies and Optimal Migration

We start by focusing on the role of external agglomeration economies.[2] Urban output $Q$, which is homogeneous and internationally traded at a given unit price, is produced by many small identical firms employing labor $N$ and capital $K$ with decreasing returns to internal scale and increasing returns to external scale:

$$Q = G(N)F(N, K) \qquad (23.1)$$

where $G' > 0$ and

$$\begin{bmatrix} F_{NN} & F_{NK} \\ F_{KN} & F_{KK} \end{bmatrix}$$

is negative definite. Firms do not see themselves as influencing city size which is given by the aggregation of their profit-maximizing labor demands. With perfectly elastic supply of private capital and labor at the going interest and wage rates $r$ and $w$ respectively, the firm's maximization problem is

$$\max[G(N)F(N, K) - wN - rK]$$

which renders the first-order conditions

$$G(N^e)F_N(N^e, K^e) - w = 0 \qquad (23.2)$$

$$G(N^e)F_K(N^e, K^e) - r = 0 \qquad (23.3)$$

and the second-order conditions

$$GF_{NN} < 0 \qquad (23.4)$$

$$(GF_{KK})(GF_{NN}) - (GF_{NK})^2 > 0 \qquad (23.5)$$

where $N^e$ and $K^e$ are the equilibrium levels of the employed labor and capital, respectively.[3]

Since firms do not incorporate the agglomeration effect in their employment decisions, the pair $(N^e, K^e)$ differs from the social optima $(N^*, K^*)$ which fulfill the first-order conditions

$$G(N^*)F_N(N^*, K^*) + G'(N^*)F(N^*, K^*) - w = 0 \qquad (23.6)$$

$$G(N^*)F_K(N^*, K^*) - r = 0 \qquad (23.7)$$

and the second-order conditions

$$GF_{NN} + 2G'F_N + G''F < 0 \qquad (23.8)$$

$$(GF_{KK})(GF_{NN} + 2G'F_N + G''F) - (GF_{NK})^2 > 0 \qquad (23.9)$$

requiring that, at the optimal level $N^*$, output increases with employment at a decreasing rate.

In order for (23.2) to entail a stable equilibrium, $G(N)F_N(N, K)$ must cut $w$ from above, and likewise for (23.6). Hence, over the relevant range, $d[G(N)F_N(N, K)]/dN < 0$. Therefore, a comparison of (23.6) with (23.2) implies $N^e < N^*$. Thus, if the externality were to be internalized, urban employment and urban size would be larger and more rural-to-urban migration would be called for. The level of this socially optimal migration is $N^* - N^e > 0$.

## 3 Ranking Policy Instruments

Having pointed out that the size of an urban area ought to be increased in order to enhance productive efficiency, we need to rank the instruments which a government may use for the purpose of externality correction. We shall address an economy of the type described in section 2 with one single urban region for which $N^* - N^e > 0$. In order to induce socially optimal urban growth and creation of additional employment we assume that the government considers recourse to output, capital, or labor subsidies.

Assume that (23.1) takes the form

$$Q = G(N)F(N, K) = BN^\gamma AN^\alpha K^\beta \qquad 0 < \gamma < 1, \alpha + \beta = 1 \qquad (23.10)$$

and that

$$w = w(N) = bN \qquad b > 0 \qquad (23.11)$$

That is, assume a positive agglomeration elasticity with the amount of output "shift" due to external economies increasing at a declining rate, a constant returns to scale internal technology, and a unitary elastic labor supply. The private problem is then given by

$$\max \left[ ABN^\gamma N^\alpha K^\beta - (bN)N - rK \right]$$

However, if the government were to award a wage subsidy, the firm's decision problem would be

$$\max [ABN^\gamma N^\alpha K^\beta - (1 - S_L)(bN)N - rK]$$

where $S_L$ is the proportion of the wage bill paid by the government. Solving the last problem gives

$$N^e = \left[\frac{\alpha}{b(1 - S_L)}\right]^{(1-\beta)/(2-2\beta-\alpha-\gamma)} (AB\beta^\beta r^{-\beta})^{1/(2-2\beta-\alpha-\gamma)} \quad (23.12)$$

This can be compared with the socially optimal city size $N^*$ given by incorporating the variability of city size in the agglomeration component of the production specification, where

$$N^* = \left(\frac{\alpha + \gamma}{b}\right)^{(1-\beta)/(2-2\beta-\alpha-\gamma)} (AB\beta^\beta r^{-\beta})^{1/(2-2\beta-\alpha-\gamma)} \quad (23.13)$$

By equating (23.12) and (23.13), that is, by capturing that amount of subsidy that will sustain the social optimum, we obtain

$$S_L = \frac{\gamma}{\alpha + \gamma} \quad (23.14)$$

We employ a similar procedure in order to derive the optimal capital subsidy, that is, we solve

$$\max [ABN^\gamma N^\alpha K^\beta - (bN)N - (1 - S_K)rK]$$

and obtain

$$S_K = 1 - \left(\frac{\alpha}{\alpha + \gamma}\right)^{(1-\beta)/\beta} \quad (23.15)$$

and derive the optimal output subsidy (for example, a sales tax concession) by solving

$$\max [(1 + S_P)ABN^\gamma N^\alpha K^\beta - (bN)N - rK]$$

and obtaining

$$S_P = \left(\frac{\alpha + \gamma}{\alpha}\right)^{(1-\beta)/\beta} - 1 \quad (23.16)$$

From the first-order conditions of the social maximization, that is, from the equivalents of (23.6) and (23.7) under (23.10) and (23.11), we obtain

$$(N^*)^2 = \frac{\alpha + \gamma}{b} Q^* \tag{23.17}$$

$$K^* = \frac{\beta}{r} Q^* \tag{23.18}$$

Drawing on (23.14), (23.15), and (23.16) we can write the total labor, capital, and output subsidies, namely $\bar{S}_L$, $\bar{S}_K$, $\bar{S}_P$, respectively as

$$\bar{S}_L = \gamma Q^* \tag{23.19}$$

$$\bar{S}_K = \beta \left[ 1 - \left( \frac{\alpha}{\alpha + \gamma} \right)^{(1-\beta)/\beta} \right] Q^* \tag{23.20}$$

$$\bar{S}_P = \left[ \left( \frac{\alpha + \gamma}{\alpha} \right)^{(1-\beta)/\beta} - 1 \right] Q^* \tag{23.21}$$

Although the capital subsidy is cheaper than the output subsidy,[4] the difference between the capital subsidy and the labor subsidy cannot be signed analytically. Fortunately, simulation experimentation (Shukla, 1984) subject to $\gamma < \alpha$ (the external condition that the labor efficiency or agglomeration parameter is lower than the internal parameter) reveals that the capital subsidy is consistently cheaper than the labor subsidy; for plausible ranges of the parameters $\gamma$ and $\alpha$, say $0.10 - 0.20$ for $\gamma$ and $0.60 - 0.70$ for $\alpha$, the capital subsidy is 20–35 percent cheaper than the labor subsidy.

Our conclusion that subsidizing capital utilization might be a more efficient means of bringing about socially optimal levels of industrial production, urban concentration, and rural-to-urban migration relates to earlier research (for example, Stark and Levhari, 1982) where we pointed out that, although migration is a labor market phenomenon, modifying its patterns could optimally assume the form of intervention in capital markets. It was argued that it is imperfections in the latter which are manifested through, and corrected by, migratory behavior. Interestingly, while it approaches migration from the production end, this chapter also suggests that intervention in the capital market could be the appropriate tool for bringing about the desirable level of migration.

## Notes

Co-authored with Vibhooti Shukla. Reprinted from *Economics Letters* 18, 1985.

1  The case where there are two urban centers is taken up in an appendix available from the authors upon request. What makes such a case particularly interesting is that the possibility of additional, namely inter-urban, migration flows opens up. Hence we critically examine in the appendix the rationale underlying dispersal from the larger to the smaller urban center.

2  External agglomeration economies have been empirically confirmed in the United States by a number of studies (for example, Sveikauskas, 1975; Segal, 1976) and in India by Shukla (1984).

3  In fact, the maximization problem renders an optimal employment level for the individual firm which we should have designated by a symbol different from $N^e$, say $n^e$ (likewise, for $K^e$). If there are $m$ identical firms, then $N^e = mn^e$. Since $N^e$ differs from $n^e$ merely by a constant factor, we adopt a short-cut and refer to $N^e$ from the start of the maximization process.

4  $\bar{S}_P/Q^* - \bar{S}_K/Q^* = (d^e - 1) - \beta[1 - (1/d)^e] = (d^e - 1)(d^e - \beta)/d^e > 0$, since $d^e > 1 > \beta$ where $d = (\alpha + \gamma)/\alpha > 1$ and $e = (1 - \beta)/\beta > 0$.

## References

Segal, David (1976) "Are There Returns to Scale in City Size?" *Review of Economics and Statistics* 58(3): 339–50.

Shukla, Vibhooti (1984) "The Productivity of Indian Cities and Some Implications for Development Policy." Ph.D Dissertation, Princeton University.

Stark, Oded (1980) "On Slowing Metropolitan City Growth." *Population and Development Review* 6(1): 95–102 (reprinted as ch. 20 in this volume).

—— and Levhari, David (1982) "On Migration and Risk in LDCs." *Economic Development and Cultural Change* 31(1): 191–6 (reprinted as ch. 4 in this volume).

Sveikauskas, Leo (1975) "The Productivity of Cities." *Quarterly Journal of Economics* 89(3): 393–413.

# 24

## Policy Comparisons with an Agglomeration Effects–Augmented Dual Economy Model

### 1 Introduction

Urbanization processes and the impetus for city growth in less developed countries (LDCs) continue to attract much interest. Underlying this interest are the recognition of the empirical association and concomitancy between urbanization and economic development as well as policy concerns with the "problems" of "excessive" cityward migration and urban unemployment. Yet an important class of urban growth models, based on considerations of external scale economies in urban production, fails to acknowledge the presence of the rural economy or of less than full employment in the urban sector. The many variants of the dual economy model of development spawned by Harris and Todaro (1970), however, which have addressed the issue of the nature of migratory responses in the face of sector-specific institutional rigidities and of the inefficiencies that might arise therefrom, do not appreciate the tremendous "pull" exercised by the economies of urban agglomeration. Yet these economies, together with infrastructure investments, appear to be the most significant factors impinging upon the expansion of the urban sector.

In this chapter we incorporate agglomeration economies in a dualistic analysis of the developing economy.[1] An effort to synthesize the two approaches is important because the normative conclusions prompted by each appear contradictory. The former argues for the productive potential of cities to be harnessed aggressively in the service of economic development (see, for example, Shukla 1984). The latter advocates combining a program of migration containment with a strong emphasis on rural development.[2] Our interest here is in examining whether the standard prescriptions associated with policy rankings under sector-specific sticky wages are sustained, strengthened, or weakened.

Accordingly, in sections 2 and 3 we combine elements of the two modeling traditions to present an integrated analysis in which several questions can be posed. In sections 4 and 5 a policy-ranking exercise of the Bhagwati and Srinivasan (1974) type[3] is performed in the context of a version of the general structural model presented in sections 2 and 3. This allows us to make comparisons with previous prescriptions. Alternative "first-best" interventions are evaluated with reference not only to benefits, but also to the costs of fiscal implementation. In section 6 we present and interpret the results of the simulations performed. Section 7 concludes with some implications of the analysis and with suggestions for future research.

## 2 The Components of the Analysis

### Agglomeration-Based Models of City Size

The idea that firms in certain industries benefit by locating in areas of large size and high concentration is hardly new in either the popular or the scientific literature on urbanization. The advantage of such location is attributed to increased opportunities for specialization and trade, better prospects for diffusing risk afforded by large numbers, better information and communication possibilities that come with spatial proximity, and various other factors stemming from larger and denser markets.

Whatever the source of the urban productivity edge, many economists have found it analytically meaningful to characterize it as technological, typically formulated as entering the set of firms' production possibilities in the form of a scale shift factor. This characterization has been matched with considerable empirical success. Suitable parametrization has usually permitted measurement of the relative gain in efficiency associated with larger city size.[4]

Invoking the fundamental idea that scale economies of some sort account for the existence of the observed uneven spatial distribution of economic activity and, consequently, of population, a respectable class of equilibrium city size models has utilized the notion of agglomeration to explain city formation and urban growth.[5] In these models, external scale economies in the manufacture of inter-regionally traded goods generate employment expansion and continuing accretion of population, whereas diseconomies in consumption and in the production of certain nontradeables create counter-pressures.

The foregoing ideas can be demonstrated in a one-factor one-good framework. Assume that identical firms in an urban area facing a fixed wage $\bar{w}$ in the aggregate produce output $X$ under the technological conditions

$$X = g(N)f(N) \qquad g', f' > 0, \;\; g'', f'' < 0 \tag{24.1}$$

with the exogenously determined output price normalized to unity. $N$, as an argument of $f(\cdot)$, is total urban area employment of labor and, as it enters $g(\cdot)$, is total urban population. By definition (assuming universal labor force participation and abstracting from dependence considerations), the two are identical, but behaviorally they are not. Firms realize that they choose employment. But they do not perceive that this choice alters city size and confers a positive externality in their manufacturing activity that leads to suboptimality of employment and consequently of city size.[6] For although private decisions lead to equilibrium size $N^e$ satisfying

$$g(N)f'(N) = \bar{w} \tag{24.2}$$

a social optimization that maximizes manufacturing sector output would yield $N^*$, which must satisfy

$$g(N)f'(N) + g'(N)f(N) = \bar{w} \tag{24.3}$$

Figure 24.1 illustrates the divergence of equilibrium from optimum that arises under our simple assumptions.

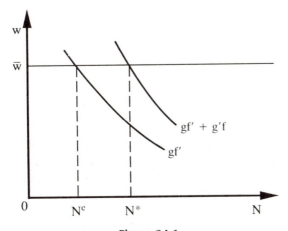

**Figure 24.1**

Naturally, the suboptimality of urban size[7] implies a suboptimality of rural-to-urban migration. We have addressed elsewhere the choice of instruments for correcting the externality that gives rise to this inefficiency (see Shukla and Stark, 1985). The issue of optimal city size, however, has mainly been addressed under assumptions of complete information and full employment spatial adjustments. In reality, rural-to-urban migration in LDCs does not often take place in response to concrete job offers, and growth in the urban workforce outpaces employment growth, prompting the concern mentioned at the outset. The dualistic expected income model captures this concern and highlights an additional efficiency problem.

## The Basic Expected-Income Framework

A basic version of the model features two sectors – manufacturing, which is wholly urban, and agriculture, which is wholly rural – each employing labor as the only variable factor. The sectors mutually exhaust the total population $\bar{N}$ so that

$$\bar{N} = N_U + N_A \tag{24.4}$$

where $N_U$ is the total labor supplied to the urban area. The price of manufacturing output and the price of farm output are given in this small open economy.[8] The former is assumed to be the numeraire; the latter is $q$. Production in the urban sector is assumed to take place under

$$X_M = \bar{f}(N_M) \qquad \bar{f}' > 0, \ \bar{f}'' < 0 \tag{24.5}$$

which, in the light of our earlier discussion, we amend to

$$X_M = g(N_M)f(N_M) \qquad g', f' > 0, \ f'', g'' < 0 \tag{24.6}$$

Agricultural production is

$$X_A = h(N_A) \qquad h' > 0, \ h'' < 0 \tag{24.7}$$

$X_M$ and $X_A$ are urban manufacturing output and rural agricultural output respectively; $N_M$ and $N_A$ are the corresponding levels of employment.

There is an institutional difference between wage formation in the two sectors: the rural labor market clears perfectly but the urban labor market is characterized by a relatively high fixed wage, conventionally attributed to minimum wage legislation, the bargaining power of unions, and so forth.

Migration by risk-neutral labor to the high-wage urban sector takes place in response to a positive expected wage differential to equilibrate

$$w_0 = \overline{w}p \tag{24.8}$$

where $w_0$ is the rural agricultural wage. The probability $p$ of securing an urban job is represented by $N_M/N_U$.

Profit-maximizing behavior by firms and farms leads to

$$g(N_M)f'(N_M) = \overline{w} \tag{24.9}$$

and

$$qh'(\overline{N} - N_U) = w_0 = \frac{\overline{w}N_M}{N_U} \tag{24.10}$$

respectively. Equations (24.4), (24.6), (24.7), (24.9), and (24.10) can be solved for $X_A$, $N_A$, $X_M$, $N_M$, and $N_U$ to yield the intersectoral equilibrium labor force allocations depicted in figure 24.2. The broken curve is the

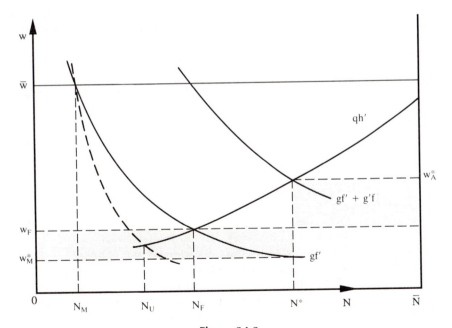

**Figure 24.2**

rectangular hyperbola on which equilibrium occurs.[9] The level of urban unemployment $U$ is given by $N_U - N_M$, and its rate by $1 - N_M/N_U$. This equilibrium is a combined consequence of urban wage fixity and the nature of the behavioral response of migrants, and it leads to market inefficiencies that invite the policy interventions we now consider.

## 3 Developmental Policy Implications

In terms of the economy's potential, the *laissez-faire* equilibrium is off the efficiency frontier. A wide range of sectoral and economy-wide[10] policies might be instituted to nudge it closer, resulting in welfare improvements. By way of a "first-best" optimal policy in the conventional Harris–Todaro context, entailing maximum welfare and no by-product distortions, Bhagwati and Srinivasan (1974) demonstrate that a wage subsidy uniform in both sectors will take the economy to full employment equilibrium, represented in figure 24.2 by the allocation $N_F$. A situation characterized by two *hypothetically* different subsidy rates $S_M^F$ and $S_A^F$, specific to the manufacturing and agricultural sectors,

$$g(N_M)f'(N_M) = \overline{w} - S_M^F \tag{24.11}$$

and

$$qh'(\overline{N} - N_U) = \frac{\overline{w}N_M}{N_U} - S_A^F \tag{24.12}$$

respectively, under the full employment identity $N_U = N_M$ and the efficiency condition

$$g(N)f'(N) = qh'(\overline{N} - N) \tag{24.13}$$

is reconcilable with $S_F = S_M^F = S_A^F$ at $N_M (= N_U) = N_F$, yielding a total cost of subsidization equal to $\overline{N}S_F$ or $\overline{N}[\overline{w} - g(N_F)f'(N_F)]$.

In the light of agglomeration effects, however, this intervention is no longer optimal: although one source of distortion has been addressed, the economy is still off the utility frontier because of the externality in urban production. Hence the possibility of further welfare improvement remains. The appropriate efficiency condition in this context is

$$g(N)f'(N) + g'(N)f(N) = qh'(\overline{N} - N) \tag{24.14}$$

which is seen to be satisfied at the "true" optimum $N^*$ rather than at $N_F$.

Let us now consider anew the problem of the optimal subsidy that will sustain *this* allocation in private markets. Denote by $w_A^*$ the optimum agricultural wage and by $w_M^*$ the optimal wage in manufacturing. An employment subsidy in agriculture must be at the level

$$S_A^* = \overline{w} - w_A^* = \overline{w} - [g(N^*)f'(N^*) + g'(N^*)f(N^*)]$$

to support socially optimal agricultural employment in equilibrium. A glance at figure 24.2 reveals that this is *lower* than the previously construed "first-best" rate $S_F$. Contrary to the case of no agglomeration effects, an identical subsidy in urban manufacturing will fail to elicit the required optimal employment response in that sector because firms' productivity perceptions lie along the $g(N)f'(N)$ curve, whereas real social benefits are represented by the curve $g(N)f'(N) + g'(N)f(N)$. A subsidy *higher* than before is now optimal for the urban sector, and is given by $S_M^* = \overline{w} - w_M^* = \overline{w} - g(N^*)f'(N^*)$.

The total cost of this new subsidization package is therefore

$$N^*[\overline{w} - g(N^*)f'(N^*)] + (\overline{N} - N^*)[\overline{w} - g(N^*)f'(N^*) - g'(N^*)f(N^*)]$$
$$= \overline{N}[\overline{w} - g(N^*)f'(N^*)] - (\overline{N} - N^*)[g'(N^*)f(N^*)] \quad (24.15)$$

It is analytically ambiguous whether this package is more or less expensive than subsidization prescribed under the assumption that no agglomeration economies prevail. The difference between subsidization costs $C^*$ with agglomeration economies and subsidization costs $C^F$ without agglomeration economies

$$C^* - C^F = \overline{N}[g(N_F)f'(N_F) - g(N^*)f'(N^*)] - (\overline{N} - N^*)[g'(N^*)f(N^*)]$$
$$(24.16)$$

cannot be signed generally. This difference can be expressed in figure 24.2 by the excess of the area of the rectangle representing the saving in agricultural subsidization costs over the area of the rectangle representing additional costs of subsidizing the manufacturing sector under the new package. A comparison of the two shaded rectangles suggests that a steeper $qh'$ curve and a relatively flat $gf'$ curve create a predisposition for the new subsidization package to be cheaper. With the aid of a specified model and under plausible ranges of the relevant parameter values, we shall now attempt to quantify the costs and benefits associated with alternative policy measures.

## 4 A Specified Model for Policy Evaluation

In this section we specify a model geared for a numerical policy ranking exercise of the type undertaken by Bhagwati and Srinivasan (1974),[11] but with the explicit incorporation of agglomeration factors. The aim is to trace the welfare effects of alternative policy responses to the problem of achieving a more efficient intersectoral allocation in the context of the general structure outlined in sections 2 and 3.

The policy options we consider are an optimal set of employment subsidies to each sector, a full employment uniform subsidy calculated under the presumption that no agglomeration economies exist, and, last, the *laissez-faire* situation. To facilitate comparison with results under the Bhagwati–Srinivasan scenario, where there are no agglomeration effects, we adopt functional specifications akin to theirs. Our innovation is to take cognizance of costs associated with alternative types of subsidization as part of a somewhat more comprehensive ranking scheme.

The model features production relationships $g(\cdot)$, $f(\cdot)$, and $h(\cdot)$ for manufacturing and agriculture, corresponding to (24.6) and (24.7), given by

$$X_M = (N_M)^\gamma (N_M)^\alpha \qquad (24.17)$$

where $g(N_M) = (N_M)^\gamma$, $\gamma$ represents what is referred to as the agglomeration elasticity, and

$$X_A = (N_A)^\beta \qquad (24.18)$$

where $0 < \alpha, \beta, \gamma < 1$. It is assumed that $N_U + N_A = N_M + N_A + U = 1$, where $U = N_U - N_M$ is urban unemployment. Under full employment $U = 0$, so that $N_M + N_A = 1$. The urban wage rate $\bar{w}$ is set exogenously and can be presented as some multiple of the prevailing rural wage $w_0 = qh'$. The price of the agricultural commodity in units of output $q$ of the manufacturing sector can be interpreted as reflecting the terms of trade given to a small open economy, or as a weight in the social welfare function $\text{SWF}(X_M, X_A) = X_M + qX_A$ of a closed economy. In the latter case, a larger $q$ reflects a heightened societal preference for the product of agriculture.

## 5 Effects of Alternative Interventions

*Laissez-Faire*

Given $\overline{w}$, equilibrium urban employment $N_M$ is determined by

$$\alpha N_M^{\alpha+\gamma-1} = \overline{w} \tag{24.19}$$

whence employment $N_A$ in agriculture or the rural workforce can be solved for by substituting $N_M$ into the migration condition

$$q\beta N_A^{\beta-1} = \frac{\overline{w} N_M}{1 - N_A} \tag{24.20}$$

$N_U = 1 - N_A$ represents total urban workforce, and equilibrium unemployment $U = N_U - N_M$ emerges.

*Uniform Wage Subsidy Without Attention to Agglomeration Effects*

The standard policy, if we ignore the need to correct for the agglomeration externality, involves uniform subsidization at the level of

$$S_F = \overline{w} - \alpha N_F^{\alpha+\gamma-1} \tag{24.21}$$

where $N_F$ is the value of $N_M$ that solves the equality corresponding to (24.13):

$$\alpha N_M^{\alpha+\gamma-1} = q\beta(1 - N_M)^{\beta-1} \tag{24.22}$$

The total cost of financing this policy is given by $C^F = \overline{N} S_F$ or, under normalization, $C^F = S_F$.

*The Optimal Solution and First-Best Package of Employment Subsidies*

The optimal allocation $(N^*, 1 - N^*)$ is obtained using $N_A = 1 - N_M$ and the optimizing condition corresponding to (24.14):

$$\alpha N_M^{\alpha+\gamma-1} + \gamma N_M^{\alpha+\gamma-1} = q\beta(1 - N_M)^{\beta-1} \tag{24.23}$$

thus it satisfies

$$(N^*)^{\alpha+\gamma-1} = q\,\frac{\beta}{\alpha+\gamma}(1 - N^*)^{\beta-1} \tag{24.24}$$

The manufacturing sector subsidy per worker $S_M^*$ that will sustain the optimal urban employment in private equilibrium is obtained as

$$S_M^* = \overline{w} - \alpha(N^*)^{\alpha+\gamma-1} \tag{24.25}$$

Similarly, the corresponding subsidy rate in agriculture $S_A^*$ is given by

$$S_A^* = \overline{w} - q\beta(1 - N^*)^{\beta-1} \tag{24.26}$$

Both subsidy rates are completely specified with the optimal employment $N^*$ from above, as is the total cost of subsidization

$$C^* = N^*S_M^* + (1 - N^*)S_A^*$$

## 6  Simulation Results

We performed a numerical simulation exercise to rank the three options of uniform wage subsidization, optimal subsidization, and *laissez-faire* (or nonintervention). The model solution was over a fairly comprehensive range of permissible values for the principal parameters $\alpha$, $\beta$, $q$, and $\overline{w}$. The objective was to trace the relative costs and benefits associated with each of the compared options. Allowing for agglomeration effects, we were particularly interested in ascertaining whether a cost advantage existed, in addition to unambiguous output and productivity increases resulting from subsidization. Clearly, in such a case a welfare improvement is gained *a fortiori*. Computations were performed under the assumption of an agglomeration elasticity in urban manufacturing of $\gamma = 0.10$, following magnitudes estimated by Shukla (1984).

Six appropriately illustrative cases are chosen for presentation in table 24.1. As expected, utility levels, as measured by the social welfare index, are consistently higher under optimal subsidization. Our results on the cost side appear to confirm the case for the relative cheapness of optimal subsidization when conditions $\alpha \geq \beta$ or $\alpha + \gamma > \beta$ are met. To see this point, consult table 24.1. With $q$ and $\overline{w}$ held at constant levels (cases 1, 2, and 3) optimal subsidization is seen to be cheaper ($C^* < C^F$) than uniform

**Table 24.1**  Effects of subsidization under agglomeration

**Case 1**  $\alpha = 0.7$, $\beta = 0.2$, $q = 1.0$, $\bar{w} = 1.0$

*Laissez-faire*

| | $X_A$ | $X_M$ | $U$ | $N_A$ | $N_M$ | $S_M$ | $S_A$ | $C$ | $qX_A + X_M$ |
|---|---|---|---|---|---|---|---|---|---|
| | 0.873935 | 0.240100 | 0.322134 | 0.509795 | 0.168070 | 0.0 | 0.0 | 0.0 | 1.114035 |

*Uniform wage subsidy*

| | $X_A^F$ | $X_M^F$ | $U^F$ | $N_A^F$ | $N_M^F$ | $S_M^F$ | $S_A^F$ | $C^F$ | $qX_A^F + X_M^F$ |
|---|---|---|---|---|---|---|---|---|---|
| | 0.723102 | 0.838438 | 0.0 | 0.197696 | 0.802304 | 0.268473 | 0.268473 | 0.268473 | 1.561540 |

*Optimal subsidization*

| | $X_A^*$ | $X_M^*$ | $U^*$ | $N_A^*$ | $N_M^*$ | $S_M^*$ | $S_A^*$ | $C^*$ | $qX_A^* + X_M^*$ |
|---|---|---|---|---|---|---|---|---|---|
| | 0.700600 | 0.862517 | 0.0 | 0.168792 | 0.831208 | 0.273633 | 0.169866 | 0.256118 | 1.563117 |

**Case 2**  $\alpha = 0.5$, $\beta = 0.5$, $q = 1.0$, $\bar{w} = 1.0$

*Laissez-faire*

| | $X_A$ | $X_M$ | $U$ | $N_A$ | $N_M$ | $S_M$ | $S_A$ | $C$ | $qX_A + X_M$ |
|---|---|---|---|---|---|---|---|---|---|
| | 0.838728 | 0.353554 | 0.119759 | 0.703464 | 0.176777 | 0.0 | 0.0 | 0.0 | 1.192281 |

*Uniform wage subsidy*

| | $X_A^F$ | $X_M^F$ | $U^F$ | $N_A^F$ | $N_M^F$ | $S_M^F$ | $S_A^F$ | $C^F$ | $qX_A^F + X_M^F$ |
|---|---|---|---|---|---|---|---|---|---|
| | 0.733892 | 0.628707 | 0.0 | 0.538597 | 0.461403 | 0.318701 | 0.318701 | 0.318701 | 1.362598 |

*Optimal subsidization*

| | $X_A^*$ | $X_M^*$ | $U^*$ | $N_A^*$ | $N_M^*$ | $S_M^*$ | $S_A^*$ | $C^*$ | $qX_A^* + X_M^*$ |
|---|---|---|---|---|---|---|---|---|---|
| | 0.661793 | 0.707710 | 0.0 | 0.437970 | 0.562030 | 0.370397 | 0.244477 | 0.315248 | 1.369503 |

(Table continued on the following page)

352

**Table 24.1** Effects of subsidization under agglomeration (*continued*)

**Case 3** $\alpha = 0.5$, $\beta = 0.6$, $q = 1.0$, $\bar{w} = 1.0$

*Laissez-faire*

| | $X_M$ | | $N_M$ | $U$ | $S_M$ | $S_A$ | $C$ | $qX_A + X_M$ |
|---|---|---|---|---|---|---|---|---|
| $X_A$ 0.834007 | 0.353554 | $N_A$ 0.738952 | 0.176777 | 0.084271 | 0.0 | 0.0 | 0.0 | 1.187560 |

*Uniform wage subsidy*

| | $X_M^F$ | | $N_M^F$ | $U^F$ | $S_M^F$ | $S_A^F$ | $C^F$ | $qX_A^F + X_M^F$ |
|---|---|---|---|---|---|---|---|---|
| $X_A^F$ 0.744832 | 0.566613 | $N_A^F$ 0.612018 | 0.387982 | 0.0 | 0.269794 | 0.269794 | 0.269794 | 1.311445 |

*Optimal subsidization*

| | $X_M^*$ | | $N_M^*$ | $U^*$ | $S_M^*$ | $S_A^*$ | $C^*$ | $qX_A^* + X_M^*$ |
|---|---|---|---|---|---|---|---|---|
| $X_A^*$ 0.659754 | 0.659754 | $N_A^*$ 0.500000 | 0.500000 | 0.0 | 0.340246 | 0.208295 | 0.274271 | 1.319508 |

**Case 4** $\alpha = 0.7$, $\beta = 0.2$, $q = 1.5$, $\bar{w} = 1.0$

*Laissez-faire*

| | $X_M$ | | $N_M$ | $U$ | $S_M$ | $S_A$ | $C$ | $qX_A + X_M$ |
|---|---|---|---|---|---|---|---|---|
| $X_A$ 0.908390 | 0.240100 | $N_A$ 0.618532 | 0.168070 | 0.213398 | 0.0 | 0.0 | 0.0 | 1.602685 |

*Uniform wage subsidy*

| | $X_M^F$ | | $N_M^F$ | $U^F$ | $S_M^F$ | $S_A^F$ | $C^F$ | $qX_A^F + X_M^F$ |
|---|---|---|---|---|---|---|---|---|
| $X_A^F$ 0.793921 | 0.738484 | $N_A^F$ 0.315417 | 0.684583 | 0.0 | 0.244885 | 0.244885 | 0.244885 | 1.929364 |

*Optimal subsidization*

| | $X_M^*$ | | $N_M^*$ | $U^*$ | $S_M^*$ | $S_A^*$ | $C^*$ | $qX_A^* + X_M^*$ |
|---|---|---|---|---|---|---|---|---|
| $X_A^*$ 0.770264 | 0.776451 | $N_A^*$ 0.271143 | 0.728857 | 0.0 | 0.254291 | 0.147760 | 0.225405 | 1.931846 |

(*Table continued on the following page*)

**Table 24.1**  Effects of subsidization under agglomeration (*continued*)

**Case 5**  $\alpha = 0.5$, $\beta = 0.5$, $q = 0.5$, $\bar{w} = 1.0$

*Laissez-faire*

| $X_A$ | $X_M$ | $N_A$ | $N_M$ | $U$ | $S_M$ | $S_A$ | $C$ | $qX_A + X_M$ |
|---|---|---|---|---|---|---|---|---|
| 0.707106 | 0.353554 | 0.500000 | 0.176777 | 0.323223 | 0.0 | 0.0 | 0.0 | 0.707107 |

*Uniform wage subsidy*

| $X_A^f$ | $X_M^f$ | $N_A^f$ | $N_M^f$ | $U^f$ | $S_M^f$ | $S_A^f$ | $C^f$ | $qX_A^f + X_M^f$ |
|---|---|---|---|---|---|---|---|---|
| 0.455574 | 0.869729 | 0.207548 | 0.792452 | 0.0 | 0.451242 | 0.451242 | 0.451242 | 1.097515 |

*Optimal subsidization*

| $X_A^*$ | $X_M^*$ | $N_A^*$ | $N_M^*$ | $U^*$ | $S_M^*$ | $S_A^*$ | $C^*$ | $qX_A^* + X_M^*$ |
|---|---|---|---|---|---|---|---|---|
| 0.390049 | 0.905723 | 0.152138 | 0.847862 | 0.0 | 0.465878 | 0.359054 | 0.449626 | 1.100746 |

**Case 6**  $\alpha = 0.7$, $\beta = 0.2$, $q = 1.0$, $\bar{w} = 1.5$

*Laissez-faire*

| $X_A$ | $X_M$ | $N_A$ | $N_M$ | $U$ | $S_M$ | $S_A$ | $C$ | $qX_A + X_M$ |
|---|---|---|---|---|---|---|---|---|
| 0.968867 | 0.047427 | 0.853731 | 0.022133 | 0.124136 | 0.0 | 0.0 | 0.0 | 1.016294 |

*Uniform wage subsidy*

| $X_A^F$ | $X_M^F$ | $N_A^F$ | $N_M^F$ | $U^F$ | $S_M^F$ | $S_A^F$ | $C^F$ | $qX_A^F + X_M^F$ |
|---|---|---|---|---|---|---|---|---|
| 0.723102 | 0.838438 | 0.197696 | 0.802304 | 0.0 | 0.768473 | 0.768473 | 0.768473 | 1.561540 |

*Optimal subsidization*

| $X_A^*$ | $X_M^*$ | $N_A^*$ | $N_M^*$ | $U^*$ | $S_M^*$ | $S_A^*$ | $C^*$ | $qX_A^* + X_M^*$ |
|---|---|---|---|---|---|---|---|---|
| 0.700600 | 0.862517 | 0.168792 | 0.831208 | 0.0 | 0.773633 | 0.669866 | 0.756118 | 1.563117 |

wage subsidization in cases 1 and 2. For case 1, where $\alpha = 0.7$ and $\beta = 0.2$, the former is about 5 percent less expensive; however, this advantage is eroded to 1 percent as we move to case 2, with $\alpha = \beta = 0.5$, and is reversed when we come to case 3, where $\alpha > \beta$ is no longer satisfied.

Recall that $\alpha$ and $\beta$ represent output elasticities with respect to the labor inputs in manufacturing and agriculture respectively. Since common sense and econometric estimates concur in leading us to believe that the inequalities $\alpha \geq \beta$ and $\alpha + \gamma > \beta$ do indeed hold, the dominance of the socially optimal policy package seems to be supported. An intuitive explanation of the significance of the conditions is best captured graphically. A high value for $\alpha$ coupled with a low value for $\beta$ corresponds to a relatively flat marginal product curve in industry and a steep curve in agriculture. As noted in section 3, a flat industry curve, allowing for the agglomeration effect, mandates only a minor increase in subsidization costs, whereas a steep agriculture curve would tend to make the *saving* relative to the case of uniform subsidization much more substantial. Indeed, cases 1 and 2 show the agriculture subsidy rates falling sharply (from $S_A^F$ to $S_A^*$) relative to those in case 3, which also registers the greatest *rise* in the rate of subsidy to the manufacturing sector ($S_M^F$ to $S_M^*$).

Note that, provided that the condition $\alpha \geq \beta$ is met, although the ranking of costs is invariant to $q$ and $\bar{w}$ their absolute magnitudes do vary with these parameter values, as evidenced in cases 4, 5, and 6. Comparison of 4 with 1, as well as of 5 with 2, shows that the greater the price $q$ of agricultural goods in units of the output of the manufacturing sector, the lower the costs. This happens because, for given $\bar{w}$, raising $q$ raises marginal value productivity in optimum and hence, in general, reduces the discrepancy that subsidization has to close. By the same token, raising $\bar{w}$ widens this discrepancy and raises the unit cost associated with both kinds of subsidization. That relative cost comparisons are neutral to the level of $\bar{w}$ can be seen by contrasting case 1 with case 6; raising $\bar{w}$ from 1.0 to 1.5 increases costs, both $C^F$ and $C^*$, by precisely 0.5.[12]

## 7 Conclusions

Having considered two intervention options, uniform wage subsidization and differential optimal subsidization, we have established, under plausible conditions, a case for the welfare superiority of subsidization with attention to agglomeration effects, over subsidization without them, on the grounds of both cost and benefit. For cases where cost superiority is not demonstrated, it may still be that the additional benefits outweigh the extra costs associated with subsidization under agglomeration.[13]

Analytically, the presence of agglomeration economies breaks down a previously construed optimal prescription involving the equal subsidization of labor in both sectors of an economy characterized by expected-income-led migration, and calls for a higher rate of assistance to urban than to rural productive activities. This might restore some balance to thinking about the relative developmental roles of the two sectors and may challenge extremist views that urban expansion is largely parasitic. To the extent that manufacturing is a predominantly urban activity, welfare effects arising from the agglomeration externality in LDCs' manufacturing generate one of the few legitimate bases of a protectionist argument for that sector (Corden, 1974).

Three important research issues need to be pursued further. First, the microfoundations of urban agglomeration economies require empirical investigation. The more clearly we understand the nature of such economies, the more policy measures can be "fine tuned" to address their internalization. Second, the financing sources and administrative costs of various subsidy options need to be explored systematically. Last, in the literature on expected-income migration cum institutionally fixed urban wage rate, explanations of the origins and functions of the high urban wage need to be reconciled with the economic behavior of the agents involved. As a step in this direction we offer elsewhere (Shukla and Stark, 1989) an agglomeration economies rationale for formal sector wage rigidity and for the existence of the urban informal sector in LDCs.

## Notes

Co-authored with Vibhooti Shukla. Reprinted from *Journal of Urban Economics* 27, 1990. Published by Academic Press Inc. This is Discussion Paper 30, Harvard University Migration and Development Program. Helpful suggestions and comments of an anonymous referee are gratefully acknowledged.

1   Since preparing the first draft of this chapter, we have become aware of a paper by Panagariya and Succar (1986) who do incorporate scale economies in manufacturing within a Harris–Todaro type of framework. Panagariya and Succar model scale economies as external to the firm but internal to the industry and focus on the comparative statics properties of their approach.

2   Consider, for example, the conclusions of Harris and Todaro (1970) and Todaro (1976).

3  An approach that has also engendered a vigorous welfare-theoretic literature in the field of international trade.
4  See, for example, Shukla (1984), where estimates based on Indian data confirm presumptions that this gain is especially significant under LDC conditions. Earlier estimates with US data can be found in Sveikauskas (1975) and Segal (1976).
5  Models using external scale economies in urban production to determine equilibrium or optimal city size have had currency in the mainstream of urban economics since the work of Dixit (1973), and more recently (for example, Henderson, 1986) have been applied to address questions of urban growth in LDCs. The present model is in the tradition of the "open city" models of this literature.
6  That this is not incompatible with perfect competition between firms is demonstrated by Chipman (1970).
7  The urban economies are assumed to be sustained positively over the entire range of city sizes. This is consistent with findings in Shukla (1984), which fail to show a significant decline in urban productivity benefits even in the upper reaches of the Indian size distribution, and reflects the presumption that, on the pure production side, there is no *a priori* reason for assuming that diseconomies should occur. More elaborate models of urban growth with production economies often render city size finite by postulating consumption-side diseconomies, or the limitedness of a site-specific factor, most commonly land, that impinges through input prices, *not* through the technology (for example, see Henderson, 1982). Of course, to the extent that external diseconomies are present on the urban scene, the sign of the difference between optimal and equilibrium city size will be moot. See Shukla (1984) for indirect evidence that consumption diseconomies may not be important in an LDC context. Further, the suboptimality of each individual urban area is viewed as being sufficient for yielding suboptimality of the aggregate urbanization level, although it is obviously not necessary. See Shukla and Stark (1986) for a discussion of comparative departures from optimality with respect to small and large urban areas.
8  Inter-industry terms of trade in the Harris–Todaro model are variously treated in the literature as endogenously determined for a closed economy through specific utility or demand functions (Harris and Todaro, 1970), as given exogenously for a small open economy (Corden and Findlay, 1975), or as obtained through a pre-specified relationship between exportables and importables in a large open economy (Srinivasan and Bhagwati, 1975). In general, the choice of treatment has hinged upon the orientation of the model and the purpose it was set up to serve. Following Bhagwati and Srinivasan (1974) we choose to have $q$ (see below) perform double duty in representing exogenous terms of trade (a formulation we consider appropriate for most LDCs) as well as a parameter in a linear social welfare index (see sections 4 and 5) to facilitate comparability with their results. Such a restriction on social preferences does not materially alter the characteristics of the equilibrium, and the likelihood that a concave utility function might imply preferences that will yield an

optimal allocation featuring a higher than *laissez-faire* agricultural product is small because of considerations of the Engel's law type.

9    The assumption implicit in figure 24.2 that $g'f$ is downsloping in the $[0, \overline{N}]$ interval is sufficient to guarantee that equilibrium exists. We do not, however, address issues of stability. See Day et al. (1987) for a statement of conditions under which unstable oscillations in a Harris–Todaro model are possible.

10   In contrast with economy-wide measures, we might mention in passing the implications of agglomeration effects for cost–benefit analyses of small interventions. The urban shadow wage in the context of expected-income migration has been variously characterized as being as high as the *laissez-faire* wage rate (Harberger, 1971) or, with declining marginal propensity to consume and migrant risk aversion, lower than this rate (Katz and Stark, 1986). The presence of agglomeration economies in urban production in either case strengthens the argument for marginal investments in urban job creation, since benefits outweigh opportunity costs, even if the latter are as high as the private sector wage. This follows from the result that, at *laissez-faire* urban employment levels, $g(N_M)f'(N_M) + g'(N_M)f(N_M) > \overline{w}$.

11   Unlike them, however, we do not attempt to rank the various second-best options; nor do we concern ourselves with the informational problems of implementability, as does Basu (1980).

12   Note that the choice of $\overline{w}$, although extraneous here, must be in conformity with plausible values of $\alpha$ and $\beta$ and consistent with realistic ranges of sectoral employment shares, the urban unemployment rate, and the factor of proportionality between urban and rural wages. The cases presented in table 24.1 feature existing agricultural employment shares ranging from about 50 percent to 85 percent of the total labor force, and an urban unemployment rate $[U/(1 - N_A)] \times 100$ ranging from about 32 percent to 85 percent. (Note, however, that the formulation does not admit the possibility of partial employment or underemployment in the urban sector.) The urban institutional wage $\overline{w} = [(1 - N_A)/N_M] w_0$ is between 1.5 and 6.6 times as high as the rural wage in *laissez-faire*.

13   The model is not closed in the costs of subsidization. There are two principal difficulties with incorporating costs into a social utility function. First, there is the standard difficulty associated with a possibly distortionary financing of the subsidy. Regrettably, much of the literature on trade distortions also stops short of explicitly characterizing the welfare effects of financing the collection costs associated with corrective measures. Second, the exogeneity of the level of the urban institutional wage in the model poses a problem for our simulation analysis. Comparison of cases 1 and 6 in table 24.1, for example, reveals that while the benefits of intervention, which are independent of $\overline{w}$, are equal in these two cases, the costs are not. Since our primary concern is with comparing costs between alternative subsidization packages that prove sensitive to arbitrary choice of the exogenous urban wage, we pursue a separate treatment of the costs of subsidization instead of burdening the utility index with the consequences of this sensitivity.

## References

Basu, K. C. (1980) "Optimal Policies in Dual Economies." *Quarterly Journal of Economics* 95(1): 187–96.

Bhagwati, J. N. and Srinivasan, T. N. (1974) "On Reanalysing the Harris–Todaro Model: Policy Rankings in the Case of Sector-Specific Sticky Wages." *American Economic Review* 64(3): 502–8.

Chipman, J. S. (1970) "External Economies of Scale and Competitive Equilibrium." *Quarterly Journal of Economics* 84(3): 347–85.

Corden, W. M. (1974) *Trade Policy and Economic Welfare*. Oxford: Oxford University Press.

—— and Findlay, R. (1975) "Urban Unemployment, Intersectoral Capital Mobility and Development Policy." *Economica* 42(165): 59–78.

Day, R. H., Dasgupta, S., Datta, S. K. and Nugent, J. B. (1987) "Instability in Rural–Urban Migration." *Economic Journal* 97(388): 940–50.

Dixit, A. (1973) "The Optimum Factory Town." *Bell Journal of Economics and Management Science* 4(2): 637–51.

Harberger, A. C. (1971) "On Measuring the Social Opportunity Cost of Labour." *International Labour Review* 103(6): 559–79.

Harris, J. R. and Todaro, M. P. (1970) "Migration, Unemployment and Development: A Two-Sector Analysis." *American Economic Review* 60(1): 126–42.

Henderson, J. V. (1982) "The Impact of Government Policies on Urban Concentration." *Journal of Urban Economics* 12(3): 280–303.

—— (1986) "Efficiency of Resource Usage and City Size." *Journal of Urban Economics* 19 (1): 47–70.

Katz, E. and Stark, O. (1986) "On the Shadow Wage of Urban Jobs in Less-Developed Countries." *Journal of Urban Economics* 20(2): 121–7 (reprinted as ch. 25 in this volume).

Panagariya, A. and Succar, P.(1986) "The Harris–Todaro Model and Economies of Scale." *Southern Economic Journal* 52(4): 984–98.

Segal, D. (1976) "Are There Returns to Scale in City Size?" *Review of Economics and Statistics* 58(3): 339–50.

Shukla, V. (1984) "The Productivity of Indian Cities and Some Implications for Development Policy." Ph.D. Dissertation, Princeton University.

—— and Stark, O. (1985) "On Agglomeration Economies and Optimal Migration." *Economics Letters* 18: 297– 300 (reprinted as ch. 23 in this volume).

—— and—— (1986) "Urban External Economies and Optimal Migration." In Oded Stark (ed.), *Research in Human Capital and Development*, vol. 4, *Migration, Human Capital and Development*. Greenwich, CT: JAI Press.

—— and —— (1989) "Why Are Urban Formal Sector Wages in LDCs Above the Market-Clearing Level?" Discussion Paper 44, Harvard University Migration and Development Program.

Srinivasan, T. N. and Bhagwati, J. N. (1975) "Alternative Policy Rankings in a Large, Open Economy with Sector-Specific, Minimum Wages." *Journal of Economic Theory* 11(3): 356–71.

Sveikauskas, L. (1975) "The Productivity of Cities." *Quarterly Journal of Economics* 89(3): 393–413.

Todaro, M. P. (1976) "Urban Job Expansion, Induced Migration and Rising Unemployment." *Journal of Development Economics* 3(3): 211–25.

# 25

# On the Shadow Wage of Urban Jobs in Less Developed Countries

## 1

A number of recent articles have directed attention once more to the expected-income model of migration into urban areas associated most closely with Todaro (1969, 1980). Addressing the issue of the shadow wage under induced migration, Heady (1981) demonstrates that the shadow wage (which we shall designate by $W^*$) should equal the market wage (which we shall designate by $W$). This result is first obtained under risk neutrality by migrants but is argued to hold equally well under risk aversion. In another recent paper Foster (1981) also claims that in a world where rural-to-urban migrants compete for scarce rent-awarding urban jobs (where rent is defined as "a wage that is higher than the supply price of labor"), $W^*$ should equal $W$. Again this result is shown to hold especially under risk neutrality by competitive rent-seekers. However, in the final part of the Foster paper it is argued that the risk neutrality assumption is nonessential in establishing the $W^* = W$ result and that it holds equally well under risk aversion. Sah and Stiglitz (1983) likewise conclude that (for the case of rural-to-urban migration under risk neutrality) "the shadow wage equals the market wage." In yet another recent paper, Schultz (1982) even goes so far as to suggest that a "crucial result" of the expected-income model of migration is that it "admits to the possibility that added urban employment could *reduce* social product; the opportunity cost of attracting labor from agriculture might exceed the social product of the new urban job, given the attendant increment to urban unemployment," that is, that $W^* > W$. Does it?

In this chapter we shall present and exploit a simple model in order to suggest that in a Todaro-type case the appropriate shadow wage for evaluating the social labor cost of a marginal (public) urban project is generally lower than the market wage, that is, that $W^* < W$. This result is shown to hold first when agents are risk averse (section 2) and consequently even when they are risk neutral (section 3).

The policy significance of determining the $W^*$, $W$ relationship need not be underscored here. It is sufficient to mention its bearing on such critical issues as the optimal choice of capital intensity in urban industry and the optimal level of employment in public urban industry (or of employment subsidies).

## 2

Let us begin with the benchmark case of risk neutrality. This appears to be the assumption upon which the result that $W^*$ is equal to $W$ may be based.

Assume that urban employment probability $P$ is given by the ratio of formal sector jobs $N$ to the total urban labor force $L$. Making this assumption maintains consistency with the established relevant literature.[1] Thus

$$P = N/L \qquad (25.1)$$

Hence, given a competitive setting *and* risk neutrality, the *expected* pecuniary gain from migration must, in equilibrium, be zero. If $W$ is the urban wage and $W_R$ is the rural wage, we have

$$PW = \frac{N}{L} W = W_R \qquad (25.2)$$

so that if urban jobs increase by one, and migration is the only source of change in the urban labor force, then

$$dL = \frac{W}{W_R} \qquad (25.3)$$

and hence the social cost associated with the creation of one urban job with wage $W$ is

$$W^* = W_R \, dL = W_R \frac{W}{W_R} = W \qquad (25.4)$$

Let us now assume that migrants are risk averse. Clearly this is a crucial assumption since, when the would-be migrants make their migration decision, they are uncertain whether or not they will obtain a job.

To show how such risk aversion affects the result, assume that all migrants are von Neumann–Morgenstern expected utility maximizers, whose utility function of wealth is $U(\cdot)$, where $U' > 0$, $U'' < 0$, and whose original wealth is $W_0$.

Now, in a competitive equilibrium, the expected utility of being in the urban area must equal the utility of being in the rural area. Hence we have that

$$\frac{N}{L} U(W_0 + W - W_R) + \left(1 - \frac{N}{L}\right) U(W_0 - W_R) = U(W_0) \quad (25.5)$$

is the competitive equilibrium condition.

Let us consider the response of migration $dL$ to the creation of one urban job as compared with the risk-neutral case. From (25.2) and (25.3) we know that under risk neutrality $dL = L/N$. Also, from (25.5), we know that under risk aversion

$$dL = \frac{U(W_0 + W - W_R) - U(W_0 - W_R)}{U(W_0) - U(W_0 - W_R)} \quad (25.6)$$

Now, what we wish to prove is that

$$dL|_{\text{risk aversion}} < dL|_{\text{risk neutrality}} \quad (25.7)$$

That is, as a result of risk aversion, fewer rural workers migrate. We prove this by contradiction. Let us make the reverse assumption that

$$\frac{U(W_0 - W - W_R) - U(W_0 - W_R)}{U(W_0) - U(W_0 - W_R)} > dL|_{\text{risk neutrality}} = \frac{W}{W_R}$$

$$(25.8)$$

Then we have that

$$\frac{[U(W_0 + W - W_R) - U(W_0 - W_R)]/W}{[U(W_0) - U(W_0 - W_R)]/W_R} > 1 \quad (25.9)$$

However, given $U'' < 0$, we know that the average slope of $U(\cdot)$ between $W_0 - W_R$ and $W_0 + W - W_R$ is *smaller* than the average slope of $U(\cdot)$

between $W_0 - W_R$ and $W_0$ (since $W > W_R$). Hence the above assumption is self-contradictory. Therefore we must have that

$$dL|_{\text{risk aversion}} < dL|_{\text{risk neutrality}} \qquad (25.10)$$

Hence we have shown that, given risk aversion, the cost of creating an urban job is less than the urban wage, since

$$W^*|_{\text{risk aversion}} = W_R dL|_{\text{risk aversion}} < W_R dL|_{\text{risk neutrality}} = W$$
$$(25.11)$$

### 3

In this section we return to the assumption of risk neutrality. Nonetheless, by considering the likely effect of migratory movements on saving patterns in less developed countries (LDCs) we show that the shadow price of urban job creation may well be below the urban wage.

Our approach is based on a well-observed feature of LDCs. Because of the absence of or imperfections in capital markets, such economies are typically characterized by a suboptimal volume of savings that implies that, at the margin, the social value of savings exceeds the social value of consumption. Since we are interested in the *cost* side, the social premium placed on savings (investment) *vis-à-vis* consumption can be expressed as $\alpha > 1$ so that, in a social cost accounting, the value of *one* unit of consumption in terms of savings is $1/\alpha < 1$. It follows that there are *two* sources of costs to the economy of using an extra laborer in a marginal new public urban project – a "production cost" and a "consumption cost." The production cost is the opportunity cost of the laborers who quit their current employment to accept, or who hope to find, new urban jobs; the consumption cost, which is also an opportunity cost, reflects the change in current consumption evaluated in terms of the (socially more valuable) change in savings.

The explicit focus on savings introduces a time dimension into our analysis and hence the treatment of time must be clearly spelled out. We adopt a very simple time framework. Individuals are assumed to live for two periods. In the first period they earn, consume, and save. In the second period they consume out of their savings.

Thus we consider individuals with utility function $U = U(C_1, C_2)$ where $C_i$ is consumption in period $i = 1, 2$ whose budget constraint is

$(W_0 + Y - C_1)r - C_2 = 0$ where $W_0$ is the initial wealth (which may be zero), $Y$ is first-period income, and $r$ is 1 plus the rate of return on savings.

To assure risk neutrality we assume that $\partial\lambda/\partial Y = 0$, where $\lambda$ is the Lagrangian multiplier associated with the constraint. This can be shown to require that

$$\begin{vmatrix} U_{11} & U_{12} \\ U_{12} & U_{22} \end{vmatrix} = 0 \qquad (25.12)$$

where $U_{ij} = \partial^2 U/\partial C_i \partial C_j$, $i = 1, 2$, $j = 1, 2$.

In addition, we assume that during his income-earning years a worker's marginal propensity to consume is a declining function of his income,[2] that is, writing $C_1 = f(Y)$,

$$\frac{\partial^2 C_1}{\partial Y^2} = f''(Y) < 0 \qquad (25.13)$$

This assumption derives from a conceptual framework of migration developed elsewhere and reflects empirical observations concerning disposition of migration income and the incidence, magnitude, and utilization of urban-to-rural migrant-to-family remittances (see Stark, 1983; Lucas and Stark, 1985).

Now, as has been shown above (see (25.3)), under risk neutrality the number of rural migrants responding to the creation of one urban job with wage $W$ is $W/W_R$. Consider the consumption of the $W/W_R$ workers. Clearly, $W/W_R - 1$ are worse off by an amount $W_R$ and one is better off by an amount $W - W_R$.

Hence the total change $\Delta c$ in consumption as a result of the creation of a new urban job is the sum of the change in consumption of the migrant who has secured the urban job and the decline in consumption incurred by the migrants who did not secure the urban job. Therefore

$$\Delta c = [f(W_0 + W - W_R) - f(W_0)]$$

$$+ \left(\frac{W}{W_R} - 1\right)[f(W_0 - W_R) - f(W_0)] \qquad (25.14)$$

Thus

$$\Delta c = (W - W_R)$$

$$\times \left[ \frac{f(W_0 + W - W_R) - f(W_0)}{W - W_R} - \frac{f(W_0) - f(W_0 - W_R)}{W_R} \right]$$

$$(25.15)$$

However, the first term in square brackets is the average slope of the arc $f(W_0)$ to $f(W_0 + W - W_R)$ and (minus) the second term is the average slope of the arc $f(W_0)$ to $f(W_0 - W_R)$. Hence, since $f'' < 0$, the average slope for the arc defined over the lower values of income is greater than the average slope defined over the higher values of income. We therefore have

$$\Delta c < 0 \qquad (25.16)$$

Hence, since total income has been kept constant by (25.2), savings must rise so that the *cost* of the urban job is the urban wage (equal to the total production cost) plus the value of the additional consumption evaluated at $1/\alpha$ per unit, that is,

$$W^* = W + \frac{1}{\alpha} \Delta c < W \qquad (25.17)$$

so that, given risk neutrality, the shadow price of an urban job is less than the urban wage.

### 4

It has been shown in this chapter that there is a good reason to believe that the urban wage exaggerates the shadow price of urban jobs. We have shown this to be the case, first, when migrants are risk averse and, second, when they are risk neutral and exhibit a declining marginal propensity to consume. It thus appears that society does not lose from the creation of additional urban jobs, even after the migration from the rural areas induced by this is fully accounted for.

# Notes

Co-authored with Eliakim Katz. Reprinted from *Journal of Urban Economics* 20, 1986. Published by Academic Press Inc. We are indebted to a referee for very helpful comments on an earlier version of this chapter.

1 Urban employment prospects may consist of formal jobs and informal jobs. In such a case $P$ would stand for a probability mixture of obtaining an urban job and $1 - P$ would be the probability of failing to obtain either a formal or an informal urban job, that is, of ending up in unemployment. Accordingly, $W$ would then be the compounded (weighted) urban wage. Note that drawing upon one's wealth (past income) or the institution of intra-familial sharing permits the survival of migrants who fail to obtain a formal sector job, as described above, or of migrants who fail to secure any (formal or informal) urban job as alluded to in this note (see Stark, 1978, 1983).

2 This requires that

$$\left[ (U_{112} - rU_{122}) \frac{\partial C_1}{\partial Y} + (U_{122} - rU_{222}) \frac{\partial C_2}{\partial Y} \right] r\Delta$$

$$- \left[ (2rU_{112} - U_{111} - r^2 U_{122}) \frac{\partial C_1}{\partial Y} + (2rU_{122} - U_{112} - r^2 U_{222}) \frac{\partial C_2}{\partial Y} \right] K < 0$$

where $\Delta$ is the bordered Hessian associated with the constrained optimization problem and $K = rU_{12} - r^2 U_{22}$.

# References

Foster, E. (1981) "The Treatment of Rents in Cost–Benefit Analysis." *American Economic Review* 71: 171–8.

Heady, C. J. (1981) "Shadow Wages and Induced Migration." *Oxford Economic Papers* 33: 108–21.

Lucas, R. E. B. and Stark, O. (1985) "Motivations to Remit: Evidence from Botswana." *Journal of Political Economy* 93: 901–18 (reprinted as ch. 16 in this volume).

Sah, R. K. and Stiglitz, J. E. (1983) "The Social Cost of Labor, and Project Evaluation: A General Approach." Working Paper 1229, National Bureau of Economic Research.

Schultz, T. P. (1982) "Lifetime Migration Within Educational Strata in Venezuela: Estimates of a Logistic Model." *Economic Development and Cultural Change* 30: 559–93.

Stark, O. (1978) *Economic–Demographic Interactions in Agricultural Development: The Case of Rural-to-Urban Migration*. Rome: UN Food and Agriculture Organization.

—— (1983) "Towards a Theory of Remittances in LDCs." Discussion Paper 971, Harvard Institute of Economic Research.

Todaro, M. P. (1969) "A Model of Labor Migration and Urban Unemployment in Less Developed Countries." *American Economic Review* 59: 138–48.

—— (1980) "International Migration in Developing Countries: A Survey." In R. A. Easterlin (ed.), *Population and Economic Change in Developing Countries*. Chicago, IL: University of Chicago Press for National Bureau of Economic Research, pp. 361–402.

# Part VII

---

## The Economic Performance of Migrants

# 26

## Why Do Migrants Fare as They Do?

### 1 Introduction

Groups of first-generation migrants who have been in their new country for a while often have a higher mean income and a greater variance in income than the indigenous (native-born) population.[1] The migrants' higher mean income may seem somewhat perplexing given the informational, language, social, institutional, and other barriers which usually stand in their way. In addition, given that migrants as a group are often economically discriminated against by the indigenous population, for example migrants are paid less, on average, than equally skilled nonmigrants, the evidence of their higher mean income becomes a formidable puzzle. Yet notwithstanding these impediments to success, migrants do in many circumstances outperform the native born. Indeed, although this result obtains with a time lag from the migrants' arrival, it does tend to hold even after various success-related attributes such as educational qualifications are normalized.

One possible explanation for this phenomenon may be found in the nature and characteristics of economically motivated migrants; those that tend to migrate for economic reasons are likely to be self-selected in a number of success-related ways. Such migrants will be younger, more enterprising, more aggressive, and less risk averse, and will have a higher amount of human capital. This human capital will be characterized by a higher average ratio of general to specific human capital than the equivalent ratio in the indigenous population. Hence the migrants' human capital will be more flexible. This vector of characteristics of economically motivated migrants is likely to be reflected in various aspects of behavior. Migrants will display high risk-taking behavior, aggression, dynamism, and keen entrepreneurship, all contributing to higher incomes. In addition, it should be noted that since in general the return to a high-risk activity has a higher mean and a higher variance than that to low-risk activity, given that migrants are prepared to take more risks than the indigenous population, they will experience a higher average income combined with greater income variance.

The purpose of this chapter is to offer another explanation for the high mean and high variance of migrants' income. This explanation is based on the relative lack of information about migrants in the receiving country, rather than on the attributes of migrants. To a large extent the explanation offered here is noncontradictory to and can be viewed as complementary with the explanation based on economic migrants' attributes presented above. Nonetheless, the argument put forward here does allow certain predictions to be made which are different from those of the explanation based on attributes. Hence discriminatory tests between the two explanations are possible.

## 2 Some Stylized Facts

Before we present our basic argument, we consider several stylized facts revealed by a study of men aged 18–64 as documented by the 1970 and 1980 US Census reports. We draw especially on the valuable summary statistics and analysis provided by Borjas (1986).

1 The probability that a person who is foreign born will be self-employed is significantly higher than the probability that a similarly skilled indigenous member of the population will be self-employed.
2 Self-employed workers have higher incomes than salaried workers. This is true for both indigenous and migrant workers.
3 A migrant's level of education has a positive correlation with his self-employment probability. That is, on average better educated migrants are more likely to be self-employed.
4 Labor market experience in a migrant's home country has a positive correlation with his self-employment probability. That is, those who have worked for some years before migrating will have a greater tendency to become self-employed in the receiving country.
5 Among the migrant population, being married has a positive correlation with being self-employed.

A theory of why foreign-born men earn more on average than US men should be capable of explaining the above five facts. It seems to us that a line of argument that draws on the theory of asymmetric information in labor markets may prove useful as the basis for such an explanation. In particular, it appears that the stylized facts as outlined above are at least as well explained by the proposed argument as by the competing explanation presented in section 1.

## 3 The Model

Our basic argument is that when migrants arrive in a new country (the United States in our case) they will tend initially to be viewed by potential employers as homogeneous in terms of their ability. This is because US employers will lack the ability to discern between the skill levels of different workers. Hence highly skilled workers will be offered the same wage as less skilled workers. In addition, it seems likely that, at least initially, all migrant workers will be paid the lowest possible wage. This is so because giving a worker a task which might be beyond his ability will, on average, be costly to the employer. The reason for this is that such a worker may, because of errors of judgment or just plain ignorance, cause damage, waste materials, bring about delays, and so on. Therefore, if the initial period is not very lengthy and since employers are risk averse, a migrant of unknown skill will tend to be initially employed in the lowest-skill (lowest-paid) job. In general, only in the long run will *all* relevant aspects of a worker's skill be fully revealed; only then will the migrant be paid the wage appropriate to his skill. As his skill is increasingly recognized, his job level and wages will rise.

Hence the present value of the lifetime earnings of a migrant employee with skill level $\theta$ can be defined as $V(\theta)$, whereas a similar but indigenous employee with skill level $\theta$ receives a present value of lifetime income $W(\theta)$ where $\partial V/\partial \theta > 0$, $\partial W/\partial \theta > 0$, and $W(\theta) > V(\theta)$ for all $\theta$.

This will tend to hold true even if some migrants possess a foreign certificate or other signal of skill achievement in their home country. For the initial wave of migrants from a given country at least, such signals will tend to be viewed with skepticism in the receiving country since there will be relatively little knowledge of what precisely they represent. Clearly, internationally recognized certificates, and especially such certificates that have the backing of the receiving country's educational authorities, *will* be of some value, but even then some employer doubt is likely to remain.

We note that the distinction between first-wave and second- and higher-order waves of migration from a given country to the United States is important. Higher-order waves of migration will arrive when US employers have had certain experience with first-wave migrants and possess more knowledge about the correlation between foreign signals and skills. In addition, there will now be a larger number of US residents (namely the first-wave migrants and their children) who are able to communicate with both the new migrants and potential employers. Such early migrants can better investigate the true skill levels of the new migrants as well as have a better understanding of the signals provided by them. Furthermore, some early-wave migrants may now be employers themselves, and they will not face the same informational asymmetry as indigenous employers. High-order-wave migrants will thus benefit from the knowledge imported to the receiving country by the first-wave migrants. First-wave migrants can thus be viewed as providing positive externalities to higher-order-wave migrants.

Let us now return to the issue of first-wave migrants. We wish to demonstrate that, as a result of market conditions in the receiving country, migrants have a greater tendency to be self-employed than indigenous workers. In order to show this as simply as possible we develop a diagram through which this and other results can be illustrated.

We begin by assuming that the present value of wages to an indigenous *employee* of a given skill level $\theta$ in a given industry $X$ is $W(\theta, X)$. Similarly, we assume that self-employment yields an indigenous employee an uncertain present value of income $\bar{W}(\theta, X)$ and that the distribution of $\bar{W}$, for a given $\theta$ and $X$, is given.

Now, let all indigenous workers defined by $(\theta, X)$ have identical preferences except in their attitude toward risk. Thus, while it is assumed that all workers are risk averse, the degree of risk aversion varies between workers. In general, self-employment tends to be riskier than being an employee. This implies that self-employment provides a higher average return and a higher variance of the return than wage employment. Hence workers with low risk aversion will most value the risk premium to self-employment whereas those who are very risk averse will put a low value on the risk premium to self-employment. Another way of looking at this is to view low-risk-aversion individuals as having a high certainty equivalent present value of income from self-employment and individuals who are more risk averse as having a low certainty equivalent present value of income from self-employment.

Hence indigenous workers can be ordered by their certainty equivalent income from self-employment. In figure 26.1, assuming continuity, this certainty equivalent wage is plotted, starting from the highest certainty equivalent wages, against the proportion of $(\theta, X)$ workers who have an equal or higher certainty equivalent wage from self-employment. This relation is depicted by SS'. Clearly, those workers at S are the least risk-averse workers and are the ones who most benefit from self-employment. As we move down SS' towards S' we encounter increasingly risk-averse workers until at S′ we find the workers with the highest level of risk aversion. These workers are least partial to self-employment. In contrast with the above (and given the homogeneity of all indigenous workers), the present value of the income from wage employment of indigenous workers in the $(\theta, X)$ class is the same for all these workers. Hence it is plotted as the horizontal line EE′ in figure 26.1. The equilibrium distribution between self-employed indigenous workers and indigenous workers who are employees will clearly occur at the intersection of SS′ and EE′. Hence the proportion of self-employed indigenous workers will be OA.

Consider now migrant workers. Following our earlier discussion, migrant employees will in general obtain a present value of income lower than that of indigenous employees. Therefore the curve relevant to wage-employed migrants in the $(\theta, X)$ class is lower than EE′. Let the migrant's employment curve be depicted by $E_M E'_M$.

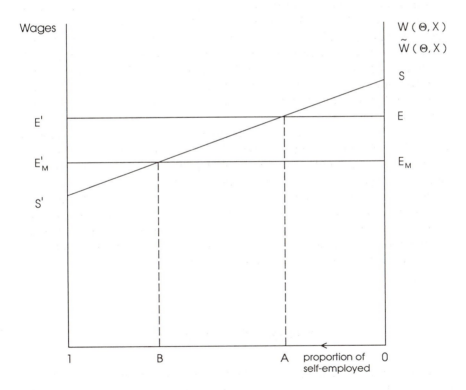

**Figure 26.1**

In contrast, let the output of self-employed migrants be accepted by consumers for the actual (and easily recognizable) skill embedded in it. Also, note our earlier comment that our result does not depend on differences in the characteristics of migrants and the indigenous population. Hence, assuming that the attitudes toward risk among migrants and among the indigenous population are identically distributed (that is, migrants do not self-select by risk aversion), the certainty equivalent curve of self-employment is SS' for migrants also. Hence the equilibrium is at the intersection of $E_M E'_M$ and SS'. It follows immediately that the proportion of self-employed migrants is OB, and this clearly exceeds the proportion of self-employed indigenous workers OA. Hence a greater proportion of migrants than indigenous workers will tend to be self-employed. On average, this provides migrants with a risk premium and makes migrants wealthier (on average) than the indigenous population. Note that this result is obtained without assuming that migrants have special attributes.

As a corollary to the above, it seems likely that as a consequence of informational asymmetry those workers with skill level $\theta_1$ lose more than workers with skill level $\theta_2$ where $\theta_1 > \theta_2$. This arises because, as argued above, initially all skill groups will tend to be treated equally by employers so that those with greater *potential* earnings (that is, those with higher skill) will lose more. In terms of figure 26.1 this implies that the $E_M E'_M$ curve will be lower for workers with higher skill levels. In turn, this suggests that higher-skilled individuals will have a greater tendency than lower-skilled individuals to be self-employed.

As noted above, our result will occur only if employers view migrant labor skills as more uncertain than the uncertainty faced by consumers when buying goods and/or services made by migrants. We suggest that this condition is likely to be satisfied for most outputs in most cases.[2] General support for our suggestion is obtained by contrasting the relatively short procedure associated with the purchase of most goods and the long procedure involved in the hiring of most labor. (This differential holds despite the fact that a great many consumer goods cannot be returned whereas labor can be fired with relatively short notice.)

## 4 Explaining the Stylized Facts

From the discussion in the preceding section it becomes clear why, in comparison with indigenous workers, migrants to the United States will tend to be proportionately more self-employed in most professions. It also becomes clear that the activities in which self-employed migrants will concentrate will be those that do not require too much consumer trust. For example, the demand by the indigenous population for a self-employed migrant doctor is likely to be small, since there will be uncertainty regarding his output (diagnosis). Hence the uncertainty about his skill may render his earnings low. Therefore, at least initially, migrant doctors will tend to work in hospitals (and be underpaid).[3] In contrast, there will be many migrants in small manufacturing or in services where the value and quality of the product is clearly and easily identifiable, for example, tailors and taxi drivers. In addition, migrants will be trusted to cook well the types of food eaten in their country of origin, so that they will often be owners of restaurants specializing in the foods of their country of origin.

Thus the first two stylized facts in section 2 have been accounted for by our model. First, we now have an explanation as to why migrants tend to be proportionately more self-employed. Second, the above point, in turn, explains why migrants have a higher average income with a higher variance than the native born.

Stylized fact 3 is also explained by our model. Migrants with higher educational levels may possess certificates indicating their years of education, but these may not be trusted by potential indigenous employers. Hence they will be paid initially as uneducated workers despite their human capital. The uncertainty of employers in the receiving country regarding levels of human capital will impose a high cost on educated migrants, and this cost will be an increasing function of their educational level (see Katz and Stark, 1987). Therefore there will be a positive correlation between a migrant's level of education and the probability of his being self-employed. Thus workers with high skills will tend to be self-employed. Stylized fact 4 is similarly explained by reference to the human capital gained through experience in the labor market. Those with the greatest human capital (in this case, with greatest work experience) will lose most by being employees and hence will tend to be self-employed.

Finally, the presence of a wife is likely to help a self-employed male migrant in the following way. The migrant's wife may work as an employee and confer a diversification advantage on the family's income. Given that women in LDCs tend to have low training and education levels, even if information were fully available, they would be paid a very low wage. Hence they lose little by being employed rather than self-employed. Thus having a wife in the United States provides the migrant family with a cheap diversification device which single migrants do not have. Indeed, in the absence of a wife to facilitate income diversification, single migrants may well choose to be employees despite the asymmetric information-induced costs of this choice.

## 5 Second- or Higher-Order-Wave Migration

One natural device which migrants might adopt in an attempt to mitigate the cost of being employees upon their migration is to enter markets where the asymmetric information problem is muted. This will probably happen if migrants work as employees for other migrants from the same country. Assuming that migrants of an earlier vintage can perfectly interpret home country signals about skill achievements, new migrants will have an incentive to locate where earlier migrants have located. This will result in a cluster-shaped distribution of migrants. (The distribution of the existing stock of migrants will thus constitute a predictor of the distribution of new migrants.) This reasoning suggests a complementary relationship between old and new migrants. Indeed, at least one study (King et al., 1986) presents results wherein, despite a continuing concentration of Hispanics (in the southwestern states, Florida, and the Northeast), the earnings of the Hispanic immigrants and the native Hispanics are *positively* correlated.[4]

The evidence of the distribution and locational choices made by second-wave and higher-order-wave migrants might be summarized as follows: "If we strive to draw general conclusions about the location choice behavior of the new immigrants to the United States, about the only thing that can be said is that all of the immigrants prefer to live in cities where their fellow countrymen are already located but this relationship is much weaker for the more educated immigrants" (Bartel, 1986, p. 31). Note that, following from the above discussion, the more educated a migrant is, the greater will be the probability of his being self-employed. Thus the better educated migrants will not benefit to the same extent from clustering as will the less educated migrants and thus will cluster less.

## 6 Discriminating Tests

Although a test distinguishing between the migrants' characteristics explanation and the asymmetric information explanation may appear quite difficult to design, at least two specific tests of this type are possible. First, consider the case of politically motivated migrants such as refugees. Usually these do not constitute an economically self-selected small group of people from a given country or region. Hence they are unlikely to possess the characteristics attributed to economically motivated migrants.

Therefore, in the case of a large group of political refugees entering a host country, economic success will constitute evidence corroborating the explanation advanced here, whereas lack of economic success will provide support for the theory based on attributes of migrants.

Second, consider migrants moving within the same country where, in their new region, the same language is spoken, the same certificates are accepted, etc. Such migrants will not be discriminated against as employees and hence will have no special motivation to become self-employed. Our theory would be supported if, in this case, the migrants and the indigenous population are self-employed in equal proportion. However, the hypothesis based on attributes of migrants would be supported if the proportion of migrants who are self-employed exceeds the same proportion for the indigenous population.

## Notes

1   For recent studies on the difference between the economic success of migrants and natives see, for the United States, Chiswick (1986) and, for Canada, Bloom and Gunderson (1989).
2   When it is not, migrants will tend not to become self-employed in that profession.
3   To protect its own reputation the work licensing entity, for example the professional association, which is also somewhat ignorant of the migrant doctor's true skill, may (implicitly or explicitly) induce him to operate as part of a large team (hospital) rather than alone.
4   These results are largely replicated in the case of illegal Mexican migrants and native Mexican Americans (see Bean et al., 1988).

## References

Bartel, Ann P. (1986) "Location Decisions of the New Immigrants to the United States." Working Paper 2049, National Bureau of Economic Research.

Bean, Frank D., Lowell, B. Lindsay and Taylor, Lowell J. (1988) "Undocumented Mexican Immigrants and the Earnings of Other Workers in the United States." *Demography* 25: 35–52.

Bloom, David E. and Gunderson, Morley K. (1989) "An Analysis of the Earnings of Canadian Immigrants." Discussion Paper 439, Department of Economics, Columbia University.

Borjas, George J. (1986) "The Self-Employment Experience of Immigrants." *Journal of Human Resources* 21: 485–506.

Chiswick, Barry R. (1986) "Human Capital and the Labor Market Adjustment of Immigrants: Testing Alternative Hypotheses." In Oded Stark (ed.), *Human Capital, Migration and Development*. Greenwich, CT: JAI Press.

Katz, Eliakim and Stark, Oded (1987) "International Migration under Asymmetric Information." *Economic Journal* 97: 718–26 (reprinted as ch. 13 in this volume).

King, Allan G., Lowell, B. Lindsay and Bean, Frank D. (1986) "The Effects of Hispanic Immigrants on the Earnings of Native Hispanic Americans." *Social Science Quarterly* 67: 673–89.

# 27

# Migrants' Savings, the Probability of Return Migration, and Migrants' Performance

## 1 Introduction

First-generation migrants who have been in the receiving country for some time often have a higher mean income than the indigenous (native-born) population. Usually this result obtains with a time lag from the migrants' arrival, and it tends to hold even after allowance is made for the standard controls such as educational qualifications.[1] The typical explanation for this phenomenon relates to the nature and characteristics of economically motivated migrants. The belief that the key to migrants' relative income is to be found in their ability, skills, and innately higher productivity has resulted in the channeling of considerable research energy in the direction of measuring, estimating, and testing for the migrants' vector of character-istics.[2] Yet the possibility that the migrants' performance could be directly attributed to migrants' incentives has escaped attention. By shifting the focus of analysis from the vector of characteristics to the structure of incentives we offer an alternative explanation for the migrants' high mean income. This explanation is based on a distinguishing characteristic of migrants *vis-à-vis* the native born, that is, the probability of return migration. Clearly, illegal participation in the host country's labor force can terminate migration.[3] Yet legal presence (in the absence of permanent status) does not preclude return migration either. When the downswing of a business cycle hits hard, migrants are often induced, requested, and even pressured to return to their home country.[4] Moreover, even in the case of legal migrants with permanent status, social pressures by alienated indige-nous population, psychological pressures arising from prolonged absence from home, and change in the status of assets left behind could compel return migration. Such considerations do not apply to natives.

Somewhat surprisingly this trait – the probability of return migration – has not been captured in the literature dealing with the differential labor market performance of migrants. Yet as will be proven below, this characteristic impinges on migrants' savings and is a critical determinant of economic performance. Furthermore, disregarding the probability of return migration has meant that policies pertaining to migrants' status, whether advocated or actually practised, appear to have erred not only in extent but, possibly, also in direction.

Even a small return probability entailing a large decline in wage income could place a wedge between the savings of migrants and those of the native born.[5] As higher savings translate into higher nonwage income, if return migration does not materialize, workers who are otherwise similar, that is, workers earning the same wage, will not have equal incomes. Migrants will outperform comparable native born.

## 2 The Probability of Return Migration and Migrants' Savings

Consider a perfectly competitive world in which economic activity is extended over infinite discrete time. The world is characterized by an overlapping generations model along the lines of Diamond (1965). In every period a single consumption good is produced using perfectly durable capital, and labor in the production process.[6] The endowment of labor is exogenously given, whereas the endowment of capital is the resources that were not consumed in the preceding period. Capital is perfectly mobile across countries and the rate of return to capital is at a stationary positive level $\bar{r}$ in terms of the consumption good.

Consider an economy that operates in the described world. In every time period the labor force in the economy is composed of natives as well as migrants (whose migration is caused by international wage differentials). The economy's stock of capital equals the resources which were not consumed in the preceding period in addition to the net international borrowing.

## Production

Production occurs within a period according to a constant returns to scale production function which is invariant through time. The output, $Y_t$, produced at time $t$ is

$$Y_t = F(K_t, L_t) \equiv L_t f(k_t) \qquad k_t = K_t/L_t \qquad (27.1)$$

where $K_t$ and $L_t$ are the capital and labor respectively employed at time $t$. The production function $f(k)$ is strictly concave and strictly monotonic increasing. Producers operate in a perfectly competitive environment. The inverse demand for factors of production is therefore given by the first-order conditions for profit maximization

$$r_t = f'(k_t) \qquad (27.2)$$
$$w_t = f(k_t) - f'(k_t)k_t \qquad (27.3)$$

where $r_t$ and $w_t$ are the interest rate and wage respectively at time $t$ and output is the numeraire.

## Equilibrium Prices

Given the unrestricted nature of the international capital markets, the economy's interest rate is exogenously given at the world level $\bar{r}$. Consequently, the capital-to-labor ratio employed in production is stationary at a level $\bar{k}$ where

$$\bar{k} = f'^{-1}(\bar{r}) \qquad (27.4)$$

and the wage rate is stationary at a level $\bar{w}$ where

$$\bar{w} = f(\bar{k}) - f'(\bar{k})\bar{k} \qquad (27.5)$$

## The Individuals

In every time period a new generation joins the labor force. A generation consists of two types of homogeneous groups of individuals: migrants (m) and natives (n). Migrants as well as natives are identical within and across generations. Individuals live for two periods. They are characterized by their intertemporal utility function and their labor endowment. The intertemporal utility function is defined over first- and second-period consumption:

$$U(c_1, c_2) = u(c_1) + \delta u(c_2) \tag{27.6}$$

where $\delta$ is the future discount factor. The utility function is strictly concave and satisfies the expected utility properties. Furthermore,

$$\lim_{c_i \to 0} u(c_i) = \infty \qquad i = 1, 2$$

Migrants differ from the native born in a single respect. They face a positive exogenous probability $\alpha$ of returning to their home country in the second period of their life and thus of earning a lower wage rate, $0 < w_h < \overline{w}$.[7,8]

In the first period of their lives individuals supply their unit endowments of labor inelastically and divide the resulting income between first-period consumption and savings so as to maximize their intertemporal utility function. The first-period consumption $c_1^i$ of individual $i$ is therefore

$$c_1^i = \overline{w} - s^i \tag{27.7}$$

where $s^i$ are the savings of individual $i$, $i = m,n$. In the second period individuals supply their unit endowments of labor inelastically, utilizing their labor income, in addition to the returns to their savings, for consumption. The second-period consumption $c_2^i$ of individual $i$, $i = m,n$, is therefore

$$c_2^i = \begin{cases} \overline{w} + (1 + \overline{r})s^i & \text{with probability } 1 - \alpha^i \\ w_h + (1 + \overline{r})s^i & \text{with probability } \alpha^i \end{cases} \tag{27.8}$$

where $\alpha^m = \alpha$ and $\alpha^n = 0$.

The optimal level of savings $s^{i*}$ for individual $i$ is therefore

$$s^{i*} = \text{argmax}(u(\overline{w} - s^i) + \delta\{\alpha^i u[w_h + (1 + \overline{r})s^i]$$
$$+ (1 - \alpha^i)u[\overline{w} + (1 + \overline{r})s^i]\}) \tag{27.9}$$

Given the properties of the utility function, $s^{i*}$ is uniquely determined by the first-order condition

$$(1 + \overline{r})\delta\{\alpha^i u'[w_h + (1 + \overline{r})s^{i*}] + (1 - \alpha^i)u'[\overline{w} + (1 + \overline{r})s^{i*}]\}$$
$$= u'(\overline{w} - s^{i*}) \tag{27.10}$$

## Savings Patterns: Migrants Versus the Native Born

### Proposition 1

*The higher the probability of return migration the higher is the level of savings.*

PROOF  Using the implicit function theorem it follows from (27.10) that

$$\frac{ds^{m*}}{d\alpha} = -\frac{(1 + \bar{r})\delta[u'(w_h + (1 + \bar{r})s^{m*}) - u'(\bar{w} + (1 + \bar{r})s^{m*})]}{u''(\bar{w} - s^{m*}) + \delta(1 + \bar{r})^2\alpha u''[w_h + (1 + \bar{r})s^{m*}] + (1 - \alpha)u''[\bar{w} + (1 + \bar{r})s^{m*}]\}}$$

$$> 0 \tag{27.11}$$

Since $w_h < \bar{w}$, the positivity of the expression in (27.11) follows, noting the strict concavity of the utility function.

### Corollary 1

*As a consequence of the possibility of return migration, migrants save more than the native born.*[9]

### Corollary 2

*If return migration does not take place, migrants' wealth outweighs the wealth of the native born.*

## 3  Concluding Remarks

In this chapter we establish a formal link between the likelihood of return migration and saving behavior. We can thus provide an explanation for the performance of migrants relative to the native born. It is shown that, given the possibility of return migration, migrants save more than the native born. Thus, if return migration does not materialize, migrants outperform the native born and migrants from countries to which the probability of return is larger will have higher mean incomes. Notice, however, that migrants who anticipate a positive return probability may transfer some of their savings as remittances to families and household members who stay behind in the sending country. By entailing a lower wealth accumulation leakage could result in a lower income differential between migrants and the native born or even in a reversal of the differential. Hence the variance in remittance propensities across migrants from different sending countries could account for the different degrees by which different groups of migrants outperform the native born. Note that, as an aside, the analysis also indicates that migrants' contribution to capital formation in the receiving economy is higher than that of comparable native born. Consequently, in a world where capital is not perfectly mobile across countries, if the latter contribution is considered by the host country to constitute a valuable attribute of migration, it pays that country to devise measures that prevent the return probability from falling to zero.

## Notes

Co-authored with Oded Galor. Reprinted from *International Economic Review* 31, 1990. This is a revised version of Discussion Paper 39, Harvard University Migration and Development Program. Helpful comments by two referees are gratefully acknowledged.
1  The difference between the economic success of migrants and that of natives is studied for the United States by Chiswick (1986a, b) and for Canada by Bloom and Gunderson (1989).
2  Particular attention has been paid to the intertemporal appreciation of the quality (for example, skills, schooling levels, etc.) of given cohorts of migrants and to the intertemporal decline of the human capital endowments of sequential cohorts of migrants. (See, for example, the recent insightful work of Borjas (1985) and Chiswick (1986a, b).)
3  Consider the status of many illegal migrants in the United States in the wake of the 1986 Immigration Reform and Control Act.
4  The recent European experience is a case in point. For example, under the FRG's Repatriation Assistance Act 1984, some 188,000 Turks returned home (OECD, 1987).
5  A referee drew our attention to a paper by Djajic (1986) which provides an analysis of the relationship between guest-workers' savings and those of the native born. On technical grounds we can view this contribution at least partly as the limiting case of the current analysis (that is, when the probability of return migration is 1). Conceptually, however, it is precisely when return migration becomes certain (as is the case with guest-worker migration) that the major observation made in our paper cannot possibly be made. The novelty of our approach lies in the observation that migrants who remain in the host country, despite an *ex ante* positive probability of return migration (which did not materialize), end up having a higher mean income relative to the native born.

6   Positive rates of capital depreciation could be introduced without altering the analysis.

7   For simplicity $\alpha$ is taken as exogenously given, regardless of the individuals' actions or preferences. A more detailed model that incorporates social and psychological pressures for return migration into the individuals' preferences will not alter the qualitative nature of the results.

8   Despite the absence of international differences in interest rates, wage rates may differ if production technologies differ across countries, thereby giving rise to incentives for international labor migration (for example Galor and Stark, 1987).

9   Interestingly, if a bequest motive were to be added to the analysis, it also could explain the higher savings of migrants *vis-à-vis* the native born. In the presence of such a motive we would expect larger bequests to be left in the high-wage country than in the low-wage country (given the same tastes and interest rates at the sending and receiving economies). A migrant to the high-wage country would then have a smaller inheritance than a native born and hence save more. This would enhance the discrepancy between migrants' savings and savings of the native born.

## References

Bloom, D. E. and Gunderson, M. K. (1989) "An Analysis of the Earnings of Canadian Immigrants." Discussion Paper 439, Department of Economics, Columbia University.

Borjas, G. J. (1985) "Assimilation, Changes in Cohort Quality, and the Earnings of Immigrants." *Journal of Labor Economics* 3: 463–89.

Chiswick, B. R. (1986a) "Human Capital and the Labor Market Adjustment of Immigrants: Testing Alternative Hypotheses." In Oded Stark (ed.), *Human Capital, Migration and Development*. Greenwich, CT: JAI Press, pp. 1–26.

—— (1986b) "Is the New Immigration Less Skilled than the Old?" *Journal of Labor Economics* 4: 168–92.

Diamond, P. A. (1965) "National Debt in a Neoclassical Growth Model." *American Economic Review* 55: 1126–50.

Djajic, S. (1986) "Migrants in a Guest-Worker System: A Utility Maximization Approach." Seminar Paper 368, Institute for International Economic Studies, Stockholm.

Galor, O. and Stark, O. (1987) "The Impact of Differences in the Levels of Technology on International Labor Migration." Discussion Paper 34, Harvard University Migration and Development Program.

OECD (Organization for Economic Cooperation and Development), Directorate for Social Affairs, Manpower and Education (1987) *Continuous Reporting System on Migration (SOPEMI)*. Paris: OECD.

# 28

## The Probability of Return Migration, Migrants' Work Effort, and Migrants' Performance

### 1 Introduction

First-generation migrants who have been in the receiving country for some time often have a higher mean income than that of the indigenous population. Given the information, knowledge, language, social, institutional, and other barriers in a migrant's way, the evidence of higher mean income is somewhat perplexing. Compounding the puzzle is the evidence that migrants as a group are often treated differently than nonmigrants by the indigenous population (for instance, on average, migrants are paid less than equally skilled nonmigrants). Yet in many circumstances migrants outperform the native born.[1]

The typical explanation for this phenomenon relates to the nature and characteristics of economically motivated migrants. Those who tend to migrate are likely to be self-selected in a number of ways. They may be more enterprising, prepared to take greater risks, younger, and possess a higher ratio of general to specific human capital than the average member of the indigenous population. This vector of characteristics is likely to be reflected in risk-taking behavior and in dynamism and entrepreneurship leading to higher income. In addition, the average return to a risky activity is higher than the average return to a nonrisky activity. Hence, given the assumption that migrants are less risk averse than the indigenous population, they will experience a higher average income, though with greater income variance.

The belief that the key to migrants' relative income is to be found in their ability, skills, and innately higher productivity has led to considerable research in the direction of measuring, estimating, and testing for migrants' vector of characteristics.[2] Yet the possibility that migrants' performance could be directly attributed to migrants' incentives has escaped attention. By shifting the focus of analysis from the vector of characteristics to the structure of incentives we offer in this chapter an alternative explanation for the migrants' high mean income. This explanation is based on a distinguishing characteristic of migrants *vis-à-vis* the native born, namely the strictly positive probability of return migration. Even after perfect adjustment is made for differences in human capital attributes, an explanation can be found for why migrants' income is higher than that of comparable counterparts. A return probability entailing a decline in wage rates could suffice to place a wedge between the economic performance of migrants and the native born. As demonstrated by Galor and Stark (1990), for a migrant who may return to a low-income economy, the desire to smooth out intertemporal consumption results in larger current savings. Consequently, if return migration does not materialize, the migrants' income is larger than that of natives. In the current chapter, in contrast, and regardless of the feasibility of savings, the possibility of return to a low-wage economy results in an intertemporal substitution in the supply of labor.[3] As greater work effort translates into higher income, migrants will outperform comparable native-born workers.

## 2 The Model

Consider individuals who operate in a two-period world. They are characterized by a unit endowment of labor in each period and by an intertemporal utility function defined over first- and second-period consumption of goods and leisure:

$$U(c_1, c_2, l_1, l_2) = u(c_1, l_1) + \beta u(c_2, l_2)$$

where $\beta$ is a discount factor and $c_i$ and $l_i$ are respectively the consumption of goods and leisure in period $i$, $i = 1, 2$; $c_i \in R_+$ and $l_i \in [0, 1]$. The utility function is strictly increasing and strictly concave, satisfying the expected utility properties. Both consumption and leisure are normal goods and the supply of labor in the second period is a nondecreasing function of the wage rate. Furthermore,

$$\lim_{c_i \to 0} u_c(c_i, l_i) = \lim_{l_i \to 0} u_l(c_i, l_i) = \infty, \, i = 1, 2.$$

In the first period of their lives individuals wish to allocate their potential earnings from their unit endowments of labor between first-period consumption $c_1$, savings $s$, and leisure $l_1$. Thus, given the wage rate $w_1$ in the first period,

$$c_1 = w_1(1 - l_1) - s \qquad (28.1)$$

The consumption good is the numeraire. In the second period of their lives individuals allocate their unit endowments of labor between work and leisure. The resulting wage income along with the returns to their savings constitute the level of their second-period consumption:

$$c_2 = w_2(1 - l_2) + (1 + \bar{r})s \qquad (28.2)$$

where $w_2$ is the wage rate in period 2 and $\bar{r}$ is the rate of return to savings.

The economy consists of two types of individuals, migrants and natives. Migrants differ from natives in a single respect. They face a positive probability $\alpha$ of return to their country of origin in the second period of their lives and of earning a lower wage rate. Thus migrants' second-period wage rate $w_2$ is a random variable with a distribution

$$w_2 = \begin{cases} \bar{w} & \text{with probability} \quad 1 - \alpha \\ \lambda\bar{w} & \text{with probability} \quad \alpha \end{cases} \qquad (28.3)$$

where $\lambda \in (0, 1)$ and $\alpha \in (0, 1)$. For simplicity it is assumed that in the receiving country the wage rate is constant over time, that is $w_1 = \bar{w}$.

Thus upon realization of the random variable $w_2$, migrants determine the optimal levels of second-period consumption of goods and leisure so as to maximize $u(c_2, l_2)$. Given the savings level in the first period, the indirect utility function $v(w_2; s)$ is

$$v(w_2; s) = \max u[w_2(1 - l_2) + (1 + \bar{r})s, l_2] \qquad (28.4)$$
$$\text{subject to } l_2 \in [0, 1]$$

Given $w_2$, the properties of the utility function imply that the optimal level of second-period leisure is

$$\frac{u_l(c_2, l_2)}{u_c(c_2, l_2)} = w_2 \qquad (28.5)$$

The expected utility $Ev(w_2; s)$ in the second period is thus

$$Ev(w_2; s) = \alpha v(\lambda\bar{w}; s) + (1 - \alpha)v(\bar{w}; s) \qquad (28.6)$$

Therefore migrants determine their optimal level of savings and first-period consumption of leisure so as to solve

$$\max\{u[\overline{w}(1 - l_1) - s, l_1] + \beta Ev(w_2, s)\} \tag{28.7}$$
$$\text{subject to } l_1 \in [0, 1]$$

Thus the optimal levels of $l_1$ and $s$ satisfy

$$\frac{u_1(c_1, l_1)}{u_c(c_1, l_1)} = \overline{w} \tag{28.8}$$

$$u_c(c_1, l_1) = \beta Ev_s(w_2, s) \tag{28.9}$$

From the envelope theorem, $v_s(w_2, s) = (1 + \overline{r})u_c[c_2(w_2, s), l_2(w_2, s)]$, and consequently

$$u_c(c_1, l_1) = \beta E(1 + \overline{r})u_c[c_2(w_2, s), l_2(w_2, s)] \tag{28.10}$$

Thus, at the optimum, (a) the first-period marginal rate of substitution between leisure and consumption is equal to the ratio of their prices and (b) the marginal utility of first-period consumption is equal to the discounted expected marginal utility of second-period consumption.

## Proposition 1

*If $u(c_1, l_1) + \beta u(c_2, l_2)$ is strictly concave, consumption and leisure are normal goods, and second-period labor supply is a nondecreasing function of the wage rate, then the higher the probability of return migration the larger is the migrant's first-period labor supply.*

PROOF   See appendix.

INTERPRETATION   In the presence of the possibility of return migration the expected price of leisure in the second period is lower than the price of leisure in the first period. Alternatively, the returns to labor are higher in the first period. Consequently, intertemporal substitution will generate higher labor supply in the first period.

**Corollary 1**

*If return migration does not materialize, migrants' income outweighs the income of the native born.*

As follows from proposition 1, in the presence of the possibility of return migration, migrants' work effort is larger than that of natives. Consequently, if the returns to labor are equal across individuals, migrants' first-period income is larger. Given the normality of all goods, higher first-period income results in higher savings. Thus if return migration does not materialize, migrants have a higher nonwage income. Therefore normality implies that migrants will experience higher consumption of both goods and leisure. Thus corollary 1 follows despite the fact that migrants work less than natives in the second period.

## 3  Concluding Remarks

In this chapter we have built on the idea that migrants consider the possibility of eventual return to their (low-wage) country of origin and thus may have an incentive to work harder in the (high-wage) country of destination. We have established a formal link between the likelihood of return migration and migrants' work effort. We can thus provide an explanation for the performance of migrants relative to native-born workers. It is shown that, given the possibility of return migration to a low-wage country of origin, migrants exert a higher level of work effort than that exerted by native-born workers. Thus if return migration does not materialize, migrants outperform native-born workers. The analysis generates an interesting testable hypothesis regarding earning patterns across migrant groups as a function of the probability of return migration. Other things being equal, migrants who have a higher probability of return migration will have steeper earning profiles than migrants who have a lower probability of return migration. The analysis suggests an additional testable hypothesis concerning the pattern of the wage differentials between migrants and native-born workers along the life-cycle. If the likelihood of return migration declines with the time period spent in the receiving country, then the wage differentials between natives and migrants would be expected to decline with age.

The analysis can be expanded to incorporate the consideration of country-specific skills. Those anticipating a higher probability of return migration (and hence supplying more effort) also have a weaker incentive to invest in skills specific to the receiving country. As a result they will undertake less on-the-job investments and possibly have flatter earnings profiles. On this account their earnings would be less likely to exceed the earnings of the native born. Furthermore, with fewer skills specific to the receiving country, migrants may experience a higher unemployment rate and hence fewer hours of work per year. A model incorporating these implications could thus generate predictions that may differ from those offered by the current model, which assumes skill homogeneity.

The probability of return migration impinges upon migrants' labor supply, their savings, and possibly their choice of the duration of stay once in the destination country. These effects coupled with their policy implications merit further study.

## Appendix: Proof of Proposition 1

Let $x_1 \equiv (c_1, l_1)$ and $x_2^j = (c_2^j, l_2^j)$; $x_2^j$ is the realized second-period consumption level in state $j$, where $j$ admits h if the migrant returns home and f if the migrant remains in the foreign country. Totally differentiating (28.5), (28.8), and (28.10) implies that

$$\frac{dl_1}{d\alpha} = \frac{\beta(1 + \bar{r})[u_c(x_2^h) - u_c(x_2^f)]}{(1/B_1)\{u_{cc}(x_1)u_{ll}(x_1) - [u_{cl}(x_1)]^2\} + \beta(1 + \bar{r})^2(A_1/B_1)\{D - [\alpha(B_2^h/A_2^h) + (1 - \alpha)B_2^f/A_2^f]\}} < 0$$

$$(28.A1)$$

where, as follows from the assumptions underlying proposition 1,

$$B_1 \equiv \frac{1}{u_c(x_1)}[u_{cc}(x_1)u_l(x_1) - u_c(x_1)u_{cl}(x_1)] < 0 \qquad (28.A2)$$

$$B_2 \equiv \frac{1}{u_c(x_2^j)}[u_l(x_2^j)u_{cc}(x_2^j) - u_l(x_2^j)u_{cl}(x_2^j)] < 0 \qquad (28.A3)$$

$$A_1 \equiv \frac{1}{[u_c(x_1)]^2}\{u_{ll}(x_1)[u_c(x_1)]^2 + u_{cc}(x_1)[u_l(x_1)]^2 - 2u_{cl}(x_1)u_c(x_1)u_l(x_1)\} < 0$$

$$(28.A4)$$

$$A_2 \equiv \frac{1}{[u_c(x_2^j)]^2} \{u_{ll}(x_2^j)[u_c(x_2^j)]^2 + u_{cc}(x_2^j)[u_l(x_2^j)]^2 - 2u_{cl}(x_2^j)u_2(x_2^j)\} < 0$$

(28.A5)

$$D \equiv [\alpha u_{cc}(x_2^h) > (1 - \alpha)u_{cc}(x_2^f)] < 0$$

(28.A6)

## Notes

Co-authored with Oded Galor. An earlier version of this chapter was presented at the Annual Meeting of the Royal Economic Society and the Association of University Teachers of Economics, Bristol, April 1989. We thank anonymous referees for their thoughtful comments.

1  This result is usually obtained with a time lag from the migrants' arrival, and it tends to hold even after allowance is made for the standard controls such as educational qualifications. For recent studies of the difference between the economic success of migrants and that of natives see, for the United States, Chiswick (1986a, b) and, for Canada, Bloom and Gunderson (1989).

2  Particular attention has been paid to the intertemporal appreciation of the quality (for example, skills, schooling levels, etc.) of given cohorts of migrants and to the intertemporal decline of the human capital endowments of sequential cohorts of migrants. See, for example, the recent work of Borjas (1985) and Chiswick (1986a, b).

3  Lucas and Rapping (1969) as well as others analyze the implications of temporary movements in the real wage on the intertemporal substitution of leisure, suggesting a possible explanation for the comovement of employment and wages over the cycle. Note that, even if the expected income in the second period remains the same, the presence of uncertainty will be sufficient to reduce first-period consumption of goods (Sandmo, 1970). However, this effect is only minor in the current analysis. Given the fact that leisure is an argument of the utility function, a reduction in the expected income generates intertemporal substitution which is the driving force in the model. The argument can be made more precise, observing that when $\alpha$ approaches 1 and uncertainty disappears, the effect on labor supply still holds.

## References

Bloom, David E. and Gunderson, Morley K. (1989) "An Analysis of the Earnings of Canadian Immigrants." Discussion Paper 439, Department of Economics, Columbia University.

Borjas, George J. (1985) "Assimilation, Changes in Cohort Quality, and the Earnings of Immigrants." *Journal of Labor Economics* 3: 463–89.

Chiswick, Barry R. (1986a) "Human Capital and the Labor Market Adjustment of Immigrants: Testing Alternative Hypotheses." In Oded Stark (ed.), *Human Capital, Migration and Development.* Greenwich, CT: JAI Press, pp. 1–26.

—— (1986b) "Is the New Immigration Less Skilled than the Old?" *Journal of Labor Economics* 4: 168–92.

Galor, Oded and Stark, Oded (1990) "Migrants' Savings, The Probability of Return Migration and Migrants' Performance." *International Economic Review* 31: 463–7 (reprinted as ch. 27 in this volume).

Lucas, Robert E. and Rapping, Leonard A. (1969) "Real Wages, Employment, and Inflation." *Journal of Political Economy* 77: 721–54.

Sandmo, Agnar (1970) "The Effect of Uncertainty on Saving Decisions." *Review of Economic Studies* 37: 353–60.

# Index